the UNAUTHORIZED GUIDE to

Microsoft® Windows Millennium Edition

Paul McFedries

201 West 103rd Street, Indianapolis, Indiana 46290

The Unauthorized Guide to Microsoft® Windows Millennium Edition

Copyright © 2000 by Que

International Standard Book Number: 0-7897-2452-9

Library of Congress Catalog Card Number: 00-101091

Printed in the United States of America

First Printing: September, 2000

02 01 00   4 3 2 1

Trademarks

Warning and Disclaimer

Associate Publisher
Greg Wiegand

Senior Acquisitions Editor
Jenny Watson

Development Editor
Todd Brakke

Managing Editor
Tom Hayes

Project Editor
Leah Kirkpatrick

Copy Editor
Julie McNamee

Indexer
Aamir Burki

Proofreader
Maribeth Echard

Technical Editor
Kyle Bryant

Team Coordinator
Sharry Lee Gregory

Interior Designer
Kevin Spear

Cover Designer
Karen Ruggles

Layout Technicians
Stacey DeRome
Ayanna Lacey
Heather Hiatt Miller

Contents

Paul McFedries is a computer consultant, programmer, and freelance writer. He is the author of more than three dozen computer books that have sold more than two million copies worldwide. His titles include *The Complete Idiot's Guide to Windows Millennium Edition*, *The Complete Idiot's Guide to Creating a Web Page,* and *The Unauthorized Guide to Windows 98 Second Edition,* published by Que. If you have any comments about the book, you can contact Paul at

Email: unauthorized@mcfedries.com

WWW: www.mcfedries.com

About the Author

To my friends and family (for being friendly and familiar) and, of course, to Karen.

Tell Us What You Think!

As the reader of this book, *you* are our most important critic and commentator. We value your opinion and want to know what we're doing right, what we could do better, what areas you'd like to see us publish in, and any other words of wisdom you're willing to pass our way.

As an associate publisher for Que, I welcome your comments. You can fax, email, or write me directly to let me know what you did or didn't like about this book—as well as what we can do to make our books stronger.

Please note that I cannot help you with technical problems related to the topic of this book, and that due to the high volume of mail I receive, I might not be able to reply to every message.

When you write, please be sure to include this book's title and author as well as your name and phone or fax number. I will carefully review your comments and share them with the author and editors who worked on the book.

Fax: 317-581-4666

Email: consumer@mcp.com

Mail: Greg Wiegand
            Que
            201 West 103rd Street
            Indianapolis, Indiana 46290 USA

Acknowledgments

I write computer books for a living, and I always tell people that I think of my job as spending a half hour figuring out how to do something in 5 minutes, and then giving the reader that 5-minute method. I hope, then, that this book makes at least a small part of your life easier and less stressful.

To make my own life easier and less stressful, I need only turn to the dedicated and hard-working folks in the Macmillan editorial department. These professionals absolutely amaze me with their knowledge, experience, and sheer competence. All I have to worry about is writing the best book that I can, knowing that the Macmillan editors are backing me up by dotting my i's and crossing my t's. Dozens of bright-eyed and energetic folks had a hand in making this book, but there are a few whom I worked with directly, so I'd like to single them out for special thanks. They include Associate Publisher Greg Wiegand, Acquisitions Editor Jenny Watson, Development Editor Todd Brakke, Production Editor Leah Kirkpatrick, Copy Editor Julie McNamee, and Technical Editor Kyle Bryant. A hearty thanks to all of you for another fantastic job.

B Y DEFINITION, WHAT PEOPLE *create* using a computer is a unique expression of who they are. Whether it's a memo, a letter, a financial model, a presentation, an email message, or a Web page, the fruit of their labors is something that only *they* could have produced.

On the other hand, *how* people use their computers—or, more to the point, how they use Windows—generally isn't unique at all. Most users follow the same Start menu paths to launch programs, use the standard techniques in programs like Windows Explorer and Outlook Express, and perform customizations that don't go much beyond changing the wallpaper. That's because most users find it easier to toe the Microsoft party line and follow the techniques outlined in the "Getting Started" booklet and the Help system. To be sure, this is a reasonable approach for novice users who are intimidated by Windows and prefer to tread carefully to avoid upsetting any digital apple carts.

However, what about those users who qualify as "post-novice"? By that I mean any person who either knows the basics of Windows or who has some computing experience and is smart enough to figure things out without having his or her hands held. For those users, doing things the "authorized" way is slower, less efficient, and less powerful because Windows Millennium was designed from the ground up so as not to confuse novice users (or, I guess, not to confuse them more than necessary). The result is default settings that restrict your flexibility, interminable wizards that turn two-step tasks into 12-step sagas, and powerful and useful programs hidden behind layers of menus and dialog boxes. To get the most out of Windows Millennium, the post-novice user needs an "unauthorized" approach that goes where the "Getting Started" booklet and the Help system fear to tread.

Introduction

Welcome to *The Unauthorized Guide to Windows Millennium Edition*. In this book, I thumb my nose at the standard-issue techniques sanctioned by Microsoft and parroted in other Windows Millennium books. Instead, I offer shortcuts for boosting your productivity, customizations for making Windows Millennium work the way you do, workarounds for known Windows Millennium problems, and warnings for avoiding Windows Millennium pitfalls. Along the way, you learn about all kinds of insider details, undocumented features, powerful tools, and background facts that help put everything into perspective.

So, is this merely a collection of tips, tricks, and traps? Not at all. This is a *guide* to Windows Millennium. That means I teach you *how* to use Windows Millennium, from setup to startup, from performing system maintenance to maintaining system performance, from getting on the Internet to getting on your network. I also cover most of the features new to Windows Millennium, including Internet Explorer 5.5, Outlook Express 5.5, the Home Networking Wizard, and much more.

The Structure of the Book

The Unauthorized Guide to Microsoft Windows Millennium Edition is structured as a work of reference. This means that you can dive in to most chapters to learn just the facts or techniques you need now without having to worry that you missed some crucial information in an earlier chapter. The exception to this is Chapter 3, "An Insider's Guide to Four Crucial Configuration Tools." That chapter discusses the Windows Millennium Registry, the System Policy Editor, the Tweak UI customization accessory, and Control Panel, and I use all four tools throughout the rest of the book.

The next few sections give you a synopsis of the book's structure.

Part I: Windows Millennium: Beyond the Basics

The book begins with three chapters that discuss some Windows Millennium basics with a beyond-the-basics approach. You get a host of Windows Millennium Setup tips and techniques and an inside look at the Windows Millennium startup process. I also discuss the Registry, System Policy Editor, Control Panel, and Tweak UI, as mentioned earlier.

Part II: Inside Windows Millennium Communication and Internet Features

The four chapters in Part II show you how to get wired with Windows Millennium. I begin by showing you how to install and configure your modem. From there, you learn how to get on the Internet and how to get the most out of Internet Explorer (for the World Wide Web) and Outlook Express (for email). I close with a look at some important Internet security considerations.

Part III: Controlling Your Files and Folders

This short section contains just three chapters, but it's jam-packed with practical and powerful tips and techniques. Chapter 8, "Expert Windows Explorer Techniques," shows you how to get the most out of Windows for file and folder chores. Chapter 9, "Powerful Techniques for File Types," discusses file types and file extensions and shows you how to modify existing file types, create new file types, customize Windows Millennium's New menu, and more. Chapter 10, "Taking Advantage of Shortcuts," teaches you about shortcuts and shortcut files, shows you how to modify shortcut properties, and provides a number of techniques for working with and customizing shortcuts.

Part IV: Windows Millennium Performance Tuning and Troubleshooting

Windows Millennium is bursting at the seams with powerful system tools, most of which are hidden in the most obscure places. The chapters in Part IV show you where to find these tools and how to make the best use of them. You learn about installing and uninstalling applications, optimizing memory, revving up your hard disk, taking advantage of FAT32, and protecting system files. For safety's sake, I also show you how to create an emergency boot disk and back up your files.

> 66
> The great challenge which faces us is to assure that, in our society of bigness, we do not strangle the voice of creativity, that the rules of the game do not come to overshadow its purpose, that the grand orchestration of society leaves ample room for the man who marches to the music of another drummer.
> —*Hubert H. Humphrey*
> 99

Part V: Advanced Windows Millennium Customizing

The two chapters in Part V offer loads of customization techniques that go beyond the standard wallpaper-and-color tweaks. You get behind-the-scenes coverage of Web integration and the Active Desktop, and powerful methods for customizing the desktop, Start menu, and taskbar.

Part VI: Windows Millennium Networking Skills

Part VI covers Windows Millennium networking. You learn network fundamentals such as the difference between peer-to-peer and client/server, networking hardware, and networking architecture. I then show you how to set up a local area network, how to work with and share network resources, and how to connect to a network remotely using Dial-Up Networking.

Part VII: High-Powered Hardware Techniques

The last three chapters of the book cover Windows Millennium's extensive hardware features. You start by learning some crucial hardware concepts, including device drivers, device settings—such as interrupt request lines and I/O ports—and Plug and Play. With that background, you then learn about installing device drivers, using Device Manager, and configuring graphics adapters, monitors, and other multimedia hardware. This section closes with a look at some notebook features, including power management, Direct Cable Connection file transfers, briefcase synchronization, and more.

Appendixes

The book finishes with a few appendixes. You get a glossary of Windows Millennium terms, a selection of World Wide Web and Usenet resources for Windows Millennium, and a complete list of Windows Millennium keyboard shortcuts.

Special Features

In the book's margins, you'll see the following six special sidebars, which I hope will help you learn more about Windows Millennium and will help you get things done quickly, efficiently, and smartly:

- **Shortcut**—Tips and shortcuts that save you time.

- **Watch Out**—Cautions that warn you about potential pitfalls and problems.

- **Remember**—Valuable information that you'll want to store away for future use.

- **Inside Scoop**—Insiders' facts and anecdotes.

- **Undocumented**—Important tidbits and techniques that you won't find in the standard documentation.

- **Quote**—Statements from real people that are intended to be prescriptive and valuable to you.

Windows Millennium: Beyond the Basics

PART I

GET THE SCOOP ON...
Installing to Maximize Performance ▪ Dual Booting with
Other Operating Systems ▪ Installing to a Clean System ▪
Creating Customized and Automated Installations ▪ Adding
and Removing Windows Millennium Components ▪
Uninstalling Windows Millennium

Ten Things You Should Know About the Windows Millennium Setup

Chapter 1

I N ITS PRESS RELEASES and documentation, Microsoft crows that the Windows Millennium Setup is the easiest operating system installation routine yet. However, what they don't say is that installing Windows Millennium is easy only under certain conditions and only if you take a few precautions in advance. What Microsoft also won't tell you is that there is often a trade-off involved in how you set up Windows Millennium. The easiest Setup route (installing over Windows 95 or Windows 98) often leads to the most problems later on, while following the hardest route (installing on a clean system) most often leads to relatively problem-free computing.

This chapter discusses these and many other Windows Millennium Setup issues. I take you behind the scenes to learn some truly useful Setup know-how that will help you prepare for the installation process and will help you get through the installation after you decide to take the plunge. You'll also learn a few Setup-related chores, such as adding and removing Windows Millennium components and uninstalling Windows Millennium.

Going Beyond the Minimum Windows Millennium Hardware Requirements

Whenever Microsoft announces the minimum system require-ments for the latest version of Windows, it usually elicits quite a few chuckles. For example, it was theoretically possible to run Windows 98 on a 486DX system equipped with 16MB of RAM, but I doubt that anyone who tried ever got any work done.

Although Microsoft has bumped up the minimum require-ments for Windows Millennium, Windows Millennium's resource requirements have also gone up to the next level. Once again, this means that a system boasting nothing more than the bare-bones hardware recommended by Microsoft will have serious performance problems.

Therefore, you should recognize that the following list of min-imum hardware requirements is only the starting point for either upgrading or purchasing a system for Windows Millennium:

- A Pentium processor running at 150MHz.

- 32MB of RAM.

- A hard disk with a partition that has enough free space to hold not only the Windows Millennium files, but also the temporary files that are installed by the Setup program. If you're upgrading over Windows 9x (that is, Windows 95 or Windows 98), you'll need at least 185MB of free space; for a clean install, the minimum is approximately 200MB.

- A VGA video card and monitor.

- A CD-ROM or DVD-ROM drive.

Depending on what you're used to, this may seem like a rea-sonable system. Such a machine would positively scream under Windows 3.x, would perform quite nicely under Windows 95, and would be fine for Windows 98. However, it's simply not good enough for serious work in Windows Millennium. The

Remember
If you're upgrad-ing over an exist-ing version of Windows, Setup can back up your existing system files, which can take up as much as 175MB of hard disk space. Also, the disk space requirements will be less if you're installing to a FAT32 partition, which stores files more efficiently (in Chapter 13, see "Making the Move to FAT32," p. 314).

most underpowered machine that I've used with Windows Millennium is a Pentium 200 desktop with 32MB of RAM, and I find it only barely usable.

Here are the *real* minimum hardware requirements for Windows Millennium:

- A system with a PCI bus and a Plug and Play–compliant BIOS.

- A Pentium II processor running at 400MHz.

- 64MB of RAM.

- A hard disk with a partition that has at least 750MB free. This will enable you to load as many of the Windows Millennium components as you want, and it gives you enough space for other applications to install their program and support files. It also gives you room to install the inevitable updates and patches that will appear over the course of Windows Millennium's lifetime.

- A Super VGA video card and monitor capable of displaying at least 65,536 colors at 1,024×768 resolution.

- A Microsoft-compatible wheel mouse; a keyboard with the Windows logo key ⊞; a sound card and speakers; a modem for online and Internet sessions; a network adapter for connecting to a network.

Other Windows Millennium features require further hardware investments. For example, if you want to take advantage of Windows Millennium's multiple-monitor support, you'll need a second video card/monitor combination. Similarly, if you want to use Windows Millennium's WebTV application or the new Movie Maker program, you need the appropriate graphics hardware.

To ensure that your system hardware is fully compatible with Windows Millennium, check out the Microsoft Windows Hardware Compatibility List:

```
http://www.microsoft.com/hwtest/hcl/
```

This page enables you to search for specific devices to see whether they are compatible with Windows Millennium, or meet Microsoft logo requirements for the PC 99 hardware specifications. For the latter, see the following Web site:

http://www.microsoft.com/hwdev/pc99.htm

Upgrading from DOS or an Existing Version of Windows

If your hardware passes muster, the next decision you have to make is how to install Windows Millennium. You have three choices:

- Upgrade from DOS or over an existing version of Windows.

- Install to dual boot with an existing operating system.

- Install to a clean hard disk that has no existing operating system.

This section discusses upgrading from DOS or Windows. Later sections discuss dual boot and clean installations.

Upgrading from DOS

If your system is running DOS only, you can "upgrade" to Windows Millennium under the following conditions:

- You must be running DOS 5.0 or later.

- You must have the full version of Windows Millennium: either the full OEM version from your computer manufacturer, or the full retail version. The upgrade version looks for an existing version of Windows 9x, so it won't work on a DOS-only machine.

What happens to your existing DOS files once Windows Millennium is installed? The original DOS directory remains in place, but certain commands that could cause problems, if they run within Windows Millennium, are renamed with the ex~ extension. (For example, defrag.exe becomes defrag.ex~.) These commands are replaced by batch files (for example,

Shortcut
If your system is DOS-only, but you do have Windows 3.x or Windows 9x on disk or CD-ROM, you don't have to install the old version of Windows in order to use the Windows Millennium upgrade. Instead, the Setup program will prompt you to insert your original disk (or disks) to verify that you have an existing version of Windows.

`defrag.bat`) that tell you to use the Windows Millennium equivalent of the program.

Note, too, that the Windows Millennium DOS is not quite the same as the old (that is, pre-Windows 95) DOS:

- The DOS commands are now stored in the `C:\Windows\Command` subfolder. (The path of this folder may be different depending on where you installed Windows Millennium.)

- You can work with long filenames at the DOS prompt.

- You can work with network resources at the DOS prompt.

- You can run Windows applications from the DOS prompt.

- The following commands have been deleted from Windows Millennium DOS:

APPEND	ASSIGN	BACKUP	CHKSTATE
COMP	DOSSHELL	EDLIN	FASTHELP
FASTOPEN	GRAFTABL	GRAPHICS	INTERLNK
INTERSVR	JOIN	LOADFIX	MEMCARD
MEMMAKER	MIRROR	MSAV	MSBACKUP
POWER	PRINT	RECOVER	REPLACE
RESTORE	SETVER	SHARE	SIZER
SMARTMON	TREE	UNFORMAT	UNDELETE
VSAFE			

Watch Out!
When working at the DOS prompt, bear in mind that you must enclose long file and path names in quotation marks, as shown in this example:

`del "long filename.txt"`

Upgrading from Windows 3.x

If you have Windows 3.x—that is, Windows 3.0 or 3.1 or Windows for Workgroups 3.1 or 3.11—you can't upgrade to Windows Millennium over your existing Windows installation. Instead, you have two choices:

- Upgrade Windows 3.x to Windows 95 or Windows 98 and then upgrade to Windows Millennium.

- Wipe out Windows 3.x and install Windows Millennium on a clean hard disk. See "Performing a Clean Installation," later in this chapter for the pros and cons of this approach.

A third option would be to install Windows Millennium into a separate folder. (You need to run the Windows Millennium installation from the DOS prompt to do this.) Unfortunately, this won't automatically mean that you can dual boot between them because Windows Millennium doesn't support dual booting. Therefore, I don't recommend doing this.

Inside Scoop

It *is* possible to set up a computer to dual boot Windows Millennium and Windows 3.*x*. However, you need a third-party boot manager program, such as System Commander (www.v-com.com) or BOOTMENU (www.bootmenu.com).

Upgrading from Windows 95 or Windows 98

Running Windows Millennium Setup as an upgrade to Windows 95 or 98 (including Windows 98 SE) is by far the easiest installation path. That's because Windows Millennium Setup processes the existing Windows 9x Registry early in the install procedure. It then uses these existing settings as the basis of Windows Millennium's configuration. This has two main advantages:

- Installation is more robust because Setup just assumes the Registry's current hardware configuration is accurate, so it doesn't run any hardware detection.

- Installation takes less time, not only because the lengthy hardware detection phase is skipped, but also because you have to respond to very few prompts.

Note, however, that you don't have a choice about whether you upgrade Windows 9x or dual boot. Windows Millennium can upgrade only an existing Windows 9x installation. And as with Windows 3.*x*, Windows Millennium doesn't support dual booting with Windows 9x. The workaround is, once again, to use a third-party boot manager program.

Dual Booting Windows Millennium with Another Operating System

As I've mentioned, Windows Millennium won't dual boot with DOS or any previous version of Windows (unless you purchase a third-party utility). That's too bad, because dual booting can be quite useful. My guess is that Microsoft just wants everyone to keep up with the Windows parade and to stop lollygagging with older versions of Windows.

However, while not easy, it is possible to dual boot Windows Millennium with other operating systems. The next few sections show you how it's done.

Partitioning for Dual Booting

A *partition* is a section of a hard disk, and is usually assigned its own drive letter. For example, the default file system used in DOS, Windows 3.*x*, and Windows 9*x* supports hard disks up to 2GB in size. If your computer comes with a 4GB hard disk, the manufacturer will have split the disk into two 2GB partitions, which will probably be assigned drive letters C and D.

If you're considering a dual boot configuration with some other PC-compatible operating system—Windows 2000, Windows NT, Linux, or OS/2—you must create a separate partition that the other OS can use to store its system files. To adjust hard disk partitions, use the DOS FDISK command.

Dual Booting with Windows 2000 or Windows NT

If you want to dual boot between Windows Millennium and Windows 2000 or Windows NT, the best approach is to install Windows Millennium first and then install 2000/NT. 2000/NT recognizes that Windows Millennium is already installed, and it adds a command for it on the startup menu:

```
Please select the operating system to start:


    Microsoft Windows 2000 Professional
    Microsoft Windows


Use ↑ and ↓ to move the highlight to your choice.
Press Enter to Choose.
```

Select the operating system you want to work with and then press Enter.

Here are a few points to bear in mind when considering this dual boot scenario:

- Make sure your hard disk has a FAT16 or FAT32 partition into which you can install Windows Millennium.

Inside Scoop
A more mundane reason that Microsoft dropped dual-boot support in Windows Millennium is that most new machines ship with massive hard drives that require the use of FAT32 (because FAT supports drives up to only 2GB). DOS and Windows 3.*x* don't understand FAT32, so dual booting would lead to all kinds of compatibility headaches.

Inside Scoop
Creating and adjusting partitions is a much easier process if you use a third-party partitioning program such as Partition Magic (www.powerquest.com).

Shortcut
If you're installing NT, select Start, Run and then enter the command *drive*:\i386\winnt /w, where *drive* is the letter of the drive that holds the NT disc. You need the /w switch to enable the Windows NT installation program to operate under Windows Millennium. If you're installing Windows 2000, you don't have to do this. However, be sure to run the winnt32.exe file to run the setup under Windows Millennium.

- 2000/NT can create FAT16 partitions up to 4GB in size. However, Windows Millennium's FAT16 doesn't support partitions of this size (the maximum is 2GB); so the Setup program won't work.

- Windows Millennium doesn't recognize 2000/NT's native NTFS file system, so you won't be able to access NTFS partitions from within Windows Millennium. Also, Windows NT won't be able to read Windows Millennium's FAT32 partitions; however, Windows 2000 is quite comfortable with them.

- The DriveSpace compression schemes used by Windows Millennium and Windows NT 3.51 are incompatible. Therefore, the two operating systems will not be able to work with each other's compressed files.

- Any applications already installed within one operating system will likely have to be reinstalled within the other. This is particularly true for any application that stores values in the Windows Registry or a Windows Millennium initialization file (such as Win.ini).

For the latter, you might not have to reinstall some applications. Certainly, any application that doesn't use the Registry or some other initialization file, and that stores all of its files in its own folder, will likely operate without a problem in both operating systems. However, many programs store DLLs and other support files either in the main Windows folder or in the System subfolder. You may be able to get these programs to work in both operating systems by adjusting the PATH variable. (This variable lists a series of folders into which Windows looks when trying to find executable files.) Here's how you do it (I'm assuming here that 2000/NT is installed in C:\Winnt and Windows Millennium is installed in D:\Windows):

- In Windows Millennium, open Autoexec.bat and edit the PATH statement as follows:

```
PATH=D:\WINDOWS;D:\WINDOWS\SYSTEM;C:\WINNT;C:\WINNT\
SYSTEM32
```

Maximum
partition
size for
FAT32 is
1024GB

- In Windows 2000, launch Control Panel and open the System icon. In the System Properties dialog box, display the Advanced tab and click Environment Variable. When the Environment Variables dialog box shows up, highlight the Path line in the System variables section, and then click Edit. In the Variable Value text box, add the following to the end of the existing value:

  `;D:\WINDOWS;D:\WINDOWS\SYSTEM`

  Click OK and then click OK in each of the other open dialog boxes.

- In Windows NT, launch Control Panel and open the System icon. In the System dialog box that appears, highlight the Path line in the System Environment Variables section. In the Value text box, add the following to the end of the existing value:

  `;D:\WINDOWS;D:\WINDOWS\SYSTEM`

  Click Set and then click OK.

What do you do if 2000/NT is already installed and you want to install Windows Millennium? That depends on how you installed NT:

- If you installed 2000/NT along with Windows 3.*x* (or DOS), the 2000/NT startup menu will have a Windows (or DOS) option. Select that option at startup and then install Windows Millennium normally.

- If 2000/NT is the only operating system, boot from a floppy disk and then run Windows Millennium Setup. When you're done, insert your 2000/NT boot floppy, restart your computer, and then follow the instructions that appear on the screen. You'll eventually end up at the Welcome to Setup screen, which has a Repair option. Press r to select that option and restore the 2000/NT boot sector that was damaged during the Windows Millennium Setup.

Watch Out!
If the PATH statement already exists and contains other folder paths, be sure not to remove those paths; otherwise, some of your programs might not work properly. Just append the 2000/NT paths (`;C:\WINNT;C:\WINNT\SYSTEM32`) onto the end of the existing PATH statement. (For Windows 2000, you also have to add `;C:\WINNT\SYSTEM32\WBEM.`)

Watch Out!
If you install
Windows
Millennium on a
Linux system,
Setup will over-
write LILO if LILO
was installed to
the Master Boot
Record. In this
case, use a
bootable Linux
floppy to restart
and then run the
LILOCONFIG utility.
If, instead, LILO
was installed
to the root
directory—or
superblock—of the
Linux partition,
Setup will deacti-
vate LILO. In this
case, use FDISK
to reactivate the
Linux partition.

Other Dual Boot Options

To conclude your look at dual booting, here are two other scenarios to consider:

Dual booting with Linux—To set this up, install Windows
Millennium and then install Linux and the Linux Loader
(LILO). The latter can recognize and work with Windows.
So, at startup LILO will offer you a choice of loading
Linux or "DOS" (that is, Windows Millennium).

Dual booting with OS/2 Warp—The best way to do this is to
install OS/2 and create a "startable" Boot Manager partition. You'll also need a "bootable" FAT16 partition to use
with Windows Millennium. (If you've already installed
OS/2, use the FDISK utility to do this.) Restart your
machine using a bootable floppy, and then install
Windows Millennium. Setup will disable Boot Manager in
order to be able to restart the system during the installation. After Windows Millennium is installed, use the OS/2
boot disk to restart your system, and then use FDISK to
restore the Boot Manager partition.

Although it does not specifically address multibooting with
Windows Millennium, Que's *Multi-Boot Configuration Handbook*
by Roderick Smith (ISBN: 0-7897-2283-6) has a wealth of information for making finicky operating systems coexist together.

Performing a Clean Installation

One of the sad facts of computing life is that system performance and reliability both degrade over time. There are a
number of system maintenance techniques that you can use to
stave off this process, and you'll learn about them in Part IV,
"Windows   Millennium   Performance   Tuning   and
Troubleshooting." Even if you were diligent about these maintenance chores in your current Windows setup, your system
will still be slower and less reliable than it was when it was new.

Why is this? The biggest culprit is the intermingling of
Windows files and application files. Windows and most programs use helper files called *dynamic link libraries*, or DLLs.

Rather than put all programming code into a single file, many functions and subroutines are split off into separate DLL files, which are loaded only when required by the program. This saves memory and enables multiple programs to easily reuse the same code. Many Windows features are also housed in DLLs, including common interface features such as the Open and Save As dialog boxes.

Many years ago, Microsoft made the fateful decision to encourage software developers to store all their programs' DLLs in the \Windows\System subfolder. Unfortunately, this has led to a number of problems, all of which contribute to system decay:

- DLLs often change over time as features get added or changed. Installation programs are supposed to check DLL version numbers and install their version only if it's more recent than an existing version on the system. However, many sloppily programmed applications don't do this.

- Some installation utilities install a program's DLLs in the program's home folder. This often means you end up with two or more copies of the same file scattered about your system.

- If a program uses a DLL with the same name as another program's DLL, the latter file will usually get overwritten.

- It's difficult to know which DLLs correspond to which programs. Unless a program comes with its own uninstall utility, DLLs tossed into the System subfolder are usually in there for good.

The best (albeit the most radical) solution is to start from scratch: Wipe your hard drive clean and then install Windows Millennium. This removes the DLL detritus that has accumulated over the years ensuring that Windows Millennium begins without having to drag around any excess DLL baggage. There are other benefits to this approach:

66

Consultant Michael Green...says that 90 percent of the GPFs [General Protection Faults] he's studied are caused by conflicting versions of DLLs.

—*Brian Livingston, InfoWorld*

99

- If you're currently running Windows 95 or Windows 98, you get to start with a fresh Registry. The Registry often gets bloated with many unused settings left over from deleted or uninstalled programs.

- You rid your system of stray temporary files that might have accumulated over the years. Many programs—and Windows itself—create temporary files while you work. These files are usually deleted when you finish working with the program, but if your system shuts down unexpectedly (due to a power failure or crash), the files remain to clutter your hard disk.

- You get rid of old device drivers and replace them with the latest versions that ship with Windows Millennium. These newer device drivers are often faster and more reliable, plus they may support new Windows Millennium features.

- It gives you a good excuse to adjust your hard disk partitions using FDISK. Since FDISK destroys all data anyway, it doesn't hurt to restructure your hard disk. This gives you a chance to create partitions to hold data files, program files, or any operating system you want to dual boot with Windows Millennium.

- You ensure that there are no computer viruses lurking anywhere on your hard disk. Although you may not have experienced any virus-like behavior, many viruses are timed to release on a certain date, so it's possible your system is infected and you don't know it.

The downside, of course, is that you must reinstall your applications and rebuild your folder structure. However, I believe these negatives are greatly outweighed by the positives previously listed.

Having said all that, you should also check with your PC manufacturer to make sure that a clean install is possible on your system. Some newer systems have hardware restrictions that may prevent a clean install from working.

Here's a general procedure to follow for installing Windows Millennium to a clean system:

1. Make backup copies of all your data files.

2. Make backup copies of initialization files and other files used to store program customization options. (If you use Microsoft Word, for example, you should back up Normal.dot and any custom templates you created.)

3. Make backup copies of the archive (for example, .zip) files for any programs that you downloaded from the Internet or some other online source.

4. Create a bootable disk. Make sure you include on this disk your system startup files—Config.sys and Autoexec.bat—as well as any real mode device drivers that are loaded within these files (particularly the drivers for your CD-ROM). You'll also need the DOS files Fdisk.exe and Format.com.

5. Insert the bootable disk in drive A and restart your computer.

6. When you get to the A:\ prompt, run FDISK to repartition your hard disk. Note that you can skip this step if you don't want to repartition the disk.

7. Format drive C by entering the command format c: /s /u. (I'm assuming here that drive C will be your bootable partition.) The /s switch makes drive C bootable by copying the system files, and the /u switch tells FORMAT not to save unformatted data.

8. If necessary, format your other partitions. Use the syntax format d: /u, where d is the drive letter of the partition.

9. Copy Config.sys, Autoexec.bat, and your startup device driver files from the bootable disk to drive C (or your bootable partition).

10. Remove the bootable disk and restart your computer so that it can boot from the hard disk.

11. Run the Windows Millennium installation.

Remember
Technically, the only partitions you need to format are your bootable partition and, if different, the partition in which your existing version of Windows is stored. If you already have a separate partition for your data files, don't bother formatting it (or backing up your data files, for that matter).

Preparing Your System

In the past, the booklet (I refuse to call it a manual) that came with Windows offered a brief "Before You Begin" section that ran through the minimum system requirements for installing Windows. After that, the only other suggested step to take to prepare your system for installing Windows Millennium was to "Close all programs."

A Preparation Checklist

For an operating system installation, such advice is woefully inadequate. Here's a list of what you *should* do to prepare your system:

Back up data files—Make backup copies of all your data files, including any custom templates that you created.

Back up application configuration files—Many applications store their current configuration in .ini files located either in the Windows folder or the application's home folder. If you're using Windows 95 or Windows 98, however, most of this configuration data will be stored in the Registry.

Back up Windows configuration files—Make backup copies of Config.sys, Autoexec.bat, Win.ini, System.ini, and all your password list (.pwl) files. If you're running Windows 3.x, back up all the program group (.grp) files in the Windows directory. If you're running Windows 95 or Windows 98, restart the computer in MS-DOS mode and make backups of the two Registry files: System.dat and User.dat (these are hidden files in the Windows folder).

Back up the Application Data folder—If you're running Windows 98 and either Outlook or Outlook Express, back up the mail, news settings, and data contained in the Windows\Application Data folder.

Back up Windows Messaging files—If you're using Windows Messaging (or Microsoft Exchange), back up your personal folder's file (usually Exchange.pst) and your personal address book (usually Exchange.pab). You'll find these files either in the Windows Messaging folder or in the Windows folder.

Check your system BIOS—Many system vendors—including Compaq, Dell, Hewlett-Packard, IBM, and Toshiba—have reported that some of their older computers won't upgrade to Windows Millennium properly unless the machines receive a BIOS update in advance. Check with your system manufacturer to see whether a BIOS update is required for your computer.

Disable the Windows 3.x permanent swap file—This not only saves some disk space, but it also enables Windows Millennium to set up its dynamic swap file. Open Control Panel, launch the 386 Enhanced icon, and then click the Virtual Memory button. If you see Permanent in the Type field, click the Change button. If you'll be installing over Windows 3.x, select None in the Type list. If, instead, you plan on dual booting Windows 3.x and Windows Millennium, select Temporary.

Clean out the Startup group or folder—Setup can migrate your Startup applications to Windows Millennium, but it's best to wait until Windows Millennium is installed and then test these applications to make sure they work properly. If they do, you can add them to Windows Millennium's Startup folder.

Do a spring cleaning on your hard disk—To free up disk space and prepare for defragmenting (discussed as follows), clean up your hard disk. This includes uninstalling applications you no longer use, removing stray files from the Windows TEMP folder (usually `C:\Windows\Temp`), and deleting the DOS backup folder (usually `C:\Old_dos.1`), if it exists.

Watch Out!
Don't delete files from the `Temp` folder while Windows is running. Always exit to DOS and then delete these files.

Perform a "thorough" ScanDisk check—The thorough check examines the surface of the disk for imperfections. It takes longer, but now is the perfect time to do it.

Run and then disable your antivirus software—If you have antivirus software, use it to check your files and system

Email folders!
(.dbx files)

C:\Windows\Application Data
\Identities\{295C4...CC265}
\Microsoft\Outlook Express\

memory for lurking viruses (make sure your virus list is up to date, first). After that's done, disable the software if it's resident in memory. The Windows Millennium Setup changes the hard disk's Master Boot Record, which, to an antivirus program, is "virus-like" activity.

Defragment your hard disk—This ensures that Windows Millennium stores its files in a defragmented state, which will improve performance. If you have Windows 3.*x*, run the DOS DEFRAG utility; if you have Windows 95 or 98, use Disk Defragmenter.

Create a bootable floppy disk—Just in case the installation procedure fails, you should have a bootable disk on hand. If you have Windows 95 or 98, create a startup disk. If you have Windows 3.*x*, insert an expendable disk in drive A, and then use one of the following methods:

- Run File Manager and select the Disk, Make System Disk command.

- At the DOS prompt, type `format a: /s` and press Enter.

Run a system report—This will give you a record of your current configuration in case you need to know what device drivers you were using, or some other bit of information useful for troubleshooting. If you have Windows 3.*x*, use the Microsoft Diagnostics utility (at the DOS prompt, type `msd` and press Enter). In Windows 95 or 98, use Device Manager (right-click My Computer, click Properties, select the Device Manager tab, and then click Print).

Close all running programs—This ensures that none of these programs can interfere with Windows Millennium Setup, and it helps Setup run faster.

Better Backup Ideas

Backing up data files and important configuration files is important, but if something goes awry during Setup, returning to your original configuration will be a time-consuming process. This section looks at some ways to make a completely recoverable backup of your system.

The first thing you need to do is get out of Windows so you avoid backing up the swap file, the existing temporary files, and other flotsam that is specific only to your current Windows session. In other words, you have to do this from DOS. That presents a whole new series of problems, including the speed of the backup and the medium you use to store the backup:

- The simplest solution would be to use the DOS XCOPY command to copy the entire boot partition to another partition on the disk, or to another hard disk altogether. For example, to copy drive C to drive D, you'd use the following command:

```
xcopy c:\ d:\ /t /e /h /k
```

This will be quite a slow process, however, and won't have any kind of built-in error checking.

- To increase speed and robustness, you need to turn to third-party programs. One such program is Partition Magic, by PowerQuest (www.powerquest.com/). You can use this program to safely make a copy of the boot partition to another hard disk. You can also use Partition Magic to resize the copied partition to remove all unused space, as well as to hide this new partition, which avoids confusion for Setup and disk utilities down the road.

- A third method is to clone the drive and store it either on another disk or on a recordable CD. Here are three programs that can clone a disk drive:

  Drive Image (www.powerquest.com)

  DiskClone (www.symantec.com/sabu/qdeck/ diskclone/mainreg.html)

  Norton Ghost (www.symantec.com/sabu/ghost/)

Remember
Drive cloning software usually creates a sector-by-sector copy of the disk, which means the clone takes up much less space than the original. This means you can fit a fairly large amount of data onto a recordable CD or small partition.

Running the Windows Millennium Setup

At last, your preparations are complete and you're just about ready to run Setup. This section looks at a couple of ways to run custom installations, and then runs through the actual Setup procedure.

Using Setup's Switches

If you'd like a bit more control over how Setup runs, you can use the various switches that are supported by Setup.exe.

The Setup.exe command uses the following general syntax:

setup [*batch*] *switches*

The optional *batch* portion specifies a Setup script that can automate much of the Setup procedure. I discuss these scripts in the next section. Table 1.1 runs through some of the more useful switches. Bear in mind that these switches are case sensitive, so enter them exactly as they appear in the table.

TABLE 1.1: SWITCHES YOU CAN USE WITH THE SETUP COMMAND

Switch	What It Does
/?	Displays a description for a few of the switches.
/C	Bypasses loading the SmartDrive disk cache.
/d	Tells Setup not to use your existing copy of Windows (that is, Setup ignores Win.ini, System.ini, and so on).
/ie	Tells Setup not to prompt you to create a startup disk.
/ih	Runs ScanDisk in the foreground (if you start Setup from within Windows 3.*x*).
/im	Bypasses the check for low conventional memory.
/is	Bypasses the ScanDisk hard disk check.
/iv	Bypasses the "billboards" that tell you about Windows features during the Setup procedure.
/IW	Tells Setup not to display the License Agreement.
/T:*dir*	Sets *dir* as the folder in which Setup should store its temporary files.

Watch Out!
Note that *all* the files in the folder specified with the /T switch are deleted when Setup is finished. Therefore, don't use a folder that contains other files you need to keep.

Creating Automated Setup Scripts

If you install Windows Millennium on a clean or DOS-only system, or if you install Windows Millennium to a separate folder on a Windows 3.*x* system, you'll be required to answer quite a few Setup prompts. These include your product ID, the folder to use for installing Windows, the components you want to install, your name and company name, and so on. There's a lot to go through, but it's not that much of a burden if you'll be running Setup only once.

However, Setup becomes quite tedious if you have to run it multiple times, either if you're running several installation tests on a single machine, or if you have to install Windows Millennium on multiple machines. Rather than trudging through every Setup step each time, you can automate Setup by creating an *installation script.*

An installation script is in an information (.inf) file that contains your answers to Setup's prompts. As you saw in the previous section, you can include the name of an installation script on the Setup command line. When you do this, Setup takes the data it needs from the script and bypasses the prompts. If you set up your script correctly (and make judicious use of Setup's switches), you can run Setup and then never touch your computer again until the installation is complete. Best of all, Windows Millennium comes with a utility called Batch 98 that makes it easy to create a script.

Here is the basic procedure for creating and using an installation script:

1. Install Windows Millennium on the first machine.

2. Install Batch 98. To get this program, you have two choices:

   - If you have a copy of the Windows 98 CD, insert it and open the \tools\reskit\batch folder. Run setup.exe and follow the prompts until the program is installed.

   - Download and install Batch 98 from the Windows 98 Resource Kit Web site:

     http://resourcelink.mspress.microsoft.com/
     reslink/win98/toolbox/default.asp

3. Select Start, Programs, Microsoft Batch 98. You see the Batch 98 window shown in Figure 1.1.

4. If you'll be using the script on the same machine, click the Gather now button. This tells Batch 98 to gather all those

Figure 1.1
Use Batch 98 to
create an auto-
mated installation
script for
Windows
Millennium.

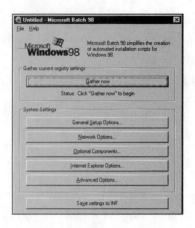

Registry settings that are related to Setup and to add them to the script.

5. To specify other Setup parameters, use the buttons in the System Settings group:

    General Setup Options—Use this button to enter information such as the Windows Millennium product ID, installation folder, user data, desktop icons to be displayed, and time zone. You can also activate or deactivate several Setup prompts.

    Network Options—Here you can specify various network components to install, including protocols, services, and clients.

    Optional Components—Click this button to choose the Windows Millennium components you want to install.

    Internet Explorer Options—This module deals with options such as which items appear in the Quick Launch toolbar, whether Web integration is turned on, security settings, and more.

    Advanced Options—Use this button to specify a Registry file to load, a system policy file, and whether Windows Update is enabled.

6. Click Save settings to INF, select a location and filename in the Save As dialog box, and then click Save.

7. To create another script, select File, New and repeat steps 4–6.

Again, you use the script by specifying its path and filename when running the SETUP command. For example, if you saved the script as msbatch.inf (the default name) to C:\, you'd launch Setup as follows (assuming drive D contains the Windows Millennium CD):

```
d:\setup c:\msbatch.inf
```

Launching Setup   See P. 26

How you get Setup underway depends on how you're installing Windows Millennium. Note that if you're starting Setup from DOS, and if you have the Windows Millennium CD, you need to make sure that the appropriate CD-ROM drivers are installed at startup.

Here's a summary of the various ways you can launch Setup (I assume in all cases that you have already inserted the Windows Millennium CD):

If you're installing to a clean system—Restart your system with a bootable floppy disk in drive A. Type *d:\setup* (where *d* is the letter of your CD-ROM drive) and then press Enter.

If you're installing to a system with only DOS or Windows 3.0—Boot to the DOS prompt and then run *d:\setup*.

If you're upgrading over Windows 9x—When you insert the Windows Millennium CD (after booting Win9x), a dialog box should show up and ask if you want to upgrade to Windows Millennium; click Yes. If no dialog box appears, select Start, Run. Enter *d:\setup*, and click OK.

If you're dual booting with another operating system—Boot to the DOS prompt, either by using the existing dual boot capabilities, if they exist, or by restarting with a bootable DOS floppy disk in drive A. Run the *d:\setup* command.

Here's a behind-the-scenes look at what happens when Setup gets underway:

1. Setup checks your hard disk for errors by running ScanDisk.

2. Setup checks for the existence of antivirus software resident in memory and, if found, asks you to disable the software before continuing.

3. Setup copies its files to a temporary folder named `Wininst0.400` on your hard disk.

4. During a Windows 9x upgrade, Setup examines the Registry to provide you with an identical Windows Millennium configuration.

5. Setup checks your system to make sure it meets the minimum system requirements.

6. Setup checks for and, if necessary, installs both an extended memory manager and a disk drive cache.

7. Setup examines RAM for any terminate-and-stay-resident programs and device drivers that are known to cause problems during installation.

8. Setup checks your hard disk for DOS uninstall information, which is typically stored in a folder named `Old_dos.1`. If found, Setup asks if you want to delete this information.

9. During a Windows 9x upgrade, Setup performs an integrity check on the Registry files.

10. If a problem occurs during the installation, Setup has a Safe Recovery option that appears the next time you run Setup. You are warned that you should use Safe Recovery the next time you reboot. This warning is put in place by adding the following two lines to `Autoexec.bat`:

    ```
    @if exist C:\WININST0.400\SuWarn.bat call
    ➥ C:\WININST0.400\SuWarn.bat
    @if exist C:\WININST0.400\SuWarn.bat del
    ➥ C:\WININST0.400\SuWarn.bat
    ```

11. The Setup wizard is loaded. This wizard takes you step-by-step through the rest of the installation. Note that a Windows 9x upgrade skips most of the following steps.

12. In the "Information Collection" phase of Setup, you're asked various questions to customize your Windows Millennium configuration. If you're upgrading, for example, Setup will ask if you want to save your existing system files (see Figure 1.2). If you're installing clean, you're asked things like which Windows Millennium components you want to install, your name and company name, your network options, and the language you want to use.

13. Setup asks if you want to create a startup disk. This is a bootable floppy disk that contains CD-ROM support and a number of troubleshooting utilities. (If you elect not to create the disk now, you can always create one later. See Chapter 15, "Preparing for Trouble," for details. Also, if you booted from a floppy, be sure to remove the disk now.)

→ **See Also** "Putting Together an Emergency Boot Disk," **p. 347.**

14. Setup begins copying the Windows Millennium files to your hard disk.

15. When the file copying is complete, Setup reboots your computer.

Shortcut
Although it takes a bit longer, selecting the Custom option gives you complete control over which components are installed. This saves you time down the road because you're less likely to have to add or remove components once the installation is complete.

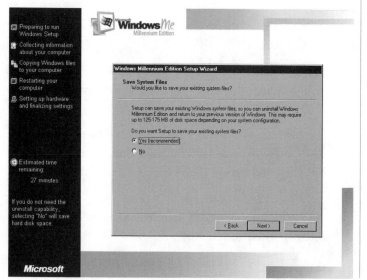

Figure 1.2
During an upgrade installation, the Setup Wizard asks if you want to save your existing system files.

Remember
The hardware detection phase can take quite a while. If the progress meter stops moving for more than a few minutes, shut off your machine. Wait for a few seconds to give all devices time to completely shut down, and then restart your computer.

16. Setup detects the Plug and Play hardware on your computer. The appropriate device drivers are installed.

17. If you're not upgrading from Windows 9x, Setup begins its hardware detection phase to look for legacy devices. Your computer may be rebooted when this phase is complete.

18. Setup prompts you to log on to Windows Millennium and your network (if applicable).

19. Setup runs through a number of chores to set up items such as the Control Panel, Start menu, and Registry. Setup also runs the WinAlign utility (which made its debut in Windows 98) to improve the startup performance of some applications. (This is the Tune Up Application Start item on Setup's checklist.)

20. When Setup is done, the Welcome to Windows Millennium dialog box appears.

Adding and Removing Windows Millennium Components

After Windows Millennium is installed, you don't have to rerun Setup to add new components or to remove installed components. You can do it right from within Windows Millennium:

1. Select Start, Settings, Control Panel to open the Control Panel window.

2. Click the Add/Remove Programs link. Windows Millennium displays the Add/Remove Programs Properties dialog box.

3. Display the Windows Setup tab. Windows Millennium takes a few seconds to figure out which components are installed, and then displays a list similar to the one shown in Figure 1.3.

4. Find the component you want to work with. Here's how to interpret the check boxes:

Figure 1.3
Use the Windows Setup tab to see which components are installed, and to add and remove components.

- An activated check box with a white background means the component is fully installed.

- An activated check box with a gray background means the component is partially installed. To see the various pieces associated with the component, click the Details button.

- A deactivated check box means the component is not installed.

5. To add a component, activate its check box; to remove a component, deactivate its check box. Repeat as necessary.

6. Click OK.

Extracting a File from the Windows Millennium Setup Files

One common Windows Millennium troubleshooting technique is to extract a single file from the Windows Millennium CD and store it on your hard disk. You most often use this technique when you need to replace an existing file that has become corrupted or has been deleted. Unfortunately, you can't simply copy the file from the disc, because most of the files are stored in special compressed archive files called *cabinets* (they use the cab extension). Here's how to extract a file from a cabinet:

Undocumented
Previous versions of Windows would usually ask you to insert your Windows CD to install the selected components. Windows Millennium doesn't do this. Why? Because during the installation, Setup copied the Millennium source files to your hard disk, so the CD isn't needed. To see the source files, check out the Windows\Options\Install\ folder.

Undocumented
To find out which cabinet contains the file you want, run a search. With the CD's `Win9x` folder highlighted, click the Search button (or press Ctrl+E). Type `*.cab` in the `Search for files or folders named` text box, type the name of the file you want to extract in the `Containing text` box, and then click Search Now.

1. Insert the Windows Millennium CD and use Windows Explorer to open the `Win9x` folder.

2. Double-click the cabinet file to open it. Windows Explorer shows a list of the files contained in the cabinet.

3. Find the file you want, drag it out of the cabinet, and then drop it on the destination folder. (Alternatively, highlight the file and then select the File, Extract command.)

Editing Your Username and Company Name

In Chapter 3, "An Insider's Guide to Four Crucial Configuration Tools," you learn about the Windows Millennium Registry, which will play a big part throughout the rest of this book. To give you a taste of what you can do with the Registry, this section shows you how to use it to change a Setup setting. (Because editing the Registry is not a task to be taken lightly, I suggest you read the Registry material in Chapter 3 before running through the techniques in this section.)

→ **See Also** "An Insider's Guide to the Registry," **p. 62.**

As I mentioned earlier, one of the chores Setup asks you to perform is to enter a username and company name. This data is stored in the Registry, and it's used in a variety of circumstances:

- Many 32-bit applications (including Microsoft Office) gather these values from the Registry and use them as the default settings during installation.

- When you open Control Panel's System icon (or right-click My Computer and then click Properties), these values are displayed in the General tab of the System Properties dialog box.

- When you select the Help, About command in most applications, these values are displayed in the About dialog box.

If you'd like to change these values, open the Registry Editor (select Start, Run, type `regedit`, and click OK) and find the following key:

```
HKEY_LOCAL_MACHINE\Software\Microsoft\Windows\Current
Version
```

Here you'll find two settings that hold your registered names:

RegisteredOwner—This is your registered username.

RegisteredOrganization—This is your registered company name.

To change a setting, double-click the setting name, edit the string in the text box that appears, and then click OK.

Uninstalling Windows Millennium

Windows Millennium isn't for everyone. Whether it's the integration of Internet Explorer, an old and treasured program that no longer runs, poor performance, or a multitude of General Protection Faults caused by installing over a previous version of Windows, you might decide your life would be better without Windows Millennium.

Fortunately, Windows Millennium does come with an uninstall feature that usually works quite well at expunging the Windows Millennium from your machine and restoring the previous operating system. However, you can use this feature only under the following conditions:

- You upgraded over Windows 3.*x*, Windows 95, or Windows 98.

- You saved the system files of your existing version of Windows during Setup, and you haven't deleted those files.

- You haven't compressed your hard disk.

- You haven't changed your hard disk partitions. (This means you haven't used Partition Magic or some other non-data-destroying partitioning utility to create or remove partitions, and that you haven't converted the drive to FAT32.)

Bill: "And the electrical outlets? The holes are round, not rectangular. How do I fix that?" Contractor: "Just uninstall and reinstall the electrical system."
—*From "Bill Gates Buys a House"*

■ Your hard disk isn't infected with a boot sector virus. (You'll need to run an antivirus program to check this.)

How can Windows Millennium uninstall itself? The secret lies within a few files stored in the root folder of your bootable partition. Here's a summary:

`Setuplog.txt`—This text file is the log of the entire Setup procedure. It contains, among many other things, a setting that records the location of the `Winundo.dat` and `Winundo.ini` files (described as follows).

`Suhdlog.dat`—This file contains a copy of the master boot record and partition boot records as they were configured when you installed Windows Millennium. This is why you can't uninstall Windows Millennium if your partition configuration has changed. Windows Millennium would restore this old partition information, and you'd almost certainly lose data.

`Winundo.dat`—This file contains a compressed backup of the system files from your old version of Windows.

`Winundo.ini`—This file is an inventory of the files that were backed up into `Winundo.dat` file. It also contains a list of the new Windows Millennium files that Setup installed.

Here are the steps to follow to uninstall Windows Millennium:

1. Select Start, Settings, Control Panel to open Control Panel, and then click the Add/Remove Programs link.

2. In the Install/Uninstall tab, highlight `Uninstall Windows Millennium`, as shown in Figure 1.4.

3. Click the Add/Remove button. A dialog box asks if you're sure you want to uninstall Windows Millennium.

4. Click Yes. Windows Millennium displays another dialog box to tell you that Uninstall is about to check for disk errors.

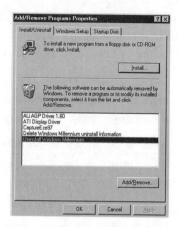

Figure 1.4
If you can uninstall Windows Millennium, the Install/Uninstall tab will sport an Uninstall Windows Millennium item.

5. Click Yes. Uninstall runs ScanDisk to check your hard disk for problems. When ScanDisk is done, another dialog box pops up to tell you that Uninstall is ready to do its thing.

6. Click Yes. Uninstall shuts down your computer, restarts, and then asks once again if you're sure you want to proceed.

7. Press **y** and then Enter. Uninstall removes the Windows Millennium files and restores your previous configuration (this process takes several minutes).

8. When Uninstall is finished, press Enter to restart your machine and load your previous operating system.

Essential Information

- To get the most out of Windows Millennium, go beyond the minimum system requirements and load your machine with a PCI bus, a Plug and Play BIOS, at least 64MB of RAM, a fast Pentium II or later processor, a large hard disk, and a Super VGA card and monitor.

- For maximum reliability, install Windows Millennium on a clean system.

Inside Scoop
If you want to uninstall Windows Millennium because you can't get it to load, you won't be able to use the Control Panel technique. Instead, boot to DOS and then run the command C:\Windows\Command\Uninstall (assuming that you installed Windows Millennium in the C:\Windows folder).

- Don't jump blindly into the Windows Millennium installation. Run through the checklist provided in this chapter to make sure your system is ready to accept Windows Millennium.

- Take advantage of Setup's switches to customize your Windows Millennium installation.

- If you'll be installing Windows Millennium multiple times or on multiple computers, use Batch 98 to create automated Setup scripts.

- Remember that you won't be able to uninstall Windows Millennium if you compressed your hard disk or changed your hard disk's partition information.

GET THE SCOOP ON...
The Intricacies of the Startup Process ▪ The Removal
of Real Mode Support in Windows ME ▪ Techniques
for Running Custom Startups ▪ The Importance of
Exiting Windows Properly ▪ Customizing the Startup
Logo and Shutdown Message

Understanding and Controlling the Windows Millennium Startup

Chapter 2

A T THE USER LEVEL, MICROSOFT has generally ignored the subject of the Windows startup. Other than perhaps briefly discussing the logon procedure, the booklets that come with each Windows version remain steadfastly mute on the subject of the startup. At first glance, this may seem reasonable. After all, isn't the startup an uneventful procedure that's nothing more than an excuse to go grab another cup of coffee? Yes, it is—*most* of the time. However, what do you do if one day Windows just refuses to run? What if an error occurs during startup?

To handle nonstandard startups, you have to understand how the startup procedure works, and you have to know how to wield the various startup tools that Windows Millennium offers. This chapter will help you do just that by giving you an inside look at the Windows Millennium startup.

How the Startup Process Works

Troubleshooting startup problems, and figuring out which of the many Windows Millennium startup options and tools you need, requires an understanding of the entire boot process. In the steps that follow, I ignore most of the hundreds of internal tasks that occur during a typical boot, and instead concentrate solely on those steps that relate to startup troubleshooting and customization:

1. During a *cold boot* (turning the power on or pressing the restart button), the microprocessor locates and runs the ROM BIOS code. On a system with a Plug and Play BIOS, the code enumerates and initializes all Plug and Play devices on the system.

2. The ROM BIOS code then runs the Power-On Self Test (POST), which tests the system memory and initializes various devices (such as the keyboard and disk drives).

3. During the POST, you have the opportunity to change your computer's startup options (these are known variously as the BIOS settings or the CMOS settings). You should see a message on the screen that tells you how to get to these options (pressing Delete is common, as is pressing Escape or Ctrl+Escape).

4. If the POST completes successfully, the computer usually beeps the speaker once.

5. The ROM BIOS code checks for a disk in drive A and, if it finds one, checks to see if the disk is bootable. If so, the system boots to the A:\ prompt. If there is no disk in drive A, the code finds the hard disk's bootable partition and boots the system from there.

6. Windows Millennium takes over at this point and processes the system file Io.sys. This little 100KB (give or take) program is all that's left of real mode DOS in Windows Millennium.

7. Io.sys runs Win.com.

8. The Windows Millennium startup logo is displayed.

9. Win.com runs the Virtual Memory Manager (Vmm32.vxd) to handle the real mode loading of virtual device drivers, or *VxDs*. These are the *static* VxDs that Windows Millennium

Remember
Step 5 shows you why a bootable disk enables you to regain control of your computer even if your hard disk isn't working. By always checking drive A first, the BIOS code can bypass the hard disk at startup. Most computers have BIOS settings that enable you to change this startup behavior (for example, you can have the BIOS codecheck the hard drive first or even boot from a removable drive).

needs immediately (as opposed to *dynamic* VxDs that only load when they're required), and they're all contained within the Vmm32.vxd file.

10. VMM32 checks the Windows\System\Vmm32 folder to see if it contains any of the VxDs that are normally found within the Vmm32.vxd file. If it does, the VxDs are loaded from that folder instead of Vmm32.vxd.

11. Vmm32 queries the Windows Millennium Registry for the list of static VxDs to load (these are Registry entries that have a StaticVxD setting). This list can be found in the following Registry key (see Chapter 3, "An Insider's Guide to Four Crucial Configuration Tools"):

    → **See Also** "An Insider's Guide to the Registry," **p. 62.**

    HKEY_LOCAL_MACHINE\System\CurrentControlSet\Services\VxD

12. VMM32 checks the System.ini file for other VxDs listed under the [386 Enh] section.

13. VMM32 switches the processor into protected mode.

14. VMM32 begins loading the protected mode Vxds for system devices and other hardware. Also, Plug and Play device drivers are loaded and the resources used by Plug and Play devices are allocated. If VMM32 detects any new or changed devices, you may be asked to insert your Windows Millennium CD-ROM.

15. The three main components of the Windows Millennium system are loaded:

    Kernel—The Kernel (Kernel32.dll and Krnl386.exe) is the heart of Windows Millennium. Its duties include loading applications, allocating virtual memory, scheduling and running program threads, and handling file input and output.

    GDI—The Graphical Device Interface (Gdi.exe and Gdi32.exe) manages Windows Millennium's graphical user interface.

    User—The User component (User.exe and User32.exe) manages input from the user (keystrokes, mouse clicks, joystick movements, and so on), and output to the user

Inside Scoop

During step 10, if Windows Millennium discovers that a VxD is missing or corrupted, the new System File Protection feature kicks in and automatically restores the problem file. I discuss System File Protection in more detail in Chapter 14, "Crucial System Maintenance Skills."

Undocumented
Windows also checks for new floppy disks at startup, which most users don't need. To avoid this check and save startup time, launch the Control Panel's System icon, display the Performance tab, and then click File System. In the Floppy Disk tab, deactivate the Search for new floppy disk drives... check box.

Shortcut
To prevent the shortcuts in the Startup folder from loading, hold down the Shift key while Windows Millennium starts.

(sending data to an open window, playing sounds in response to events, and so on).

16. The Windows Millennium shell is loaded.

17. Windows and network logon dialog boxes are displayed.

18. Shortcuts for programs, documents, and other files are processed from the Startup folder. Also, the Registry's various Run keys are processed. See Chapter 11, "Getting the Most out of Your Applications."

→ **See Also** "Launching Applications Automatically at Startup," **p. 276.**

Say Goodbye to Real Mode in Windows Millennium

You can scour the steps outlined in the previous section all you want, but you won't find any references to Config.sys or Autoexec.bat. These two files have been startup stalwarts since the early days of DOS (around the time of Windows 1.0!) and have been used since those ancient times to load device drivers, set environment variables, and run programs at startup. Since Windows 95, they've represented the *real mode* (pure DOS) portion of Windows.

With Windows Millennium, however, Microsoft has finally made that long-awaited (and long overdue) break with the past and has eliminated real mode support. From a startup perspective, this means two things:

- The files Config.sys and Autoexec.bat are not processed during startup.

- There is no direct way to "boot to DOS" at startup. Instead, the only way to get to DOS is to create a Windows Millennium emergency boot disk, as explained in Chapter 15, "Preparing for Trouble."

→ **See Also** "Putting Together an Emergency Boot Disk" **p. 347.**

If `Config.sys` and `Autoexec.bat` are ignored at startup, does that mean older applications that rely on settings within these files will break? Probably not. The reason is that Windows Millennium handles `Config.sys` and `Autoexec.bat` settings in two ways.

The first occurs during the Windows Millennium installation. Setup removes all settings from both files, discards those that have protected mode equivalents (such as CD-ROM device drivers), and stores the rest inside the Windows Millennium Registry. See the following key:

```
HKEY_LOCAL_MACHINE\System\CurrentControlSet\Control\Session
Manager\Environment
```

`Config.sys` and `Autoexec.bat` are still available in the root folder, but they're hidden from view and modified: `Config.sys` is stripped completely and `Autoexec.bat` is given a few SET statements for compatibility.

The second way that Windows Millennium handles `Config.sys` and `Autoexec.bat` is to watch for changes to these files from older setup programs. The next time you start Windows, it removes the new settings from the files, discards whatever isn't needed, and stores the rest in the Registry.

Working with the Windows Millennium Startup Menu

Unlike Windows 3.*x*, Windows Millennium launches automatically at startup. What do you do if you need to prevent Windows Millennium from loading, maybe because you're having trouble getting Windows Millennium to run? For these situations, you can invoke the Windows Millennium Startup menu, which offers various startup options.

To get to the Startup menu, restart your computer and hold down the Ctrl key during the POST. After the POST is complete, the Startup menu appears:

```
Microsoft Windows Millennium Startup Menu
=====================================

1. Normal
2. Logged (\BOOTLOG.TXT)
```

Remember

Real mode is a single-tasking processor mode that can address only 1MB of memory and that gives applications direct access to system hardware. *Protected mode* is a multitasking mode that can address memory beyond 1MB (virtual memory) and takes advantage of the microprocessor's built-in protection features that enable multiple programs to safely share the same system resources.

3. Safe mode
4. Step-by-step confirmation

To select an item, type its number and then press Enter.

If you're familiar with the Startup menu from Windows 9x, it's likely you're surprised at the relatively small number of commands in the Windows Millennium version. That's because, as I mentioned earlier, Windows Millennium doesn't support booting to DOS; so the Startup menu commands relating to DOS booting have been removed. Let's examine the four remaining commands.

Normal—Not surprisingly, this option starts Windows Millennium in the usual way, so it requires no further elaboration.

Logged   (\BOOTLOG.TXT)—This option starts Windows Millennium normally, but records each step of the boot procedure to a text file named Bootlog.txt, which is stored in your system's root folder. Use this option when Windows Millennium won't start and you want to see where in the boot process the failure occurs. Here's the general procedure for using this option:

1. Restart your computer and then run the Logged (\BOOTLOG.TXT) option.

2. When Windows Millennium fails to load, insert your emergency boot disk and restart your computer.

3. At the DOS prompt, type **edit bootlog.txt** and press Enter to open Bootlog.txt in the MS-DOS Editor.

4. Search for a line that contains LoadFailed:

   ```
   [000DE95B] Loading Vxd = CONFIGMG
   [000DE95B] LoadFailed = CONFIGMG
   ```

5. Reinstall the offending driver or file:

   • If the line shows only a filename without an extension or path (for example, CONFIGMG), it's a VxD that's loading from within Vmm32.vxd. In this case, extract the VxD file (see Chapter 1, "Ten Things You Should

Watch Out!
Holding down Ctrl may interfere with some POST chores, such as setting up the keyboard or initializing a SCSI controller. If this happens, just release Ctrl until the POST resumes, and then hold it down again. If you have a lot of trouble with this, forget about Ctrl and wait until you hear the POST beep; then immediately press F8.

Know About the Windows Millennium Setup") and copy it to the `C:\Windows\System\Vmm32` folder.

→ **See Also** "Extracting a File from the Windows Millennium Setup Files," **p. 33.**

- If the line shows a filename with an extension but no folder (for example, `JAVASUP.VXD`), it's a VxD that's loading from the `C:\Windows\System` folder. Extract the file from the Windows Millennium source files (or wherever) and then replace the existing file in the `C:\Windows\System\` folder.

- If the line shows a full path (folder plus filename), reinstall the file to that folder.

Safe mode—This command launches a bare-bones version of Windows Millennium. This means that the Registry isn't processed, only necessary device drivers are loaded (such as those for the keyboard and mouse), and the display is set to a 16-color, 640×480 resolution using the Standard VGA display driver. This minimal configuration should enable you to load Windows Millennium successfully. From there, you can (hopefully) troubleshoot the problem.

Step-by-step confirmation—This command tells Windows Millennium to ask you for confirmation before performing a startup task:

`Process the system registry [Enter=Y,Esc=N]?`

Pressing Enter or Y loads the driver or runs the command. To bypass the task, press Esc or N. This is one of the best methods for isolating a problem. As you step through the tasks, press Enter or Y to load each one. Keep an eye on the screen to see if any error messages show up. If you see such a message, or if your system hangs, then you've found the culprit and you can take the necessary steps to repair the problem. For example, if it's a Windows device driver, replace the driver (as described earlier).

Undocumented
Not all `LoadFailed` lines indicate a problem. In some cases, a driver may fail to load simply because the necessary hardware doesn't exist on your system. For example, the driver VPOWERD will fail to load if your system doesn't support Advanced Power Management. False `LoadFailed` lines may appear with the following drivers: DSOUND, EBIOS, NDIS2SUP, VPOWERD, VSERVER, and VSHARE.

Shortcut
You can bypass the Startup menu and select `Safe` `mode` automatically by holding down the Shift key during the POST. Alternatively, press F5 as soon as you hear the beep that signals the end of the POST.

Shortcut
The shortcut key
for the Step-by-
step confirmation
command is
Shift+F8.
Remember to
press this key
combination as
soon as your hear
the beep that
announces the
end of the POST.

Controlling Startup Using the System Configuration Utility

If Windows Millennium won't start, troubleshooting the problem usually involves trying various Startup menu commands and experimenting with different step-by-step sequences. It's almost always a time-consuming and tedious business.

However, what if Windows Millennium *will* start, but you encounter problems along the way? Or, what if you want to try a few different configurations to see if you can eliminate startup items or improve Windows Millennium's overall performance? For these scenarios, don't bother trying out different startup configurations by hand. Instead, take advantage of Windows Millennium's System Configuration Utility, which gives you a graphical front end that offers precise control over how Windows Millennium starts.

To launch the System Configuration Utility, you have two choices:

- Select Start, Programs, Accessories, System Tools, System Information. When the System Information window appears, select Tools, System Configuration Utility.

- Select Start, Run, type **msconfig**, and click OK.

Either way, the System Configuration Utility window appears, as shown in Figure 2.1.

Figure 2.1
Use the System
Configuration
Utility to select
different startup
configurations.

The General tab has three startup options:

Normal startup—This option loads Windows Millennium normally.

Diagnostic startup—This option is equivalent to selecting `Step-by-step confirmation` in the Windows Millennium Startup menu.

Selective startup—When you activate this option, the check boxes below become available. Use these check boxes to select which portions of the startup should be processed.

For a selective startup, you control how Windows Millennium processes items in five categories:

System.ini—This file contains system-specific information about your computer's hardware and device drivers. Most hardware data is stored in the Registry, but `System.ini` retains a few settings that are needed for backward compatibility with older programs.

Win.ini—This file contains configuration settings relating to Windows Millennium and to installed Windows applications. Again, the bulk of this data is stored in the Registry, but `Win.ini` is kept around for compatibility.

Static VxDs—Deactivate this check box to prevent static VxDs from loading at startup, as described earlier (see "How the Startup Process Works").

➔ **See Also** "Understanding Device Drivers," **p. 468**.

Startup—This refers to items in your Windows Millennium Startup group (identified in the Startup tab as a `Per-User Run` item; see Figure 2.2), `Win.ini`, or the Registry. For the latter, the settings are stored in the following key (as explained in Chapter 11, "Getting the Most out of Your Applications"):

➔ **See Also** "Launching Applications Automatically at Startup," **p. 276**.

```
HKEY_LOCAL_MACHINE\Software\Microroft\Windows\
CurrentVersion
```

This includes items in the Run subkey (identified in the Startup tab as a Machine Run item) and the RunServices subkey (identified in the Startup tab as a Machine Service item).

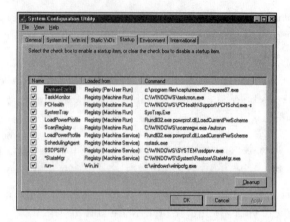

Environment—This is a section of memory that stores the values of a number of *variables*, such as the location Windows uses for its temporary files and the prompt you see at the DOS command line.

To control these startup items, the System Configuration utility gives you two choices:

- To prevent Windows Millennium from loading every item in a particular category, activate Selective startup in the General tab and then deactivate the check box for the category you want. For example, to disable all items in Win.ini, deactivate the Process Win.ini file check box.

- To prevent Windows Millennium from loading only specific items in a category, display the category's tab and then deactivate the check box beside the item you want to bypass at startup.

Clicking the General tab's Advanced button displays the Advanced Troubleshooting Settings dialog box, shown in Figure 2.3. Here's a summary of the settings in this dialog box:

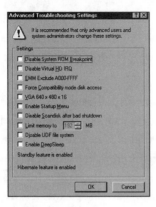

Figure 2.3
Click the
Advanced button
to display these
advanced startup
settings.

Disable System ROM Breakpoint—When you activate this check box, Windows Millennium won't use the ROM address space between F000:0000 and 1MB for a system breakpoint (an internal code used by Windows). This setting was designed only for systems that run the QEMM or 386Max memory managers, so you shouldn't need to activate this option.

Disable Virtual HD IRQ—When you activate this check box, you're telling Windows Millennium not to use its virtual handler for interrupt requests from the hard disk controller. Instead, these requests will be handled by the ROM code that processes controller interrupts.

EMM Exclude A000-FFFF—When activated, this check box tells Windows Millennium not to look for unused memory blocks in the Upper Memory Area (that is, the addresses from A000 to FFFF).

Force Compatibility mode disk access—When you activate this check box, Windows Millennium uses only real mode drivers for disk access. When a disk drive uses real mode drivers, it is said to be in *compatibility mode.*

VGA 640 x 480 x 16—Activate this check box to load Windows Millennium using the Standard VGA display driver, which uses 640×480 resolution and only 16 colors.

Inside Scoop
If video problems prevent you from using the System Configuration Utility, you can still configure Windows Millennium to use the Standard VGA driver by editing System.ini. Boot to the DOS prompt using an emergency boot disk and enter the command **edit c:\windows\system.ini** to load System.ini into the MS-DOS Editor. Find the display.drv line and change it to display.drv=vga.drv.

Undocumented
The design of Intel's TX chipset allows only a maximum of 64MB to be cached. Therefore, anything loaded above 64MB must be accessed from main memory instead of the faster cache. Windows loads its files from the top of memory on down, so its services are not cached, and therefore overall performance suffers.

Enable Startup Menu—If you activate this check box, the Windows Millennium Startup menu appears automatically when you boot. You don't have to hold down Ctrl during the POST.

Disable Scandisk after bad shutdown—If you shut off or reboot your computer without exiting Windows Millennium, ScanDisk is run automatically during Startup to check for disk errors. If you find yourself constantly rebooting after Windows Millennium hangs during startup, these ScanDisk checks can waste time. In this case, activate this check box and then run ScanDisk later after the problem is solved.

Limit memory to x MB—Use this check box to restrict memory usage on your machine to the first x megabytes. For example, some Intel processors suffer performance problems when more than 64MB is installed.

Disable UDF file system—Activating this check box tells Windows Millennium not to use the Universal Disk Format file system for removable media, including DVD discs. You may need to activate this check box if you have a DVD player that doesn't support UDF.

Controlling Startup Using Msdos.sys

Inside Scoop
Activating Enable DeepSleep tells Windows that it can put your system into the "S3" sleep state (assuming your system supports it). This is part of the ACPI specification (see Chapter 23); it's a low-power mode where everything but main memory is shut down.

Msdos.sys is a special system file that controls various aspects of the Windows Millennium startup. For example, you can use Msdos.sys to tell Windows Millennium to always display the Startup menu, to adjust the length of time Windows Millennium waits before selecting the default Startup menu command, or to disable the Windows Millennium startup logo.

Msdos.sys contains some powerful options. So, to prevent novice users from accidentally editing or deleting this file, Windows Millennium sets the file's read-only, hidden, and system attributes. The first thing you must do is make sure that Windows Millennium is displaying hidden files:

1. Run Windows Explorer and select the Tools, Folder Options command to display the Folder Options dialog box.

2. Select the View tab.

3. Activate the Show hidden files and folders option button.

4. Deactivate the Hide protected operating system files check box, and then click Yes when Windows asks if you're sure.

5. While you're here, you should also deactivate the Hide file extensions for known file types check box.

6. Click OK.

To set up Msdos.sys for editing, you have to perform the following tasks:

1. In the root folder, right-click Msdos.sys and then click Properties. The file's property sheet appears.

2. Deactivate the Read-only check box and click OK.

3. Right-click Msdos.sys again, but this time click Open With in the shortcut menu.

4. When Windows worries that you're attempting to open a system file, click Open With.

5. In the Open With dialog box, highlight Notepad (or some other text editor), make sure the Always use this program to open these files check box is deactivated, and then click OK.

6. Edit the file, save your changes, and then exit the text editor.

That's an awful lot of work to go through just to make some edits to Msdos.sys. To avoid this drudgery, create a batch file that performs all of these steps automatically:

1. Right-click the desktop, and then click New, Text Document.

Watch Out!
To ensure that Msdos.sys isn't accidentally deleted or modified, reinstate the read-only attribute. Right-click Msdos.sys, click Properties, activate the Read-only check box in the dialog box that appears, and then click OK. You should also consider making a backup copy of this file before making changes.

2. Type **Edit Msdos.sys.bat** and press Enter. (When Windows Millennium asks if you're sure you want to change the extension, click Yes.)

3. Right-click the new file and then click Edit.

4. In Notepad, enter the following lines:

```
@ECHO OFF
ATTRIB -R -H -S C:\Msdos.sys
START /W NOTEPAD C:\Msdos.sys
ATTRIB +R +H +S C:\Msdos.sys
```

5. Save the file and exit Notepad.

Figure 2.4 shows a typical Msdos.sys file opened in Notepad.

Figure 2.4
Notepad showing
a typical
Msdos.sys file.

Msdos.sys contains three sections:

■ The [Paths] section contains settings that specify the main Windows Millennium folder (WinDir), the Windows Millennium boot folder (WinBootDir), and the letter of the drive from which Windows Millennium boots (HostWinBootDrv). You shouldn't change any of these settings.

- The [Options] section contains settings that determine various Windows Millennium startup options. I discuss the available settings as follows.

- The lines that consist mostly of the letter x are there to ensure compatibility with older programs. For example, some older virus checkers expect Msdos.sys to be larger than 1,024 bytes. (Msdos.sys used to be a DOS system file.) All those extra lines are there to make sure that the Msdos.sys file size is at least 1,024 bytes.

The real meat of Msdos.sys is the [Options] section, which accepts various settings for customizing the Windows Millennium startup. The default Msdos.sys may contain only four or five settings (depending on your system), but there are many more you can use:

AutoScan—Controls whether Windows Millennium runs ScanDisk after an improper shutdown. There are three values you can use:

> AutoScan=0—Windows Millennium does not run ScanDisk after a bad shutdown.

> AutoScan=1 (the default)—Windows Millennium runs ScanDisk automatically after a bad shutdown.

BootGUI—This setting used to control whether the Windows Millennium graphical user interface (GUI) was loaded at startup. Windows Millennium doesn't support booting to DOS, so this setting is no longer supported.

BootKeys—Controls whether the Windows Millennium Startup menu's shortcut keys are enabled:

> BootKeys=0—The shortcut keys are disabled.

> BootKeys=1 (the default)—The shortcut keys are enabled.

BootMenu—Controls whether the Windows Millennium Startup menu appears automatically:

Remember
You must press a Startup menu shortcut key immediately after you hear the beep that signals the end of the POST. Windows 95 supported an extra Msdos.sys option called BootDelay that enabled you to specify the number of seconds Windows would wait for a keypress. This option is not supported in Windows Millennium.

`BootMenu=0` (the default)—You must hold down Ctrl during the POST to display the Startup menu.

`BootMenu=1`—The Startup menu appears automatically.

BootMenuDefault—Specifies the Startup menu command that is highlighted automatically when the menu is first displayed. Set this value equal to the number of the menu command, where 1 is the `Normal` command, 2 is the `Logged` (`\BOOTLOG.TXT`) command, and so on.

BootMenuDelay—Specifies the length, in seconds, of the countdown that appears when you display the Startup menu. The default value is 30.

BootMulti—This setting used to control whether Windows Millennium could dual boot with your previous version of DOS. This is no longer supported in Windows Millennium.

BootSafe—Controls whether Windows Millennium boots in Safe mode automatically:

> `BootSafe=0` (the default)—You can start Windows Millennium in Safe mode only by selecting one of the Safe mode options from the Startup menu.

> `BootSafe=1`—Windows Millennium starts in Safe mode automatically.

BootWarn—Controls whether Windows Millennium starts in Safe mode automatically if it encountered problems on the previous boot:

> `BootWarn=0`—Windows Millennium loads normally, even if the previous boot failed.

> `BootWarn=1` (the default)—If `Io.sys` detects that the most recent boot failed, it displays the Startup menu, sets the `Safe mode` option as the default, and displays a warning message.

BootWin—This setting used to control whether your system would boot to Windows Millennium or your previous version of DOS. This is not supported in Windows Millennium.

Logo—Controls whether the Windows Millennium logo is displayed at startup:

Shortcut
You can also bypass the Windows Millennium logo at startup by pressing Esc once the logo appears.

> Logo=0—The logo isn't displayed. Use this setting if you have a video card that can't handle the graphics mode switch that is required to display the logo.
>
> Logo=1 (the default)—The logo is displayed.

Shutting Down Windows Millennium

Shutting down Windows Millennium isn't difficult, but there are a few issues to consider, which is what you'll do in this section.

How the Shutdown Process Works

First off, you should know that Windows Millennium continues the use of Windows 98's *fast shutdown* feature that shuts down your system quite a bit faster than Windows 95. This feature basically just bypasses the unloading of device drivers and other device shutdown chores. The upshot is that your system should shut down in just a few seconds, instead of the 10 or 15 seconds that was typical of Windows 95.

Certainly the most important aspect of shutdown to bear in mind is that you should always exit Windows before you shut off your computer. There are a number of reasons why you need to do this:

" Don't turn off your computer until you see a message telling you that shutdown is complete. If you turn off your computer without shutting it down correctly, you risk losing information. —*Microsoft* "

- Windows Millennium doesn't record some Registry settings until the shutdown process is underway. You'll lose these unsaved settings if you turn off your machine before exiting Windows Millennium.

- Windows Millennium waits for idle processor time before committing some changed data to disk (this is called *write-behind caching*). If you shut down your machine before exiting Windows Millennium, you'll lose this changed data.

- When you exit Windows Millennium, it checks to see if any network users are connected to any of the resources you share with the network. If you turn off your machine without exiting Windows Millennium, network users could get cut off in the middle of a file transfer or print operation.

The Shutdown Procedure

Here's the proper Windows Millennium shutdown procedure:

1. Close all your applications and save all your work.

2. Select the Start, Shut Down command. Windows Millennium displays the Shut Down Windows dialog box shown in Figure 2.5.

Figure 2.5
Selecting the Shut Down command displays this dialog box.

3. Select the shut down command you want to use:

Shut down—Prepares your computer to be turned off. A few seconds later, a bitmap appears with the message It's now safe to turn off your computer. Note that some newer Advanced Power Management computers will turn themselves off automatically at this point.

Restart—Exits Windows Millennium and then cold boots the computer to restart it.

Stand by—Places your computer in standby mode, which powers down the monitor and hard disk. This option is available only if your system has support for Advanced Power Management.

Inside Scoop
Previous versions of Windows displayed *two* bitmaps at shutdown. The first bitmap (it displayed a Windows is shutting down message) has been removed from Windows Millennium.

4. Click OK. Windows Millennium runs the selected shut-down option.

Creating Shutdown Shortcut

Shutting down Windows can take four or five mouse clicks, depending on the current state of the Shut Down Windows dialog box. However, one of the fundamental goals of an unauthorized approach to Windows is to save as many mouse clicks and keystrokes as possible. To that end, here's how to reduce the shutdown procedure to a single click:

1. Right-click an empty section of the desktop and then click New, Shortcut.

2. In the Create Shortcut dialog box, enter the following into the Command line text box and then click Next:

   `c:\windows\rundll32.exe User,ExitWindows`

3. In the Select a name for the shortcut text box, enter **Shut Down Windows** (or whatever you prefer) and click Finish. Windows Millennium adds a new icon to the desktop.

4. Drag that icon and drop it beside (not on) one of the existing icons in the taskbar's Quick Launch toolbar.

Now you need only click the Shut Down Windows icon to initiate the shutdown procedure.

Creating Custom Startup and Shutdown Screens

When you start Windows Millennium, a startup logo is displayed to give you something nicer to look at than the boot text displayed during the POST. You also saw in the previous section that Windows Millennium displays a bitmap during the shutdown process. Interestingly, Windows Millennium is happy to display custom bitmaps in place of either of these two images. Here's how:

- To replace the startup bitmap, create a new image or edit an existing image and then save it as Logo.sys in your system's root folder.

■ The It's now safe to turn off your computer bitmap is a file named Logos.sys in the C:\Windows folder. You can either modify this file, or replace it with a new or modified image that you save as Logos.sys in the C:\Windows folder.

Note that, in all cases, the file you create or modify must have a width of 320 pixels and a height of 400 pixels, and it must be saved as a 256-color bitmap.

Here are the steps to follow to replace a logo screen with a new file.

1. To ensure that the existing file doesn't get overwritten, rename it (with, say, an old extension).

2. Select Start, Programs, Accessories, Paint to launch the Paint program.

3. Select Image, Attributes to display the Attributes dialog box. (You can also press Ctrl+E.)

4. Type **320** in the Width text box, type **400** in the Height text box, and then click OK.

5. Use Paint's tools and colors to construct your image.

6. Select File, Save (or press Ctrl+S) to display the Save As dialog box.

7. Save the file as follows (click Save when you're done):

   • In the File name text box, enter either **logo.sys** (for the startup logo) or **logos.sys** (for the shutdown logo).

   • Select either the boot drive root (for the startup logo) or C:\Windows (for the shutdown logo).

   • In the Save as type list, be sure 256 Color Bitmap is selected.

Here are the steps to follow to convert an existing image:

1. To ensure that the existing file doesn't get overwritten, rename it (with, say, the old extension).

2. Select Start, Programs, Accessories, Paint to launch the Paint program.

3. Select File, Open (or press Ctrl+O) to display the Open dialog box, highlight the file you want to work with, and then click Open.

4. Select Image, Attributes (or press Ctrl+E) to display the Attributes dialog box, note the current values in the Width and Height text boxes, and then click OK.

5. To adjust the width of the image to 320 pixels, select Image, Stretch/Skew (or press Ctrl+W), enter an appropriate percentage in the Stretch group's Horizontal text box, and then click OK.

6. To adjust the height of the image to 400 pixels, select Image, Stretch/Skew (or press Ctrl+W), enter an appropriate percentage in the Stretch group's Vertical text box, and then click OK.

7. Select Image, Attributes (or press Ctrl+E) to confirm that the image's width is 320 pixels and its height is 400 pixels. If you're just a few pixels off, type **320** in the Width text box, type **400** in the Height text box, and then click OK.

8. Use Paint's tools and colors to modify your image, if necessary.

9. Select File, Save As to display the Save As dialog box.

10. Save the file as follows (click Save when you're done):

    - In the File name text box, enter either **logo.sys** (for the startup logo) or **logos.sys** (for the shutdown logo).

    - Select either the boot drive root (for the startup logo) or C:\Windows (for the shutdown logo).

    - In the Save as type list, be sure 256 Color Bitmap is selected.

Shortcut
You may decide to start with one of the existing logo screens and modify it. Because these screens use sys extensions (or old if you renamed them), they won't appear in the Open dialog box. To work around this, select All Files in the Files of type drop-down list. Make sure, as well, to use the File, Save As command to save the modified file under a new name.

Essential Information

- Windows Millennium no longer supports real mode; therefore, it doesn't process `Config.sys` and `Autoexec.bat`.

- Hold down Ctrl during the Power-On Self Test to invoke the Windows Millennium Startup menu, from which you can select various startup options, such as loading Windows Millennium in safe mode.

- Windows Millennium's new System Configuration Utility gives you an easy-to-use graphical front end for many of Windows Millennium's startup options.

- `Msdos.sys` is a hidden, read-only text file that supports a large number of options for controlling the Windows Millennium startup.

- Before turning off your computer, always select Start, Shut Down to exit Windows Millennium properly and ensure that you don't lose data.

- You can customize the startup and shutdown bitmaps by using Paint to create or modify 320×400-pixel images and saving them as `C:\logo.sys` (for the startup bitmap) or `C:\Windows\logos.sys` (the `It's now safe to turn off your computer` bitmap).

GET THE SCOOP ON...
The Importance of the Registry ▪ Techniques for Backing
Up and Keeping the Registry Error-Free ▪ Understanding
the Structure of the Registry ▪ Using the Registry Editor ▪
Installing and Using the System Policy Editor ▪ Installing
and Using Tweak UI ▪ Understanding the Control Panel

An Insider's Guide to Four Crucial Configuration Tools

Chapter 3

M Y GOAL IN THIS BOOK is to help you get the most out of Windows Millennium, and my premise is that this goal can't be met by "toeing the line" and doing only what the manual or Help system tells you. Rather, I believe you can only reach this goal by taking various "unauthorized" routes that go beyond Windows orthodoxy.

This chapter is a perfect example. The four tools that I discuss—the Registry, system policies, Tweak UI, and the Control Panel—aren't difficult to use, but they put an amazing amount of power and flexibility into your hands. I discuss them in this early chapter because you'll be using these important tools throughout the rest of the book. However, you can scour the Windows Millennium manual and Help system all day long and you'll find only a few scant references to the Registry and the Control Panel, and nothing at all on system policies or Tweak UI. To be sure, Microsoft is just being cautious since these *are* powerful tools, and the average user can wreak all kinds of havoc if these features are used incorrectly. However, your purchase of this book is proof that you are not an "average user"; so, by following the instructions in this chapter, I'm sure you'll have no trouble at all using these tools.

An Insider's Guide to the Registry

Let's begin with the Registry, which most experts agree is the most important feature on the Windows landscape. In the next few sections, you'll learn why the Registry is so important, how to keep the Registry safe from harm, how the Registry is structured, and how to work with Registry settings. I'll be referring to the Registry constantly in the chapters to come, so your mastery of this material will go a long way in helping you get your money's worth not only out of this book, but also out of Windows itself.

Why Is the Registry So Important?

One of the main reasons that a computer is a more useful tool than, say, a washing machine, is that computers can remember things. Files that you create or install are remembered, of course, simply by virtue of being stored on your hard disk. But computers are also very good at remembering settings and configurations. If you customize an application's toolbar, for example, chances are the application will remember your customization and display it the next time you use the program. Windows has always done a lot of this. Things like the settings you entered during Setup, the color of the desktop, and the arrangement of the icons are all saved for later use.

In the pre-Windows 95 world, any settings that Windows wanted to remember were stored in simple text files. At first, just Config.sys and Autoexec.bat were used. Subsequent versions of Windows turned to initialization files such as Win.ini and System.ini to hold an ever-growing list of configuration data.

The problem with this design was that these text files were too easily modified or deleted. Also, the sheer number of INI files that eventually came to be used made it difficult to find the setting you wanted to work with.

So, one of the many innovations born with Windows 95 was the concept of a central storage area to hold all (or almost all) Windows configuration data. This database is called the Registry, and it contains a lot of data:

- Information about all the hardware installed on your computer.

- The resources used by those devices.

- A list of the device drivers that get loaded at startup.

- Settings used internally by Windows Millennium.

- File type data that associates a particular type of file with a specific application.

- Object linking and embedding data.

- Wallpaper, color schemes, and other interface customization settings.

- Other customization settings for things like the Start menu and the taskbar.

- Settings for accessories such as Windows Explorer and Internet Explorer.

- Internet and network connections and passwords.

- Settings and customization options for many applications.

That may seem like a long list, but it's only a tiny fraction of what's contained within the Registry's walls. The sheer wealth of data stored in one place makes the Registry convenient, but it also makes it very precious. If your Registry went missing somehow, or if it got corrupted, Windows Millennium simply would not work.

Keeping the Registry Safe

Now that you see why the Registry is an important piece of business, let's take a moment to run through a few protective measures. The techniques in this section should ensure that Windows Millennium never goes down for the count because of a Registry problem.

Copying the Registry Database Files

The first thing you need to understand is that the Registry consists of three files—User.dat, Classes.dat, and System.dat:

Remember
The Registry may have taken over as Windows' memory, but that doesn't mean that INI files have no place in Windows Millennium. Many older applications still expect to store and retrieve settings from INI files such as Win.ini, so Windows Millennium still ships with many of its old INI files to ensure compatibility with these legacy programs.

❝
WARNING: Using Registry Editor incorrectly can cause serious problems that may require you to reinstall Windows. Microsoft cannot guarantee that problems resulting from the incorrect use of Registry Editor can be solved. —*From the Microsoft Knowledge Base*
❞

- User.dat is a hidden, read-only, system file in the Windows folder. Its job is to store user-specific data, including your Windows Millennium customizations, your program configurations, and so on.

- Classes.dat is also a hidden, read-only, system file in the Windows folder. It contains data related to file extensions and their associated programs, as well as OLE (Object Linking and Embedding) and DDE (Dynamic Data Exchange) information. In previous versions of Windows, this data was housed in System.dat.

- System.dat is another hidden, read-only, system file that resides in the Windows folder. It stores system-specific data, such as your machine's hardware configuration, settings used internally by Windows Millennium, and settings required by some 32-bit applications.

So, one of the simplest ways to keep the Registry safe is to make copies of User.dat, Classes.dat, and System.dat. Bear in mind, however, that these files are quite large. In particular, both Classes.dat and System.dat will be between 1.5MB and 2MB to start with, and can easily grow to be 4MB or 5MB in size. (User.dat begins around 150KB and can grow to several times that size.) This means you can't back up these files to a floppy disk. Instead, you'll have to copy these files to another hard disk, a network folder, or a removable disk such as a Zip or Jaz disk.

Backing Up the Registry

The Backup program that came with Windows 95 left a lot to be desired. One of its strangest quirks was that it wouldn't allow you to include the Registry files as part of a backup job! The only way to include these files in a backup was to use the default "Full System Backup" set, which was inconvenient, to say the least.

Happily, this absurd behavior was fixed in Windows 98 and remains absent from the Windows Millennium version of Backup. I'll be discussing the Backup utility in detail in

Chapter 15, "Preparing for Trouble." For now, here are the steps to follow to include the Registry files in a backup job:

→ **See Also** "Backing Up Your Files," **p. 354.**

1. Select Start, Programs, Accessories, System Tools, Backup. (Note that you might need to install Backup from the Windows Millennium CD. I explain how this is done in Chapter 15.)

→ **See Also** "Installing Microsoft Backup," **p. 355.**

2. If the Microsoft Backup dialog box appears, click Close.

3. Click Options to display the Backup Job Options dialog box.

4. Select the Advanced tab, as shown in Figure 3.1.

Figure 3.1
Windows Millennium's Backup program is only too happy to include the Registry files as part of a backup job.

5. Activate the Back up Windows Registry check box.

6. Click OK.

Using the Registry Checker

The only protection Windows 95 offered for the Registry was to make backup copies of the Registry files each time you shut down or restarted your system. Windows 98 beefed up Registry protection considerably thanks to its new Registry Checker utility, which is also part of Windows Millennium. Registry Checker does three things:

Undocumented
Microsoft Backup will *not* back up the Registry if you don't include either the Windows folder or at least one file from your computer's boot partition (usually drive C) in the backup job.

- It makes daily backup copies (up to five in all) of the Registry files.

- It checks for corrupted Registry data and tries to fix any problems it finds. If it can't fix the problem, it restores the previous day's backup.

- It checks for unused data blocks. If enough empty blocks are found (more than 500KB), the Registry is optimized to remove the unused space.

Remember
A cab file is a *cab-inet archive* file that stores multiple files in a compressed format.

Windows Millennium itself uses Registry Checker. For example, during a Windows 9x upgrade, Setup runs Registry Checker to ensure that the Windows 9x Registry is working properly. Also, Windows Millennium runs Registry Checker each time you start your computer. In this case, Registry Checker makes copies of the Registry files (Win.ini and System.ini are also included for good measure) and combines everything into a cab file. This file is then stored in the Windows\Sysbckup folder. Registry Checker stores up to five backups, and they usually take the filenames rb000.cab through rb004.cab.

When Registry Checker runs at startup, it will automatically restore the previous day's backup if it detects a problem with the Registry. However, you can also restore the previous day's backup by booting to DOS and running the following command at the DOS prompt:

```
SCANREG /RESTORE
```

Registry Checker loads and then displays a list of the available backups and the dates on which they were created. Select the cab file you want to use and then click Restore.

If you're in Windows Millennium, you can restore any previous backup and any individual file within that backup by following these steps:

1. Use Windows Explorer to open the Windows\Sysbckup folder.

2. Find the rb00x.cab file you want to work with (select View, Details to use Explorer's Details view to see the file dates).

3. Open the file. Windows Millennium displays the contents of the .cab file in a folder window.

4. Highlight the file or files you want to restore and then select File, Extract. The Browse for Folder dialog box appears.

5. Highlight the Windows folder and then click OK.

Registry Checker actually comes in two versions:

- Scanreg.exe is the real mode version, which is suitable for use at the DOS prompt. This file is located in the Windows\Command folder.

- Scanregw.exe is the protected mode version, which you can use while within Windows. This file is located in the Windows folder.

Here's the syntax used by these files:

```
SCANREG [/BACKUP] [/RESTORE] [/FIX] ["/COMMENT=text"]
SCANREGW [/BACKUP] [/AUTORUN] [/FIX] ["/COMMENT=text"]
```

/BACKUP	Backs up the system files, even if they have already been backed up today.
/RESTORE	Displays a list of backups so you can select the one you want to restore.
/AUTORUN	Runs Registry Checker without prompting. If you don't include this switch and today's backup has already been created, Registry Checker asks if you want to back up the files again.
/FIX	Repairs and optimizes the Registry if no backup copy is available.
"/COMMENT=text"	Adds the string specified by text (29 characters maximum) to the CAB file. This string is displayed instead of the backup's CAB filename when you run scanreg/restore.

Shortcut
You should include Scanreg.exe in your Windows Millennium emergency boot disk. (In Chapter 15, see "Putting Together an Emergency Boot Disk.") This will enable you to run scanreg /restore just in case a Registry problem prevents you from starting Windows Millennium.

Inside Scoop
The bigger the Registry, the more conventional memory Registry Checker requires. You may need to optimize conventional memory to get Registry Checker to run.

Registry Checker maintains a small list of settings that control how the program runs. As you can imagine, it would make no sense to store these settings within the Registry itself. Instead, the settings can be found in the file Scanreg.ini in the Windows folder.

Select Start, Run, type **scanreg.ini**, and then click OK to open this file in Notepad. When you do, you see four settings:

Backup—When this value is set to 1, Registry Checker backs up the configuration files. If you set this value to 0, Registry Checker doesn't perform the backup.

Optimize—When this value is set to 1, Registry Checker looks for blank space within the Registry files and then removes that space to optimize the file. (The optimization occurs only when there is more than 500KB of unused space.) If you set this value to 0, Registry Checker doesn't perform the optimization.

Watch Out!
By using the MaxBackupCopies setting, you can tell Registry Checker to save up to 99 backups. However, when you run scanreg /restore at the DOS prompt, you see only the last five backups.

MaxBackupCopies—This setting specifies the maximum number of backups that Registry Checker can store in Sysbckup. The default value is 5. If you're thinking about increasing this value, remember that each .cab backup file consumes from 500KB to over 1MB, depending on the size of the original files.

BackupDirectory—When this setting is blank, Registry Checker uses the Windows\Sysbckup folder to store the cab backup files. If you'd prefer to use another location (say, on a separate hard disk or on a removable disk), enter the full path you want to use.

Scanreg.ini also lets you specify one or more other files to include in the backup. You do this by adding one or more lines with the following syntax:

```
Files=[dir code,]file1,file2,file3
```

Here, dir code is a two-digit code that represents a predefined path, as described in Table 3.1.

TABLE 3.1:   DIRECTORY CODES FOR USE IN SCANREG.INI

Code	What It Represents
10	The main Windows Millennium folder (usually C:\Windows).
11	The System subfolder (usually C:\Windows\System).
30	Your system's boot folder (usually c:\).
31	Your system's boot host folder (usually c:\). If your boot drive is compressed, this will be the root folder of the host drive (such as H:\).

Remember
If you restore a backed-up Registry, any Registry settings that were modified since that backup was made will be lost. So, for example, you may need to reinstall any programs that you set up after the backup, or you may need to reconfigure any Windows settings that you changed since the backup.

Otherwise, you just enter the full path and filename of the file(s) you want to include in the backup. Here are some examples:

```
Files=10,control.ini,paul.pwl
Files=11,desktop.ini,folder.htt
Files=30,msdos.sys
Files=c:\msoffice\normal.dot
```

Launching the Registry Editor

The Registry dat files are binary files, so you can't edit them directly. Instead, you use a program called the Registry Editor, which enables you to view, modify, add, and delete any Registry setting. It also has a search feature to help you find settings, and export and import features that enable you to save settings to and from a text file.

There are two methods you can use to launch Registry Editor:

- Select Start, Run to display the Run dialog box, type **regedit**, and then click OK.

- In Windows Explorer, open the Windows folder and then launch the file Regedit.exe.

Figure 3.2 shows the Registry Editor window. Here are some notes about this window:

- The left side of the window—which I'll call the *Keys pane*—contains a hierarchical list of the Registry's *keys*. I'll explain what keys are in the next section.

Remember
You can adjust the size of the panes by using your mouse to drag the vertical split bar that separates the two panes. Alternatively, select View, Split, use the left and right arrow keys to move the split bar, and then press Enter.

- To see more keys, either click the plus sign (+) beside a key, or highlight a key and then press the plus sign (+) on your keyboard's numeric keypad.

- To hide exposed keys, either click the minus sign (-) beside a key, or highlight a key and then press minus (-) on your keyboard's numeric keypad.

- The Registry has many levels of keys. To keep straight where you are in the hierarchy, watch the status bar, which always shows the full path of the currently highlighted key.

- The right side of the window—which I'll call the *Settings pane*—displays the settings found within the currently highlighted key.

- The Settings pane is divided into two columns. The Name column shows the name of each setting, and the Data column shows the value associated with each setting.

- Registry settings come in three types: String values, binary values (a series of hexadecimal numbers), and DWORD values.

Figure 3.2
Use the Registry Editor to work with Registry settings.

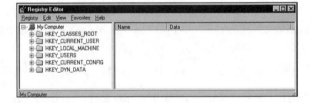

Inside Scoop
DWORD is short for *double word*. In programming circles, a *word* is a 16-bit value. Therefore, a double word is a 32-bit value. Registry DWORD values are 32-bit hexadecimal values arranged as eight digits.

How the Registry Is Structured

When you first open the Registry Editor, you see My Computer at the top, followed by six keys. These are known as the Registry's *root keys*. Here's a summary of what kind of data is stored within each root key:

HKEY_CLASSES_ROOT—This key is mostly concerned with file types (which file extensions are associated with which applications). For example, it's thanks to this key that Windows Millennium knows that a file with a .txt extension should be opened using the Notepad text editor. This key also contains data related to object linking and embedding. All of this data is what's stored in the Classes.dat Registry file. Note, too, that this key is exactly the same as the following key:

```
HKEY_LOCAL_MACHINE\Software\Classes
```

HKEY_CURRENT_USER—This key contains a number of user-specific settings, such as the current wallpaper and color scheme. (This is, in other words, the data from User.dat.) If you set up Windows Millennium with multiple user profiles, this key contains the settings for whichever user is currently logged on.

HKEY_LOCAL_MACHINE—This key (which is basically System.dat) contains a large number of settings related to your hardware and software. In particular, the bulk of the settings used by Windows Millennium can be found here:

```
HKEY_LOCAL_MACHINE\Software\Microsoft\Windows\
CurrentVersion
```

HKEY_USERS—If you haven't set up Windows Millennium for user profiles, this key contains the same data as HKEY_CURRENT_USER. Otherwise, this key contains three subkeys: DEFAULT (which contains default settings for users logging in for the first time), Software (which can be ignored), and a key for the current user (which is the same as HKEY_CURRENT_USER).

HKEY_CURRENT_CONFIG—This key contains settings related to the current hardware profile.

HKEY_DYN_DATA—Changes to the Registry files are written to disk periodically. For fast access, however, some data needs to remain in memory. This data is stored in the HKEY_DYN_DATA key.

Working with Registry Keys and Settings
Now let's examine the Registry Editor techniques that you'll need throughout the rest of this book. In particular, you need to know how to find data, edit settings, rename, create, and delete keys and settings, and how to import and export Registry data. The next few sections provide the specifics.

Finding a Key, Setting, or Value

The Registry contains hundreds of keys and thousands of values, so it helps to know how to search for the item you want to work with. To run a search, follow these steps:

1. Select a starting point for the search. For example, if you know the item you want is in the HKEY_LOCAL_MACHINE root key, highlight HKEY_LOCAL_MACHINE in the Keys pane. If you're not sure, highlight My Computer at the top of the Keys pane.

2. Select Edit, Find, or press Ctrl+F, to display the Find dialog box, shown in Figure 3.3.

Figure 3.3
Use the Find dialog box to search for strings within the Registry.

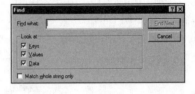

3. Use the Find what box to enter the text you want to locate.

4. Use the check boxes in the Look at group to specify what parts of the Registry you want to search.

Shortcut
After you close the Find dialog box, you can resume your search without having to display the dialog box all over again. To do so, select Edit, Find Next, or press F3.

5. Find usually tries to match your string with any part of a key or setting. If you prefer to find the exact string you entered, activate the Match whole string only check box.

6. Click Find Next until you find the string you want (or until the entire Registry has been checked).

Two New Features That Make It Easier to Navigate the Registry

When using the Registry Editor in previous editions of Windows, two shortcomings cropped up all the time to make navigating the Registry a pain:

- Each time you started the Registry Editor, you always had to begin at the top and then drill down into the keys and settings.

- There was no easy way to navigate to extremely popular keys, such as the main Windows key:

```
HKEY_LOCAL_MACHINE\Software\Microsoft\Windows\
CurrentVersion
```

Fortunately, Windows Millennium's version of the Registry Editor solves both problems rather neatly:

- When you launch the Registry Editor, it displays not the topmost key (My Computer), but the key you were in the previous time you ran the program.

- If you have keys that you visit often, you can save them as "favorites." To do this, navigate to the key and then select Favorites, Add to Favorites. In the Add to Favorites dialog box, edit the key name, if necessary, and then click OK. To navigate to a favorite key, pull down the Favorites menu and select the key name from the list that appears at the bottom of the menu.

Changing the Value of a String Setting

Most of the Registry settings that you'll work with will be strings. To edit a string setting, follow these steps:

1. Find the string setting you want to work with.

2. Double-click the setting or highlight it and press Enter. (The official route is to highlight the setting and then select Edit, Modify.) The Edit String dialog box appears, as shown in Figure 3.4.

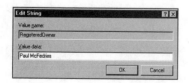

3. Use the Value data text box to edit the string.

4. Click OK.

Shortcut
You can also open a setting for editing by double-clicking it, or by right-clicking it and then clicking Modify in the shortcut menu.

Figure 3.4
You use the Edit String dialog box to modify a string setting.

Changing the Value of a Binary Setting

Working with binary settings is slightly different than working with strings. Here are the steps to follow:

1. Find the binary setting you want to work with.

2. Double-click the setting or highlight it and press Enter. The Edit Binary Value dialog box appears, as shown in Figure 3.5.

Figure 3.5
You use the Edit Binary Value dialog box to modify a binary setting.

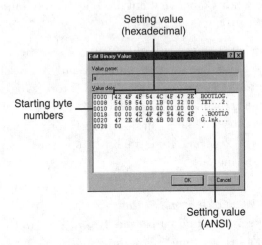

Setting value
(hexadecimal)

Starting byte
numbers

Setting value
(ANSI)

3. Use the Value data text box to edit the value. You use the text box's three columns:

   - The left column contains the starting byte numbers. You can't edit these values.

   - The middle column contains the value of the setting expressed as hexadecimal numbers. This value is displayed in rows consisting of eight two-digit hexadecimal numbers, where each two-digit number represents one byte. You can edit these values.

   - The right column contains the value of the setting expressed as ANSI characters. That is, each character is the ANSI equivalent of the corresponding hexadecimal byte value in the middle column. You can edit these values.

4. Click OK.

Renaming a Key or Setting

You won't often need to rename existing keys or settings. Just in case, though, here are the steps to follow:

1. Find the key or setting you want to work with and then highlight it.

2. Select Edit, Rename, or press F2.

3. Edit the name and then press Enter.

Creating a New Key or Setting

Many Registry-based customizations don't involve editing an existing setting or key. Instead, you have to create a new setting or key. Here's how you do it:

Watch Out!
Rename only those keys or settings that you've created yourself. If you rename any other key or setting, Windows Millennium might not work properly.

1. Highlight the key in which you want to create the new sub-key or setting.

2. Select Edit, New. (Alternatively, right-click an empty section of the Settings pane and then click New.)

3. In the cascade menu, select one of the following: Key, String Value, Binary Value, or DWORD Value.

4. Type a name for the new key or setting.

5. Press Enter.

Deleting a Key or Setting

Here are the steps to follow to delete a key or setting:

1. Highlight the key or setting that you want to delete.

2. Select Edit, Delete, or press Delete. The Registry Editor asks if you're sure.

3. Click Yes.

Exporting a Key to a Registration (.reg) File

Earlier, I showed you a number of methods for backing up the Registry. Another approach is to back up only part of the Registry. For example, if you're about to make changes within the HKEY_CURRENT_USER key, you could back up just that key.

The way you do this is to export the key to a registration file, which is a text file that uses the .reg extension. Here's how it works:

1. Highlight the key you want to export.

2. Select Registry, Export Registry File to display the Export Registry File dialog box shown in Figure 3.6.

3. Select a location for the file.

4. Use the File name text box to enter a name for the file (without the extension).

Inside Scoop
If you need to make global changes to the Registry, export the entire Registry and then load the resulting registration file into WordPad or some other word processor or text editor. Use the application's Replace feature (carefully!) to make changes throughout the file. You can then import the changed file back into the Registry (as described in the next section).

5. If you want to export only the currently highlighted key, make sure the Selected branch option is activated. If you'd prefer to export the entire Registry, activate the All option.

6. Click Save.

If you want to make changes to the registration file, highlight the file in Windows Explorer and then select File, Edit. Windows Millennium will open the file in Notepad (unless the file is too large, in which case Windows Millennium uses WordPad, instead).

Importing a Registration (.reg) File

If you need to restore the key that you backed up to a registration file, follow these steps:

1. Select Registry, Import Registry File to display the Import Registry File dialog box.

2. Find and highlight the file you want to import.

3. Click Open.

Shortcut
You can also import a registration file without opening the Registry Editor. To do so, highlight the file using Windows Explorer and then select the File, Merge command (you can also double-click the file).

Note, too, that you can create registration files from scratch and then import them into the Registry. This is a handy technique if you have some customizations that you want to apply to multiple systems. Here's the general structure of a registration file:

```
REGEDIT4

[KEY_PATH]
"StringSetting"="String value"
"BinarySetting"=hex:xx,yy,,zz
"DWORDSetting"=dword:nnnnnnnn
etc.
```

Here's what the various placeholders mean:

KEY_PATH	The full path of the Registry key that will hold the settings you're adding.
StringSetting	The name of a string setting. Notice the name is surrounded by quotation marks.
String value	The value of the string setting, surrounded by quotation marks.
BinarySetting	The name of a binary setting. Again, the name is surrounded by quotation marks.
hex:*xx,yy,zz*	The binary value of the setting. Separate each two-digit hexadecimal number with a comma.
DWORDSetting	The name of a DWORD setting, surrounded by quotation marks.
dword:*nnnnnnnn*	The 8-digit DWORD value of the setting.

You can add as many keys and as many settings as you like. Here's an example:

```
REGEDIT4


[HKEY_LOCAL_MACHINE\Software\Microsoft\Windows\
CurrentVersion]
"RegisteredOwner"="Paul McFedries"
"Install Type"=hex:03,00


[HKEY_CURRENT_USER\Software\Microsoft\Windows\
CurrentVersion\Policies\WinOldApp]
"NoRealMode"=dword:00000001
```

An Insider's Guide to System Policies

Another measure of the importance of the Registry is the number of front ends that Windows Millennium offers for working with Registry settings:

The Registry Editor—As you've seen, the Registry Editor gives you a hierarchical menu of all the keys and settings available with the Registry.

System Configuration Utility—As you saw in Chapter 2, "Understanding and Controlling the Windows Millennium Startup," this utility controls a number of startup options, several of which are Registry related.

➜ **See Also** "Controlling Startup Using the System Configuration Utility," **p. 46.**

Device Manager—This tool provides a summary of many of the hardware-related Registry items. See Chapter 21, "Taking the Mystery out of Hardware."

➜ **See Also** "Dealing with Device Manager," **p. 479.**

System Information Utility—This program offers a more complete picture of the hardware and software items in the Registry. See Chapter 14, "Crucial System Maintenance Skills."

➜ **See Also** "The System Information Utility," **p. 328.**

System Policy Editor—This feature gives you access to a number of *system policies*, which are customization options set by adding or modifying Registry values.

Tweak UI—This utility offers a long list of interface customization options, many of which control Registry settings.

This section discusses system policies and the System Policy Editor. I'll discuss Tweak UI later in this chapter.

To reiterate, system policies are settings that control how Windows Millennium works. You can use them to customize the Windows Millennium interface, specify your own folders for things like the Start menu, the desktop, and the Startup group, restrict access to certain areas, and much more.

System policies are mostly used by system administrators who want to make sure that novice users don't have access to dangerous tools (such as the Registry Editor); or it is used by those who want to ensure a consistent computing experience across multiple machines. However, system policies are also useful on standalone machines, as you'll see throughout this book.

Installing the System Policy Editor

To work with system policies, you use the System Policy Editor, which shipped with Windows 98 (but not, unfortunately, with Windows Millennium). Here's how to install this tool:

- If you don't have a copy of the Windows 98 CD, download NETADMIN.EXE from the Windows 98 Resource Kit Web site:

  `http://resourcelink.mspress.microsoft.com/reslink/win98/toolbox/default.asp`

- Insert the Windows 98 CD and then follow these steps:

1. Select Start, Settings, Control Panel and, in the Control Panel window, launch the Add/Remove Programs icon.

2. Display the Windows Setup tab. Windows Millennium takes a few moments to collect data on the installed components.

3. Click Have Disk. The Install From Disk dialog box appears.

66

Using System Policy Editor (Poledit.exe) incorrectly can cause serious problems that may require you to reinstall Windows. Microsoft cannot guarantee that problems resulting from the incorrect use of System Policy Editor can be solved. Use System Policy Editor at your own risk. —*From the Microsoft Knowledge Base*

99

Remember
When you insert the Windows 98 disc, you normally see the Windows 98 CD-ROM window. To avoid seeing this window, hold down Shift while inserting the disc. This will bypass the AutoRun program on the CD.

4. Type the following path into the Copy manufacturer's files from text box, where *d* is the letter of your CD-ROM drive (you can also use the Browse button to select this path):

   d:\tools\reskit\netadmin\poledit\

5. Click OK. The Have Disk dialog box appears.

6. Activate the System Policy Editor check box.

7. Click Install. Windows Millennium installs the System Policy Editor.

8. Click OK.

With the System Policy Editor installed, you can run it by selecting Start, Programs, Accessories, System Tools, System Policy Editor.

Working with a Local Registry

As I've said, the System Policy Editor acts as a front-end for various Registry settings. So, the first step in working with the System Policy Editor is to open this front-end, which you do by selecting the File, Open Registry command. This adds two icons to the System Policy Editor, as shown in Figure 3.7:

Local Computer—This icon contains system policies that correspond to some of the settings in the Registry's HKEY_LOCAL_MACHINE key.

Local User—This icon contains system policies that correspond to some of the settings in the Registry's HKEY_CURRENT_USER key.

To work with individual system policies, double-click either Local Computer or Local User. The dialog box that appears contains a hierarchical menu of policy categories. In Figure 3.8, for example, I opened the Local Computer icon, and then opened Windows 98 System, Network Paths.

Shortcut
If you're a network administrator, you don't have to install System Policy Editor on every machine. Instead, you can select File, Connect to open a machine's registry remotely. Note that the remote computer must have user-level access, and it must have the Remote Registry service installed.

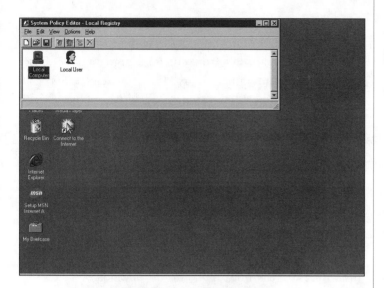

Figure 3.7
The Local
Computer and
Local User icons
appear when you
open the Registry.

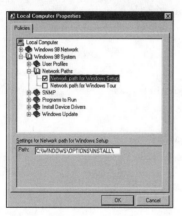

Figure 3.8
The System Policy
Editor's icons
offer a hierarchi-
cal list of policies.

As you can see, each policy has a check box that toggles the policy on and off. In many cases, activating the policy's check box also activates a text box or some other control, which appears in the Settings area in the bottom half of the dialog box. For example, the Network path for Windows Setup policy has a Path text box in the Settings area. In this case, you would use this text box to specify the location of the Windows Millennium source files. This corresponds to the SourcePath setting in the following Registry key:

```
HKEY_LOCAL_MACHINE\Software\Microsoft\Windows\
CurrentVersion\Setup
```

Inside Scoop
If you think you'll be reinstalling Windows Millennium down the road, or if you'd like to apply a set of policies to another computer, create a policy (.pol) file. Select File, New Policy, set up your policies, and then select File, Save and save the settings as Config.pol. To use this policy file, open Local Computer and select Windows Millennium Network, Update, Remote Update. Select Manual as the Update Mode and use the Path for manual update box to enter the name and location of Config.pol.

66

Great care has been taken to ensure that Tweak UI operates as it should. But please keep in mind, this tool is not a part of Windows and is not supported by Microsoft. For this reason, Microsoft Technical Support is unable to answer questions about TweakUI.
—From the POWERTOY folder's README.TXT file

99

Installing and Running Tweak UI

The next Windows Millennium tool you need to know about is Tweak UI, which acts as a front-end for a large number of user interface customization options. Most of these options are controls for adding and working with Registry settings. As with the Registry Editor and the System Policy Editor, I'll be using various Tweak UI settings throughout the rest of this book.

Installing Tweak UI

Tweak UI isn't part of the main Windows Millennium package, but as this book went to press, Microsoft announced that a version of Tweak UI for Windows Millennium will be made available around the time that Windows Millennium ships. No details were available, so check out the Millennium Web site (www.microsoft.com/windowsme/) for the download.

Just in case, you can also get the Windows 98 version of Tweak UI using either of the following methods:

- Insert the original Windows 98 CD (not the Windows 98 Second Edition CD), display the \tools\reskit\powertoy folder, right-click tweakui.inf, and then click Install in the shortcut menu.

- Go to the following Web site:
  http://www.winmag.com/windows/win98/software.

Running Tweak UI

To launch Tweak UI, select Start, Settings, Control Panel and then open the Tweak UI icon. (If you don't see the icon, click the view all Control Panel options link.) You'll see the window shown in Figure 3.9. Some notes about this window:

- The tabs across the top take you to different categories of options.

- Many of the tabs have a Restore Factory Settings button. Click this button to reset a tab's settings to their Windows Millennium defaults.

An Insider's Guide to the Control Panel

The Control Panel is a folder that contains a large number of icons—there are well over two dozen in the default Windows Millennium setup, but depending on your system configuration, there could be 30 or more icons available. Each of these icons deals with a specific area of the Windows Millennium configuration: Hardware, applications, fonts, printers, multimedia, and much more.

Figure 3.9
Tweak UI offers a simple interface for customizing a wealth of Windows Millennium options.

Opening an icon displays a dialog box containing various properties related to that area of Windows. For example, you saw back in Chapter 1, "Ten Things You Should Know About the Windows Millennium Setup," that you can use the Add/Remove Programs icon to add and remove Windows Millennium components.

→ **See Also** "Adding and Removing Windows Millennium Components," **p. 32.**

The Control Panel is a folder. However, unlike the Windows 3.x Control Panel, which was a mere program group like any other, the Windows Millennium Control Panel is a special Windows Millennium system folder. (It's actually an ActiveX component.) This gives you much more flexibility when working with the Control Panel:

- The Control Panel folder can appear within Windows Explorer and My Computer.

- You can hide Control Panel icons.

- Other applications can easily add new icons to the Control Panel.

- You can display the Control Panel just about anywhere you like, including the Start menu and taskbar.

I'll discuss these and other Control Panel techniques through-out this section.

To display the Control Panel folder, use any of the following techniques:

- Select Start, Settings, Control Panel.

- In Windows Explorer's All Folders list, select the Control Panel folder.

- Open the desktop's My Computer icon and then open Control Panel.

Controlling the Control Panel

To help you get the most out of the Control Panel, this section runs through a few techniques for controlling how this folder operates. You learn about the files that are at the heart of the Control Panel, how to hide and display Control Panel icons, how to customize Control Panel dialog boxes, and more.

Easier Access to the Control Panel Icons

When you first launch the Control Panel, the window displays only seven icons. This is yet another scheme to protect the novice user from the intricacies of the operating system. That's reasonable, but the implementation isn't particularly well thought out because the default folder view excludes such potentially useful icons as Folder Options, Fonts, Mouse, and Power Options.

In any case, this default format is a pain for experienced users because they have to click the view all Control Panel options link to see the full complement of icons. Fortunately, Windows Millennium is smart enough to remember this choice and will display all the icons the next time you open the Control Panel.

One of the things I've always disliked about the Control Panel was that you often had no direct route to the icons. You had to open the folder, launch the icon, and then close the folder again. (See the next section, "Alternative Methods for Opening Control Panel Icons," for some exceptions.) In Windows 9x, there was an obscure Start menu trick you could perform to create a cascading menu of the icons. That trick is no longer necessary in Windows Millennium because it offers a much easier way to get the Control Panel icons on a menu:

1. Select Start, Settings, Taskbar and Start Menu (or launch the Control Panel's Taskbar and Start Menu icon).

2. Display the Advanced tab.

3. In the Start menu and Taskbar list, activate the Expand Control Panel check box.

4. Click OK.

With this tweak, selecting Start, Settings, Control Panel now presents you with a submenu that contains all the Control Panel icons. (I explain the rest of the options in the Advanced tab in Chapter 17, "Customizing the Windows Millennium Interface.")

→ **See Also** "Renovating the Start Menu," **p. 397.**

Alternative Methods for Opening Control Panel Icons

Access to many Control Panel icons is scattered throughout the Windows Millennium interface, meaning that there's more than one way to skin a Control Panel cat. Many of these methods are faster and more direct than using the Control Panel folder. Here's a summary:

Date/Time—Double-click the clock in the taskbar's system tray.

Dial-Up Networking—Select Start, Settings, Dial-Up Networking.

Display—Right-click the desktop and then click Properties.

Folder Options—In Windows Explorer, select Tools, Folder Options.

Fonts—In Windows Explorer, select the Windows\Fonts folder.

Infrared—Double-click the infrared icon in the taskbar's system tray.

Internet Options—Right-click the desktop's Internet Explorer icon and then click Properties in the shortcut menu. Alternatively, in Internet Explorer, select Tools, Internet Options.

Modems—Available through various Windows Millennium components, including Dial-Up Networking, HyperTerminal, and Device Manager.

Network—Right-click the desktop's My Network Places icon and then click Properties.

PC Card (PCMCIA)—Double-click the PC Card icon in the taskbar's system tray.

Power Options—Right-click the Power Meter icon in the taskbar's system tray.

Printers—Select Start, Settings, Printers.

System—Right-click the desktop's My Computer icon and then click Properties.

Taskbar and Start Menu—Select Start, Settings, Taskbar and Start Menu.

Understanding Control Panel Files

Each Control Panel icon is represented by a *Control Panel extension* file, which uses the cpl extension. All of these files reside in the Windows\System folder. When you open the Control Panel, Windows Millennium scans the System folder looking for these cpl files, and then displays an icon for each one. (Windows Millennium also checks Control.ini to see if any icons are not supposed to be displayed. More on this later in this chapter; see "Hiding and Displaying Control Panel Icons.")

These cpl files offer an alternative method for launching individual Control Panel dialog boxes. The idea is that you run Control.exe and specify the name of a cpl file as a parameter. This bypasses the Control Panel folder and opens the icon directly. Here's the syntax:

```
C:\Windows\Control.exe Cplfile.cpl [module]
```

Cplfile.cpl   The name of the cpl file.

module   An optional module name for Main.cpl, which contains several Control Panel modules.

Table 3.2 lists the various Control Panel icons and the appropriate command line to use.

TABLE 3.2: COMMAND LINES FOR LAUNCHING INDIVIDUAL CONTROL PANEL ICONS

Control Panel Icon	Command Line
Accessibility Options	Control.exe Access.cpl
Add/Remove Programs	Control.exe Appwiz.cpl
Automatic Updates	Control.exe Wuaucpl.cpl
Date/Time	Control.exe Timedate.cpl
Desktop Themes	Control.exe Themes.cpl
Display	Control.exe Desk.cpl
Fonts	Control.exe Main.cpl Fonts
Internet	Control.exe Inetcpl.cpl
Game Controllers	Control.exe Joy.cpl
Keyboard	Control.exe Main.cpl Keyboard
Modems	Control.exe Modem.cpl
Mouse	Control.exe Main.cpl Mouse
Multimedia	Control.exe Mmsys.cpl
Network	Control.exe Netcpl.cpl
ODBC Data Sources (32bit)	Control.exe Odbccp32.cpl
Passwords	Control.exe Password.cpl
Power Management	Control.exe Powercfg.cpl
Printers	Control.exe Main.cpl Printers
Regional Settings	Control.exe Intl.cpl
System	Control.exe Sysdm.cpl
Telephony	Control.exe Telephon.cpl
Tweak UI	Control.exe Tweakui.cpl

Remember
Not all the Control Panel icons appear in Table 3.2 because a few—particularly Add New Hardware, PCMCIA (PC Card), and Sounds—can't be accessed by running Control.exe.

Hiding and Displaying Control Panel Icons

If you find your Control Panel folder is bursting at the seams, you can trim it down to size by removing the icons you never use. Windows Millennium offers four methods for doing this:

- Move Control Panel files

- Customize Control.ini

- Use Tweak UI

- Use the System Policy Editor

The next four sections discuss each of these techniques.

Moving Control Panel Files

To remove a Control Panel icon, the most obvious point of attack is simply to take the appropriate cpl file out of the Windows\System folder. That way, when Windows Millennium scours the System folder for cpl files, it won't find the moved file and it won't display the icon. Because you never know when you might need the icon again in the future, don't delete the cpl file. Instead, I recommend creating a subfolder within the System folder (named, say, CplBackup) and moving the unwanted cpl files into that subfolder.

Watch Out!
Don't try to move a cpl file while the Control Panel is open. If you do, Windows Millennium may display an error message telling you the file is in use.

Customizing with Control.ini

Rather than messing with the cpl files directly, you can prevent an icon from appearing in the Control Panel folder by modifying the Control.ini file. Here's how it's done:

1. Select Start, Run, type **control.ini** in the Run dialog box, and then click OK. This opens the file in Notepad.

2. Scroll down until you come to the section named [don't load].

3. Directly under that section name, type the name of the cpl file for the icon you want to hide, followed by =no. For example, to hide the Telephony icon, you'd add the following line:

   ```
   telephon.cpl=no
   ```

4. Save the file and exit Notepad.

5. If the Control Panel is already open, switch to it and press F5 to update the icons. (Note that you may need to press F5 twice to refresh the icons completely.)

You may think that changing a [don't load] value in Control.ini from no to yes would display the icon once again. Unfortunately, that's not the case. Instead, you either have to delete the line completely, or "comment out" the line by adding a semicolon (;) at the beginning.

Customizing Control Panel with Tweak UI

Perhaps the easiest way to hide and display Control Panel icons is to use Tweak UI. As you can see in Figure 3.10, Tweak UI's Control Panel tab offers check boxes for each cpl file. Activate a check box to display the icon; deactivate a check box to hide the icon.

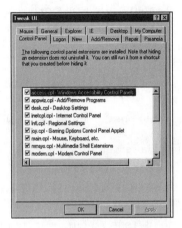

Figure 3.10
Use Tweak UI's Control Panel tab to toggle Control Panel icons on and off.

Customizing Control Panel with the System Policy Editor

The System Policy Editor enables you not only to hide and display Control Panel icons, but also to customize the dialog boxes that are displayed by several of the icons. Specifically, you can hide one or more dialog box tabs.

To see how this works, follow these steps:

1. Select Start, Programs, Accessories, System Tools, System Policy Editor.

2. Run the File, Open Registry command to load the Registry.

3. Open the Local User icon and select Windows 98 System, Control Panel. This branch contains five sub-branches that correspond to five Control Panel icons: Display, Network, Passwords, Printers, and System.

4. Open the subbranch you want to work with, and then activate the check box. For example, if you want to work with the Display icon, open the Display branch and activate the Restrict Display Control Panel check box.

5. To hide the icon in Control Panel, activate the Disable *icon* Control Panel check box, where *icon* is the name of the icon (for example, Disable Display Control Panel).

6. To hide a tab within the icon's dialog box, activate the appropriate Hide *tab* page check box, where *tab* is the name of the dialog box tab (for example, Hide Background page).

7. When you're done, click OK.

8. Select File Save to put the settings into effect.

If you elected to hide certain dialog box tabs, the settings for this are stored in the following Registry key:

```
HKEY_CURRENT_USER\Software\Microsoft\Windows\CurrentVersion
\Policies\System
```

Each hidden tab is represented by a setting that has a DWORD value of 1. For example, if you hide the Background tab in the Display Properties dialog box, a setting named NoDispBackgroundPage is added to this key. You can reinstate the tab by setting this value to 0 (or, of course, by using the System Policy Editor).

Control Panel and the Registry

You saw in the previous section that the Registry plays a hand in hiding individual tabs from the Control Panel icon dialog boxes. The Registry and the Control Panel have other ties, as well, and I will tell you about them in this section.

Windows Millennium settings that can be modified via the Control Panel are scattered throughout the Registry. However, one location in particular stores almost all the interface customizations you'll be working with in Part V, "Advanced Windows Millennium Customizing." That location is the following Registry key:

`HKEY_CURRENT_USER\Control Panel\`

The number of subkeys you see depends on your system configuration and on whether you've adjusted any settings using particular Control Panel icons (such as Keyboard). Most of the subkeys are straightforward. For example, the Accessibility subkey stores the settings from Control Panel's Accessibility icon. Here's a quick look at the most useful of the other subkeys:

Appearance—This subkey stores the settings from Control Panel's Display icon. In particular, it deals with the various interface appearance schemes that you can work with in the Appearance tab of the Display Properties dialog box.

Colors—This subkey stores the settings from Control Panel's Display icon. It tracks the colors you can apply to various Windows Millennium interface components in the Appearance tab of the Display Properties dialog box.

Cursors—This subkey stores the settings from Control Panel's Mouse icon. It tracks and lists the mouse pointer scheme—as specified in the Pointers tab of the Mouse Properties dialog box.

Desktop—This subkey stores the settings from Control Panel's Display icon. It deals with the desktop-related settings from the Background and Effects tabs of the Display Properties dialog box.

Besides the storage of settings, the Registry also contains data about the Control Panel ActiveX control. Here's the key to look for:

`HKEY_CLASSES_ROOT\CLSID\{21EC2020-3AEA-1069-A2DD-08002B30309D}`

Essential Information

- The Registry is a central storage area for thousands of settings related to your hardware and software.

Inside Scoop
The CLSID key
contains a long
list of subkeys
that are all 16-
byte (32-digit
hexadecimal) val-
ues. These are the
class IDs for all
the registered
ActiveX objects,
and they're unique
(hence, they're
also known as
Globally Unique
Identifiers, or
GUIDs).

- Because the Registry is so crucial, always make a backup copy before making major changes.

- The Registry Editor (Regedit.exe) offers a hierarchical view of the Registry's keys and settings. You can use the Registry Editor to change values, add new keys and settings, delete keys and settings, and more.

- System policies are settings that control various aspects of Windows Millennium. Each policy corresponds to a Registry setting. The System Policy Editor provides a convenient front end for working with these settings.

- Tweak UI is another Registry front-end that provides an easier method for setting up user interface customizations.

- The Control Panel is a special Windows Millennium system folder that stores numerous icons for customizing and tweaking hardware, software, the Windows Millennium interface, and more.

- Select Start, Settings, Control Panel to open the Control Panel folder. You can also view this folder from within Windows Explorer.

Inside Windows Millennium Communication and Internet Features

PART II

GET THE SCOOP ON...

Setting Up Your Modem ▪ The Information Required to Set Up an Internet Connection ▪ Creating a Dial-Up Internet Connection ▪ Automating Dial-Up Connections Using Scripts ▪ Using TCP/IP to Create an Internet Connection Through Your Network ▪ Working with PING and Other Windows Internet Utilities

Getting on the Internet

Chapter 4

T HE INTERNET HAS BEEN A BIG DEAL since about the mid-'90s. Since that time, thousands of books, stories, and articles have been published in an effort to explain what the Internet is, to outline what users can do with it, and to come to grips with this phenomenon's good, bad, and ugly sides. This is to say, in other words, that the Internet needs no introduction.

So there's no doubt you'll be happy to hear that you won't be getting any kind of "Internet 101" from me. This chapter assumes you've had it up to here with the "it all began with the Department of Defense" histories, "network of networks" definitions, and gee-whiz descriptions of how great the Web and email are. You already know the what and why. Now all you need to know is the how. This chapter provides you with plenty of that. I tell you the information you need to get started, and then show you how to put that data to good use in setting up a dial-up Internet connection. If you're on a local area network that has an Internet gateway, I show you how to get your machine to access that connection. You also learn about some of Windows Millennium's Internet utilities, connection tricks, and much more.

How to Get on the Internet Using a Phone Line

Most home users access the Internet by using a dial-up connection over a phone line. These accounts typically offer a certain number of hours of connection time for a monthly fee, with extra time being billed hourly. Connecting these accounts is usually straightforward, and some Internet service providers (ISPs) make it very easy:

- Online services such as America Online offer Internet gateways as part of their regular service. In these cases, getting on the Internet is a simple matter of installing the service's software. If this is the route you want to take, open the desktop's Online Services icon and then open the icon for the service you want to install.

- Some ISPs offer installation programs that will create the appropriate connection for you automatically (as well as install some Internet software).

All other connections require some sort of setup within Windows Millennium. The next few sections show you how to get your connection established.

Installing a Modem

If Windows Millennium didn't detect your modem during Setup, or if you have a new modem, you need to install your modem before you can use it with any communications software. This section shows you how to install and test a modem in Windows Millennium.

Many newer modems support Plug and Play, so it's possible that Windows Millennium may recognize your modem after you install it and restart your computer. In this case, Windows Millennium will offer to search for the best driver for the modem. When choosing search locations, be sure to include the location of your Windows Millennium source files. If you also have the manufacturer's drivers, specify their location, as well. (Windows will choose the best one for the job.) See Chapter 21, "Taking the Mystery out of Hardware," to learn more about installing device drivers.

→ **See Also** "Installing Device Drivers," **p. 470.**

If Windows Millennium didn't recognize your modem at startup, you can install it by using the Add New Modem wizard.

Before doing so, run through the following modem installation checklist:

■ Many non-Plug and Play modems offer different configurations for things like the IRQ line. Internal modems use jumper switches, whereas external modems use DIP switches. See your modem's documentation to check whether the default configuration will conflict with an existing device on your system.

■ Windows Millennium will send signals to the serial port in an attempt to communicate with the modem. Therefore, make sure your external modem is turned on and connected to the serial port. If you have a USB modem, make sure it's attached to a USB port.

■ Make sure you shut down any communications software (that is, any software that interacts with your modem, such as a fax program).

■ If you have a device driver from the manufacturer, insert the disk in the appropriate drive so that it's ready for use.

Running the Add New Modem Wizard
The Add New Modem wizard takes you step-by-step through the installation process. How you launch this wizard depends on whether you're setting up your first modem:

If you're setting up your first modem—Open the Control Panel's Modems icon and the Install New Modem wizard will automatically appear.

If you're setting up another modem—Opening the Control Panel's Modems icon displays the Modems Properties dialog box. To launch the Add New Modem wizard, click the Add button.

With the wizard up and running, follow these steps to install your modem:

1. In the initial wizard dialog box, click Next. The wizard interrogates your system's serial ports to look for an

Remember
The purpose of the Location Information dialog box is to set up an initial *dialing location*. I discuss dialing locations in detail later in this chapter; see "Setting Dialing Properties," **p. 100**.

attached modem, and then displays a dialog box showing the name of the modem.

2. Click Next. The wizard installs your modem.

3. If this is your first modem installation, you may see the Location Information dialog box. If so, choose your country and enter your area code. You might also need to enter a number to access an outside line and to choose whether your phone system uses Tone dialing or Pulse dialing. Click Next when you're done.

4. Click Finish. The wizard opens the Modems Properties dialog box with your modem displayed, as shown in Figure 4.1.

Figure 4.1
The Modems Properties dialog box lists your installed modems.

If the wizard failed in its quest to find your modem, or if you prefer to install the manufacturer's drivers, you can install the modem by hand. There are three ways to get started:

- Launch the Add New Modem wizard and, in the initial dialog box, activate the Don't detect my modem; I will select it from a list check box. Then click Next.

- If the wizard found the wrong modem, click the Change button in the dialog box that shows the name of the modem.

- If the wizard didn't find any modem, it will display a dialog box to let you know. Click Next.

You now see the Install New Modem dialog box shown in Figure 4.2.

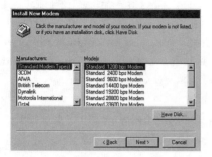

Here are the steps to follow:

1. If you want to load the Windows Millennium drivers, use the Manufacturers list to highlight the modem maker, use the Models list to highlight your modem, and then click Next. If you want to install the manufacturer's drivers, instead, click Have Disk and follow the instructions that appear.

2. The next dialog box asks you to select the port to which the modem is attached. The correct port should be selected already (if not, click the port), so click Next to install the modem.

3. Fill in the Location Information dialog box, if it appears, and click Next.

4. Click Finish to return to the Modems Properties dialog box.

Shortcut
If you're not sure what type of modem you have, select (Standard Modem Types) in the Manufacturers list, and then use the Models list to select one of the standard types.

Running Modem Diagnostics

With your modem installed, you should run a test to make sure Windows Millennium can communicate with the modem. Here are the steps to follow:

1. In the Modems Properties dialog box, display the Diagnostics tab.

2. If you have multiple modems, click the port that corresponds to the modem you want to test.

Watch Out!
Outside of the obvious reasons (modem not turned on, cable not connected, and so on), one common reason that a modem may fail to respond is an IRQ conflict with the serial port. COM1 and COM3 both use IRQ 4, and COM2 and COM4 both use IRQ 3. If you have, say, a mouse on COM1 and an internal modem on COM3, the resulting conflict will cause problems. Either adjust the modem's jumpers to use another IRQ, or use Device Manager to change a port's IRQ.

3. Click More Info.

4. If Windows Millennium can communicate with your modem, it displays the More Info dialog box with data such as the port, IRQ, I/O address, UART type, highest speed, and a list of AT commands. Otherwise, you get an Error dialog box that tells you the modem failed to respond. Click OK in either case.

Setting Dialing Properties

When you set up your modem, Windows Millennium probably asked you for information about your location, such as your country code, your area code, whether you use tone or pulse dialing, and so on. For most users, that information stays constant over time. However, a growing number of users take notebook computers on the road with them (or just back and forth between home and the office). For these users, their location data often changes, so how they dial the phone changes, as well. For example, dialing a number in the 317 area code from your home may be a long distance call, but it will be a local call when you're in the 317 area. Similarly, travelers often need to use a calling card or a long distance service, and those usually require entering ID numbers, passwords, and other extra digits.

All of this affects how your modem dials, as well. To help you manage this, Windows Millennium enables you to set up different *dialing locations* that specify an area code, numbers to dial to get an outside line, calling card numbers, and much more.

To set up and modify dialing locations, open the Control Panel's Modems icon. When the Modems Properties dialog box appears, click the Dialing Properties button to get the Dialing Properties dialog box onscreen, as shown in Figure 4.3.

Let's look at the options in this dialog box:

I am dialing from—This is the list of defined dialing locations. A new location is automatically started for you. Feel free to edit the New Location name. To create another new location, click New, and then click OK when Windows Millennium tells you the new location was created. Finally, edit the new location name.

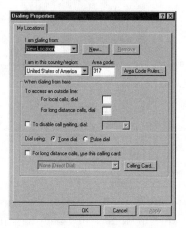

Figure 4.3
Use this property sheet to set up and customize dialing locations.

I am in this country/region—This is the location's country code.

Area code—This is the location's area code.

Area Code Rules—Click this button to display the Area Code Rules dialog box, shown in Figure 4.4. There are two groups (click OK when you're done):

    When calling within my area code—If your phone company requires that you use 10-digit dialing (area code plus phone number) when making calls to your own area code, activate the Always dial the area code (10-digit dialing) check box. If some calls to your own area code are long distance calls, click New to specify the phone number prefixes that Windows Millennium must dial as long distance.

    When calling to other area codes—If your phone company has split off part of your area code into a separate area code, it's likely that calls between the two codes aren't treated as long distance. To tell

Windows Millennium not to dial calls to the other area code as long distance, click New and specify the other area code.

Figure 4.4
Use the Area
Code Rules dialog
box to set up
10-digit dialing.

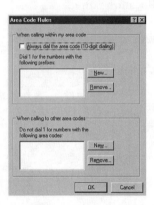

To access an outside line—If you're dialing through a PBX system at an office or hotel, you usually have to dial a number to get an outside line. Use these text boxes to enter the appropriate numbers to get an outside line for local calls (such as 9) and long distance calls (such as 8).

To disable call waiting, dial—Activating this check box tells Windows Millennium to disable call waiting by sending whatever code you select from the list (such as *70) or enter by hand.

Dial using—Select the type of dialing used by the phone system: Tone dial or Pulse dial.

For long distance calls, use this calling card—If you want to use a calling card or a long distance carrier, activate this check box and then select the card or carrier you want to use from the list.

Calling Card—Click this button to customize an existing calling card or carrier or define a new calling card or carrier. I explain how this works as follows.

Watch Out!
Call waiting signals an incoming call by sending extra tones. Unfortunately, those tones can throw the modem for a loop and disrupt communications. Therefore, you should always disable call waiting.

If you plan on using a calling card, you need to modify the card setup to add your PIN number. And if Windows Millennium doesn't come with a predefined calling card or long distance carrier that you use, you must define a new one. Here are the steps to follow:

1. In the Dialing Properties dialog box, click the Calling Card button. Windows Millennium displays the Calling Card dialog box, shown in Figure 4.5.

2. You have two ways to proceed:

   • If you want to work with an existing item, use the list box at the top of the dialog box to select the calling card or long distance carrier.

   • If you want to create a new item, click New, enter a name for the new item, and then click OK. When Windows Millennium tells you that you must enter dialing rules, click OK.

3. If you're working with a calling card, enter your PIN number in the `Personal ID Number (PIN Number)` text box.

4. Use the `To use this calling card for long distance calls...` text box to enter the access number that must be dialed to initiate a long distance call.

5. Use the `To use this calling card for international calls...` text box to enter the access number that must be dialed to initiate an international call.

6. Calling card and long distance calls must follow a sequence. For example, you dial the number, wait for a tone, enter your PIN, and so on. To adjust the sequences

used for calls, click the Long Distance Calls and International Calls buttons. In each case, the dialog box that appears has various steps that you can fill in. Enter what should be dialed and what the system should wait for before moving on to the next step in the sequence. Click OK when you're done.

7. Click OK. Windows Millennium returns you to the Dialing Properties dialog box.

8. Click OK.

Information You Need Before Getting Started

The Internet is all about information, so it's appropriate (or ironic, depending on how you look at it) that the key to getting connected to the Internet is having adequate information. Fortunately, most ISPs are pretty good at supplying you with the information you need. The following list runs through all the data that you *might* need to get your connection going (note, however, that many setups require only some of these items):

- The phone number you must dial to connect to the ISP.

- The username and password for your ISP account.

- Whether logging in to the ISP requires any special instructions.

- Whether you need to enable or disable certain modem features—such as error control and data compression—to connect to the ISP successfully.

- The type of flow control used by the ISP's modems.

Remember
IP is the fundamental protocol of the Internet. It defines the structure of all the data that's sent over the Internet, as well as the addresses of all the Internet's resources.

- Whether the ISP assigns you an *IP (Internet Protocol) address* automatically when you log in. If not, you need to know your permanent IP address and the *subnet mask* that goes along with it. (Your IP address identifies your computer when you're on the Internet. That is, when you request data, it's sent to your IP address. Each IP address uses *dotted-decimal notation*, which takes the form *aaa.bbb.ccc.ddd*, where *aaa* and so on are numbers between 1 and 255.)

- Whether the ISP assigns the IP address of their *DNS (Domain Name System) server* automatically when you log in. If not, you need to know the address of the DNS server. Most ISPs give you addresses for both a primary DNS server and a secondary DNS server. (A *domain name* is an English language equivalent to an IP address. For example, the IP address of my Web server is 216.208.33.130, but its domain name is www.mcfedries.com. The DNS is a technology that handles the translation of IP addresses to domain names, and vice versa.)

- The type of connection. Most ISPs use PPP (Point-to-Point Protocol) connections, although some still use SLIP (Serial Line Interface Protocol) connections.

If you plan on using Internet email, you need to gather the following:

- Your email account username and password, if they're different from your login username and password.

- The type of email account (POP3 or IMAP).

- The domain name of the ISP's incoming (POP3 or IMAP) email server and its outgoing (SMTP) email server. Note that most ISPs use the same server for both incoming and outgoing mail.

With this information at the ready, Windows Millennium offers two ways to create the connection:

- Use the Internet Connection Wizard.

- Create a Dial-Up Networking connection by hand.

The next two sections explore both routes.

Using the Internet Connection Wizard

The Internet Connection Wizard takes you through the process of setting up an Internet connection in the usual wizardly, step-by-step fashion. You get things started either by launching the desktop's Connect to the Internet icon, or by

> 66
> Using the Internet Connection wizard, you can quickly set up an Internet account and connection. After you set up a connection, you can also use the wizard to set up e-mail, newsgroups, and directory services.
> —*From the "Getting Started" booklet*
> 99

selecting Start, Programs, Accessories, Communications, Internet Connection Wizard. Either way, the Internet Connection Wizard appears, as shown in Figure 4.6.

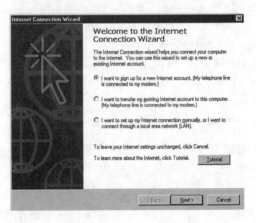

The initial dialog box offers three choices:

I want to sign up for a new account—Choose this option to open an account via one of Windows Millennium's preselected ISPs.

I want to transfer my existing Internet account to this computer—If you already have an account, the wizard may be able to download its settings automatically by choosing this option. Note, however, that only certain ISPs support this feature (the wizard supplies you with a list of those ISPs).

I want to set up my Internet connection manually...—This is the option to choose if you'll be specifying the account details by hand.

After you activate the I want to set up my Internet connection manually... option and click Next, you then follow these steps:

1. In the next wizard dialog box, activate the I connect through a phone line and a modem option, and then click Next.

2. The wizard checks your system and may perform one or more of the following tasks:

- It may display the Location Information dialog box, which I discussed earlier in this chapter.

- It may launch the Install New Modem wizard if you haven't yet installed a modem.

- If you have multiple modems installed, it will ask which modem you want to use for the connection.

3. The wizard now displays a dialog box named Step 1 of 3. Enter the `Telephone number` of your ISP, as well as the `Area code` and `Country/region name and code`, if necessary. If this will be a local call, be sure to deactivate the `Dial using the area code and country code` check box.

4. Click the Advanced button to get to the Advanced Connection Properties dialog box, shown in Figure 4.7. You use the Connection tab to specify the connection type (`PPP` is the most common by far) and the logon procedure (`None` is the right choice for most ISPs).

5. Display the Addresses tab, shown in Figure 4.8. (When you click the Addresses tab, the wizard may display a warning about file and printer sharing and TCP/IP. If so, be sure to click Yes to have the wizard disable file and printer sharing on the Internet connection. I talk more about this in Chapter 7, "Implementing Windows Millennium Internet Security Features.") Use the `IP address` group to enter your permanent IP address (ISPs rarely assign these

nowadays). Use the DNS Server address group to enter the IP address of your ISP's DNS server (or servers).

→ **See Also** "Internet Security and the TCP/IP Protocol," **p. 182.**

Figure 4.8
Use the
Addresses tab to
enter IP
addresses for
your computer
and your ISP's
DNS server(s).

6. Click OK to return to the wizard's Step 1 of 3 dialog box.

7. Click Next. The Step 2 of 3 dialog box appears.

8. Enter your User name and Password and click Next. The Step 3 of 3 dialog box appears.

9. Edit the Connection name, if you like, and then click Next.

From here, the wizard asks if you want to set up your Internet email account. I talk about that in Chapter 6, "Outlook Express and Internet Email."

→ **See Also** "Setting Up Mail Accounts," **p. 157.**

Using Dial-Up Networking

Using the Internet Connection Wizard is a good way to make sure you don't miss anything when setting up your Internet connection. However, it's not the quickest or the most efficient way to go about things. This is particularly true when you real-ize that all the wizard is really doing is gathering data to create a Dial-Up Networking connection. If you already have Dial-Up Networking installed, and you've already told Windows Millennium about your modem, it's often easier to set up your connection directly from the Dial-Up Networking folder. Here's how to do it:

1. Select Start, Programs, Accessories, Communications, Dial-Up Networking.

2. The next step depends on how Dial-Up Networking started:

   • If this is the first time you've launched Dial-Up Networking, the Welcome to Dial-Up Networking dialog box appears. In this case, click Next.

   • Each subsequent time you launch Dial-Up Networking, the Dial-Up Networking folder appears. In this case, open the Make New Connection icon.

3. In the initial dialog box, enter a name for your connection and, if you have multiple modems, choose the modem you want from the Select a device list.

4. If your ISP requires you to log in, click Configure to display the modem's property sheet, select the Options tab, activate the Bring up terminal window after dialing check box, and click OK.

5. Click Next.

6. In the next dialog box, enter the ISP's Area code, Telephone number, and Country code, and then click Next.

7. Click Finish. An icon for your new connection appears in the Dial-Up Networking folder.

8. Highlight the connection and then select File, Properties to display the connection's property sheet.

9. Display the Networking tab.

10. If your ISP uses a PPP server, make sure you select the PPP option in the Type of Dial-Up Server list. If your provider uses SLIP, choose the SLIP option, instead.

11. Activate or deactivate the other check boxes in the Advanced options group, as necessary. (For most connections, you can use the default selections.)

12. In the Allowed network protocols group, deactivate the NetBEUI and IPX/SPX check boxes.

Shortcut
You can also get to the connection's property sheet by highlighting the icon and then clicking the Properties button in the toolbar, or by right-clicking the icon and then clicking Properties.

Undocumented
Windows
Millennium makes
it easy to share
Dial-Up
Networking con-
nections with
other Windows
Millennium
machines or
users. Open the
Dial-Up
Networking folder
and copy the con-
nection you want
to work with to a
floppy disk,
removable disk,
or network drive.
On the other
machine, open
the Dial-Up
Networking folder
and then copy the
connection into
that folder. Adjust
the properties of
the copied con-
nection to select
a different
modem, if
necessary.

13. Make sure the TCP/IP check box is activated and click the TCP/IP Settings button to display the TCP/IP Settings dialog box.

14. Choose one of the following options:

   Server assigned IP address—Select this option if your ISP assigns you an IP address each time you log in.

   Specify an IP address—Select this option if your ISP has assigned you a permanent IP address. Use the IP address boxes to enter your address.

15. Choose one of the following options:

   Server assigned name server address—Select this option if your ISP assigns a DNS server IP address each time you log in.

   Specify name server addresses—Select this option if your ISP has given you IP addresses for its DNS server. Use the Primary DNS and Secondary DNS boxes to enter the addresses (see Figure 4.9).

16. Click OK to return to the connection's property sheet. At this point, you might want to leave this dialog box open because you need it in the next section.

Figure 4.9
Use this dialog
box to fill in your
IP address and
your ISP's DNS
server addresses,
if necessary.

Setting a Few More Connection Properties

Your Internet connection is now ready to go. Before connecting, however, there are a few other settings that you might want to work with. To see these settings, open the Dial-Up Networking folder and display the property sheet for your connection (if it isn't still open from the previous section). Display the Dialing tab, shown in Figure 4.10.

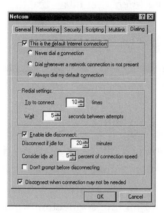

Figure 4.10
Use this dialog box to adjust some settings related to your Internet connection.

Let's run through the available options in this dialog box:

This is the default Internet connection—Activate this check box to set this connection as the default. This means that Windows Millennium uses the connection automatically when you attempt to access an Internet resource. This also enables the following three options:

- **Never dial a connection**—Activate this option to prevent Windows Millennium from connecting to the Internet automatically. This is a good choice if you always want to initiate the connection yourself.

- **Dial whenever a network connection is not present**—Activate this option to tell Windows Millennium to only dial your Internet connection when your computer isn't on a local area network. This is a good choice for notebook computers that have part-time access to an Internet-enabled network.

■ **Always dial my default connection**—Activate this option to have Windows Millennium always dial this connection when you access an Internet resource.

Try to connect x times—Use this spinner to set the maximum number of dial-up attempts Windows Millennium performs if it can't connect with the ISP.

Wait x seconds between attempts—Use this spinner to set the amount of time Windows Millennium waits before attempting another connection.

Enable idle disconnect—Leave this check box activated to have Windows Millennium automatically disconnect from your ISP if the connection goes idle. Use the following three options to control this feature:

■ **Disconnect if idle for x minutes**—Use this spinner to specify the number of minutes of idle time that must pass before you're disconnected. The most common cause for an idle connection would be an ISP problem (such as a down or overtaxed server) that causes packets to slow to a trickle. Packets still come in, but they're being received so slowly that you may as well be disconnected rather than running up wasted connection time.

■ **Consider idle at x percent of connection speed**— Use this spinner to set the percent of your original connection speed that Windows Millennium will use to consider the connection idle.

■ **Don't prompt before disconnecting**—When it detects an idle connection, Windows Millennium normally displays a dialog box warning you that you'll be disconnected in 30 seconds (see Figure 4.11). If you don't want to see this warning, activate this check box.

Disconnect when connection may not be needed—When this check box is activated, Windows Millennium offers to disconnect if you close the program that initiated the Internet connection in the first place.

Figure 4.11
Windows
Millennium dis-
plays this dialog
box when it
detects an idle
Internet connec-
tion.

Making the Connection

Once your connection is defined, Windows Millennium gives
you a number of ways to get online. Here's a summary:

- Launch an Internet application such as Internet Explorer
  or Outlook Express.

- Use Dial-Up Networking by first selecting Start, Programs,
  Accessories, Communications, Dial-Up Networking. When
  the Dial-Up Networking window appears, double-click the
  icon. (You can also highlight the icon and then either
  select Connections, Connect or click the toolbar's Dial
  button.)

- Enter an Internet address in Windows Explorer's
  Address bar.

- Select Start, Run and enter an Internet address in the Run
  dialog box.

Whichever method you use, Windows Millennium displays the
Connect To dialog box, shown in Figure 4.12.

Shortcut
For faster access
to a Dial-Up
Networking con-
nection, create a
shortcut for the
icon either on the
main Start menu,
the desktop, or
the Quick Launch
toolbar.

Figure 4.12
When you initiate
a Dial-Up
Networking con-
nection, the
Connect To dialog
box appears.

Remember
If you elect to have Windows Millennium enter your password automatically, there's a good chance you'll eventually forget the password through disuse. You should write down your password and store it in a safe place just in case Windows Millennium ever "forgets" the password (believe me, it happens).

Now follow these steps:

1. Make sure the User name and Password fields are filled in correctly.

2. The following two check boxes can save you a bit of work in the future:

   • **Save password**—Activating this option tells Windows Millennium to enter your password automatically.

   • **Connect automatically**—Activating this check box tells Windows Millennium to bypass the Connect To dialog box and proceed directly to the connection when you launch the icon. This is a good idea if you find that you never change any of the data in the Connect To dialog box. (To turn off this feature, head for the Dial-Up Networking window, highlight the icon, and select File, Properties. In the Security tab, deactivate the Connect automatically check box, and then click OK.)

3. Adjust the Phone number field, if necessary.

4. If you have multiple dialing locations defined, select the location you want to use from the Dialing from list. You can also click Dial Properties to adjust the selected dialing location.

5. Click Connect. Dial-Up Networking dials your modem to connect to the ISP. If you have to log in (and if you activated the Bring up terminal window after dialing option, as described earlier), Windows Millennium displays the Post-Dial Terminal Screen, shown in Figure 4.13.

Figure 4.13
Some users require the Post-Dial Terminal Screen to log in to their ISP.

6. Fill in the prompts to log in, and then either click Continue or press F7. Dial-Up Networking displays the Connection Established dialog box.

7. This dialog box doesn't give you much useful data, so you can avoid having it displayed in subsequent dial-ups by activating the Do not display this message in the future check box.

8. Click Close.

Creating Scripts to Automate Dial-Ups

Connecting to the Internet can become quite a chore if you find yourself dialing up your ISP several times a day and you have to enter login data each time. To streamline the login, Windows Millennium supports *scripts* that look for prompts (such as Login:) and then sends the appropriate responses (such as your username) automatically.

A script is a text file that uses the scp extension and contains simple programming commands and functions. Let's begin by examining the four most commonly used scripting commands: delay, halt, waitfor, and transmit.

The delay command tells Dial-Up Networking to wait for a specified number of seconds before moving on to the next command in the script:

delay *seconds*

seconds   This is the number of seconds Dial-Up Networking must wait.

The halt command tells Dial-Up Networking to stop processing the script. This is useful if a problem occurs and you need to abandon the login.

The waitfor command tells Dial-Up Networking to check the incoming characters from the ISP and look for a specific string:

waitfor "*string*" [, matchcase] [then *label*] [until *seconds*]

string   This is the remote text Dial-Up Networking should watch for.

Inside Scoop
If you told the Internet Connection Wizard not to use the area code when dialing, then it's likely that the Dialing from list and Dial Properties buttons will be disabled in the Connect To dialog box. If so, you can enable them by clicking Properties and activating the Use area code and Dialing Properties check box. To still bypass the area code in the number, leave the Area code field blank.

Remember
When you complete the login, you may see a stream of garbage characters appear in the Post-Dial Terminal Screen. This is normal and it goes away after you click Continue.

matchcase	This optional parameter tells Dial-Up Networking to look for text that exactly matches the uppercase and lowercase letters used in *string*.
then *label*	This optional parameter tells Dial-Up Networking to jump to the script line that begins with *label* when it receives the *string* prompt.
until *seconds*	This optional parameter sets the number of *seconds* that Dial-Up Networking waits for the *string* prompt.

Consider the following example:

```
waitfor "User Name:" then Continue until 30
halt
Continue:
waitfor "Password:"
...
```

This partial script uses waitfor to look for the User Name: prompt. If it arrives within 30 seconds, the script jumps down to the Continue: label. Otherwise, the script just runs the halt command to stop the script.

The transmit command tells Dial-Up Networking to send text to the ISP's computer:

```
transmit "string" [,raw]
```

string	This is the text you want to send.
raw	This optional parameter tells Dial-Up Networking to treat the *string* as is and not interpret it as a string literal. For example, "^M" is a string literal that represents a carriage return. If you include raw, the string is sent just as a caret and the letter M.

Table 4.1 lists the string literals supported by the transmit command.

TABLE 4.1: STRING LITERALS YOU CAN USE WITH THE transmit COMMAND

String Literal	Sends
^*char*	A control character. For example, "^M" sends Ctrl+M, which is the control character for a carriage return.
<cr>	Carriage return
<lf>	Line feed
\"	Quotation mark
\^	Caret
\<	Less-than sign
\\	Backslash

Inside Scoop
To use the $USERID and $PASSWORD variables, you must enter your correct username and password in the Connect To dialog box. If you activate the Save password check box, Dial-Up Networking will remember your username and password and enter them automatically the next time you connect. You can then opt not to display the Connect To dialog box, as outlined earlier.

Scripts also recognize several system variables. These are outlined in Table 4.2.

TABLE 4.2: SYSTEM VARIABLES SUPPORTED BY DIAL-UP NETWORKING SCRIPTS

Variable	What It Represents
$USERID	The contents of the User name field in the Connect To dialog box.
$PASSWORD	The contents of the Password field in the Connect To dialog box.
$SUCCESS	True or false. Commands such as waitfor set the value of this variable. For example, if waitfor doesn't find the prompt it's looking for, it sets $SUCCESS to false.

Remember
Dial-up scripting supports a few more commands, as well as programming constructs such as if...endif and while...endwhile. To learn about these other features, see the file Script.doc in the Windows folder.

Place all your script commands within the following structure:

```
proc main
    Type your commands in here.
endproc
```

Here's a sample script that automates a simple login that requests a username and password:

```
proc main
    ; Delay for 3 seconds to allow the remote system
    ; enough time to send the initial characters.
    delay 3
    ; Now wait for the remote system to prompt for
    ; the user name. When it does, send the $USERID
    ; followed by a carriage return.
```

Shortcut
Windows Millennium ships with some sample scripts for automating CompuServe dial-ups, logins that require selecting menu choices, and more. You'll find them in the `C:\Program Files\Accessories` folder. If you create your own script, save it in this folder for easier access later on.

```
waitfor "user name:"
transmit $USERID
transmit "<cr>"
; Now wait for the remote system to prompt for
; the password. When it does, send the $PASSWORD
; followed by a carriage return.
waitfor "Password:"
transmit $PASSWORD
transmit "<cr>"
endproc
```

After your script is ready, follow these steps to assign it to a Dial-Up Networking connection:

1. In the Dial-Up Networking folder, display the property sheet for the connection you want to work with.

2. Select the Scripting tab.

3. Use the `File name` text box to enter the path and filename for your script (see Figure 4.14). Alternatively, click Browse to select the script file using the Open dialog box.

Figure 4.14
Use the Scripting tab to assign a script to a Dial-Up Networking connection.

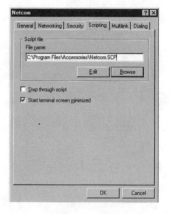

4. To test your script, activate the `Step through script` check box. With this option turned on, Dial-Up Networking will step through the script one line at a time. This will enable you to watch the progress of the login to ensure that everything works properly. Once you're sure your script is working, deactivate this check box.

5. To follow the prompts from the ISP, leave the `Start terminal screen minimized` check box deactivated. Once your script is working, you can activate this check box to avoid displaying the terminal screen.

6. Click OK to return to the Dial-Up Networking folder.

Disconnecting from Your ISP

After you've completed your Internet labors, you can disconnect from your ISP by using any of the following techniques:

- Double-click the Dial-Up Networking icon in the system tray, and then click Disconnect.

- Right-click the Dial-Up Networking icon in the system tray, and then click Disconnect.

- In the Dial-Up Networking folder, right-click the connection's icon and then click Disconnect.

- If you connected by running an Internet application, close the application. When Windows Millennium asks if you want to disconnect, click Yes.

Notes on Broadband (Cable or DSL) Connections

For many people, even a 56Kbps connection over a V.90 modem just isn't fast enough. For one thing, you never get the full 56Kbps connection. Instead, because of line noise and technical restrictions, you're more likely to get a connection between 40Kbs and 50Kbps. For another, Web pages are getting fatter and fatter as Web designers cram in more graphics, sounds, and other e-gadgetry. As a result, Web surfers spend much of their time in "blue bar land," waiting for sites to download. (The phrase "blue bar land" comes from the blue progress bar that Internet Explorer displays in the status bar while a page loads.)

Many intrepid souls are now foregoing slow-as-molasses dial-up connections and replacing them with *broadband* connections via cable or a digital subscriber line (DSL). Depending on the

Watch Out!
Because you no longer have to enter login data by hand, make sure you tell Dial-Up Networking not to display the Post-Dial Terminal Screen. To do so, display the connection's property sheet, click Configure, select the Options tab, and then deactivate the `Bring up terminal window after dialing` check box.

Watch Out!
The "always on"
nature of cable
and DSL connec-
tions makes them
convenient, but it
also makes your
computer a prime
target for attacks
from nefarious
hackers. For some
solutions, see
Chapter 7's
"'Always On'
Connections and
Personal
Firewalls" section,
p. 182.

Undocumented
If your computer
uses another net-
work card for net-
work access,
make sure you
keep the two
cards distinct dur-
ing the configura-
tion. If the two
cards are identi-
cal, check the
properties of each
card to determine
which one the
network uses. If
you can't tell,
remove one, con-
figure the other
for cable or DSL
access, then rein-
stall the first card
and configure it
for your network.

provider, the connection, and (in the case of cable) the number of nearby users, these alternatives offer connection speeds
measured in megabits per second (Mbps) as opposed to mere
kilobits per second (Kbps).

Although there are broadband setups that require high-end
hardware (such as a router) and specialized installation, the
setup for most individual users is relatively simple. In most
cases, it requires just three extra pieces of equipment:

A special modem—A cable modem that connects to a cable TV
line, or a DSL modem that connects to a phone line.

A network card—This card is inserted in the computer and
acts as the network connection point. This is required only
if you use an external cable or DSL modem; internal models don't require an extra network card.

A network cable—This connects the modem and the network
card.

After this hardware is installed, most providers have software
that sets up the hardware and configures the Internet connection automatically. If you don't have such software, or if you'd
rather do it yourself to maintain control over what happens to
your PC, it's usually not hard to set things up.

The specifics are very similar to those I describe later in this
chapter for setting up a computer to use a network gateway
(see "Installing and Configuring the TCP/IP Protocol").
Here's a list of what's different:

- When you configure TCP/IP, use the instance of TCP/IP
  that's bound to the network card connected to the cable
  or DSL modem (instead of the TCP/IP that's bound to
  the Dial-Up Adapter).

- Most cable and DSL providers assign IP addresses automatically. If not, you need your permanent IP address as
  well as the subnet mask that goes along with your address.

- You need the IP address of your provider's Internet
  gateway.

- You need your computer's hostname (sometimes called the client ID) and your provider's domain name.

- You need the IP address of your provider's DNS server (as well as that of the secondary DNS server, if they have one).

How to Get on the Internet Using a Local Area Network

If your computer is part of a local area network (LAN) that has an Internet gateway, connecting to the Internet requires a different configuration. Specifically, you have to set up the TCP/IP networking protocol to use your network's gateway as your connection to the Internet. This section shows you how it's done.

It's worth noting at this point that the instructions in this section don't apply if you're setting up a home or small office network and want to be able to share a single Internet connection among the computers. If that's what you're looking to do, see Chapter 19, "Setting Up Your Own Local Area Network."

→ **See Also** "Running the New Home Networking Wizard," p. 434.

Information You Need Before Getting Started

Before starting, you need to gather information from your network administrator. Here's a checklist that tells you the information you need to set up the connection:

- Whether your network assigns you an IP address automatically. If not, you need your permanent IP address as well as the subnet mask that goes along with your address.

- Whether your network uses the Windows Internet Name System (WINS) or the Dynamic Host Configuration Protocol (DHCP) to resolve computer network names and IP addresses. If your LAN uses WINS, you'll need the IP address of one or more WINS servers.

- The IP address of your network's Internet gateway.

- Your computer's hostname and your network's domain name.

- The IP address of one or more DNS servers used by your network.

- Whether your network uses a proxy server and, if so, the name of the proxy server.

Installing and Configuring the TCP/IP Protocol

With all your data in hand, here are the steps to follow to set up TCP/IP for the Internet connection:

Shortcut
A quick way to get to the Network dialog box is to right-click the desktop's My Network Places icon and then click Properties.

1. Open the Control Panel's Network icon to display the Network dialog box. In the Configuration tab, check the list of installed components to see if the TCP/IP protocol is bound to your network adapter. This will appear as TCP/IP -> Adapter, where Adapter is the name of your adapter (see Figure 4.15). If you see this, skip to Step 4.

Figure 4.15
Find the component that represents TCP/IP bound to the network adapter.

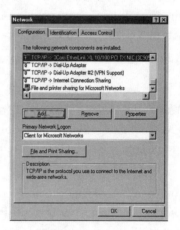

2. Click Add, highlight Protocol, and click Add again. The Select Network Protocol dialog box appears.

3. Highlight Microsoft in the Manufacturers list, highlight TCP/IP in the Network Protocols list, and then click OK.

4. In the list of components, highlight the item that represents TCP/IP bound to your network adapter (again, see Figure 4.15), and then click Properties.

5. In the IP Address tab, select one of the following options:

   Obtain an IP address automatically—Select this option if your network assigns you an IP address automatically.

   Specify an IP address—Select this option if you have a permanent network IP address. In this case, fill in the IP Address and Subnet Mask boxes.

6. In the WINS Configuration tab, activate the Enable WINS resolution option if your network uses WINS. Use the WINS Server Search Order box to add the IP address for one or more WINS servers. If your LAN uses DHCP, activate the Use DHCP for WINS Resolution option, instead.

7. In the Gateway tab, enter the IP address of one or more Internet gateways used by your LAN.

8. In the DNS Configuration tab, enter your computer's Host name and your network's Domain name. Use the DNS Server Search Order box to enter the IP address of one or more DNS servers used by your LAN.

9. In the Bindings tab, deactivate the check box File and printer sharing for Microsoft Networks.

10. Click OK to return to the Network dialog box.

11. Click OK.

12. When Windows Millennium asks if you want to restart your computer, click Yes.

If your Internet access is filtered through a proxy server, you need to configure the proxy server by following these extra steps:

1. Open the Control Panel's Internet icon and, in the Internet Properties dialog box that appears, select the Connection tab.

2. Click the LAN Settings button to display the Local Area Network (LAN) Settings dialog box.

3. Activate the Use a proxy server check box.

Watch Out!
Disabling the File and printer sharing for Microsoft Networks check box in the Bindings tab tells Windows Millennium not to bind file and print sharing to TCP/IP. In other words, you're preventing your shared resources from being shared with the entire Internet! For details on this, see Chapter 7's "Internet Security and the TCP/IP Protocol" section, page 182.

4. Enter the proxy server's Address and Port.

5. If you want to specify proxy servers for specific protocols, click Advanced and use the Proxy Settings dialog box to enter addresses and ports for the various protocols. Note, too, that you can also use the Exceptions group to enter IP addresses (such as 123.231.*.*) or domain names (such as *.mcfedries.com) for sites that shouldn't go through the proxy server. Click OK.

6. If you don't want to use the proxy server for intranet addresses, activate the Bypass proxy server for local addresses check box.

7. Click OK.

Some Internet Utilities You Should Know

Now that you can actually get on the Internet, the next three chapters will focus on various Internet applications and tools. Before that, let's take a quick look at some useful TCP/IP utilities:

Inside Scoop
To use PING to test your Internet connection, first try pinging the loopback address: 127.0.0.1. If that doesn't work, uninstall and then reinstall TCP/IP. Next try your IP address. If that ping doesn't work, check your IP address and the subnet mask for errors. Next try your LAN's Internet gateway. If that doesn't work, make sure TCP/IP is bound to your network adapter.

PING—You use the PING utility to see if you can access a remote system. The idea is that PING sends out special IP *echo packets* that ask the remote server to send back a response. If the response is received, then you know the remote computer is accessible. At the DOS prompt, type **ping *host***, where ***host*** is the IP address or domain name of the remote host you want to use. This syntax sends out four packets. If you'd prefer to have PING send out packets indefinitely, use the syntax ping -t *host*. (You can interrupt the pinging by pressing Ctrl+C.)

TRACERT—This utility also sends out echo packets, but it traces the route that the packets take. If PING can't reach a remote host, it could be because the echo packets are getting stuck at some intermediate host. TRACERT (trace route) can tell you if this is the case. At the DOS prompt, enter **tracert *host***, where ***host*** is the IP address or domain name of the remote host. If the trace stops at a particular point, then you've found the culprit.

WINIPCFG—This utility can tell you your current IP address, which is often useful if your ISP or network assigns IP addresses dynamically. To launch this utility, select Start, Run, type **winipcfg.exe**, and then click OK. In the IP Configuration dialog box that appears, click More Info to get the expanded version of the dialog box shown in Figure 4.16.   *Also: IPCONFIG /ALL*

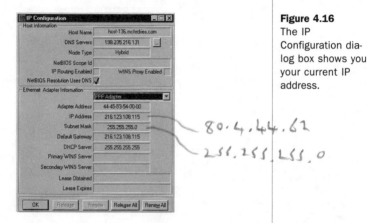

80.4.44.62
255.255.255.0

Figure 4.16
The IP Configuration dialog box shows you your current IP address.

Essential Information

- To install a modem and work with modem properties, open the Control Panel's Modems icon.

- To specify dialing location settings (such as the country code, area code, calling card data) and how to disable call waiting, click Dialing Properties in the Modems Properties dialog box.

- Before creating your Internet connection, gather the information you need, such as the dial-up number, your username and password, your IP address, the IP addresses of your ISP's DNS servers, and so on.

- To run the Internet Connection Wizard, launch the desktop's Connect to the Internet icon.

- To create a connection by hand, select Start, Programs, Accessories, Communications, Dial-Up Networking and then open the Make New Connection icon.

- To connect to your ISP, either launch the icon from the Dial-Up Networking folder, or open an Internet application or resource.

- Connecting to the Internet via a LAN gateway requires installing and configuring the TCP/IP protocol.

GET THE SCOOP ON...
Internet Explorer's Browsing Tools and Techniques ▪
Address Bar Tips and Tricks ▪ Setting Up Pages for
Offline Reading ▪ Taking Control of Internet Explorer's
Temporary Files ▪ Internet Explorer's Advanced
Options

Expert Internet Explorer Techniques

THE WINDOWS MILLENNIUM desktop boasts icons for both Internet Explorer and Outlook Express. These two programs also have shortcut icons in the taskbar's Quick Launch toolbar. That these icons get privileged positions on the Windows Millennium desktop isn't surprising because Web surfing and email represent the two most popular online activities. This chapter shows you how to use Internet Explorer to browse sites on the World Wide Web. (Outlook Express is covered in the next chapter.)

My approach will be to pass quickly over the basics of Web browsing and to concentrate more on Internet Explorer's powerful features, including the Search bar, the Address bar, the Favorites folder, offline pages, and Internet Explorer's customization options. See also Chapter 7, "Implementing Windows Millennium Internet Security Features," to learn about implementing security in Internet Explorer.

➜ **See Also** "Internet Explorer's Security Features," **p. 184.**

Basic Browsing Techniques

Browsing is Internet Explorer's bread and butter, and that's reflected in the sheer number of techniques it offers for getting from one Web page to another. This section offers a quick synopsis of all the ways you can use Internet Explorer to browse the Web.

Understanding Web Page Addresses

Let's begin by examining that strange creature, the World Wide Web address, officially known as a *Uniform Resource Locator* (URL). A Web page's address usually takes the following form:

```
http://host.domain/directory/file.name
```

host.domain	The domain name of the host computer where the page resides.
directory	The host computer directory that contains the page.
file.name	The page's filename. Note that most Web pages use the extensions html and htm.

Here are some notes about URLs:

- The http part of the URL signifies that the TCP/IP protocol to be used to communicate with the server is HTTP (Hypertext Transfer Protocol), which is used for standard Web pages. Other common protocols are https (Secure Hypertext Transfer Protocol: secure Web pages) and ftp (File Transfer Protocol: file downloads).

- Most Web domains use the www prefix and the com suffix (for example, www.mcfedries.com). Other popular suffixes are edu (educational sites), gov (government sites), net (networking companies), and org (nonprofit sites). Note, too, that most servers don't require the www prefix (for example, mcfedries.com).

- Directory names and filenames are case sensitive on most Web hosts (those that run UNIX servers, anyway).

Inside Scoop
Most Web sites use one or more default filenames, the most common of which are index.html and index.htm. If you omit the filename from the URL, the Web server will display the default page.

Opening and Browsing Pages

Using Internet Explorer to open and surf Web pages is straightforward and easy (which is one reason Microsoft decided to adapt the browsing metaphor to folders, disk drives, and other local resources). Here's a review of the techniques you can use to open a page:

Type a URL in the Run dialog box—Select Start, Run, type the URL you want in the Run dialog box, and click OK.

Type a URL in any Address bar—Internet Explorer and all folder windows have an Address bar. To open a page, type the URL in the Address bar and press Enter.

Select a URL from the Address bar—Internet Explorer's Address bar doubles as a drop-down list that holds the last 25 addresses you entered.

Use the Open dialog box for remote pages—Select File, Open (or press Ctrl+O) to display the Open dialog box, type the URL, and click OK.

Use the Open dialog box for local pages—If you want to view a Web page that's on your computer, display the Open dialog box, enter the full path (drive, folder, and filename), and click OK. Alternatively, click Browse, find the page, click Open, and then click OK.

Click a Links bar button—The Links bar contains seven buttons that take you to predefined Web pages. For example, the Microsoft button takes you to the Microsoft home page. (You can add buttons to the Links bar, remove existing buttons, and more. See "Customizing the Links Bar," later in this chapter.)

Once you've opened a page, there are more techniques you can use to navigate to other pages:

Click a link—Most Web pages contain several *hypertext links*: text that, when clicked, loads another page into the browser. Links usually appear underlined and in a different color from the rest of the text. To see the URL of a linked page before you go there, hover the mouse pointer over the link and the URL appears in the status bar.

Inside Scoop
If you have a mouse with a wheel button, hold down Ctrl while pressing and turning the wheel. This changes the onscreen font size on-the-fly.

Click an image map—Some Web page graphics are *image maps* where different sections of the image are linked to different Web pages.

Open a link in another window—If you don't want to leave the current page, you can force a link to open in another Internet Explorer window by right-clicking the link and then clicking Open in New Window. (You can open a new window for the current page by selecting File, New, Window, or by pressing Ctrl+N.)

Retrace the pages you've visited—Click Internet Explorer's Back button to return to a page you visited previously in this session. (Alternatively, select Go, Back or press Alt+Left arrow.) After you've gone back to a page, click the Forward button to move ahead through the visited pages. (You can also select Go, Forward or press Alt+Right arrow.) Note, too, that the Back and Forward buttons also serve as drop-down lists. Click the downward-pointing arrow to the right of each button to see the list.

Return to the start page—When you launch Internet Explorer without specifying a URL, you end up at MSN, the default start page (http://www.msn.com/). You can return to this page at any time by selecting View, Go To, Home Page, or by clicking the Home button in the toolbar (you can also press Alt+Home).

Use the History bar—If you click the toolbar's History button or select the View, Explorer Bar, History command, Internet Explorer adds a History bar to the left side of the window. This bar lists the sites you've visited over the past 20 days. Just click a URL to go to a site. Note that the items you see in the History bar are based on the contents of the Windows\History folder.

The default Internet Explorer toolbar is just as strangely configured as the default Windows Explorer toolbar. Fortunately, the customization steps are identical. See Chapter 8's "Customizing the Standard Buttons Toolbar" section, **p. 227.**

Undocumented
Hold down Shift and click a link to open that link in a new browser window.

Inside Scoop
To change the home page, first surf to the page you want to use. Then select Tools, Internet Options, display the General tab, and click Use Current. Alternatively, drag the icon from the Address bar and drop it on the Home toolbar button.

Searching for Sites

Although most new Web users prefer just to surf around and see what serendipity brings, most veteran users prefer a more targeted approach that enables them to find information and do research. The bad news is that the Web is home to hundreds of millions of pages, so finding what you want is no easy task. The good news is that there's no shortage of indexes and search engines that can at least narrow things down a bit. To help you get started, Internet Explorer offers some default searching options.

For quick searches, use the Search bar:

- Click the Search toolbar button.

- Select View, Explorer Bar, Search.

Internet Explorer adds a Search bar to the left side of the window, as shown in Figure 5.1. The Search bar offers a scaled-down version of a Web search engine, such as the MSN Search engine shown in Figure 5.1. The layout of the Search bar depends on the engine, but in all cases you get a text box where you can enter your search terms. You then click Search (or Seek or Find or whatever) and the bar is updated with the results. You then click a resulting match to display the page in the main part of the Internet Explorer window.

Remember
You can adjust some History folder settings by selecting Tools, Internet Options. In the General tab, use the Days to keep pages in history spinner to determine the maximum number of days that Internet Explorer will store a URL in its History list. Click the Clear History button to remove all URLs from the History folder.

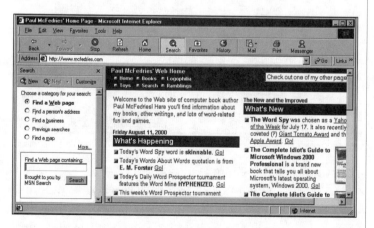

Figure 5.1
Use the Search bar to enter quick searches.

Inside Scoop

Most good search engines offer *Boolean* searches. This means you separate search terms with particular keywords. For example, separating two terms with AND means you only want to match sites that contains both terms. Similarly, OR means you want to match sites that match at least one of the terms. You can also use NOT to exclude sites that contain a particular term.

Figure 5.2
Use this window to customize the Search bar.

If you prefer to use another search engine, the Search bar is easily customizable. Here's a review:

Repeating the same search on a different search engine—After you've run a search, the Search bar's Next button becomes enabled. Click this button to repeat the search using the next search engine in the list. Alternatively, drop down the Next list and click the search engine you want to use.

Customizing the list of search engines—You can customize the Next list by clicking the Search bar's Customize button. Internet Explorer displays the Customize Search Settings window, shown in Figure 5.2. In the Find a Web page section, use the check boxes to add or remove search engines from the Next list.

Reordering the search engines—The order in which the search engines appear in the Next list is determined by the order in which they appear in the Find a Web page list. You can change this order by highlighting an engine and then clicking the up and down arrows below the list.

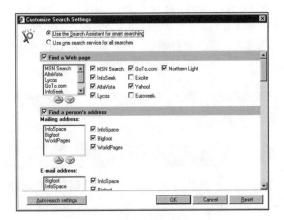

Customizing the Links Bar

I like the *idea* of the Links bar: one-click access to Web sites. However, I don't really like the *execution* of the Links bar because I use only a couple of the predefined Web sites. I get the impression Microsoft isn't all that thrilled with the Links bar, either, because the default is to hide it to the right of the Address bar. To bring the Links bar into view, drag its left edge to the left, or drop it below the Address bar.

Here's a list of the techniques you can use to customize the Links bar:

Removing a button—To delete a button from the Links bar, right-click it and then click Delete.

Changing a button's URL—Right-click the button and then click Properties to display the button's property sheet. Use the URL text box to change the URL, and then click OK.

Renaming a button—Right-click the button and then click Rename. Use the Rename dialog box to edit the name, and then click OK.

Adding a button for the current page—Drag the icon in the Address bar and drop it inside the Links bar.

Adding a button for a link—Drag the link and drop it inside the Links bar. If you've already saved the page as a Favorite, pull down the Favorites menu, drag the icon from the menu, and drop it inside the Links bar. If the page title is long, you'll likely want to rename it to something shorter to avoid wasting precious Links bar space.

Moving a button—Drag the button left or right within the Links bar.

Address Bar Tricks

One of Windows 98's new features was the expansion of the Address bar's territory from Internet Explorer to all folder windows (as well as to Windows Explorer). When you enter a URL into the Address bar of a folder window and then click Go (or press Enter), the window morphs into Internet Explorer—complete with the appropriate toolbars and menus. You can even place a version of the Address bar on the taskbar. Right-click an empty section of the toolbar, and then click Toolbars, Address. Entering a URL into this Address bar loads Internet Explorer to display the page.

Shortcut
Internet Explorer supports searches from the Address bar. When you enter a word or phrase, the Address bar list drops down and you see Search for "text", where text is the word or phrase you typed. Press the down arrow and then Enter to run a search on the text. To specify the search engine used for this type of search, display the Customize Search Settings window, click Autosearch settings, and then use the dialog box that shows up to choose the search engine.

Inside Scoop
The Links bar buttons are URL shortcut files located in the Windows\Favorites \Links folder. You can use this folder to work with the shortcuts directly, add subfolders, and so on.

Shortcut
After you have
your Links bar cus-
tomized to suit
your style, you can
make it even more
convenient by dis-
playing it as part
of the taskbar. To
do this, right-click
an empty section
of the taskbar,
and then click
Toolbars, Links.

66

By default, the
Address Bar
shows your cur-
rent location,
whether it's a
folder or a Web
page. You can
browse to
another location
by typing an
address—a URL,
a path, or even
a program
name.
—*Microsoft*

99

However, the Address bar is more than a mere type-and-click mechanism. It's useful for many things, and comes with its own bag of tricks for making it even easier to use. Here's a run-down:

- Press F4 to select the Address bar text and drop down its list. Use the Up and Down arrow keys to select an item from the list.

- If you just want to edit the Address bar text, press Alt+D to select it.

- You can create a shortcut for whatever object is displayed in the Address bar by dragging the object's icon (it's on the left side of the text box) and dropping it on the desktop or some other location.

- The Address bar's AutoComplete feature monitors the address as you type. If any previously entered addresses match your typing, those addresses appear in a list. To choose one of those addresses, use the down arrow to select it and then press Enter.

- Internet Explorer assumes any address you enter is for a Web site. Therefore, you don't need to type the `http://` prefix because Internet Explorer will add it for you automatically.

- Internet Explorer also assumes that most Web addresses are in the form `www.something.com`. Therefore, if you simply type the "something" part and press Ctrl+Enter, Internet Explorer will automatically add the `www` prefix and the `com` suffix. For example, you can get to my home page (`www.mcfedries.com`) by typing `mcfedries` and pressing Ctrl+Enter.

- Some Web sites use *frames* to divide a Web page into multiple sections. Some of these sites offer links to other Web sites but, annoyingly, those pages appear within the first site's frame structure. To break out of frames, drag a link into the Address bar.

Using the `Favorites` Folder to Save Sites

If you come across a Web page that you want to read later or that you think you'll be visiting regularly, you can use the `Windows\Favorites` folder to store a shortcut that points to the page's URL. Here's how you do it:

1. Open the Web page you want to save. (If you want to set up a link as a favorite, right-click the link, click Add to Favorites, and then skip to step 3.)

2. Select Favorites, Add to Favorites to get the Add Favorite dialog box onscreen.

3. I discuss offline pages in the next section, so for now make sure the `Make available offline` option is deactivated.

4. If you want to place the page into a subfolder, click the Create in button to expand the dialog box as shown in Figure 5.3. From here, either click the folder you want to use, or else click New Folder to add a folder to the Favorites hierarchy.

5. Click OK.

Shortcut
Internet Explorer offers two methods for quickly adding a site to the `Favorites` folder. If the current page has a link to the site you want to save, drag the link to the Favorites menu. If you want to save the current page, instead, drag the icon from the Address bar to the Favorites menu. When the menu pulls down, drag the item to the position you want (you can even hover over sub-menus to open them) and then drop the item.

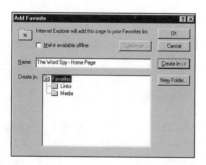

Figure 5.3
The expanded version of the Add Favorite dialog box.

Opening Favorite Sites

To browse to a favorite site, use any of the following techniques:

- In Internet Explorer, Windows Explorer, or any folder window, pull down the Favorites menu and then select the favorite.

- In Internet Explorer, Windows Explorer, or any folder window, either click the Favorites button in the toolbar, or select View, Explorer Bar, Favorites. This adds a Favorites bar to the left side of the window. From there, click the favorite you want to open.

- Select Start, Favorites and then click the favorite. (I show you how to add the Favorites item to the Start menu in Chapter 17, "Customizing the Windows Millennium Interface.")

→ **See Also** "Renovating the Start Menu," **p. 397.**

- In Windows Explorer, open the Windows\Favorites folder and then double-click the icon for the favorite.

Sharing Favorites and Netscape Bookmarks

Many users like to run both Internet Explorer and Netscape Navigator on their machines. Unfortunately, the two browsers store saved sites differently: Internet Explorer uses favorites while Navigator uses bookmarks. However, Internet Explorer has a feature that enables you to either export favorites to a bookmark file, or import bookmarks as favorites. Here's how it's done:

1. In Internet Explorer, select File, Import and Export. The Import/Export Wizard makes an appearance.

2. Click Next.

3. Highlight one of the following:

Import Favorites—Select this option to import Navigator bookmarks as favorites. When you click Next, the wizard asks you for the path to the bookmark.htm file. Click Next when you're done.

Export Favorites—Select this option to export your favorites as Navigator bookmarks. When you click Next, the wizard first asks you which Favorites folder you want to export. Click Next again and the wizard prompts you to enter the path to the bookmark.htm file. Click Next once you've done that.

4. This wizard performs the requested operation and then displays a dialog box to let you know when it's complete. Click Finish.

Maintaining Favorites

Once you have a large number of favorites, you need to do some regular maintenance to keep things organized. This involves creating new subfolders, moving favorites between folders, changing URLs, deleting unused favorites, and more. Here's a summary of a few maintenance techniques you'll use most often:

- To change the URL of a favorite, pull down the Favorites menu, find the item you want to work with, and right-click it. In the shortcut menu, click Properties and then use the property sheet to adjust the URL.

- To move a favorite, pull down the Favorites menu, find the item you want to work with, and then drag the item to another spot on the menu (or into a submenu).

- To delete a favorite, pull down the Favorites menu, find the item you want to work with, right-click it, and then click Delete.

- To work with the Favorites folder, select Favorites, Organize Favorites to display the dialog box shown in Figure 5.4.

- You can also work with the Favorites folder directly by launching Windows Explorer and selecting the Windows\Favorites folder.

Undocumented
You can also open the Organize Favorites dialog box by pressing Ctrl+B. Note, too, that this dialog box is sizable. Use your mouse to drag any edge to get the size you want.

Figure 5.4
Use the Organize
Favorites dialog
box to perform
maintenance
chores on the
URL shortcut
files.

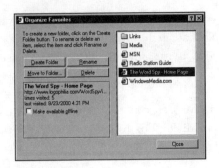

Reading Pages Offline

After you spend some time on the Web, you'll likely find you have a long list of favorites, and that they fall into one of the following three categories:

- Sites that remain relatively constant over time. These are sites that contain good information for research or fun features for entertainment. You usually access them only as needed.

- Sites that change frequently. These are sites that have constantly updated information, such as news or "something-of-the-day" features. (For an example of the latter, see my Word Spy site: www.wordspy.com.) To keep up with these sites, you might consider storing them in a Favorites subfolder named, say, Daily Links and browsing each favorite daily to look for new content.

- Sites that change content only occasionally. These are sites that update on an irregular schedule. They're problematic because you never know when the content will change.

The latter two categories are workable if you have just a few sites in each category. However, they quickly chew up a lot of connection time if you end up with a large number of these sites. If you have many frequently changing sites, you spend a great deal of connection time reading the new content; if you have many occasionally changing sites, you waste a lot of connection time looking for changed content.

In other words, there are two connection time problems to solve:

- Reading a large number of frequently changing sites.

- Searching for changed content in a large number of occasionally changing sites.

Internet Explorer solves both problems with its offline pages feature. The idea is that for each of your pages saved as a favorite, you can tell Internet Explorer to also make the page available offline. This means that a local copy of the page is stored in the Windows\Offline Web Pages folder. There is also an associated synchronize feature that you can run to tell Internet Explorer to go online and check for (and download) updated versions of the offline pages. These features solve the preceding problems as follows:

- Having the changed pages on your computer means that you can read them without going online.

- After the synchronization is complete, Internet Explorer indicates which pages have changed, so you know from a glance which ones to read.

Setting Up a Page for Offline Reading

To set up a page for offline reading, you have two ways to get started:

For a page that's already set up as a favorite—Pull down the Favorites menu, right-click the favorite, and then click Make available offline.

For all other pages—Open the page in Internet Explorer and then select Favorites, Add to Favorites. In the Add Favorite dialog box, activate the Make available offline check box and then click Customize.

Either way, the Offline Favorite Wizard appears. Here's how to wield this wizard:

1. The first dialog box just offers an introduction, so click Next. (You might want to activate the In the future, do

not show this introduction screen check box to avoid this useless dialog box down the road.)

2. As shown in Figure 5.5, the next wizard dialog box wonders if you also want to view pages that are linked to the favorite page (which could be pages on the same site or one different sites):

> **No**—Activating this option tells Internet Explorer not to bother downloading linked pages.
>
> **Yes**—Activating this option tells Internet Explorer to download the linked pages. Use the Download pages *x* links deep from this page spin box to specify how many levels of links you want downloaded.

Figure 5.5
Use the Offline
Favorite Wizard to
set up a page for
offline viewing.

3. Click Next. The wizard now asks how you want the page synchronized:

> **Only when I choose Synchronize from the Tools menu**—Choose this option to perform the synchronization by hand. Click Next and skip to step 5.
>
> **I would like to create a new schedule**—Choose this option to set up a schedule for automatic synchronizations. Click Next and proceed to step 4.

4. If you elected to set up a schedule, the wizard displays a dialog box with the following controls (click Next when you're done):

> **Every x days**—Set the interval, in days, that Internet Explorer uses to run the synchronization.

at—Set the time at which Internet Explorer runs the synchronization.

Name—Make up a name for this new synchronization schedule.

If my computer is not connected...—Activating this check box tells Internet Explorer to connect to the Internet automatically to perform the synchronization.

5. The wizard now asks if the page requires a password. If not, activate No; if so, activate Yes and then enter your User name and Password (twice).

6. Click Finish.

Synchronizing Offline Pages

With all that done, you can synchronize your offline content at any time by using either of the following techniques:

- Select the Tools, Synchronize command. In the Items to Synchronize dialog box, leave the check boxes activated for the pages you want to download, and then click Synchronize.

- To synchronize an individual page, pull down the Favorites menu, right-click the page, and then click Synchronize.

When that's done, you can go offline (by activating the File, Work Offline command) and view the updated content by selecting the pages from the Favorites menu. You can tell the pages that have changed content by looking for a small, red dot in the upper-left corner of the page's icon on the Favorites menu (see Figure 5.6).

Changing Offline Page Properties

To change any options for an offline page, follow these steps:

1. Select Tools, Synchronize to display the Items to Synchronize dialog box.

Watch Out!
Having Internet Explorer connect automatically is great for running unattended synchronizations (in the middle of the night, for example). However, this will work only if you connect to your ISP without having to input login data using the Post-Dial Terminal Screen.

Changed pages
have a red dot
on their icons.

Figure 5.6
Internet Explorer
uses a red dot to
indicate offline
pages with
changed content.

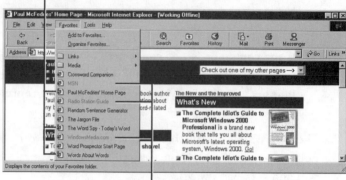

Grayed-out pages
aren't available offline.

2. Highlight the item you want to work with and then click Properties. Internet Explorer displays a property sheet for the offline page.

3. In the Web Document tab, use the Make this page available offline check box to toggle offline availability on and off.

4. The Schedule tab offers two options that control how the page is synchronized:

   Only when I choose Synchronize from the Tools menu—Choose this option to run the synchronization by hand.

   Using the following schedule(s)—Choose this option to synchronize the page on a schedule. In the list below it, activate the check boxes beside each schedule you want to use. Use the Add, Remove, and Edit buttons to create, delete, and change schedules.

5. The Download tab, shown in Figure 5.7, is loaded with useful options:

   Download pages x links deep from this page—Use this spin box to set the number of linked pages that are downloaded.

Follow links outside of this page's Web site—If you leave this check box activated, Internet Explorer will download a linked page even if it's not within the same site as the offline page. If you prefer to stick to the offline page's site, deactivate this check box.

Limit hard-disk usage for this page to x Kilobytes— Activate this check box and use the associated spin box to restrict the amount of hard disk space used by the offline page. This is a good idea if you decide to download pages more than one level deep because that could easily lead to hundreds of pages being downloaded.

Advanced—Click this button to display the Advanced Download Options dialog box, which you use to tell Internet Explorer not to download certain page components (such as image, sound, and video files, ActiveX controls, and Java applets).

When this page changes, send e-mail to—Activate this check box if you want Internet Explorer to alert you via email when an offline page has new content. You also need to fill in the E-mail address and the Mail Server (SMTP) text boxes.

If the site requires a user name and password—If you have to login to the Web site, click Login and use the resulting dialog box to specify your username and password.

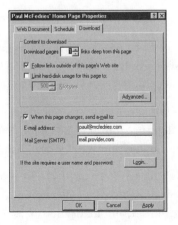

Figure 5.7
Use the Download tab to control various options related to how the offline page is downloaded to your computer.

6. Click OK to return to the Items to Synchronize dialog box.

7. Click Close.

Changing Synchronization Settings

Besides properties for individual offline pages, Internet Explorer also maintains a separate collection of settings that apply to the synchronization feature as a whole. These settings provide you with alternative ways to set up automatic synchronizations (such as when you log on or when your computer has been idle for a while).

To work with these settings, first select Tools, Synchronize to display the Items to Synchronize dialog box, and then click the Setup button. Internet Explorer displays the Synchronization Settings dialog box shown in Figure 5.8.

Figure 5.8
Use the Synchronization Settings dialog box to set up Internet Explorer for automatic synchronizing of offline pages.

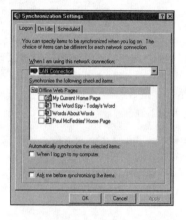

This dialog box sports three tabs:

Logon—Use this tab to select offline pages that you want automatically synchronized when you log on to your network (or just when you log on to your computer).

On Idle—Use this tab to select offline pages that you want automatically synchronized when your computer has been idle. To set the idle time, click Advanced.

Scheduled—Use this tab to create and edit *synchronization tasks*. A synchronization task is a collection of offline pages that gets synchronized automatically on a regular schedule.

Clicking the Add button invokes the Schedule Synchronization Wizard, which takes you through the process of creating a synchronization task.

When you're done, click OK to return to the Items to Synchronize dialog box and then click Close.

Controlling the Web Page Cache

In the same way that a disk cache stores frequently used data for faster performance, Internet Explorer also keeps a cache of files from Web pages you've visited recently. This cache is the Windows\Temporary Internet Files folder, and Internet Explorer uses these saved files to display Web pages quickly the next time you ask to see them.

To control the cache, select Tools, Internet Options and display the General tab. Use the following buttons in the Temporary Internet files group:

Delete Files—Clicking this button cleans out the Temporary Internet Files folder.

Settings—Clicking this button displays the Settings dialog box (see Figure 5.9).

Figure 5.9
Use this dialog box to control how the Internet Explorer cache works.

You have the following options:

Check for newer versions of stored pages—Choose an option to determine when Internet Explorer checks for updated versions of cache files. Choosing Every visit to the page always ensures that you see the most current data, but it can delay the loading of a page. Choosing Every time you start Internet Explorer causes the cache to be updated only at startup. To let Internet Explorer determine the best method for updating the cache, choose Automatically. If you don't want the cache checked at all, choose Never.

Amount of disk space to use—Use this slider to set the size of the cache, as a percentage of the hard disk's capacity. A larger cache speeds up Web site browsing but also uses more hard drive space.

Move Folder—Clicking this button enables you to change the folder used for the cache. Note that you must restart your computer if you move the cache folder.

View Files—Clicking this button displays the Temporary Internet Files folder.

View Objects—Clicking this button displays the Downloaded Program Files folder, which holds the Java applets and ActiveX controls that have been downloaded and installed on your system.

Remember
No matter which cache update option you choose, you can view the most up-to-date version of a page at any time by selecting the View, Refresh command. (You can also press F5 or click the Refresh button.)

Internet Explorer's Advanced Options

To complete our look at Internet Explorer, this section examines the huge list of customization features found in the Advanced tab of the Internet Explorer property sheet. To begin, use any of the following techniques to get the Internet Explorer Properties dialog box onscreen:

- In Internet Explorer, select Tools, Internet Options.

- Open the Control Panel's Internet Options icon.

- Right-click the desktop's Internet Explorer icon and then click Properties.

Whichever method you choose, select the Advanced tab, shown in Figure 5.10.

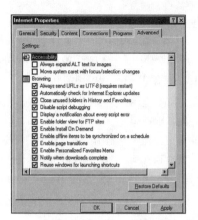

Figure 5.10
The Advanced tab is crammed with Internet Explorer customization settings.

The Accessibility group has two options:

Always expand ALT text for images—Most Webmasters define a text description for each image they include on a page. If you tell Internet Explorer not to show images (see the following discussion of the Show pictures check box), all you see are boxes where the images should be, and each box contains the text description (which is known as *alt text*, where alt is short for alternate). Activating this check box tells Internet Explorer to expand the image box horizontally so the alt text appears on a single line.

Move system caret with focus/selection changes—Activating this check box tells Internet Explorer to move the system caret whenever you change the focus. This is useful if you have a screen reader or screen magnifier that uses the position of the system caret to determine what part of the screen should be read or magnified.

The Browsing branch boasts quite a few options:

Always send URLs as UTF-8—When activated, this check box tells Internet Explorer to send Web page addresses using the UTF-8 standard, which is readable in any language. If you're having trouble accessing a page that uses non-English characters in the URL, the server may not be able to handle UTF-8, so deactivate this check box.

Remember
The system caret is a visual indication of what part of the screen currently has the focus. If a text box has the focus, the system caret is a blinking, vertical bar; if a check box or option button has the focus, the system caret is a dotted outline of the control name.

Automatically check for Internet Explorer updates—When activated, this option tells Internet Explorer to check (approximately every 30 days) to see whether a newer version of the program is available.

Close unused folders in History and Favorites—When this check box is activated, Internet Explorer keeps unused folders closed when you display the History bar and the Favorites bar. That is, if you open a folder and then open a second folder, Internet Explorer automatically closes the first folder.

Disable script debugging—This check box toggles the script debugger (if one is installed) on and off.

Display a notification about every script error—If you activate this check box, Internet Explorer displays a dialog box to alert you to JavaScript or VBScript errors on a page. If you leave this option deactivated, Internet Explorer displays an error message in the status bar. To see the full error message, double-click the status bar message.

Enable folder view for FTP sites—When this option is activated and you access an FTP (File Transfer Protocol) site, Internet Explorer displays the contents of the site using the familiar Windows folder view. This makes it easy to drag and drop files from the FTP to your hard disk (and possibly perform other file maintenance chores, depending on what permissions you have at the site).

Enable Install On Demand—When this check box is activated, Internet Explorer examines each Web page for elements that require a specific browser feature. If that feature isn't installed, the program asks if you want to install it.

Enable offline items to be synchronized on a schedule—This check box toggles the synchronization updates on and off. Deactivating this check box is a good idea if you're going out of town for a few days and don't want offline pages updated while you're away.

Enable page transitions—This check box toggles Internet Explorer's support for page transitions on and off. Web sites that use a server that supports FrontPage extensions can define various page transitions (such as wipes and fades). However, these transitions often slow down your browsing, so turning them off is recommended.

Enable Personalized Favorites Menu—When this check box is activated, Windows Millennium's new "personalized" menu feature gets applied to Internet Explorer's Favorites menu. This means that Internet Explorer hides favorites that you haven't visited in a while. To see the hidden favorites, click the downward-pointing arrow at the bottom of the menu.

Notify when downloads complete—If you leave this check box activated, Internet Explorer leaves its download progress dialog box onscreen after the download is complete (see Figure 5.11). This enables you to click Open to launch the downloaded file or to click Open Folder to display the file's destination folder. If you deactivate this check box, Internet Explorer closes this dialog box as soon as the download is over.

Remember
You can also force Internet Explorer to close the Download complete dialog box automatically by activating the `Close this dialog box when download complete` check box.

Figure 5.11
When Internet Explorer completes a file download, it leaves this dialog box onscreen to help you deal with the file.

Reuse windows for launching shortcuts—When this check box is activated, Windows looks for an already-open Internet Explorer window when you click a Web page shortcut (such as a Web address in an Outlook Express email message). If such a window is open, the Web page is loaded into that window. If you deactivate this option, Windows always loads the page into a new Internet Explorer window.

Show friendly HTTP error messages—When this check box is activated, Internet Explorer intercepts the error messages generated by Web servers and replaces them with its own messages that offer more information as well as possible solutions to the problem.

Show friendly URLs—This check box determines how URLs appear in the status bar when you hover the mouse over a link or image map. Activate this check box to see only the filename of the linked page; deactivate this check box to see the full URL of the linked page.

Show Go button in Address bar—When this check box is activated, Internet Explorer adds a Go button to the right of the Address bar. You click this button to open whatever URL is shown in the Address bar. The usefulness of this button is dubious, but it doesn't hurt anything.

Show Internet Explorer on the desktop—This check box toggles the desktop's Internet Explorer icon on and off.

Underline links—Use these options to specify when Internet Explorer should format Web page links with an underline. The Hover option means that the underline only appears when you position the mouse pointer over the link.

Use inline AutoComplete—This check box toggles the Address bar's AutoComplete feature on and off.

Use Passive FTP for compatibility with some firewalls and DSL modems—In a normal FTP session, Internet Explorer opens a connection to the FTP server (for commands) and then the FTP server opens a second connection back to the browser (for the data). If you're on a network with a firewall, however, incoming connections from a server aren't allowed. With *passive FTP*, the browser establishes the second (data) connection itself. So, if you're on a firewalled network (or are using a DSL modem) and you can't establish an FTP connection, activate this check box.

Use smooth scrolling—This check box toggles a feature called *smooth scrolling* on and off. When you activate this check

Inside Scoop
Internet Explorer's AutoComplete feature also applies to Web forms. That is, AutoComplete can also remember data that you've typed into a form—including usernames and passwords—and then enter that data automatically when you use the form again. You can control this portion of AutoComplete by selecting Tools, Internet Options and then clicking the Content tab's AutoComplete button.

box to enable smooth scrolling, pressing Page Down or Page Up causes the page to scroll down or up at a preset speed. If you deactivate this check box, pressing Page Down or Page Up causes the page to instantly jump down or up.

The check boxes in the HTTP 1.1 settings branch determine whether Internet Explorer uses the HTTP 1.1 protocol:

Use HTTP 1.1—This check box toggles Internet Explorer's use of HTTP 1.1 to communicate with Web servers. (HTTP 1.1 is the standard protocol used on the Web today.) You should deactivate this check box only if you're having trouble connecting to a Web site. This tells Internet Explorer to use HTTP 1.0, which may solve the problem.

Use HTTP 1.1 through proxy connections—This check box toggles on and off the use of HTTP 1.1 only when connecting through a proxy server.

The check boxes in the Microsoft VM branch are related to Internet Explorer's Java Virtual Machine:

Java console enabled—This check box toggles the Java console on and off. The Java console is a separate window in which the output and error messages from a Java applet are displayed. If you activate this option (which requires that you restart Internet Explorer), you can view the Java console by selecting the View, Java Console command.

Java logging enabled—This check box toggles Internet Explorer's Java logging on and off. When it's on, Internet Explorer logs Java applet error messages to a file named Javalog.txt in the Windows\Java folder. This is useful for troubleshooting Java problems.

JIT compiler for virtual machine enabled—This check box toggles Internet Explorer's internal "just-in-time" Java compiler on and off. This compiler is used to compile and run Java applets using native Windows code. In many

Undocumented
When reading a Web page, you can scroll down one screenful by pressing the spacebar. To scroll up one screenful, press Shift+Spacebar.

cases, this causes the Java applet to run much faster than the regularly compiled code. However, it may break some applets, or cause them to run slower than normal.

The options in the Multimedia branch toggle various multimedia effects on and off:

Always show Internet Explorer (5.0 or later) Radio toolbar— When this check box is activated, Internet Explorer adds a new Radio toolbar. You can use this toolbar to listen to a radio station using streaming audio. However, this feature is useful only if you have a fast connection.

Play animations—This check box toggles animated GIF images on and off. If you want to view an animation, right-click the box and then click Show Picture.

Play sounds—This check box toggles Web page sound effects on and off. Because the vast majority of Web page sounds are extremely bad MIDI renditions of popular tunes, turning off sounds will save your ears.

Play videos—This check box toggles Internet Explorer's support for inline AVI files on and off. If you turn this setting off, the only way to view a video is to turn the option back on and then refresh the page.

Show image download placeholders—If you activate this check box, Internet Explorer displays a box that is the same size and shape as the image it is downloading.

Show pictures—This check box toggles Web page images on and off. If you're using a slow connection, turn off this option and Internet Explorer will show only a box where the image would normally appear. (If the designer has included alt text, that text will appear inside the box.) If you want to view a picture, right-click the box and then click Show Picture.

Smart image dithering—This check box toggles image dithering on and off. Dithering is a technique that slightly alters an image in order to make jagged edges appear smooth.

In the `Printing` branch, the `Print background colors and images` check box determines whether Internet Explorer includes the page's background when you print the page. Many Web pages use solid colors or fancy images as backgrounds, so you'll print these pages faster if you deactivate this setting.

The options in the `Search from the Address bar` branch control Internet Explorer's Address bar searching:

Display results and go to the most likely site—Activate this option to display the search engine's results in the Search bar and to display the best match in the main browser window.

Do not search from the Address bar—Activate this option to disable Address bar searching.

Just display the results in the main window—Activate this option to display in the main browser window a list of the sites that the search engine found.

Just go to the most likely site—Activate this option to display the search engine's best match in the main browser window.

The `Security` branch has many options related to Internet Explorer security. I'll hold off discussing these until I discuss security in Chapter 7.

→ **See Also** "Internet Explorer's Security Features," **p. 184.**

Essential Information

- Web page addresses are called Uniform Resource Locators (URLs) and take the form `http://host.domain/directory/file.name`, where `file.name` is the name of the page, `directory` is the name of the directory that contains the page, and `host.domain` is the domain name of the Web site.

- You enter URLs using the Address bar, the Open dialog box (select File, Open), or the Run dialog box (select Start, Run).

- Internet Explorer offers a number of Explorer bars (View, Explorer Bar), including History (displays the pages you've visited over the past 20 days), Search (displays a search engine), and Favorites (displays the contents of the Favorites folder).

- To maintain your favorites, either select Favorites, Organize Favorites (or press Ctrl+B) or work with the Favorites folder directly.

- For sites that have content that changes irregularly, set up a subscription by selecting Favorites, Add to Favorites and then selecting one of the two subscription options.

Outlook Express and Internet Email

Chapter 6

T HE WORLD WIDE WEB IS POPULAR because it offers lots of eye candy and, once in a while, some useful information. But study after study has shown that the main reason people get connected to the Internet is to send email messages. Whether it's client contact, communicating with peers, or keeping in touch with friends and family, folks from the four corners of the world are busy sending out over a *billion* email messages each day.

The huge popularity of Internet email was not lost on the Windows design team. They realized that Windows 95's email client, Windows Messaging (original name: Microsoft Exchange), was woefully inadequate for the rigors of Internet email. So, in Windows 98 they dropped Windows Messaging and replaced it with a new client called Outlook Express that was built from the ground up to handle only Internet email. Outlook Express uses Internet standards such as SMTP, POP3, IMAP, and LDAP. It can handle multiple email accounts, and it supports goodies such as automatic signatures, HTML messages, and digital ID security.

Remember
Windows
Messaging may
be gone, but it's
not completely
forgotten. It's still
available, tucked
away in an
obscure nook in
the Windows
Millennium CD.
Look in the
tools\
oldwin95\
message\us
folder. Run
wms.exe to install
Windows
Messaging, and
run awfax.exe to
install Microsoft
Fax. If you want
to use only
Microsoft Fax,
you still need to
install Windows
Messaging,
although it works
with Microsoft
Outlook (*not*
Outlook Express)
as well.

66

Outlook Express
ranks among the
best mail pro-
grams in exis-
tence and is built
into the operat-
ing system.
—*Edward
Mendelson, PC
Magazine*

99

This chapter takes you through most of these features as well as some of the new features in Outlook Express 5.5 that ships with Windows Millennium. (See Chapter 7, "Implementing Windows Millennium Internet Security Features," to learn about the Outlook Express security features.) My emphasis is on those tools and techniques that help you get the most out of Outlook Express and help you communicate efficiently. If you're new to Internet email, you might want to take a look at the email primer that I have on my Web site:

http://www.mcfedries.com/Ramblings/email-primer.html

➔ **See Also** "Using a Digital ID for Secure Email," **p. 193.**

A Quick Look at Some Outlook Express Email Basics

Let's begin by running through some of the day-to-day chores that you'll perform most often with Outlook Express, including setting up accounts, sending messages, retrieving and reading messages, and sending out replies and forwards.

To get started, use any of the following techniques to launch Outlook Express:

- Select Start, Programs, Outlook Express.

- Click the Launch Outlook Express icon in the Quick Launch toolbar.

- Double-click the desktop's Outlook Express icon.

- If you have Internet Explorer open, select Tools, Mail and News, Read Mail. To make sure Outlook Express is your default mail client, select Tools, Internet Options, display the Programs tab, and then select Outlook Express in the E-mail list.

If you didn't set up your email account when you configured your Internet connection, the Internet Connection Wizard appears and jumps directly to its email account setup. In this case, see the next section, "Setting Up Mail Accounts," for details.

Otherwise, Figure 6.1 shows the Outlook Express window that appears.

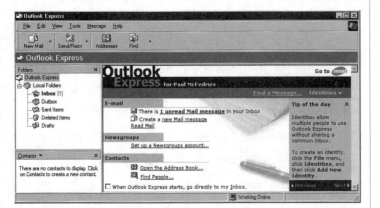

The left side of the window contains a hierarchical list of the Outlook Express folders, which are used to store messages. There are five default folders:

Inbox—Messages that you've received.

Outbox—Messages waiting to be sent.

Sent Items—Messages that have been sent.

Deleted Items—Messages that you've deleted.

Drafts—Messages that you're currently working on (that is, they've been saved but not sent to the Outbox for delivery).

Outlook Express opens with the top-level Outlook Express folder selected. When this folder is selected, the right side of the window displays various icons for common tasks.

The left side of the window also includes a Contacts list, which displays the names of the people in your Address Book.

Setting Up Mail Accounts

If you didn't define your Internet email account when you set up your Internet connection, or if you have multiple accounts and need to set up others, this section shows you how to do it within Outlook Express.

Shortcut
It's more efficient to start with the Inbox folder selected, so activate the When Outlook Express starts, go directly to my Inbox check box.

Remember
It *is* possible to send a message using any of your accounts. However, sending a message using anything other than the default account requires an extra step. See "Sending a Message," later in this chapter.

As I mentioned earlier, the Internet Connection Wizard may appear automatically when you first launch Outlook Express. If not, you can load it by first selecting Tools, Accounts to display the Internet Accounts dialog box. Then click Add, Mail. The wizard will ask you to enter the following data:

- A display name. This is the name that will appear in the From field when you send a message.

- The email address for the account.

- The type of email server (POP3 or IMAP) and the server domain names for incoming and outgoing mail.

- The account username and password.

When the wizard completes its labors, your new account appears in the Mail tab of the Internet Accounts dialog box, as shown in Figure 6.2. While you're in this dialog box, this is as good a time as any to check out some account properties.

Figure 6.2
Your Internet email accounts are listed in the Mail tab.

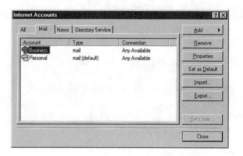

The first property to work with is the default account. If you have multiple accounts, the default account is the one Outlook Express uses automatically when you send a message. To set the default account, highlight it in the Mail tab and then click Set as Default.

To work with the other properties, highlight an account and then click Properties. The property sheet that appears contains five tabs:

General—Use this tab to set the name of the account, as well as your display name, organization name, and email address. By default, replies to your messages are sent to your email address. If you prefer to have replies sent somewhere else, use the Reply address field to enter the other address. There's also a check box named Include this account when receiving mail or synchronizing. As you'll see later, Outlook Express has a Send and Receive command that normally works with all accounts. If you prefer to exclude this account from the Send and Receive operation, deactivate this check box.

Servers—Use this tab to set the mail server domain names, and the account username and password.

Connection—Use this tab to set the type of Internet connection you use and, for dial-ups, the Dial-Up Networking connection to use.

Security—Use this tab to specify a digital ID for secure messages. Again, I discuss email security in Chapter 7.

Advanced—This tab contains a large number of relatively obscure options. However, there are useful settings in the Sending and Delivery groups. In the Sending group, activate the Break apart messages larger than x KB check box if you'll be sending messages to older servers that can't handle large messages. In the Delivery group, activate the Leave a copy of messages on server check box to download only a copy of each incoming message while leaving the original messages intact on the server. This is useful if you need to download the messages using another email program or another computer. The two other check boxes in this group determine when Outlook Express deletes the messages from the server:

- **Remove from server after x day(s)**—Activate this check box to specify the number of days after which the messages are deleted from the server.

- **Remove from server when deleted from 'Deleted Items'**—Activate this check box to have Outlook Express delete the items from the server only when you delete the

Shortcut
If you've been
using another
email client, you
can make your life
easier by import-
ing the client's
address book,
message, and
accounts into
Outlook Express.
Select File, Import
and then select
one of the follow-
ing commands:
Address Book,
Messages, or Mail
Account Settings.

downloaded copies from the Deleted Items folder. Note that this means that any items you store in a different folder remain on the server indefinitely, which your ISP may not appreciate.

Sending a Message

With your email account (or accounts) set up, it's time to try things out. Here are the steps to follow to compose a message:

1. Use any of the following techniques to get started:

   - Select Message, New Message, or press Ctrl+N.

   - Click the New Mail toolbar button.

   - In Internet Explorer, select Tools, Mail and News, New Message.

   - If you want to use one of Outlook Express' prede-fined stationery patterns as a background, select Message, New Message Using and then select a sta-tionery from the submenu that appears. Alternatively, drop down the New Mail toolbar but-ton and click the stationery you want to use.

2. Figure 6.3 shows the New Message window that appears. If you have multiple accounts, use the From list to select the account you want to use to send the message.

Figure 6.3
Use this window
to compose your
message.

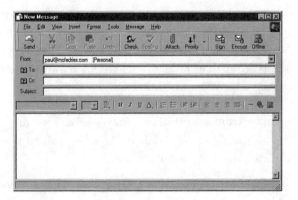

3. Use the To and Cc (carbon copy) text boxes to enter the addresses of the recipients. (If you also want to include a blind carbon copy, select View, All Headers to add the Bcc text box.) In each text box, you can enter multiple addresses by separating each one with a semicolon (;).

4. Enter a brief description for the email in the Subject text box.

5. Pull down the Format menu and select the message style: Rich Text (HTML) or Plain Text. Note that if you select the Rich Text (HTML) command, your recipient must have an email client (such as Outlook Express, Outlook 98 or later, or Netscape Mail) that can handle HTML formatting.

6. Use the large text box below the Subject line to compose the message body. If you selected the Rich Text (HTML) style, use the Formatting toolbar and the commands on the Format menu to format the message.

7. Complete your message by using any of the following techniques:

Check the spelling—Select Tools, Spelling (you can also press F7 or click the Spelling button). Note, however, that the Spelling feature is available only if your system has a program (such as Microsoft Word) that offers a spell checker. Outlook Express uses that checker for its own devices.

Attach a file to the message—Select Insert, File Attachment (or click the Attach toolbar button), find the file in the Insert Attachment dialog box, and then click Attach.

Request a read receipt—Activate the Tools, Request Read Receipt command. A *read receipt* is a message that the recipient's system sends to you when they have read your message. (Not all systems support this feature.) If you always want a read receipt, select Tools, Options, display the Receipts tab, and activate the Request a read receipt for all sent messages check box.

Remember
Click the icons to the left of the To, Cc, and Bcc fields to open the Windows Address Book. From there, you can define commonly used recipients and then insert them into the To, Cc, and Bcc fields. Note, too, that the Address Book is also available within Outlook Express by selecting Tools, Address Book, pressing Ctrl+Shift+B, or by clicking the Address Book toolbar button.

Inside Scoop
To set the default message format, select Tools, Options, display the Send tab, and in the Mail Sending Format group activate either HTML or Plain Text. To change the default font (see Step 6), display the Compose tab and click the Font Settings button beside Mail in the Compose Font group.

Inside Scoop
To create a signature, switch to the Outlook Express window and select Tools, Options, display the Signatures tab, and click New. Enter the signature in the Text box. (Alternatively, select File and specify a text file or HTML file that contains the signature text.) If you want Outlook Express to add the signature automatically, activate the Add signatures to all outgoing messages check box.

Watch Out!
Once Outlook Express connects to the server and sends the messages, it does *not* hang up the connection. If you'd prefer that Outlook Express hang up after it's finished, select Tools, Options, select the Dial-Up tab, and activate the Hang up when finished check box.

Set the message priority—Select Message, Set Priority and then select High, Normal, or Low in the submenu that appears. You can also drop down the Priority toolbar list. (Note that the priority doesn't change how the message is sent. All it means is that the recipient sees some indication of the selected priority when they receive the message. If they use Outlook Express or Outlook, for example, high-priority messages appear with an upward-pointing red arrow, and low-priority messages appear with a downward-pointing blue arrow.)

Insert a signature—If you've defined a signature, you can add it to the message by selecting Insert, Signature. If you have multiple signatures, choose the one you want from the submenu that appears.

Once the message is ready to ship, how you send it depends on whether you have multiple accounts and on whether you want to send the message now or later:

- If you want to send the message now, select File, Send Message (alternatively, press Alt+S or click the Send button).

- If you prefer to send the message later (which is a good idea if you're using a dial-up connection and you're composing multiple messages), select File, Send Later. Outlook Express displays a dialog box letting you know that the message will be stored in the Outbox folder. When you're ready to send the Outbox messages, return to Outlook Express and select the Tools, Send and Receive, Send All command. When the Connect To dialog box appears, click Connect.

The Outlook Express default is to send messages immediately. To change that, first select Tools, Options to display the Options dialog box. In the Send tab, deactivate the Send messages immediately check box, and then click OK.

Retrieving Messages

To receive the messages that have been sent to your account, Outlook Express offers a number of options:

- If you have a single email account, select Tools, Send and Receive, or click the Send/Recv toolbar button. (You can also press Ctrl+M or, if you're in the Inbox folder, F5.) Note that this method not only receives the incoming messages, but it also sends any messages waiting in the Outbox folder.

- If you have multiple email accounts, click the Send/Recv toolbar button (or press Ctrl+M or F5) to send and receive messages from the default account.

- If you have multiple email accounts, select Tools, Send and Receive, or pull down the Send/Recv toolbar list and then select the account you want to work with.

Reading a Message

The messages you receive are stored in the Inbox folder, which has five columns:

Exclamation mark—Indicates the priority of the message: a red exclamation mark means high priority, and a blue, downward-pointing arrow means low priority.

Paper clip—A paper clip icon in this column indicates that the message has an attached file.

Flag—You can put a flag icon in this column (as described in the next section) to remind yourself to take some kind of action on the message.

From—The name (or sometimes just the email address) of the person who sent the message.

Subject—The Subject line of the message.

Received—The date and time the message was received from the server.

Messages that you haven't read yet are displayed in bold. To read a message, you have two choices:

- Highlight the message to view it in the preview page.

Shortcut
Outlook Express can check for new messages automatically. Select Tools, Options and, in the General tab of the Options dialog box, activate the Check for new messages every *x* minutes check box. Use the spinner to set the frequency of the checks (between 1 and 480 minutes). For this to work, you also need to choose one of the Connect... options in the If my computer is not connected at this time list.

Inside Scoop
If a sender requests a read receipt, when you first read their message, Outlook Express will ask if it's okay to send the receipt (click Yes or No). You control this behavior by selecting Tools, Options and displaying the Receipts tab. Use the options in the `Returning Read Receipts` group to determine whether Outlook Express never sends a receipt, asks you if it's okay, or always does.

Watch Out!
When you reply to a message, Outlook Express has an annoying habit of adding the author of the original message to your Address Book. To turn off this dumb behavior, select Tools, Options, display the Send tab, and deactivate the `Automatically put people I reply to in my Address Book` check box.

- Open the message in its own window by double-clicking it. Alternatively, highlight the message and press Enter or Ctrl+O, or select File, Open.

Dealing with a Message After You've Read It

Here's a list of actions you can take after you've read a message:

Reply to the author of the message—Select Message, Reply to Sender. (The alternatives are to press Ctrl+R or click the Reply toolbar button). Outlook Express appends Re: to the Subject line and the existing message text is included in the reply.

Reply to all the message recipients—Select Message, Reply to All (alternatively press Ctrl+Shift+R or click the Reply All button).

Forward the message—Select Message, Forward (or press Ctrl+F or click the Forward button). Outlook Express appends Fw: to the Subject line and the existing message text is included in the forward.

Forward the message as an attachment—Select Message, Forward As Attachment. Outlook Express appends Fw: to the Subject line and the existing message is attached. Use this option if you want the recipient to see the message exactly as you received it.

Add the sender to your address book—Open the message and then select Tools, Add To Address Book, Sender. Alternatively, right-click the sender and then click Add To Address Book. To do this from the Outlook Express window, drag the message header and drop it on the Contacts list.

Save an attachment—In the preview pane, click the paper clip icon in the upper-right corner, and then click Save Attachments. If the message is open, select File, Save Attachments. In the Save Attachments dialog box, make sure the file is highlighted, and then click Save. You can also drag the file's icon from the message.

Move the message to another folder—Drag the message header from the Inbox folder and drop it on the destination folder. If the message is open, select File, Move To Folder.

Copy the message to another folder—Hold down Ctrl and drag the message header from the Inbox folder and drop it on the destination folder. If the message is open, select File, Copy To Folder.

Print the message—Select File, Print (alternatively, press Ctrl+P or click the Print button).

Flag the message—Select Message, Flag Message. This adds a flag icon beside the message to the Flag column. This is useful if you want to remind yourself to take some kind of action on the message.

Delete the message—In the Inbox folder, select Edit, Delete, or press Delete. If the message is open, select File, Delete, or press Ctrl+D. You can also drag the message header to the Deleted Items folder.

Working with Outlook Express Folders

No savvy user would ever consider organizing her hard disk so that all data files were stored in a single folder. But that, essentially, is the way Outlook Express is organized by default. The messages that you don't delete remain in the Inbox folder. That's not a big deal at first, but it gets messy once you have a few dozen messages stored. To reduce the clutter and help you find messages, you should create new folders and subfolders to store related messages. Here's how it's done:

1. Select File, Folder, New (or press Ctrl+Shift+E). Outlook Express displays the Create Folder dialog box.

2. Enter the name of the new folder in the Folder name text box.

3. Use the list to highlight the folder in which you want to create the new folder.

4. Click OK. Outlook Express creates the folder.

Watch Out!

Most virus programs now propagate via email messages. They come as benign-looking attachments with names such as Happy99.exe or Pretty Park.exe. When you open them, you may see an innocuous display (such as an animation), but the virus is busy infecting your system behind-the-scenes. The moral of the story is that you should *never* open any attachment (particularly an executable file) unless you're certain of the file's contents.

Watch Out!

If you delete a message by accident, open the Deleted Items folder and move the message to another folder. If you want to permanently delete a message, delete it from the Deleted Items folder. To clean out the folder, right-click it and then click Empty 'Deleted Items' Folder.

Undocumented
For each folder,
Outlook Express
maintains a .dbx
file on the hard
disk. (For more
about where
these files are
stored, see
"Working with
Identities," later
in this chapter.)
Deleting mes-
sages causes
gaps to appear in
these files.
Compacting the
folder removes
these gaps and
reduces the size
of the files.

The File, Folder submenu contains a number of other commands. Here's what they do:

Move—Moves the highlighted folder to another location.

Rename—Renames the highlighted folder. (You can also highlight the folder and press F2.)

Delete—Deletes the highlighted folder. As with messages, this
just moves the folder to the Deleted Items folder.

Compact—Reduces the size of the files that store the highlighted folder's contents.

Compact All Folders—Reduces the size of the folder files for
all the existing folders.

Filtering Incoming Messages

Just a couple of years ago, my email chores took up only a few
minutes of each workday. Now it takes me up to two or three
hours to get through the hundreds of messages I receive every
day. What's interesting about this is that it's by no means
unusual. Most people find that once they really get into
Internet email, the messages really start to pile up quickly.

To help ease the crunch, Outlook Express offers *mail rules*. You
can set up these rules to handle incoming messages for you
automatically. Of course, these rules are limited in what they
can do, but what they *can* do isn't bad:

- If you'll be out of the office for a few days, or if you go on
  vacation, you can create a rule to mail out an automatic
  reply that lets the sender know you received their message
  but won't be able to deal with it for a while.

- If you have multiple email accounts, you can set up a rule
  to redirect incoming messages into separate folders for
  each account.

- You can create a rule to redirect incoming messages into
  separate folders for specific people, projects, or mailing
  lists.

- If you receive unwanted messages from a particular source (such as a spammer), you can set up a rule to automatically delete those messages.

For the latter, note that Outlook Express also comes with a Blocked Senders list. If you put an address on this list, Outlook Express watches for messages from that address and deletes them automatically. To use this feature, follow these steps:

1. Highlight a message that comes from the address you want to block.

2. Select Message, Block Sender. Outlook Express adds the address to the Blocked Senders list and asks if you want to delete all messages from that address.

3. Click Yes to delete the messages, or click No to let them be.

To view the Blocked Senders list, select Tools, Message Rules, Blocked Senders List. Outlook Express opens the Message Rules dialog box and displays the Blocked Senders tab. From here, you can Add another blocked sender, or Modify or Delete an existing blocked sender.

For more general situations, you need to set up mail rules. Here's how it works:

1. Select the Tools, Message Rules, Mail command. Outlook Express displays the New Mail Rule dialog box.

2. In the Select the Conditions for your rule list, activate the check box beside the rule condition you want to use to pick out a message from the herd. Outlook Express adds the condition to the Rule Description text box, as shown in Figure 6.4. Note that you're free to select multiple conditions.

3. The condition shown in the Rule Description text box will probably have some underlined text. You need to replace that underlined text with the specific criterion you want to use (such as a word or an address). To do that, click the

Inside Scoop
One of the problems with redirecting messages to other folders is that it's less convenient to read those messages. Outlook Express helps by bolding the name of any folder that contains unread messages. (It also tells you how many unread messages are in each folder.) Outlook Express also opens the folder tree to reveal any folders that have unread messages. (To make sure this option is turned on, select Tools, Options and, in the General tab, check that the Automatically display folders with unread messages setting is activated.)

underlined text, enter the criterion in the dialog box that appears, and click Add. Most conditions support multiple criteria (such as multiple addresses or multiple words in a Subject line), so repeat this step as necessary. When you're done. click OK.

Figure 6.4
Use this dialog box to set up a mail rule for filtering incoming messages.

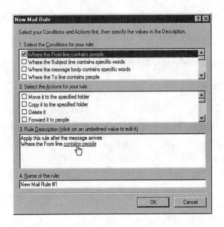

Inside Scoop
You can make each criterion adhere to Boolean principles such as AND, OR, and NOT. To do this, click the Options button in the dialog box that appears in step 3. To make an AND criterion, activate Message matches all of the x below (where x depends on the condition): to make an OR criterion, activate Message matches any one of the x below: to make a NOT criterion, activate Message does not contain the x below.

4. In the Select the Actions for your rule list, activate the check box beside the action you want Outlook Express to take with messages that meet your criteria. Again, you may have to click underlined text in the Rule Description text box to complete the action. Also, you can select multiple actions.

5. If you selected multiple conditions, Outlook Express assumes that all the conditions must be true before invoking the rule (Boolean AND). To change this, click and in the Rule Description text box, activate the Messages match any one of the criteria option, and click OK.

6. Use the Name of the rule text box to enter a descriptive name for the rule.

7. Click OK. Outlook Express drops you off at the Mail Rules tab of the Message Rules dialog box.

Whichever method you used, here are a few notes to bear in mind when working with the list of rules:

Toggling rules on and off—Use the check box beside each rule to turn the rule on and off.

Setting rule order—Some rules should be processed before others. For example, if you have a rule that deletes spam, you want Outlook Express to process that rule before sending out a vacation reply. To adjust the order of a rule, highlight it and then click either Move Up or Move Down.

Modifying a rule—To edit a rule, highlight it and click Modify.

Applying a rule—If you want to apply a rule to existing Inbox messages or to messages in a different folder, click Apply Now. Highlight the rule you want to apply (or click Select All to apply them all). To choose a different folder, click Browse. When you're ready, click Apply Now.

Deleting a rule—Highlight the rule and click Remove. When Outlook Express asks if you're sure, click Yes.

Finding a Message

Although you'll delete many of the messages that come your way, it's unlikely that you'll delete all of them. So, over time, you'll probably end up with hundreds, or more likely thousands, of messages stored throughout various folders. What happens if you want to find a particular message? Even if you curmudgeonly delete everything that comes your way, your Sent Items folder will still eventually contain copies of the hundreds or thousands of missives you've shipped out. What if you want to find one of those messages?

For both incoming and outgoing messages, Outlook Express offers a decent Find Message feature that can look for messages based on addresses, subject lines, body text, dates, and more.

Simple Searches

If you're not fussy about what part of the message Find uses to look for a particular word, and if you already know which folder holds the message you want, Outlook Express 5.5 offers a simplified Find feature for quick-and-dirty searches. Here are the steps to follow:

1. Use the Folders list to highlight the folder in which you want to search.

2. Select Edit, Find, Message in this Folder. (Alternatively, either press Shift+F3 or pull down the Find toolbar list and select Message in this Folder.) Outlook Express displays the Find dialog box shown in Figure 6.5.

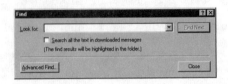

3. Use the Look for text box to enter a word or two that you want to use as the search criteria. Find will look in the From, To, and Subject fields for the search text. If you also want Find to look in the body of the messages, activate the Search all the text in the downloaded messages check box.

4. Click Find Next. Find examines the messages and, if it locates a match, it highlights the message.

5. If this isn't the message you're looking for, select Edit, Find, Next. (You can also either press F3 or pull down the Find toolbar list and select Next.)

Inside Scoop
When entering
your search crite-
ria, bear in mind
that if you enter
multiple words,
Find will only
match messages
that contain all
the words. Also,
Find matches
whole words only,
so it won't match
partial words, and
the search is not
case sensitive.

Advanced Searches

If you want to search specific message fields, if you want to specify different criteria for each field, or if you want to include specialized criteria such as the message date or whether a message has attachments, then you need to use the full-fledged Find Message feature.

To try it out, you have two ways to get started:

- Select the Edit, Find, Message command. (The alternatives are to press Ctrl+Shift+F or to click the Find toolbar button.)

- If you have the Find dialog box displayed, click the Advanced Find button.

Figure 6.6 shows the Find Message dialog box that appears. Use the following controls to set the search criteria:

Browse—Select the folder to search. If you want the search to include the subfolders of the selected folder, leave the Include subfolders check box activated.

From—Enter one or more words that specify the email address or display the name of the sender you want to find.

To—Enter one or more words that specify the email address or display name of the recipient you want to find

Subject—Enter one or more words that specify the Subject line you want to find.

Message—Enter one or more words that specify the message body you want to find.

Received before—Select the latest received date for the message you want to find.

Received after—Select the earliest received date for the message you want to find.

Message has attachment(s)—Activate this check box to find only messages that have attached files.

Message is flagged—Activate this check box to find only messages that have been flagged.

After your search criteria are defined, click Find Now. If Outlook Express finds any matches, it displays them in a message list at the bottom of the dialog box. From here, you can open a message or use any of the commands in the menus to work with the messages (reply, forward, move to another folder, delete, and so on).

Remember
As with Find, the individual Find Message criteria match only those messages that contain *all* the words you enter, match only whole words, and are not case sensitive. Note, too, that Find Message looks only for messages that match all the criteria you enter.

Figure 6.6
Use the Find
Message dialog
box to look for
specific messages
in a folder.

Finding a Person

In an effort to create a kind of White Pages for the Internet, a
number of companies have set up *directory servers* that contain
databases of names and email addresses. Using a standard
Internet protocol called the Lightweight Directory Access
Protocol (LDAP), email clients and other programs can use
these directory servers to perform simple searches for names
and addresses.

Remember
To get more infor-
mation about the
selected directory
service, click the
Web Site button
to open the ser-
vice's home page
in Internet
Explorer. Note,
too, that in most
cases you can
use the Web site
to add your own
name and address
to the service.

Outlook Express supports LDAP and is set up to provide ready
access to several of the most popular directory servers. To see
the complete list, select Tools, Accounts and then display the
Directory Service tab. If your company runs its own directory
server, you can add it to this list by clicking Add, Directory
Service and following the Internet Connection Wizard's dialog
boxes.

To perform a search on a directory server, or to search the
Windows Address Book, follow these steps:

1. Select the Edit, Find, People command. (Alternatively,
   press Ctrl+E or pull down the Find toolbar list and select
   People.) Outlook Express displays the Find People
   dialog box.

2. Use the Look in list to select either Address Book (to search
   the Windows Address Book) or a directory service.

3. You have two searching options:

   • If you know the name of a person and want to find
     out his email address, use the Name text box to enter
     the person's name. (You can enter the exact name or
     a partial name.)

- If you know the email address of a person and want to find out her name, use the E-mail text box to enter the person's exact email address.

4. Click Find Now. Outlook Express accesses the directory server and runs the query. If the server reports any matches, they're displayed at the bottom of the dialog box.

Working with Identities

Sharing a computer with colleagues or family members is problematic on many levels. For example, one person's soothing wallpaper might be another person's constant eyesore, and a younger person's high-resolution screen might be an older person's text-too-tiny-to-read squintfest.

These sorts of cosmetic differences can be overcome with compromises or, in a pinch, by setting up different users. (In the Control Panel, open the Users icon.) The differences grow more profound when two or more people have to share a single copy of Outlook Express. Yes, you can create separate accounts for each user and, yes, you can set up mail rules to filter each user's messages into a specific folder. However, the possibility remains that anybody who uses Outlook Express can read everybody else's mail.

To overcome this obvious drawback, Outlook Express 5.5 offers a new feature called *identities*, and it works much like Windows' users feature. That is, you configure Outlook Express so that each person using it has their own identity. Only one person can be "logged on" to Outlook Express at a time, and that person sees only their own accounts and their own folders. For extra protection, each identity can be protected by a password.

Creating a New Identity

Outlook Express already has a default identity in place, and its called Main Identity (I show you how to rename identities a bit later). Follow these steps to set up another identity:

1. Select File, Identities, Add New Identity. Outlook Express displays the New Identity dialog box.

2. Enter the name of the new identity in the Type your name text box.

3. To protect the identity with a password, activate the Require a password check box. Outlook Express displays the Enter Password dialog box. Type the password in both the New Password and Confirm New Password text boxes, and then click OK to return to the New Identity dialog box.

4. Click OK. Outlook Express asks if you want to switch to the new identity.

5. Click Yes. Outlook Express closes, restarts, and launches the Internet Connection Wizard to set up the initial account for the new identity.

6. Run through the wizard's dialog boxes as described earlier in this chapter (see "Setting Up Mail Accounts").

When the wizard is complete, you're dropped off at the Outlook Express window, which is logged on to the new identity. To reiterate, being logged on to an identity means the following:

- Only that identity's accounts are available.

- Only that identity's messages and folders are visible.

- Only that identity's contacts are listed in the Address Book and Contacts list.

- That identity can customize Outlook Express and the new settings will affect only that identity's version of the program.

Switching Identities

To switch from one identity to another, follow these steps:

1. Select File, Switch Identity. The Switch Identities dialog box appears.

Inside Scoop
Although the logged on identity sees only their contacts, it's possible to share contacts among identities. In the Address Book, add the contacts you want to share to the Shared Contacts folder. For contacts that already exist, drag them from the identity's Address Book and drop them on the Shared Contacts folder.

2. Use the list of identities to highlight the one you want to use.

3. Use the Password text box to enter the identity's password, if applicable.

4. Click OK. Outlook Express closes and then restarts with the chosen identity logged on.

Managing Identities

If you need to change the name or password for an identity, delete an identity, or perform some other identity maintenance, follow these steps:

1. Select File, Identities, Manage Identities. (Alternatively, click the Manage Identities button in the Switch Identities dialog box.) Outlook Express displays the Manage Identities dialog box, shown in Figure 6.7.

2. Use the Identities list to highlight the identity you want to work with.

3. Besides the New button (which enable you to create a new identity from here), there are two other command buttons available:

Remove—Click this button to delete the highlighted identity. (Note that you can't delete the Main Identity.)

Properties—Click this button to change the highlighted identity's name or password.

Remember
How do you know which identity is currently logged on? The easiest way to tell is to look at the Outlook Express title bar. For example, if the Inbox folder is currently displayed, the title bar will say Inbox - Outlook Express - *Identity*, where *Identity* is the name of the current identity.

Figure 6.7
Use the Manage Identities dialog box to make changes to your Outlook Express identities.

4. Other programs may also be "identity aware" (an example is the MSN Messenger program that ships with Windows Millennium). To determine which identity gets logged on when you start those programs, make sure the Use this identity when starting a program check box is activated, and then use the drop-down list to choose which identity you want logged on.

5. If an identity-ignorant program needs to request that Outlook Express create a new email message, the program won't be able to ask you (or Outlook Express) which identity to use. For these situations, pick out the default identity from the Use this identity when a program cannot ask you to choose an identity list.

6. Click Close.

Remember
Another way to log off Outlook Express is to select File, Switch Identities and then click the Log Off Identity button in the Switch Identities dialog box.

Logging Off Your Identity

As a convenience, Outlook Express leaves you logged on to your identity when you exit the program in the usual way (that is, by selecting File, Exit or by pressing Alt+F4). This means Outlook Express uses your identity the next time you start the program.

However, if someone else starts the program in the meantime, they'll be logged on to your identity and will have access to all your accounts and messages. That obviously defeats the purpose of identities. To prevent this from happening, always *log off* your identity when you shut down Outlook Express. You do that by selecting File, Exit and Log Off Identity.

The next time you (or anyone else) launches Outlook Express, the first thing that appears is the Identity Login dialog box. Highlight the identity you want to use, enter a Password, if necessary, and click OK.

Identities—Storage Locations and the Registry

I mentioned earlier that Outlook Express maintains a .dbx file for each folder. To see these files, first go to the \Windows\Application Data\Identities folder. Here you find a subfolder for each Outlook Express identity. Unfortunately, the folder names are obscure 32-character "user IDs" that bear no resemblance to the identity name. How do you know which folder applies to which identity (say, for backup purposes)? The only way to tell is to head for the following Registry key:

`HKEY_CURRENT_USER\Identities`

Here, you find subkeys that use the same 32-character user IDs. Highlight the subkey you want and then look for the `Username` setting, which tells you the identity name.

Once you know which folder is which, open it and head for the `Microsoft\Outlook Express` subfolder, which is where the `.dbx` files are stored.

Customizing Outlook Express

I close this look at Outlook Express with a few pointers for customizing the program. I discuss sorting messages, customizing the message columns, changing the Outlook Express layout, creating a custom toolbar, and much more.

Reorganizing the Message List Columns

As you've seen, the columns in the message list display the basic header data associated with each message. You can also use these columns to sort the messages, change the order of the header data, and even display other header fields. Here's a summary (in all cases, first use the `Folders` list to select the folder with which you want to work):

Sorting the messages—Click a column heading to sort the messages on the values in that column. Clicking the heading repeatedly toggles between a descending sort and an ascending sort. (You can also right-click the column heading and then click either Sort Ascending or Sort Descending.) Alternatively, select the View, Sort By command, and then select a column from the submenu that appears.

Displaying only unread messages—Select the View, Current View, Hide Read Messages command. To display all the messages again, select View, Current View, Show All Messages.

Changing the column width—Move your mouse to the right edge of the heading of the column you want to adjust. Then, drag the mouse left (to create a narrower column) or right (to create a wider column).

Moving a column—Drag the column heading left or right.

Changing the size of the message list—To change the width of the message list, drag the vertical split bar that separates the folder list from the message list and the preview pane. To change the height of the message list, drag the horizontal split bar that separates the message list pane from the preview pane.

Adding and removing columns—Select View, Columns to display the Columns dialog box, shown in Figure 6.8. To add a column, activate its check box in the list. To remove a column, deactivate its check box. Note, too, that you can reposition a column by highlighting it and clicking the Move Up and Move Down buttons.

Figure 6.8
Use this dialog box to add and remove columns, and to change the column order.

Rearranging the Layout of the Outlook Express Window

One of the nice features of Outlook Express is that its window layout is quite flexible and customizable. To see how, select the View, Layout command to display the Window Layout Properties dialog box, shown in Figure 6.9.

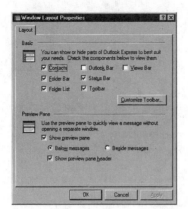

Figure 6.9
Use this dialog
box to rearrange
the Outlook
Express window
to your liking.

The Basic group enables you to toggle certain window features on and off by using the following check boxes:

Contacts—This is the Contacts list that's displayed under the Folder list.

Folder Bar—This is displayed above the message list. It shows the name of the currently selected folder.

Folder List—This is the folder list.

Outlook Bar—This is displayed as a strip down the left side of the Outlook Express window. It contains icons for the Outlook Express folders.

Status Bar—This is the status bar that runs across the bottom of the window.

Toolbar—This is the toolbar that runs across the window below the menu bar.

Views Bar—This is a drop-down list that is displayed below the toolbar. You can use this list as a quick way to change the view.

Customize Toolbar—Click this button to display the Customize Toolbar dialog box. (In Outlook Express, you can also right-click the toolbar and then click Customize.) This is the same dialog box as the one used to customize the Windows Explorer toolbar, that I discuss in Chapter 8, "Expert Windows Explorer Techniques."

Inside Scoop
If you decide to hide the folder list, Outlook Express offers a number of alternative folder navigation techniques. For starters, press Ctrl+Shift+I to select the Inbox folder. If you're in a subfolder, you can move up the parent folder by pressing Backspace. Finally, you can move to any folder by selecting View, Go to Folder or by pressing Ctrl+Y.

➜ **See Also** "Customizing the Standard Buttons Toolbar," **p. 227.**

The Preview Pane group enables you to customize several aspects of the preview pane:

Show preview pane—Toggles the preview pane on and off.

Below Messages—Positions the preview pane below the message list (this is the default position).

Beside Messages—Positions the preview pane between the folder list and the message list.

Show preview pane header—Toggles the header that appears at the top of the preview pane on and off.

Essential Information

- Select Tools, Accounts to define new email accounts and to adjust the properties of existing accounts.

- To send a message, select Message, New Message, enter the recipient addresses, the Subject line, and the message text, and then click Send.

- To retrieve a message, select Tools, Send and Receive and, if you have multiple accounts, select the account you want to use.

- Organize your incoming messages by creating folders to store related messages, such as those from specific people, projects, or mailing lists.

- Select the Tools, Message Rules, Mail command to set up rules to filter incoming messages based on the recipient, Subject line, account, and more.

- Select the File, Identities, Add New Identity command to create a new Outlook Express identity.

- To customize Outlook Express, select View, Columns to add and remove columns, and select View, Layout to rearrange the Outlook Express Window.

GET THE SCOOP ON...
Avoiding Security Holes Created by the TCP/IP
Protocol ▪ Broadband Connections and Personal
Firewalls ▪ Internet Explorer Security Options ▪
Implementing Digital IDs for Secure Email in Outlook
Express

Implementing Windows Millennium Internet Security Features

Chapter 7

A S MORE PEOPLE, BUSINESSES, and organizations establish a presence online, the world becomes an increasingly connected place. And the more connected the world becomes, the more opportunities arise for communicating with others, doing research, sharing information, and collaborating on projects. The flip side to this new connectedness is the increased risk of connecting with a remote user whose intentions are less than honorable. It could be a "packet sniffer" who steals your password or credit card number, a cracker who breaks into your Internet account, a virus programmer who sends a Trojan Horse virus attached to an email, or a Web site operator who uses Web browser security holes to run malicious code on your machine.

Admittedly, online security threats are relatively rare and are no reason to swear off the online world. However, these threats *do* exist and people fall victim to them every day. Luckily, protecting yourself from these and other e-menaces doesn't take much effort or time, as you'll see in this chapter, in which I discuss the Internet security tools built into Windows Millennium.

> **❝**
> **packet sniffer,**
> **noun** Software that monitors network traffic to steal passwords, credit card numbers, and other sensitive data. Also, the person who uses such software.
> —*The Word Spy*
> (www.WordSpy.com)
> **❞**

Internet Security and the TCP/IP Protocol

When you launch your Internet connection, you might see the System Security Check dialog box shown in Figure 7.1. This warning appears if your system has the TCP/IP protocol bound to the file and printer sharing service. TCP/IP is used for connecting to the Internet and file and printer sharing is used to enable network users to see and work with shared files and printers on your computer. (It's also used with the Direct Cable Connection feature.) If the two are bound together, then it could mean that someone on the Internet would be able to work directly with the files on your computer!

Figure 7.1
This dialog box appears if your Internet connection isn't secure.

Remember
If you don't see this dialog box when you connect, make sure Windows Millennium is set up to perform the security check. Open the Control Panel's Internet Options icon and display the Connections tab. Make sure the Perform system security check before dialing check box is activated.

Note, however, that this scenario applies only to the version of TCP/IP that's bound to whatever mechanism you use to connect to the Internet:

- If you use a dial-up connection, it applies only to the TCP/IP protocol bound to the Dial-Up Adapter.

- If you use a local area network connection, it applies only to the TCP/IP protocol bound to your network adapter.

The easiest way to fix this problem is to click Yes in the System Security Check dialog box. Alternatively, open the Control Panel's Network icon, highlight the appropriate TCP/IP component, as described previously, and click Properties. Display the Bindings tab and deactivate the File and printer sharing for Microsoft Networks check box.

"Always On" Connections and Personal Firewalls

Disabling file and printer sharing on your TCP/IP Internet connection is particularly important if you access the Net using a broadband—cable modem or DSL—service. These are "always on" connections, so there's a much greater chance that a malicious hacker could find your computer and have his (they're almost always male) way with it.

You might think that with millions of people connected to the Internet at any given moment, there would be little chance of a "script kiddy" finding you in the herd. Unfortunately, one of the most common weapons in a black-hat hacker's arsenal is a program that runs through millions of IP addresses automatically, looking for "live" connections. The problem is compounded by the fact that many cable systems and some DSL systems use IP addresses in a narrow range, thus making it easier to find the "always on" connections.

Although disabling file and printer sharing is a must, it's not enough. That's because when a hacker finds your IP address, he has many other avenues with which he can access your computer. Specifically, your TCP/IP connection uses many different "ports" for sending and receiving data. For example, Web data and commands typically use port 80, email uses ports 25 and 110, FTP uses ports 20 and 21, DNS uses port 53, and so on. In all, there are dozens of these ports, and every one is an opening through which a clever cracker (a malicious hacker) can gain access to your computer.

As if all this wasn't enough, hackers also can check your system to see if some kind of "Trojan horse" virus is installed. (Those nasty email virus attachments I told you about in the previous chapter sometimes install these programs on your machine.) If the hacker finds one, he can effectively take control of your machine and either wreak havoc on its contents or use your computer to attack other systems (in which case, your machine is called a *zombie computer*).

Again, if you think your computer is too obscure or worthless for someone else to bother with, think again. My computer gets "probed" for vulnerable ports or installed Trojan horses at least a couple of times a day. My server gets probed or outright attacked several *dozen* times a day.

If you want to see just how vulnerable your computer is, several good sites on the Web will test your security:

> 66
>
> **script kiddies,**
> **noun**
> Inexperienced and unskilled 'hackers' who attempt to infiltrate or disrupt computer systems merely by running programs designed to crack those systems.
> —*The Word Spy*
> (*www.WordSpy.com*)
>
> 99

- Gibson Research: grc.com/

- DSL Reports: www.dslreports.com/secureme_go

- HackerWhacker: www.hackerwhacker.com

The bad news is Windows Millennium doesn't include any tools to combat these threats. The good news is many programs called *personal firewalls* are now available. These programs lock down your ports and prevent unauthorized access to your machine. The best of them make your computer *invisible* to the Internet (although you can still surf the Web and work with email normally). First, check with your provider to see if it implements any personal firewall technology. If not, check out these good software programs:

- BlackIce Defender: www.networkice.com

- ZoneAlarm: www.zonelabs.com

- McAfee Personal Firewall: www.mcafee.com

- Norton Internet Security 2000: www.symantec.com

Internet Explorer's Security Features

Internet Explorer implements security along two different lines:

Outgoing security—This involves data that you send, which could be a credit card number, data in a form, or a username and password.

Incoming security—This involves data sent to your computer, which could be a Java applet or ActiveX control embedded inside a page, a script, or a file download.

For outgoing security, Internet Explorer offers the following features:

- A warning dialog box displays when you enter or leave a secure site. (A secure site uses encryption and other features to ensure that the data you send can't be read by a third party.)

- A lock icon appears in the status bar (see Figure 7.2).

- If the site uses Netscape's Secure Sockets Layer (which implements RSA encryption, among other things), the URL protocol is displayed as https—Secure Hypertext Transport Protocol (again, see Figure 7.2).

The protocol

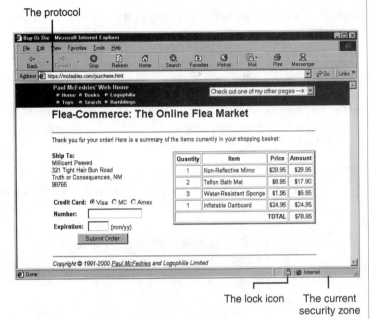

Figure 7.2
When you access a secure page, Internet Explorer displays a lock icon in the status bar and changes the protocol to https.

The lock icon   The current security zone

Remember
Some sites—particularly online banks—allow you to access their secure pages only if you have a browser that implements 128-bit encryption. Thankfully, the version of Internet Explorer that ships with Windows Millennium supports 128-bit encryption right out of the box. This is approximately 300 trillion trillion times more secure than the 40-bit encryption that came with the Windows 9x version of Internet Explorer.

The next couple of sections discuss the long list of Internet Explorer features that deal with incoming security.

Working with Internet Explorer's Security Zones

When implementing security for Internet Explorer, Microsoft realized that different sites have different security needs. For example, it makes sense to have fairly stringent security for Internet sites, but you can probably scale the security back a bit when browsing pages on your corporate intranet.

To handle these different types of sites, Internet Explorer defines various *security zones*, and you can customize the security requirements for each zone. The current zone is displayed in the status bar (refer to Figure 7.2).

To work with these zones, either select Tools, Internet Options in Internet Explorer, or open the Control Panel's Internet Options icon. In the Internet Properties dialog box that appears, select the Security tab, shown in Figure 7.3.

The list at the top of the dialog box shows icons for the four types of zones available:

Internet—Web sites that aren't in any of the other three zones. The default security level is Medium.

Local intranet—Web pages on your computer and your network (intranet). The default security level is Medium-low.

Trusted sites—Web sites that implement secure pages and that you're sure have safe content. The default security level is Low.

Restricted sites—Web sites that don't implement secure pages or that you don't trust, for whatever reason. The default security level is High.

Figure 7.3
Use the Security
tab to set up
security zones
and customize the
security options
for each zone.

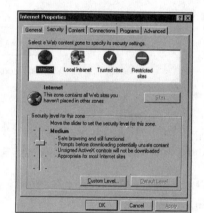

Adding and Removing Zone Sites

Three of these zones—Local intranet, Trusted sites, and Restricted sites—enable you to add sites. To do this, select the zone you want to work with and then click Sites.

If you selected the Local intranet zone, you see a dialog box with three check boxes:

- **Include all local (intranet) sites not listed in other zones**—When activated, this option includes all intranet sites in the zone. If you add specific intranet sites to other zones, those sites aren't included in this zone.

- **Include all sites that bypass the proxy server**—When this check box is activated, sites that you've set up to bypass your proxy server (if you have one) are included in this zone.

- **Include all network paths (UNCs)**—When this check box is activated, all network paths that use the Universal Naming Convention are included in this zone.

If you want to add sites, click Advanced. This displays a dialog box like the one shown in Figure 7.4 that appears for the Trusted sites zone.

Two of these dialog boxes (Local intranet and Trusted sites) have a Require server verification (https:) for all sites in this zone check box. If you activate this option, then each site address you enter must begin with the https protocol.

To add a site, enter the address in the Add this Web site to the zone text box, and then click Add. Note, too, that you can include an asterisk as a wildcard character, as shown in Figure 7.4. For example, the address http://*.microsoft.com adds every microsoft.com domain, including www.microsoft.com, support.microsoft.com, windowsupdate.microsoft.com, and so on.

Watch Out!
Outlook Express also supports two of these security zones: Internet and Restricted sites. To prevent malicious code embedded in email from running on your system, be sure to choose the Restricted sites zone. To do that, select Tools, Options, display the Security tab, and then activate the Restricted sites zone option.

Figure 7.4
Use this dialog box to add sites to a zone.

To remove a site, highlight it and then click Remove.

Remember
The Universal
Naming
Convention is a
standard format
used with net-
work addresses.
They usually take
the form
server\
resource, where
server is the
name of the net-
work server and
resource is the
name of a shared
network resource.

Changing a Zone's Security Level

To change the security level for a zone, select it in the list and
then use the slider to set the level. To set up your own security
settings, click Custom Level. This displays the Security Settings
dialog box shown in Figure 7.5.

The dialog box provides you with a long list of possible security issues, and your job is to specify how you want Internet
Explorer to handle each issue. You usually have three choices:

- **Enable**—Security is turned off. For example, if the issue is
  whether to run an ActiveX control (a small program
  embedded in a Web page), the control is run automatically.

- **Prompt**—You're asked how you want to handle the issue.
  For example, whether you want to accept or reject an
  ActiveX control.

- **Disable**—Security is turned on. For example, if the issue is
  whether to run an ActiveX control, the control is not run.

Figure 7.5
Use this dialog
box to set up cus-
tomized security
levels for the
selected zone.

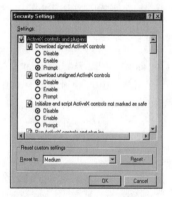

Let's take a quick look at the various security issues that are
covered in this dialog box. I'll begin with the options in the
ActiveX controls and plugins branch:

Download signed ActiveX controls—Determines whether
  ActiveX controls that have a valid security signature can be
  downloaded.

Download unsigned ActiveX controls—Determines whether ActiveX controls that don't have a valid security signature can be downloaded.

Initialize and script ActiveX controls not marked as safe—Determines whether Web page scripts can interact with ActiveX controls that don't have a digital signature that marks them as safe for scripting.

Run ActiveX controls and plugins—Determines whether ActiveX controls embedded in a Web page, as well as browser plug-in modules required by Web page objects, can be run.

Script ActiveX controls marked safe for scripting—Determines whether Web page scripts can interact with ActiveX controls that have a security certificate that marks them as safe for scripting.

The options in the Cookies branch determine whether Internet Explorer accepts cookies. A cookie is a small text file that a remote site stores on your computer in the Windows\Cookies folder. Cookies are normally used to *preserve state*—that is, to remember selections you've made so that they can be referred to in other pages you visit. There are two settings:

Allow cookies that are stored on your computer—Determines whether Internet Explorer accepts stored cookies.

Allow per-session cookies (not stored)—Determines whether Internet Explorer accepts cookies that are valid only for the current browser session.

The Downloads branch has two settings:

File download—Determines whether file downloads are enabled.

Font download—Determines whether font downloads are enabled.

Remember
A *security certificate* is your assurance that a control comes from a reputable publisher. Certificates are issued by trusted signing authorities (such as VeriSign—see www.verisign.com) and they guarantee that a control is safe to use.

Watch Out!
Some sites require cookies and won't work properly if you disable them. On the other hand, some sites use cookies only to track your movements within their site. In subsequent visits, the sites might use this data to display targeted advertising. Most (but not all) reputable sites warn you when cookies are required.

The Java permissions branch controls the permissions that are assigned to Java applets that run within the zone. Java applets are executed on your computer, so they can potentially work with your local files and network resources, run programs, display dialog boxes (including the Open dialog box), access system information, print documents, and create temporary files. Select one of the following: Low safety, Medium safety, High safety, or Disable Java. Alternatively, you can define your own permissions by selecting Custom and then clicking the Java Custom Settings button that appears.

The Miscellaneous branch contains a grab bag of security settings:

Inside Scoop
The "Cross-Frame Navigation" vulnerability is a bug that enables a malicious Web site operator to use JavaScript to open a text or HTML file from your computer (they would need to know the exact path and name of the file) and then send that file to an arbitrary host.

Access data sources across domains—This is the fix for a security bug called the "Cross-Frame Navigation" vulnerability. Leave this option disabled to ensure that this problem never affects you.

Don't prompt for client certificate selections when no certificates or only one certificate exists—Toggles whether Internet Explorer prompts you to choose a client certificate if you have fewer than two certificates.

Drag and drop or copy and paste files—Determines whether Web page files (such as graphics) can be dragged or copied from the Web page and then dropped or pasted locally.

Installation of desktop items—Determines whether Active Desktop items can be installed.

Launching applications and files in an IFRAME—Determines whether programs can be run and files can be downloaded from a floating frame window (defined by the <IFRAME> tag in HTML).

Navigate subframes across different domains—This is the fix for an Internet Explorer bug called the "Frame Spoof" vulnerability. To ensure that you don't fall victim to this spoof, disable this option.

Software channel permissions—Determines whether an Active Channel can download and install software. Choose one of Low safety (the software is downloaded and installed automatically), Medium safety (the software is downloaded automatically and then you're prompted to launch the installation), or High safety (you're prompted to launch the download and the installation).

Submit nonencrypted form data—Determines whether forms can be submitted from sites that don't use SSL (that is, that don't encrypt the form data).

userData persistence—Determines whether Internet Explorer allows persisted userData structures in a Web page. The userData structure enables a Web developer to maintain (persist) data about users across sessions (similar to what a cookie does).

The Scripting branch contains three options:

Active scripting—Determines whether Web page scripts are allowed to run.

Allow paste operations via script—Determines whether Internet Explorer allows Web page scripts to paste data into Explorer controls.

Scripting of Java applets—Determines whether Web page scripts can interact with Java applets.

The User Authentication branch determines how HTTP authentication is implemented for sites that require a username and password:

Anonymous logon—You're logged in as a Guest on the server.

Automatic logon only in Intranet zone—On your intranet only, uses Windows NT Challenge/Response to supply the server with your current username and password.

Automatic logon with current username and password—Uses Windows NT Challenge/Response to supply the server with your current username and password.

Inside Scoop
The "Frame Spoof" bug enables malicious Web site operators to create a Web page frame that encapsulates the page of a legitimate site. If the user attempts to send data to the legitimate site, it is sent instead to the malicious user.

Watch Out!
The vast majority of large sites use some form of JavaScript on their pages. Therefore, for the best surfing experience, don't disable the Active scripting option.

Inside Scoop
Yet another security issue is the "Untrusted Scripted Paste" bug which could enable a Web site operator to download a file (such as your Windows password file) from your computer. If the user knows the exact path of a file, they could use a script to paste the path and filename into Internet Explorer's built-in upload control. The remote script could then submit a form behind the scenes, and the file will be included in the submission. Setting the Submit nonencrypted form data option to Prompt (this is the default for Medium security) will thwart this bug. If you're prompted about submitted unencrypted data, but there's no form in sight, then you know a malicious site is trying to submit data secretly.

Prompt for username and password—Displays a dialog box asking you for your username and password.

More Security Settings

While you have the Internet Properties dialog box onscreen, display the Advanced tab and scroll down to the Security branch. You find the following settings:

Check for publisher's certificate revocation—If you enable this option, Internet Explorer examines a site's digital security certificates to see if they have been revoked.

Check for server certificate revocation—When activated, this option also checks the security certificate for the Web page's server.

Do not save encrypted pages to disk—If you enable this option, Internet Explorer won't store encrypted files in the Temporary Internet Files folder.

Empty Temporary Internet Files folder when browser is closed—If you enable this option, Internet Explorer removes all files from the Temporary Internet Files folder when you exit the program.

Enable Profile Assistant—Toggles the Profile Assistant on and off. Your *profile* is just an extra entry in the Windows Address Book that stores your personal information (name, address, and so on). The Profile Assistant can work with some Web sites to share this data, which prevents you from having to enter this data by hand. To edit your profile, see the options in the Content tab's Personal information group.

Use Fortezza—When this option is activated, Internet Explorer can set up a secure connection to any Fortezza Web site. (Fortezza is U.S. Department of Defense cryptographic security standard.)

Use PCT 1.0—Toggles support for Microsoft's Private Communications Technology security protocol on and off. PCT is an upgrade to SSL.

Use SSL 2.0—Toggles support for the Secure Sockets Layer Level 2 security protocol on and off. This version of SSL is currently the Web's standard security protocol.

Use SSL 3.0—Toggles support for SSL Level 3 on and off. SSL 3.0 is more secure than SSL 2.0 (it can authenticate both the client and the server), but isn't currently as popular as SSL 2.0.

Use TLS 1.0—Toggles support for Transport Layer Security (TLS) on and off. This is a relatively new protocol, so few Web sites implement it.

Warn about invalid site certificates—When activated, this option tells Internet Explorer to display a warning dialog box if a site is using an invalid digital security certificate.

Warn if changing between secure and not secure mode—When activated, this option tells Internet Explorer to display a warning dialog box whenever you enter and leave a secure site.

Warn if forms submit is being redirected—When activated, this option tells Internet Explorer to display a warning dialog box if a form submission is going to be sent to a site other than the one hosting the form.

Using a Digital ID for Secure Email

When you connect to a Web site, your browser sets up a direct connection—called a *channel*—between your machine and the Web server. Because the channel is a direct link, it's relatively easy to implement security because all you have to do is secure the channel, which is what PCT and SSL do.

However, email security is entirely different and much more difficult to set up. The problem is that email messages don't have a direct link to an SMTP email server. Instead, they must usually "hop" from server to server until the final destination is reached. Combine this with the open and well-documented email standards used on the Internet, and you end up with three email security issues:

The privacy issue—Because messages often pass through other systems and can even end up on a remote system's hard disk, it isn't that hard for someone with the requisite know-how and access to the remote system to read a message.

The tampering issue—Because a user can read a message passing through a remote server, it comes as no surprise that he can also change the message text.

The authenticity issue—With the Internet email standards an open book, it isn't difficult for a savvy user to forge or *spoof* an email address.

To solve these issues, the Internet's gurus came up with the idea of *encryption*. When you encrypt a message, a complex mathematical formula scrambles the message content to make it unreadable. In particular, a *key value* is incorporated into the encryption formula. To unscramble the message, the recipient feeds the key into the decryption formula.

This *single-key encryption* works, but its major drawback is that the sender and the recipient must both have the same key. *Public-key encryption* overcomes that limitation by using two related keys: a *public key* and a *private key*. The public key is available to everyone, either by sending it to them directly or through an online key database. The private key is secret and is stored on the user's computer.

Here's how public-key cryptography solves the issues discussed earlier:

Solving the privacy issue—When you send a message, you obtain the recipient's public key and use it to encrypt the message. The encrypted message can now be decrypted using only the recipient's private key, thus assuring privacy.

Solving the tampering issue—An encrypted message can still be tampered with, but only randomly because the content

Inside Scoop
As a further anti-tampering measure, the secure email system—it's called S/MIME or Secure Multipurpose Internet Mail Extension—uses an algorithm that creates a unique digest of the message. If the digest created by the recipient's mail client doesn't match the original digest, then the message has been tampered with.

of the message can't be seen. This thwarts the most important skill used by tamperers: making the tampered message look legitimate.

Solving the authenticity issue—When you send a message, you use your private key to digitally sign the message. The recipient can then use your public key to examine the digital signature to ensure the message came from you.

If there's a problem with public-key encryption, it is that the recipient of a message must obtain the sender's public key from an online database. (The sender can't just send the public key because the recipient would have no way to prove that the key came from the sender.) Therefore, to make all this more convenient, a *digital ID* is used. This is a digital certificate that states the sender's public key has been authenticated by a trusted certifying authority. The sender can then include her public key in her outgoing messages.

Setting Up an Email Account with a Digital ID

To send secure messages using Outlook Express, you first have to obtain a digital ID. Here are the steps to follow:

1. In Outlook Express, select Tools, Options to display the Options dialog box.

2. Display the Security tab.

3. Click Get Digital ID. Internet Explorer loads and takes you to the Outlook Express digital ID page on the Web.

4. Click a link to the certifying authority (such as VeriSign) you want to use.

5. Follow the authority's instructions for obtaining a digital ID. (Note that digital IDs cost money, typically about $15 per year.)

With your digital ID installed, the next step is to assign it to an email account:

1. In Outlook Express, select Tools, Accounts to open the Internet Accounts dialog box.

2. Use the Mail tab to highlight the account you want to work with and then click Properties. The account's property sheet appears.

3. Display the Security tab.

4. In the Signing certificate group, click Select. Outlook Express displays the Select Default Account Digital ID dialog box.

5. Make sure the certificate you installed is highlighted and then click OK. Your name appears in the Security tab's first Certificate box.

6. Click OK to return to the Internet Accounts dialog box.

7. Click Close.

Obtaining Another Person's Public Key

Before you can send an encrypted message to another person, you must obtain their public key. How you do this depends on whether you have a digitally signed message from that person.

If you do have a digitally signed message, open the message, as described later in this chapter in the "Receiving a Secure Message" section. Outlook Express adds the digital ID to the Address Book automatically:

- If you have one or more contacts whose email addresses match the address associated with the digital ID, the digital ID is added to each contact (see the Digital IDs tab).

- If there are no existing matches, a new contact is created.

If you don't have a digitally signed message for the person you want to work with, you have to visit a certifying authority's Web site and find the person's digital ID. For example, you can go to the VeriSign site (www.verisign.com) to search for a digital ID and then download it to your computer. After that, follow these steps:

1. Open the Windows Address Book.

2. Open the person's contact info, or create a new contact.

Inside Scoop
To make a backup copy of your digital ID, open Internet Explorer and select Tools, Internet Options. Display the Content tab and click Certificates to see a list of your installed certificates (be sure to use the Personal tab). Click your digital ID and then click Export.

Inside Scoop
If you don't want Outlook Express to add digital IDs automatically, select Tools, Options, display the Security tab, and click Advanced. In the dialog box that appears, deactivate the Add senders' certificates to my address book check box.

3. Enter one or more email addresses, and fill in the other data as necessary.

4. Display the Digital IDs tab.

5. In the Select an E-Mail address list, select the address that corresponds with the digital ID you downloaded.

6. Click the Import button to display the Select Digital ID File to Import dialog box.

7. Find and highlight the downloaded digital ID file, and then click Open.

8. Click OK.

Sending a Secure Message

After your digital ID is installed, you can start sending out secure email messages. You have two options:

- **Digitally sign a message to prove that you're the sender—** With the New Message window open, either activate the Tools, Digitally Sign command, or click the Sign toolbar button. A small, red "seal" icon appears to the right of the From field.

- **Encrypt a message to avoid snooping and tampering—** In the New Message window, either activate the Tools, Encrypt command, or click the Encrypt toolbar button. A blue lock icon appears to the right of the From field.

Receiving a Secure Message

The technology and mathematics underlying the digital ID are complex, but there's nothing complex about dealing with incoming secure messages. Outlook Express handles everything behind the scenes, including the authentication of the sender (if the message was digitally signed) and the decryption of the message (if the message was encrypted). For the latter, a dialog box tells you that your private key has been used to decrypt the message.

As you can see in Figure 7.6, the preview pane gives you a few visual indications that you're dealing with a secure message:

- The message text doesn't appear in the preview pane.

- The preview pane title is Security Help and the subtitle tells you the type of security used: Digitally Signed and/or Encrypted.

Figure 7.6
For a secure message, the preview pane describes the type of security used.

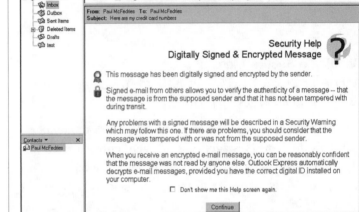

Undocumented
If you change your mind and decide you want to see the preview screen, you have to edit the Registry. Open the Registry Editor and head for the key named HKEY_CURRENT_USER\Identities. Open your 32-character identity key and then open the Software\Microsoft\Outlook Express\5.0\Dont Show Dialogs subkey. Open the Digital Signature Help setting and change its value to 0.

- The preview pane text described the security used in the message.

To read the message, click the Continue button at the bottom. (If you don't want to see this security preview in the future, activate the Don't show me this Help screen again check box.)

Essential Information

- Make sure you don't have the TCP/IP protocol bound to file and printer sharing, or you could end up sharing your resources with the entire Internet.

- If you access the Internet using an "always on" broadband connection, be sure to install a personal firewall program to prevent hackers from compromising your system.

- The Security tab in the Internet Options dialog box enables you to select a security level for various zones and to customize the security level for each zone.

- In Outlook Express, use a digital ID to sign a message for authenticity and to encrypt a message for privacy.

Controlling Your Files and Folders

PART III

Expert Windows Explorer Techniques

WHETHER YOU'RE LOOKING TO MASTER Windows Millennium or just get your work done quickly and efficiently, a thorough knowledge of the techniques available for working with files, folders, and floppy disks is essential. Or perhaps I should say that a thorough knowledge of *certain* techniques is essential. That's because, like the rest of Windows Millennium, Windows Explorer (the file management accessory) offers a handful of methods for accomplishing most tasks. Not all of these techniques are particularly efficient, however. Therefore, my goal in this chapter is to not only tell you *how* to do file management chores, but also to tell you the *best* ways to do those chores.

My Computer or Windows Explorer?

With Windows Millennium, Microsoft seems to be downplaying Windows Explorer in favor of My Computer. How can I tell? Because they've maintained My Computer's prominent desktop perch and pushed Windows Explorer deeper into the Start menu by moving it from Programs to Accessories. My Computer gets the red-carpet treatment because it's geared more toward inexperienced users:

- It has a friendlier name and a name, moreover, that jibes with the whole lame "Windows Me" marketing pitch and

Shortcut
To get easy
access to
Windows Explorer,
right-drag the
Windows Explorer
shortcut from the
Accessories menu
and drop it on the
desktop or in the
Quick Launch tool-
bar. In the short-
cut menu that
appears, click
Copy Here.

with the "My This" and "My That" name theme that
abounds in Windows Millennium.

- It doesn't display the Folders bar by default, and I assume
  Microsoft thinks the Folders bar is a bit intimidating for
  the novice.

Cute names aside, the key idea here is the Folders bar because
that's what makes Windows Explorer so much more useful
than My Computer, at least to non-novice users. Unfortunately,
as I've said, getting to Windows Explorer is now a four-click
workout: Start, Programs, Accessories, Windows Explorer.
Fortunately, Windows Millennium does offer several simpler
techniques for getting to a My Computer window that displays
the Folders bar:

- Double-click the desktop's My Computer icon and then
  click the Folders toolbar button.

- Right-click the My Computer icon and then click Explore
  in the shortcut menu.

- If you have a keyboard with the Windows logo key (),
  press ()+E.

The upshot of all this is that in Windows Millennium, My
Computer and Windows Explorer are identical. In fact, you
can view My Computer as a special instance of Windows
Explorer that displays the My Computer folder without the
Folders bar. Therefore, throughout the rest of this chapter, I'll
use the phrase "Windows Explorer" to refer to either the
Windows Explorer program or to My Computer displaying the
Folders bar.

Basic File and Folder Chores: The Techniques Used by the Pros

As shown in Figure 8.1, the Windows Explorer screen is
divided into three main areas:

Folders bar—Shows the contents of your computer: the disk
   drives, the folders within those drives, and a few other special folders.

Information panel—Displays information about the currently selected object. In Figure 8.1, for example, the information panel displays data about the space usage on a hard drive partition. Note that Windows Millennium now shows the information panel full time. In Windows 98, you saw this area only if you activated the View, as Web Page command. (To learn how to turn off this "Web content," see "Customizing Windows Explorer," later in this chapter.)

Contents list—Displays the files and other objects that reside in the currently selected folder.

Folders button

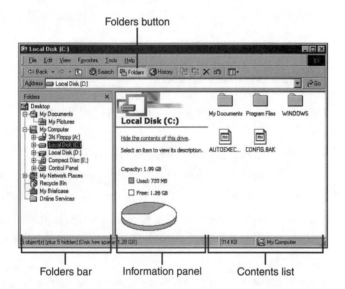

Folders bar   Information panel   Contents list

Figure 8.1
The Windows Explorer window.
Folders button
Folders bar
Information panel
Contents list

With Windows Explorer ready for action, it's time to put it through a workout. The next few sections take you through a few basic file and folder chores: selecting, moving and copying, and renaming.

Selecting Files and Folders

Before you can do anything in Windows Explorer—whether it's copying a file, renaming a folder, or deleting a shortcut— you have to *select*—or *highlight*—the object or objects you want to work with. (For simplicity's sake, I use the generic term *object* to refer to any file or folder.)

Watch Out!
If you're using the keyboard selection techniques while Web integration is turned on, first move the mouse away from any objects. Otherwise, if the mouse pointer is hovering over an object, Windows Explorer may keep trying to select that object, which will undermine your keyboard efforts.

Inside Scoop
If you need more room for your selecting, you can place Windows Explorer in *full-screen* mode by holding down Ctrl and clicking the Maximize button. This mode takes over the entire screen, shrinks the toolbar buttons, and removes the title bar, menu bar, status bar, and Address bar. To restore the window, click the Restore button or press Alt+Spacebar and then select the Restore command.

Selecting a Single Object

Selecting a single object with the mouse is straightforward: Click the object's name. (Note that you use a slightly different technique if Web integration is turned on. See Chapter 16, "An In-Depth Look at Web Integration.")

➜ **See Also** "The Integration Interface I: Opening and Selecting Objects," **p. 368.**

From the keyboard, follow this two-step procedure:

1. Pressing Tab cycles you through the Folders bar, the Contents list, the Address bar, and the Folders bar's Close button. Therefore, press Tab to move the highlight into the area you want.

2. Use the up and down arrow keys to move the highlight to the object you want to select.

Here are some notes to keep in mind when using the keyboard to select an object:

- If the Contents list shows objects displayed in two or more columns, use the left and right arrow keys to move between columns.

- If the current folder contains a large number of items, use the Page Up and Page Down keys to jump through the list quickly.

- Press Home to select the first object in the list; press End to select the last object in the list.

- If you press a letter, Windows Explorer will jump down to the first object that has a name that begins with that letter. Press that letter again to move to the next object that begins with the letter.

Selecting Multiple Objects

To select two or more objects, click the first object, then hold down Ctrl and click the rest of the objects. If the objects are contiguous, click the first object, then hold down Shift and click the last object. (Again, see Chapter 16 to learn how to do this when Web integration is activated.)

From the keyboard, use the following techniques:

- To select objects individually, use the navigation keys (the arrow keys, Page Up and Page Down, and so on) to select the first object. Now hold down the Ctrl key. For each of the other objects you want to select, use the navigation keys to move the selector to the object, and then press the spacebar.

- To select multiple contiguous objects, use the navigation keys to select the first object, then hold down the Shift key, and then use the navigation keys to select the last object.

- To select every object in the current folder, run the Edit, Select All command, or press Ctrl+A.

- To reverse the current selection—that is, to deselect everything that's currently highlighted and to select everything that's not currently highlighted—run the Edit, Invert Selection command.

Making Sense of Windows Millennium's Rules for Moving and Copying

If you've used Windows before, you know that you can move text from one part of a document to another by cutting it and then pasting it in the new location. One of Windows 95's innovations was to bring this cut-and-paste metaphor to file and folder copying and moving:

- If you want to copy an object, select it and then run the Edit, Copy command, or press Ctrl+C. If you want to move an object, instead, select it and then run Edit, Cut, or press Ctrl+X.

- To perform the move or copy, go to the destination folder and then select Edit, Paste, or press Ctrl+V.

An alternative—and often faster—method for moving and copying objects is to drag and drop them. This means that you use your mouse to drag the object to a specific destination and then drop it there.

Undocumented
The Windows Explorer status bar shows you how many objects you've selected and the total size of the selected objects. However, it doesn't take into account any objects that might be inside a selected subfolder. To allow for subfolders, right-click the selection and then click Properties. Windows Millennium counts all the files, calculates the total size, and then displays this data in the property sheet that appears.

Undocumented
A quick way to make a backup copy of a file or folder is to highlight it, press Ctrl+C, and then Ctrl+V. This makes a copy of the object with "Copy of" appended to the name in the same location as the original file.

Undocumented
If your right mouse button doesn't work, you can simulate a right-drag by holding down both Ctrl and Shift while you drag and drop using the left mouse button.

You can use this drag-and-drop technique to move or copy files. Unfortunately, Windows Millennium uses a fairly arcane set of rules for how this works:

- If you drag an object to a destination on the *same* drive, Windows Millennium will move the object.

- If you drag an object to a destination on a *different* drive, Windows Millennium will copy the object. While you're dragging, the mouse pointer sprouts a small plus sign (+) as a visual indicator that you're copying the object.

- If you drag an executable file, Windows Millennium will create a shortcut for the object. While you're dragging, the mouse pointer displays a small arrow to indicate that you're creating a shortcut for the object.

To work around the last rule, and to avoid trying to remember the first two rules, use the following techniques:

To move an object—Hold down the Shift key while you drag and drop.

To copy an object—Hold down the Ctrl key while you drag and drop.

Right-drag an object—Right-drag means that you drag the object while holding down the *right* mouse button. In this case, when you drop the object Windows Millennium displays a shortcut menu similar to the one shown in Figure 8.2. Click the command you want to run.

Figure 8.2
When you right-drag an object and then drop it, Windows Millennium displays this shortcut menu.

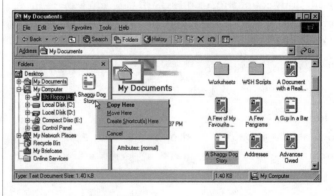

Expert Drag-and-Drop Techniques

You'll use drag and drop throughout your Windows career. To make drag and drop even easier and more powerful, here are a few pointers to bear in mind:

"Lassoing" multiple files—If the objects you want to select are displayed in a block within the Contents list, you can select them by dragging a box around the objects, as shown in Figure 8.3. This is known as *lassoing* the objects.

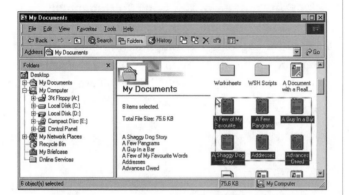

Figure 8.3
To select multiple objects, drag a box around the objects to "lasso" them.

Drag and scroll—Most drag-and-drop operations involve dragging an object from the Contents list and dropping it on a folder in the Folders bar. If you can't see the destination in the Folders bar, drag the pointer to the bottom of the Folders bar. Windows Explorer will scroll the list up. To scroll the list down, drag the object to the top of the Folders bar.

Drag and open—If the destination is a subfolder within an unopened folder branch, drag the object and hover the pointer over the unopened folder. After a second or two, Windows Explorer opens the folder branch.

Inter-window dragging—You can drag an object outside the window and then drop it on a different location, such as the desktop.

Drag between Explorers—Windows Millennium lets you open two or more copies of Windows Explorer. If you have to use several drag and drops to get some objects to a

Inside Scoop
You can't drop an object on a running program's taskbar icon, but you can do the next best thing. Drag the mouse over the appropriate taskbar button and wait a second or two. Windows will then bring that application's window to the foreground, and you can then drop the object within the window.

Remember
Windows Explorer
doesn't show hid-
den files and fold-
ers by default.
To learn how to
display hidden
objects, see
"Exploring the
View Options,"
later in this
chapter.

particular destination, open a second copy of Windows Explorer and display the destination in this new window. You can then drag from the first window and drop into the second window.

Canceling drag and drop—To cancel a drag and drop operation, either press Esc or click the right mouse button. (If you're right-dragging, click the left mouse button to cancel.)

Taking Advantage of the Send To Command

For certain destinations, Windows Millennium offers an easier method for copying or moving files or folders—the Send To command. To use this command, select the objects you want to work with and then run one of the following techniques:

- Select File, Send To.

- Right-click the selection and then click Send To in the shortcut menu.

Either way, you see a submenu of potential destinations, as shown in Figure 8.4. Note that the items in this menu are taken from a hidden folder named Windows\SendTo that contains shortcut files for each item. This means that you can customize the Send To menu by adding, renaming, and deleting the shortcut files in the SendTo folder. I explain how to work with shortcuts in detail in Chapter 10, "Taking Advantage of Shortcuts."

➜ **See Also** "Creating a Shortcut," **p. 253.**

Figure 8.4
The Send To com-
mand offers a
menu of possible
destinations.

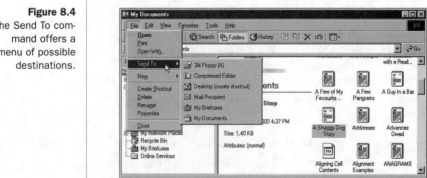

Click the destination you want and Windows Millennium will send the object there. What do I mean by "send"? I suppose "drop" would be a better word because the Send To command acts like the drop part of drag and drop. Therefore, Send To follows the same rules as drag and drop:

- If the Send To destination is on a different disk drive, the object is copied.

- If the Send To destination is on the same disk drive, the object is moved.

Undocumented
As with drag and drop, you can force the Send To command to copy or move an object. To force a move, hold down Shift when you select the Send To command. To force a copy, hold down Ctrl when you select the Send To command.

Creating New Folders and Files

You'll find yourself requiring a new folder quite often. For example, Windows Millennium creates the My Documents folder, which you can use to store the documents that you create. This is a good start, but it makes no sense to stuff all your documents into a single folder. Instead, you'll want to create a number of subfolders to store different types of documents (memos, worksheets, presentations, and so on).

Here are the steps to follow to create a new folder:

1. Use Windows Explorer to open the folder in which you want to create the new folder. For example, if you want to create a subfolder within My Documents, open the My Documents folder.

2. Select File, New, Folder. (You can also right-click an empty part of the Contents list and then click New, Folder.) Windows Millennium creates a new folder and surrounds its name with a text box.

3. Edit the text box with the name of your folder, and then press Enter.

When you select the New command, notice that the submenu that appears contains not only the Folder command, but a number of other commands: Shortcut, Text Document, Bitmap Image, and so on. Selecting any of these commands creates a new file of the selected type. This new file is empty, of course, so you need to open it to add your content.

Shortcut
There are three
other methods you
can use to get the
text box around
an object's name:
Press F2; right-
click the object
and then click
Rename; click the
object's name,
wait a second or
two, and then
click the object's
name again.

I show you how to customize the New menu in Chapter 9, "Powerful Techniques for File Types."

➜ **See Also** "Customizing the New Menu," **p. 246.**

Renaming Files and Folders

Renaming files and folders is very easy in Windows Millennium:

1. Select the file or folder you want to rename. (You can work with only one object at a time.)

2. Select File, Rename. Windows Millennium places a text box around the name.

3. Edit the name and then press Enter.

Bear in mind that you should rename only objects that you've created yourself. Renaming objects used by Windows or any of your applications can cause all kinds of problems.

Working with Zip Files (Compressed Folders)

When you download files from the Internet, they often arrive as Zip files (they use the .zip extension). These are compressed archive files that contain one or more files that have been compressed for faster downloading. Prior to Windows Millennium, you had to use a simple command-line decompression program (such as PKUNZip.EXE; see www.pkunzip.com) or a Windows decompression program (such as WinZip; see www.winzip.com) to extract the files from the Zip. However, Windows Millennium now offers built-in support for these files, which is a welcome addition.

In Windows Millennium, a Zip file is called a *compressed folder*. Why a "folder"? Because a Zip file contains one or more files, just like a regular folder. As you'll see, this makes it easy to deal with the files within the Zip, and it enables Windows Millennium to offer a few useful compression and decompression features.

Viewing a Zip File

To see what's inside a Zip file, double-click it. Windows Millennium opens a new folder window (see Figure 8.5) that shows the name of the Zip in the Folders bar and the files within the Zip in the Contents list.

Figure 8.5
Double-click a Zip file and Windows Millennium displays its contents within a folder window.

From here, use the following techniques to work with the archived files:

- To extract some of the files, highlight them, drag them out of the compressed folder, and then drop them on the destination folder. (You can also select the Edit, Copy command, open the destination folder, and then select Edit, Paste.)

- To extract all the files, select them and then drag and drop them on the destination. Alternatively, select File, Extract All to launch the Extract Wizard, shown in Figure 8.6. Use the text box to enter a destination for the extracted files and then click Next. In the next wizard dialog box, activate the Show extracted files check box to open a window for the destination folder (this is optional), and then click Finish.

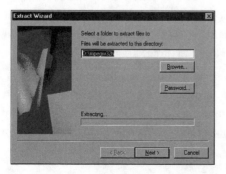

Figure 8.6
Select File, Extract All to launch the Extract Wizard.

- To run a file (such as a program's setup file) from the compressed folder, double-click the file.

Creating a Zip File

Besides viewing existing Zip files, Windows Millennium also enables you to create new Zip files. There are two methods you can use:

- Highlight the objects you want to store in the Zip file and then run the File, Send To, Compressed Folder command. Windows Millennium creates a Zip file with the same primary name as the first highlighted file. For example, if the first file is memo.doc, the compressed folder is memo.zip.

- Create a new, empty Zip file by running the File, New Compressed Folder command. Windows Millennium creates a new Zip file with an active text box. Edit the name and press Enter. You can then drag the files you want to archive and drop them on the Zip file.

Inside Scoop
If you don't want just anyone to be able to extract files from a Zip, Windows Millennium enables you to encrypt a Zip with a password. To do this, right-click the Zip file and then click Encrypt. Use the Encrypt dialog box to enter a password (twice) and click OK.

The Recycle Bin: Deleting and Recovering Files and Folders

In my conversations with Windows users, I've noticed an interesting trend that has become more prominent in recent years: People don't delete files as often as they used to. I'm sure the reason for this is the absolutely huge hard disks that are offered these days. Even entry-level systems come equipped with multigigabyte disks, and double-digit gigabyte capacities (10GB and up) are no longer a big deal. So, unless someone's working with digital video files, even a power user isn't going to put a dent in these massive disks any time soon. So why bother deleting anything?

While it's always a good idea to remove files and folders you don't need (it makes your system easier to navigate, it speeds up defragmenting, and so on), avoiding deletions does have one advantage: You can never delete something important by accident.

Just in case you do, however, Windows Millennium's Recycle Bin can bail you out. The Recycle Bin icon on the Windows Millennium desktop is actually a front-end for a collection of hidden folders named Recycled that exist on each hard disk partition. The idea is that when you delete a file or folder, Windows Millennium doesn't actually remove the object from your system. Instead, the object is just moved to the Recycled folder on the same drive. If you delete an object by accident, you can go to the Recycle Bin and return the object to its original spot. Note, however, that the Recycle Bin can hold only so much data. When it gets full, it permanently deletes its oldest objects to make room for newer ones.

Inside Scoop
If you're absolutely sure you don't need an object, you can permanently delete it from your system (that is, bypass the Recycle Bin) by highlighting it and pressing Shift+Delete.

Deleting a File or Folder

To delete a file or folder, use either of the following methods:

- Highlight the object (or objects) and then select File, Delete. Pressing the Delete key, right-clicking the selection and clicking Delete, and clicking the Delete toolbar button will also work.

- Drag the object and drop it either on the desktop's Recycle Bin icon, or on the Recycled folder in the same drive.

Whichever method you use, Windows Millennium displays a dialog box asking if you're sure you want to send the object to the Recycle Bin. Click Yes to continue with the deletion, or click No to cancel it.

Please note that Windows Millennium bypasses the Recycle Bin and permanently deletes an object under the following circumstances:

- You delete the object from a floppy disk or any removable drive.

- You delete the object from the DOS prompt.

- You delete the object from a network drive.

However, there *is* a method you can use to recover these sup-
posedly permanent deletions, and I'll show you that method a
bit later (see "Recovering a 'Permanently' Deleted File or
Folder").

Setting Some Recycle Bin Options

The Recycle Bin has a few properties you can set to control
how it works. To view these properties, right-click the desktop's
Recycle Bin icon and then click Properties. Windows
Millennium displays the property sheet shown in Figure 8.7.

Figure 8.7
Use this property
sheet to configure
the Recycle Bin
to your liking.

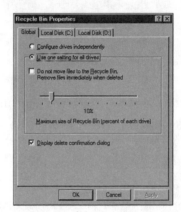

Here's a rundown of the various controls:

Configure drives independently—By default, the Recycle Bin
    uses the same settings on all your partitions (drives). To set
    up separate configurations for each partition, activate this
    option and then click the other tabs to configure the par-
    titions.

Use one setting for all drives—This is the default setting for
    the Recycle Bin. It means that, for the next two controls,
    the configuration that you select is used for all your drives.

**Do not move files to the Recycle Bin. Remove files immedi-
    ately when deleted**—If you activate this option, all dele-
    tions are permanent.

Maximum size of Recycle Bin (percent of each drive)—Use
    this slider to set the maximum size of the Recycle Bin, as a
    percentage of the total capacity of the drive. The higher

the percentage, the more deleted files the Recycle Bin can hold, but the less disk space you'll have available. (Unless you work with very large files, a maximum size of 3–5 percent is more than adequate.)

Display delete confirmation dialog—If you don't want Windows Millennium to ask for confirmation when you delete an object, deactivate this option.

Click OK to put the new settings into effect.

Recovering a File or Folder

If you accidentally delete the wrong file or folder, you can return it to its rightful place by using the following method:

1. Open the desktop's Recycle Bin icon, or open any `Recycled` folder in Windows Explorer.

2. Highlight the object.

3. Select File, Restore. (You can also right-click the file and then click Restore.)

Recovering a "Permanently" Deleted File or Folder

According to the official Microsoft party line, an object is permanently deleted from your system under the following circumstances:

- You deleted the object from a floppy disk, removable disk, or the DOS prompt.

- You bypassed the Recycle Bin with Shift+Delete.

- You deleted the object from the Recycle Bin or you emptied the Recycle Bin.

Microsoft may call these deletions permanent, but they're not totally unrecoverable. The reason is that under all of the circumstances mentioned previously, Windows Millennium doesn't delete the file's contents. Instead, it changes the first letter of the file's name to the Greek lowercase sigma (σ), and it alerts the file system that the file's clusters are free to be used by another file. Therefore, as long as you act before the file's clusters are overwritten, the file *can* be recovered.

Remember
You can clean out your Recycle Bin at any time by right-clicking the desktop's Recycle Bin icon and then clicking Empty Recycle Bin. The Recycle Bin contents can also be purged using Windows Millennium's Disk Cleanup utility.

Inside Scoop
If deleting the file or folder was the last action you performed in Windows Explorer, you can recover the object by selecting the Edit, Undo Delete command. Note, too, that Windows Millennium lets you undo the 10 most recent actions.

When you empty the Recycle Bin, all the items in it are permanently deleted from your computer.
—Microsoft

99

Remember
Here's the general rule that Windows uses for creating an 8.3 filename out of a long filename. For the primary name, remove all the spaces and other illegal characters, take the first six remaining characters, and append "~1". For the extension, take just the first three characters. Note that if this would result in two files having the same 8.3 name, then Windows uses "~2" instead of "~1" in the primary name.

How? By using the DOS UNDELETE command, which you can run from your original DOS disks if you have them. Failing that, you can obtain a copy here:

`http://www.ou.edu/pub/simtelnet/msdos/microsft/pd0646.zip`

Extract the file named UNDELETE.EXE and place it on your emergency boot disk. (I tell you how to create such a disk in Chapter 15, "Preparing for Trouble.")

→ **See Also** "Putting Together an Emergency Boot Disk," p. 347.

Here are the steps to follow:

1. Use your emergency boot disk to boot to DOS.

2. You must give the UNDELETE command direct access to the disk. Therefore, when you get to the DOS prompt, type **lock** and press Enter. (The LOCK command gives an application direct access to the disk, something Windows doesn't normally allow.)

3. When you're asked to confirm, press **y** and Enter.

4. Change to the folder from which you deleted the file.

5. Type **undelete** *filename*, where *filename* is the 8.3 name of the file you want to recover. UNDELETE displays a message similar to this:

```
Directory C:\
File Specification: SAVEME.TXT

    Delete Sentry control file not found.

    Deletion-tracking file not found.

    MS-DOS directory contains    1 deleted files.
    Of those,    1 files may be recovered.

Using the MS-DOS directory method.

    ?AVEME    TXT    41894    2-28-99  5:47p  ...A
Undelete (Y/N)?
```

6. Press **y**. UNDELETE displays the following prompt:

   ```
   Please type the first character for ?AVEME   .TXT:
   ```

7. Press the appropriate character. UNDELETE recovers the file.

8. Type **unlock** and press Enter to disable direct disk access.

9. Restart Windows Millennium.

Watch Out!
If the file you recover had a long filename, this name will be lost and the recovered file will use only its 8.3 filename.

File Maintenance Using the Open and Save As Dialog Boxes

One of the best-kept secrets of Windows Millennium is the fact that you can perform many of these file maintenance operations within two of Windows Millennium's standard dialog boxes:

Open—In most applications, you display this dialog box by selecting the File, Open command, or by pressing Ctrl+O.

Save As—You usually display this dialog box by selecting File, Save As, or, if you're working with a new, unsaved file, by selecting File, Save, or by pressing Ctrl+S.

There are three techniques you can use within these dialog boxes:

- To perform maintenance on a particular file or folder, right-click the object to display a shortcut menu like the one shown in Figure 8.8.

- To create a new object, right-click an empty section of the file list, and then click New to get the New menu.

- To create a new folder within the current folder, click the Create New Folder button.

Powerful Search Techniques for Finding Files

I mentioned earlier that hard disks are getting huge, so people don't delete as much as they used to. Another consequence of these large disk capacities is that users don't move files to archival storage as much as they used to. Why bother when a multigigabyte drive can store tens of thousands of files? Keeping the file on disk is much more convenient, but *only* if you can find the file you want, and there's the rub.

The Create New
Folder button

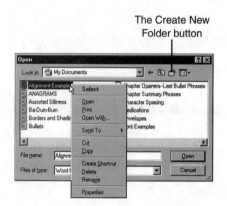

Figure 8.8
You can perform
most basic file
and folder mainte-
nance right from
the Open and
Save As dialog
boxes.

66
Data expands to
fill the space
available for
storage.
—*Parkinson's
Law of Data*
99

Shortcut
If you have a key-
board with the
Windows logo key
🔳 , you can start
Search by press-
ing 🔳 +F. Also, if
you're in Windows
Explorer or if you
click the desktop,
you can start
Search by press-
ing F3.

Fortunately, Windows Millennium comes with a revamped Search utility that offers some reasonably powerful search options for tracking down files.

Here's how to get started:

- To search within a specific folder, highlight the folder in Windows Explorer, and then click the Search toolbar button, or press Ctrl+E. (You can also select View, Explorer Bar, Search.)

- Select Start, Search, For Files or Folders.

Figure 8.9 shows the Search bar that appears.

Here are the steps to follow to run a search:

1. Use the Search for files or folders named text box to enter the name of the file you want to locate (this is optional). If you're not sure of the exact name, you can enter a *file specification,* which uses a partial name or a wild-card character or two. Here are some pointers for using this text box:

   - Search doesn't differentiate between uppercase and lowercase letters.

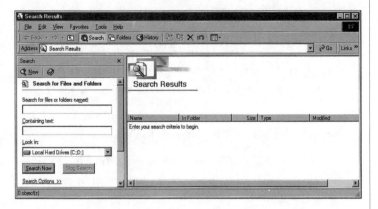

- If the filename contains one or more spaces, surround the name with quotation marks.

- Search always looks for filenames that *contain* the text you enter. Therefore, if you're not sure about a filename, just enter part of the name.

- Another way to broaden your search is to use wildcard characters. Use the question mark (?) to substitute for a single character (for example, memo5?.txt); use an asterisk (*) to substitute for a group of characters (for example, *.doc).

- To search for multiple file specifications, separate each one with a space, comma, or semicolon.

2. Use the Containing text box to enter a word or phrase contained within the file (this is optional). Note that if you enter multiple words, Search will match documents that contain only the exact phrase you enter.

3. Use the Look in combo box to either type the drive and/or folder you want to check or select one of the predefined locations. To specify multiple locations, separate each path with a semicolon.

4. To narrow down your search even more, click the Search Options link. This displays four check boxes:

Remember
If you entered a complex set of criteria that you think you might use again, you can save your search by selecting File, Save Search. Find gathers the search criteria and then prompts you to save them to a file. Open this file to display the Search bar with your saved criteria.

Date—Activate this check box to search using the file date and time stamps. Of the controls that appear, first use the list to select files Modified, files Created, or files Last Accessed. You then choose the date range by activating in the last x month(s), in the last x day(s), or between x and y.

Type—Activate this check box and use the drop-down list to choose the type of file you want to find.

Size—Activate this check box and use the first list to select either at least or at most. Then, use the spinner to enter a size in kilobytes.

Advanced Options—Activate this check box to see two more check boxes. Deactivate the Search Subfolders check box if you don't want Search to examine all the folders contained within the Look in location. Activate the Case sensitive check box if you want Search to exactly match the uppercase and lowercase letters you specify in the Containing text box.

5. Click the Search Now button to begin the search. If Find locates any matching files, they appear in a list in the Contents area.

Customizing Windows Explorer

I close this chapter by examining various ways to customize the Windows Explorer interface. You'll likely be spending a lot of time with Windows Explorer over the years, so customizing it to your liking will make you more productive.

Changing the View

The icons in Windows Explorer's Contents list can be viewed in five different ways. To see a list of these views, either pull down the View menu or pull down the Views button in the toolbar. Here are your choices:

Large Icons—Increases the size of the Contents list icons and displays those icons in rows across the list pane.

Small Icons—Decreases the size of the icons and displays them in columns that you must scroll vertically.

List—Icons are the same size as in the Small Icons view, but the icons are arranged in columns that you must scroll horizontally.

Details—Displays a vertical list of icons, where each icon has four columns: Name, Size, Type, and Modified.

Thumbnails—Displays the contents of each file instead of just its name. This works for many graphics formats—including BMP, GIF, JPG, and TIF—as well as for Web pages (HTML files).

Here are some techniques to remember when working with the Details view:

- You can change the order of the columns by dragging the column headings to the left or right.

- You can adjust the width of a column by pointing the mouse at the right edge of the column's heading (the pointer changes to a two-headed arrow) and dragging the pointer left or right.

- You can adjust the width of a column so that it's as wide as its widest data by double-clicking the right-edge of the column's heading.

Undocumented
To adjust all the columns so that they're exactly as wide as their widest data, press Ctrl+plus sign (+), where the plus sign is the one on your keyboard's numeric keypad.

Sorting Files and Folders

The icons in the Contents list are sorted alphabetically by name, with folders displayed before files. You can change this sort order by selecting View, Arrange Icons (or right-clicking the Contents list and clicking Arrange Icons), and then selecting one of the following commands:

by Name—Select this command to sort the folder alphabetically by name (this is the default).

by Type—Select this command to sort the folder alphabetically according to file type.

Shortcut
An easier way to sort a folder is to click the column headers in Details view. For example, click the Size column to sort the folder by file size. Clicking the same column header toggles the sort order between ascending and descending.

by Size—Select this command to sort the folder numerically according to file size, with the smallest sizes at the top.

by Date—Select this command to sort the folder by date, with the most recent dates at the top.

Auto Arrange—Activate this command to have Windows Explorer sort the folder automatically whenever you move icons or change the size of the window. Note that this command works only with the Large Icons and Small Icons views.

Exploring the View Options

The Windows Millennium version of Windows Explorer boasts a large number of customization options that you need to be familiar with. To see these options, you have two choices:

- In Windows Explorer, select the Tools, Folder Options command.

- Select Start, Settings, Control Panel, click the view all Control Panel options link, if necessary, and then open the Folder Options icon.

Either way, the view options can be found, appropriately enough, on the View tab, as shown in Figure 8.10.

Figure 8.10
The View tab has quite a few options for customizing Windows Explorer.

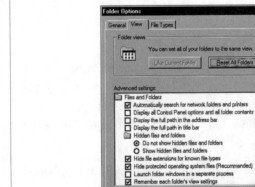

The `Folder views` group contains two command buttons that you use to define a common view for all your folders:

Like Current Folder—Use Windows Explorer's View menu to customize a folder the way you want. Then display the Folder Options dialog box and click Like Current Folder. (Note that this button is available only if you display the dialog box from Windows Explorer.) This tells Windows Explorer to display every folder using the same view options as the current folder.

Reset All Folders—If you prefer to set up a unique view for each folder, click Reset Folders to revert everything to the default Windows Millennium view.

Here's a complete look at the various options in the `Files and Folders` branch:

Automatically search for network folders and printers—When this check box is activated, Windows Millennium examines your network and displays all the shared folders and printers in the new My Network Places window. If your network has lots of shares, you may prefer to deactivate this feature.

Display all Control Panel options and all folder contents—If you activate this check box, Windows Millennium will always display the entire collection of Control Panel icons, so you won't have to click the annoying `view all Control Panel options` link. Activating this setting also means that Windows Millennium won't hide the contents of certain folders, including the root of the boot drive, `Program Files`, `Windows`, and `Windows\System`. Note that in each case the information panel displays a `Hide the contents of this folder/drive` link that you can click to resume hiding the contents.

Display the full path in address bar—Activate this check box to place the full pathname of the current folder in the Windows Explorer title bar. The full pathname includes the drive, the names of the parent folders, and the name of the current folder. This is a good idea because it enables you to quickly see where you are in the folder hierarchy, particularly if you're deep within a set of subfolders. It also means that you're able to edit the path and then move to the new folder by pressing Enter (or clicking Go).

Display the full path in title bar—This is the same as the pre-vious setting, except that the path appears in the title bar, which is less useful.

Hidden files and folder—Windows Millennium hides certain types of files by default. These files include the root files Autoexec.bat, Config.sys, and Bootlog.txt. This makes sense for novice users because they could accidentally delete or rename an important file. However, it's a pain for more advanced users who may require access to these files. You can use these options to tell Windows Explorer which files to display:

- **Do not show hidden files and folders**—Activate this option to avoid displaying objects that have the hid-den attribute set.

- **Show hidden files and folders**—Activate this option to display the hidden files.

Hide file extensions for known file types—When you read Chapter 9, "Powerful Techniques for File Types," you'll see that file extensions are one of the most crucial Windows Millennium concepts. That's because file extensions define the file type and automatically associate files with certain applications. Microsoft figures that, crucial or not, the file extension concept is just too hard for new users to grasp. Therefore, right out of the box, Windows Explorer doesn't display file extensions. To overcome this limita-tion, deactivate this check box.

Hide protected operating system files—When this check box is activated, Windows Millennium hides files that have the System attribute activated. This is not usually a problem because you rarely have to do anything with the Windows system files. However, if you do need to see one of these files (such as Msdos.sys; see Chapter 2, "Understanding and Controlling the Windows Millennium Startup"), deactivate this check box. When Windows Millennium asks if you're sure, click Yes.

➜ **See Also** "Controlling Startup Using Msdos.sys," **p. 50.**

Launch folder windows in a separate process—Activating this check box tells Windows Millennium to create a new thread in memory for each folder you open. This makes Windows Explorer more stable because a problem with one thread won't crash the others. However, this also means that Windows Explorer requires far greater amounts of system resources and memory. Activate this option only if your system has plenty of resources and memory.

Remember each folder's view settings—Activate this check box to have Windows Explorer keep track of the view options you set for each folder. The next time you display a folder, Windows Explorer will remember the view options and use them to display the folder.

Show My Documents on the Desktop—This check box toggles the desktop's My Documents icon on and off.

Show pop-up description for folder and desktop items—Some icons display a pop-up banner when you point the mouse at them. For example, the default desktop icons display an InfoTip that describes each icon. Use this check box to turn these pop-ups on and off.

Customizing the Standard Buttons Toolbar

The Windows Explorer toolbar (known officially as the Standard Buttons toolbar) has been revamped for Windows Millennium. For example, the old Cut, Copy, and Paste buttons have been removed, and new Explorer Bar buttons have been added. (The Explorer Bar buttons toggle the Search, Folders, and History bars on and off.) If, like me, you used the Cut, Copy, and Paste buttons quite often, you probably won't be all that enthusiastic about this new arrangement.

Another thing that's less than overwhelming about the new toolbar is its peculiar design. For example, why does the Back button have a text label, but the Forward button doesn't?

All these peculiarities add up to bad toolbar news, but the good news is that they can be remedied because the toolbar is customizable. Here's how it works:

1. Right-click the toolbar and then click Customize in the shortcut menu. The Customize Toolbar dialog box appears, as shown in Figure 8.11.

Figure 8.11
Use this dialog
box to create a
more sensible
toolbar.

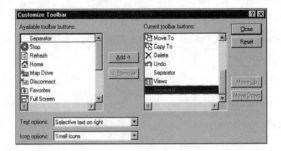

2. To add an extra button to the toolbar, highlight it in the `Available toolbar buttons` list and then click Add. Use the `Separator` item to add a vertical bar to the toolbar. This is normally used to separate groups of related buttons.

3. To remove a button from the toolbar, highlight it in the `Current toolbar buttons` list and then click Remove.

4. To change the order of the buttons, highlight any button in the `Current toolbar buttons` list and click Move Up or Move Down.

5. To control the button text, use the `Text options` list:

   - **Show text labels**—This option adds text to every button. This makes the buttons much easier to figure out, so I recommend going with this option.

   - **Selective text on right**—This is the default option, and it displays text on only some buttons.

- **No text labels**—This option displays every button using just its icon. If you already know what each icon represents, selecting this option will give you a bit more room because the toolbar will be at its narrowest.

6. The size of the icons is controlled by the items in the Icon options list. Select either Small icons (this is the default) or Large icons.

7. Click Close to put your new settings into effect.

Using Windows Explorer's Command-Line Options

The Windows Explorer executable file is Explorer.exe, and it resides in the Windows folder. Explorer.exe supports various command-line parameters, which you can take advantage of to control how Windows Explorer starts. Here's the syntax for Explorer.exe:

```
explorer [/n]|[/e][,/root,folder][,subfolder]
```

/n	Starts Windows Explorer using the My Computer view (just the Contents list).
/e	Starts Windows Explorer using the Explorer view (both the Folders bar and the Contents list).
/root,folder	Tells Windows Explorer to display folder at the top of the Folders bar. You can only view folder and all of its subfolders.
subfolder	Specifies a subfolder that will be highlighted in the Folders bar.

The following command opens Windows Explorer with C:\Windows as the root:

```
explorer /e,/root,c:\windows
```

The following command opens Windows Explorer with C:\My Documents highlighted:

```
explorer /e,c:\my documents
```

Essential Information

- To select multiple objects with your mouse, hold down Ctrl and click each object. For contiguous objects, click the first object, hold down Shift, and click the last object. (If Web integration is on, replace "click" with "hover over.")

- Windows Millennium copies objects dragged to a different drive, and moves objects dragged to the same drive. To force a move, hold down Shift; to force a copy, hold down Ctrl.

- Select the File, Send To command to send objects to a floppy drive, removable drive, or another predetermined destination.

- To rename an object, highlight it and either select File, Rename or press F2.

- Deleted items are sent to the Recycle Bin, which represents the `Recycled` folders on your hard disks. To restore an accidentally deleted file, highlight it in the Recycle Bin and select File, Restore.

- Select View, Folder Options to customize Windows Explorer view options.

Powerful Techniques for File Types

A MAZINGLY, A LONG LIST OF USEFUL and powerful Windows Millennium features are either ignored or given short shrift in the official Microsoft documentation. Whether it's the Windows Millennium startup options, the Registry, or the Web view templates (to name a few that I discuss in this book), Microsoft prefers that curious users figure these things out for themselves. (With, of course, the help of their favorite computer book authors.)

The subject of this chapter is a prime example. The idea of the *file type* can be described, without hyperbole, as the very foundation of the Windows Millennium file system. Not only does Microsoft offer scant documentation and tools for working with file types, but also they seem to have gone out of their way to hide the whole file type concept. As usual, the reason is to block out this aspect of Windows Millennium's innards from the sensitive eyes of the novice user. Ironically, however, this just creates a whole new set of problems for beginners, and more hassles for experienced users.

This chapter brings file types out into the open. You'll learn the basics of file types and then see a number of powerful techniques for using file types to take charge of the Windows Millennium file system.

Understanding File Types

To get the most out of this chapter, you need to understand some background about what a file type is and how Windows Millennium determines and works with file types. The next couple of sections tell you everything you need to know to get you through the rest of the chapter.

File Types and File Extensions

One of the fictions that Microsoft has tried to foist on the computer-using public is that we live in a "document-centric" world. That is, that people care only about the documents they create and not about the applications they use to create those documents.

This is pure hokum. The reality is that applications are still too difficult to use and the capability to share documents between applications is still too problematic. In other words, you can't create documents unless you learn the ins and outs of an application, and you can't share documents with others unless you use compatible applications.

Unfortunately, we're stuck with Microsoft's worship of the document and all the problems that this worship creates. A good example is the hiding of file extensions. As you learned in Chapter 8, "Expert Windows Explorer Techniques," Windows Millennium turns off file extensions by default. Here are just a few of the problems this allegedly document-centric decision creates:

→ **See Also** "Exploring the View Options," **p. 224**.

Document confusion—If you have a folder with multiple documents that use the same primary name, it's often difficult to tell which file is which. For example, Figure 9.1 shows a folder with 15 different files named Project. Windows Millennium unrealistically expects users to tell files apart just by examining their icons.

The inability to rename extensions—If you have a file named index.txt and you want to rename it to index.html, you can't do it with file extensions turned off. If you try, you just end up with a file named index.html.txt.

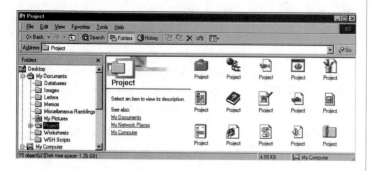

Figure 9.1
With file exten-
sions turned off,
it's often difficult
to tell one file from
another.

The inability to save a document under an extension of your choice—Similarly, with file extensions turned off, Windows Millennium forces you to save a file using the default extension associated with an application. For example, if you're working in Notepad, every file you save must have a txt extension.

You can overcome all these problems by turning on file extensions. Why does the lack of file extensions cause such a fuss? Because file extensions *solely and completely* determine the file type of a document. In other words, if Windows Millennium sees that a file has a txt extension, then it knows the file uses the Text Document file type. Similarly, a file with the extension bmp uses the Bitmap Image file type.

The file type, in turn, determines the application that's associated with the extension. If a file has a txt extension, Windows Millennium associates that extension with Notepad, so the file will always open in Notepad (or if it's fairly large, WordPad). Nothing else inherent in the file determines the file type so, at least from the point of view of the user, the entire Windows Millennium file system rests on the shoulders of the humble file extension.

This method of determining file types is, no doubt, a poor design decision. (For example, there is some danger that a novice user could render a file useless by imprudently renaming its extension.) However, it also leads to some powerful methods for manipulating and controlling the Windows Millennium file system, as you'll see in this chapter.

Undocumented
There are two ways to get around the inability to save a document under an extension of your choice. 1) In the Save As dialog box, surround the filename you want to use with quotation marks. 2) In the Save as type list, select the All Files (*.*) option, if it exists.

Remember
One way to turn on file extensions is to select Windows Explorer's Tools, Folder Options command, display the View tab, and deactivate the Hide file extensions for known file types check box.

File Types and the Registry

As you might expect, everything Windows Millennium knows about file types is defined in the Registry. You use the Registry to work with file types throughout this chapter, so let's see how things work. Open the Registry Editor and then examine the HKEY_CLASSES_ROOT key. Notice that it's divided into two sections:

Inside Scoop
HKEY_CLASSES_ROOT also stores information on ActiveX controls in its CLSID subkey. Many of these controls also have corresponding subkeys in the second half of HKEY_CLASSES_ROOT.

- The first part of HKEY_CLASSES_ROOT consists of dozens of file extension subkeys (such as .bmp and .txt). There are well over 200 such subkeys in a basic Windows Millennium installation, and there could easily be double that number on a system with many applications installed. Each of these subkeys represents a file extension that has been *registered* with Windows Millennium.

- The second part of HKEY_CLASSES_ROOT lists the various file types that are associated with the registered extensions.

To see what this all means, take a look at Figure 9.2. Here, I've highlighted the .txt key, which has txtfile as its Default value.

Figure 9.2
The first part of the HKEY_CLASSES_ ROOT key contains subkeys for all the registered file extensions.

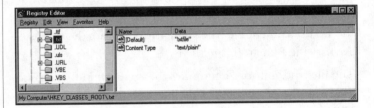

That Default value is a pointer to the extension's associated file type subkey in the second half of HKEY_CLASSES_ROOT. Figure 9.3 shows the txtfile subkey associated with the txt extension. Here are some notes about this file type subkey:

- The Default value is a description of the file type (Text Document, in this case).

- The DefaultIcon subkey defines the icon that's displayed with any file that uses this type.

- The shell subkey determines the *actions* that can be performed with this file type. These actions vary depending on the file type, but open and print are common. The open action determines the application that's associated with the file type. For example, the open action for a Text Document file type is the following:

```
C:\WINDOWS\NOTEPAD.EXE %1
```

The File Types Tab: A Front-End for HKEY_CLASSES_ROOT

For much of the work you do in this chapter, you won't have to deal with the Registry's HKEY_CLASSES_ROOT key directly. Instead, Windows Millennium offers a dialog box tab that acts as a front-end for this key. Follow these steps to display this tab:

1. In Windows Explorer, select Tools, Folder Options to display the Folder Options dialog box.

2. Select the File Types tab.

Figure 9.4 shows the File Types tab. The Registered file types list shows all the file types known to Windows Millennium, as well as their extensions. When you highlight a file type, the Opens with line in the Details area shows you the icon and name of the program associated with the file type.

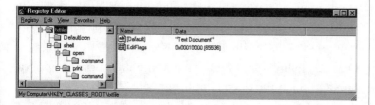

Opening a Document with an Unassociated Application

From the preceding discussion, you can see the process that Windows Millennium goes through when you double-click a document:

Inside Scoop
The "%1" at the end of the command is a placeholder that refers to the document being opened (if any). If you double-click a file named memo.txt, for example, the %1 placeholder is replaced by memo.txt, which tells Windows to run Notepad and open that file.

Shortcut
You can also get to the Folder Options dialog box by launching the Control Panel's Folder Options icon.

Figure 9.3
The second part of HKEY_CLASSES_ROOT contains the file type data associated with each extension.

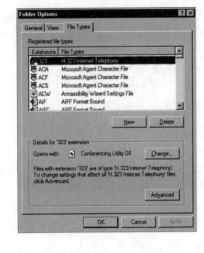

1. Look up the document's extension in HKEY_CLASSES_ROOT.

2. Examine the Default value to get the name of the file type subkey.

3. Look up the file type subkey in HKEY_CLASSES_ROOT.

4. Get the Default value in the shell\open\command subkey to get the command line for the associated application.

5. Run the application and open the document.

What do you do if you want to bypass this process and have Windows Millennium open a document in an *unassociated* application? (That is, an application other than the one with which the document is associated.) For example, what if you want to open a text file in WordPad?

One possibility would be to launch the unassociated application and open the document from there. To do so, you'd run the File, Open command (or whatever) and, in the Open dialog box, select All Files (*.*) in the Files of type list.

That will work, but it defeats the convenience of being able to launch a file directly from Windows Explorer or some other folder window. Here's how to work around this:

1. In Windows Explorer, highlight the document you want to work with.

2. Select File, Open With.

3. For most files, Windows Millennium goes directly to the Open With dialog box. However, if you run the Open With command on a system file, Windows asks if you're sure you want to open the file. In this case, click Open With.

4. In the Choose the program you want to use list, highlight the unassociated application in which you want to open the document (see Figure 9.5). If the application you want to use isn't listed, click Other and then select the program's executable file from the dialog box that appears.

5. To prevent Windows Millennium from changing the file type to the unassociated application, make sure the Always use this program to open these files check box is deactivated.

6. Click OK to open the document in the selected application.

One of the small but useful interface improvements in Windows Millennium is that the system "remembers" the unassociated applications that you choose in the Open With dialog box. As you can see in Figure 9.6, right-clicking the file (or any file with the same extension) and clicking Open With displays a menu that includes the associated program (Notepad, in this case) and the unassociated program you chose earlier (WordPad). Note, too, that there is also a Choose Program command that you can run to display the Open With dialog box.

Shortcut
A faster method for displaying the Open With dialog box is to right-click the document, and then click Open With in the shortcut menu.

Figure 9.5
Use the Open With dialog box to select the unassociated application you want to use to open the document.

Undocumented
You can add an unassociated application to the Open With list by editing the program's file type subkey in HKEY_CLASSES_ROOT. Create a new \shell\open\command subkey and set the Default value to the path of the program's executable file, followed by a space and "%1".

Working with Existing File Types

In this section, you'll learn how to work with Windows
Millennium's existing file types. I'll show you how to change
the file type description, modify the file type's actions, associate an extension with another file type, and disassociate a file
type and an extension.

Editing a File Type

To make changes to an existing file type, follow these steps:

1. Open the Folder Options dialog box and display the File
   Types tab, as described earlier.

2. Use the `Registered file types` list to highlight the file type
   you want to work with.

3. Click Advanced. The Edit File Type dialog box appears.
   Figure 9.7 shows the Edit File Type dialog box for the Text
   Document type.

4. The text box at the top holds the description of the file type, which can be edited. This description appears in the `Registered file types` list and in the New menu (right-click a folder and then click New).

5. You can also work with the following controls:

Change Icon—Click this button to display the Change Icon dialog box. Use this dialog box to select a new icon for the file type. (I describe this dialog box in Chapter 17, "Customizing the Windows Millennium Interface.")

→ **See Also** "Changing an Icon," **p. 387.**

Actions—This list shows the actions defined for the file type. I'll discuss file type actions in more detail in the next section.

Confirm open after download—When this check box is activated and you attempt to download a file from the Web, Internet Explorer displays the File Download dialog box (see Figure 9.8) that asks whether you want to save or open the downloaded file. Otherwise, Internet Explorer just opens the file using its associated application. Here are two points to bear in mind:

- Despite the name of this check box, Internet Explorer displays the File Download dialog box *before* you download the file.

- The File Download dialog box includes a check box named `Always ask before opening this type of file`. Deactivating this check box is the same thing as deactivating the Confirm open after download check box.

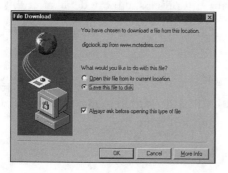

Figure 9.8
If the Confirm open after download check box is activated, Internet Explorer displays this dialog box.

Undocumented
What if you want
Windows
Millennium to
never show a file
type's extension,
even if extensions
are turned on
globally? To set
this up, find the
appropriate file
type subkey in
HKEY_CLASSES_
ROOT, and add a
new string
value named
NeverShowExt, and
leave its value as
the empty string.
You may need to
restart Windows
to put this into
effect.

Shortcut
When you want to
open a folder win-
dow in the two-
paned Explorer
view, you have to
right-click the
folder and then
click Explore. To
make the latter
the default action
for a folder, edit
the Folder file
type, highlight
explore in the
Actions list, and
then click Set
Default.

Always show extension—If you activate this check box, Windows Millennium shows this file type's extension even if you hide extensions globally.

Browse in same window—When this check box is activated, the file type opens within Internet Explorer instead of its associated application. This applies only to Microsoft Office file types that are capable of being displayed within Internet Explorer.

6. Click OK to return to the File Types tab.

7. Click Close.

Working with File Type Actions

In the Edit File Type dialog box, the Actions list displays the defined actions for the file type. You usually see two types of actions:

- An action shown in boldface represents the default action for the file type. This is the action that's performed when you double-click one of these files (or highlight a file and press Enter). This action also appears in bold on the file type's shortcut menu (the menu that appears when you right-click a file of that type).

- All other actions are listed on the shortcut menu for the file type.

The buttons beside the Actions list enable you to work with the file type's actions:

New—Click this button to create a new action for the file type. I describe this process in more detail after this list.

Edit—Click this button to make changes to the highlighted action.

Remove—Click this button to delete the highlighted action.

Set Default—Click this button to make the highlighted action the default for this file type.

To demonstrate how these actions work, let's run through an example. In this case, I'll create a new action for the Text Document type. Specifically, I'll create an "Open in MS-DOS Editor" action that opens a text file in the MS-DOS Editor (Edit.com):

1. In the Edit File Type dialog box, click New. Windows Millennium displays the New Action dialog box.

2. In the `Action` text box, type in a name for the new action. This name will appear in the file type's shortcut menu.

3. In the `Application used to perform action` text box, enter the drive, path, and filename of the executable file you want to use. Here are a few notes to keep in mind:

   - If the action will be opening the file, add the `%1` placeholder at the end.

   - If you want the action to print the file, add `/P` at the end.

   - If the path or filename contains spaces, enclose the text within quotation marks.

4. Figure 9.9 shows a completed dialog box. Click OK when you're done. Windows Millennium adds your new action to the `Actions` list.

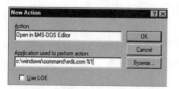

5. If you want the new action to be the default, highlight it and click Set Default.

6. Click OK to return to the File Types tab.

7. Click Close.

In Figure 9.10, I right-clicked a text file. Notice how the new action appears in the shortcut menu.

Inside Scoop
You can assign an accelerator key to the action by preceding a letter in the action name with an ampersand (&). For example, if you enter `Open in &MS-DOS Editor` (see Figure 9.9), the "M" becomes the accelerator key.

Figure 9.9
Use the New Action dialog box to define a new action for the file type.

Figure 9.10
The new action appears in the file type's context menu.

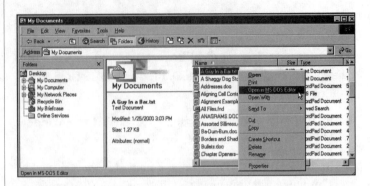

Associating an Extension with a Different Application

There are many reasons you might want to override Windows Millennium's default associations and use a different program to open an extension. For example, you might prefer to open text files in WordPad instead of Notepad. Similarly, you might want to open HTML files in Notepad or some other text editor rather than Internet Explorer.

In these cases, you need to associate the extension with the application you want to use instead of the Windows default association. Windows Millennium gives you two ways to go about this:

The Open With dialog box—With this method, right-click any file that uses the extension and then click Open With. (If you've used the Open With dialog box on this extension before, click the Choose Program command from the menu that appears.) In the Open With dialog box, select the program you want to use, activate the Always use this program to open these files check box, and click OK.

The File Types tab—With this method, first display the File Types tab, highlight the file type or extension, and click Advanced. In the Actions list, highlight open and click Edit. Modify the Application used to perform action text box so that it displays the full pathname of the application you want to use, followed by a space and %1.

Disassociating an Application and an Extension

One of the most annoying things a newly installed program can do is change your existing file type associations. Some programs (such as the latest versions of Netscape) are courteous enough to ask you if they can change some associations. However, many other programs make the changes without permission. In these cases, you often want to undo the damage by disassociating the new application from the affected extensions. You have two ways to proceed:

- If you want to revert the association to its original application, use either of the procedures from the previous section.

- If you prefer to have no associated application at all, first display the File Types tab. Then, highlight the file type or extension, and click Advanced. In the Actions list, highlight Open and click Remove.

Creating a New File Type

Windows Millennium comes with a long list of registered file types, but it can't account for every extension you'll face in your computing career. For rare extensions, it's best just to use the Open With dialog box. However, if you have an unregistered extension that you encounter frequently, you should register that extension by creating a new file type for it. The next two sections provide a couple of methods for doing this.

Using Open With to Create a Basic File Type

Our old friend the Open With dialog box provides a quick-and-dirty method for creating a simple file type for an unregistered extension:

1. In Windows Explorer, highlight the file you want to work with.

2. Select File, Open With. (Again, if you've used the Open With dialog box on this extension before, click the Choose Program command from the menu that appears.) The Open With dialog box appears.

Inside Scoop
Text files, in particular, seem to come with all kinds of nonstandard (that is, unregistered) extensions. Rather than constantly setting up file types for these extensions or using the Open With dialog box, I created a shortcut for Notepad in my Windows\SendTo folder. That way, I can open any text file by right-clicking it and then selecting Send To, Notepad.

3. Use the Description for files of this type text box to enter a description for the new file type.

4. In the Choose the program you want to use list, highlight the application you want to use to open the file. (Or click Other to choose the program from a dialog box.)

5. Make sure the Always use this program to open these files check box is activated.

6. Click OK.

This method creates a new file type with the following properties:

- In the File Types tab, the new file type appears in the Registered file types list under the name you entered into the Description for files of this type box.

- The file type has only a single action: open.

- The icon associated with the file is the same as the one used by the associated application.

- In the Registry, the new HKEY_CLASSES_ROOT file type name is ext_auto_file, where ext is the file's extension.

Using the File Types Tab to Create a More Advanced File Type

If you want more control over your new file type, use the File Types tab instead of the Open With dialog box. This method enables you to select a different icon, set up multiple actions, and more. Here are the steps to follow:

1. Open the Folder Options dialog box and display the File Types tab.

2. Click New. Windows Millennium displays the Create New Extension dialog box shown in Figure 9.11.

3. Enter the File Extension for the new file type.

Figure 9.11
Use the Create
New Extension dia-
log box to define
your new file type.

4. Click OK to return to the File Types tab.

5. Make sure the new extension is highlighted in the Registered file types list.

6. To associate an application with the file type, click Change and use the Open With dialog box to select the program.

7. When you're back in the File Types tab, click Advanced and fill in the other options as described earlier in the "Working with Existing File Types" section.

Associating Two or More Extensions with a Single File Type

The problem with creating a new file type is that you often have to reinvent the wheel. For example, let's say you want to set up a new file type that uses the .1st extension. These are usually text files (such as readme.1st) that provide preinstallation instructions, so you probably want to associate them with Notepad. However, this means repeating some or all of the existing Text Document file types. To avoid this, it's possible to tell Windows Millennium to associate a second extension with an existing file type.

In Windows 9x, you had to do this via the Registry, but Windows Millennium offers an easier route:

1. Open the Folder Options dialog box and display the File Types tab.

2. Click New. Windows Millennium displays the Create New Extension dialog box.

3. Enter the File Extension for the new file type.

4. Click Advanced. The dialog box expands as shown in Figure 9.12.

Figure 9.12
The expanded version of the Create New Extension dialog box.

Figure 9.12
The expanded version of the Create New Extension dialog box.

5. Use the `Associated File Type` list to select the file type for the new extension (such as Text Document).

6. Click OK to return to the File Types tab.

Customizing the New Menu

In Chapter 8, I showed you how to create new documents by using the New menu. That is, you either select File, New or right-click and then click New in the shortcut menu. As you can see in Figure 9.13, the New menu includes a Folder command, and commands for seven different file types. (You may see more commands, depending on which applications you have installed.)

Inside Scoop
The Windows Millennium version of the New menu has a new member: Compressed Folder. This creates a Zip file, as explained in Chapter 8.

→ **See Also** "Creating New Folders and Files," **p. 211.**

→ **See Also** "Working with Zip Files," **p. 212.**

Figure 9.13
The New menu enables you to create new documents on-the-fly.

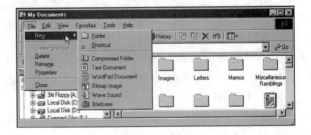

The New menu is a handy tool, but it gets even handier if you customize it by adding your own commands and by removing existing commands that you don't need. This is all possible through the Registry.

To understand how this works, let's see how those New menu commands got there in the first place. In the Registry, open `HKEY_CLASSES_ROOT` and then open the `.bmp` subkey. As you can see in Figure 9.14, this subkey includes a `ShellNew` subkey. The existence of `ShellNew` tells Windows Millennium to include this file type on the New menu.

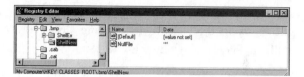

Figure 9.14
If an extension key has a `ShellNew` subkey, Windows Millennium includes the file type on the New menu.

How Windows Millennium creates the new file is determined by extra settings (other than `Default`) in `ShellNew`. There are four different settings used:

`NullFile`—When Windows Millennium sees this string setting, it creates an empty document of the associated file type. This is the method used by the Bitmap Image (`.bmp`), Text Document (`.txt`), and Compressed Folder (`.zip`) file types.

`FileName`—The value of this string setting is always a filename. When Windows Millennium sees this setting, it looks in the hidden `Windows\ShellNew` folder for that filename, and then creates the new file by making a copy of the file that's in `ShellNew`. This method is used by the Wave Sound (`.wav`) and WordPad Document (`.doc`) file types. For the latter, the filename (`winword.doc`) is defined in the following key:

`HKEY_CLASSES_ROOT\.doc\Wordpad.Document.1\ShellNew`

`Command`—The value of this string setting is a command. When Windows Millennium sees this setting, it creates the new document by running the command. This is the method used by the Shortcut (`.lnk`) and Briefcase (`.bfc`) file types.

`Data`—This setting is a binary value. When Windows Millennium sees this setting, it creates a new document of the associated file type and copies the binary value into the document.

Remember
The `ShellNew` folder contains a dozen (or more) templates, including files named `Excel.xls` and `Lotus.wk4`. The reason these items don't show up on the New menu is that they don't have a corresponding registered file type.

Given all this, it's relatively easy to add file types to and remove file types from the New menu:

To add a file type to the New menu—In `HKEY_CLASSES_ROOT`, find the extension subkey for the file type and add a new subkey named ShellNew. Within this new subkey, create a setting using one of the four names listed previously: NullFile, FileName, Command, or Data.

To remove a file type from the New menu—In HKEY_CLASSES_ROOT, open the extension subkey for the file type and delete the ShellNew subkey.

Figuring Out Browser File Types: Internet Explorer Versus Netscape

One of the unfortunate consequences in the ongoing Battle of the Browsers is that Internet Explorer and Netscape often use your computer as a battleground. That is, each program wants to be your default browser, and they often use unscrupulous means to achieve this end. In this section, I show you how to make peace reign on your desktop.

The first thing you should do is make sure the browser you want to use as your default is set up as such. That is, the next time you start the browser, if it asks you if it can be your default browser, click Yes to make it so.

Note that the browser's executable is stored in the various URL file types, such as URL:Hypertext Transfer Protocol and URL:File Transfer Protocol. (In each case, the file extension is listed as N/A.) You see over a dozen of these file types in the File Types tab. In most cases, these file types refer to the protocol prefix used in an Internet address. For example, the URL::Hypertext Transfer Protocol is used in Web page addresses that begin with http. Note, too, that each of these file types has a corresponding Registry entry at HKEY_CLASSES_ROOT*protocol*, where *protocol* is the protocol prefix. For example, data on the URL::Hypertext Transfer Protocol file type can be found here:

```
HKEY_CLASSES_ROOT\http
```

Now you need to force both browsers to stop pestering you to make them your default browser.

To do this in Internet Explorer, select Tools, Internet Options to display the Internet Options dialog box. Display the Programs tab and then deactivate the Internet Explorer should check to see whether it is the default browser check box.

To tell Navigator not to check whether it's the default browser, start the program. If Internet Explorer is currently your default browser, at startup Netscape will ask if you want to register Navigator as the default. Make sure you activate the Do not perform this check in the future check box and then select No.

Essential Information

- The file type of a document is determined solely by its extension.

- Registered file extensions and their associated file types are stored in the Registry in the HKEY_CLASSES_ROOT key.

- To open a document in an unassociated application, select File, Open With.

- Use the File Types tab (in Windows Explorer, select Tools, Folder Options) to edit existing file types and create new file types.

- The items in the New menu are determined by the various ShellNew subkeys in the extension keys in HKEY_CLASSES_ROOT.

Remember
You can also display the Internet Options dialog box by opening Control Panel's Internet Options icon.

Taking Advantage of Shortcuts

O NE OF THE PROBLEMS WITH the "authorized" way of doing things in Windows Millennium is that it tends to be the long and inefficient way, as well. Whether it's a needlessly tedious wizard, a poorly laid out Start menu structure, or faulty defaults, doing Windows "by the book" is often not the best way to work. Fortunately, as you've seen throughout this book, there are plenty of "unauthorized" detours you can take to route around Windows' inefficiencies.

In this chapter, you see one of those rare instances in which the authorized Windows way is actually pretty good. As their name implies, *shortcuts*—the topic of this chapter—offer all kinds of opportunities to streamline your work. I run through these opportunities, and along the way I explain how shortcuts work and offer a few undocumented tricks for getting even more out of this useful feature.

Understanding Shortcuts

You see and work with shortcuts quite often in this book:

▪ Some of the items on the default Windows Millennium desktop—such as the Connect to the Internet icon—are shortcuts.

66
shortcut An icon that links to a file or folder. When you double-click a shortcut, the original item opens.—*Microsoft*
99

- Other than the built-in items (from Programs on down), everything you see on the Start menu is a shortcut.

- The items on the Send To menu are shortcuts stored in the Windows\SendTo folder.

- Some of the items in the Quick Launch toolbar—such as the Launch Internet Explorer icon—are shortcuts.

From all this, it's not hard to figure just what a shortcut is: a special file that points to another object, such as a program's executable file or a document. From this definition, you might be tempted to conclude that Windows Millennium shortcuts are more or less the same as the program items found in Windows 3.x program groups. That's not true, however. The crucial difference is that Windows Millennium shortcuts are standalone files. By contrast, each Windows 3.x program item was merely an element within a program group (.grp) file. Having a shortcut as a separate file offers two main advantages:

- You can create, copy, or move shortcuts within any Windows Millennium folder.

- Like all files in Windows Millennium, shortcuts have properties that you can customize.

The other big advantage enjoyed by Windows Millennium shortcuts is flexibility. Whereas Windows 3.x program items could point to only application executables and documents, Windows Millennium shortcuts can also point to folders, printers, disk drives, and much more.

Shortcuts for Windows objects are stored in special files that use the lnk (short for *link*) extension. If you examine HKEY_CLASSES_ROOT (as described in the previous chapter), you see that the lnk extension is associated with the lnkfile file type:

> → **See Also** "File Types and the Registry," **p. 234.**

```
HKEY_CLASSES_ROOT\lnkfile
```

> **"**
> A shortcut
> doesn't change
> the location of a
> file—the short-
> cut is just a
> pointer that lets
> you open the file
> quickly. If you
> delete the short-
> cut, the original
> file isn't
> deleted.—
> *Microsoft*
> **"**

As you can see in Figure 10.1, this subkey's Default value is Shortcut, and it also includes three other settings:

EditFlags—When this value is 1 (0x00000001 in hex), Windows Millennium prevents this file type from appearing in the File Types tab of the Folder Options dialog box.

IsShortcut—When this setting is present, Windows Millennium overlays a small arrow on the file's icon to indicate that it's a shortcut.

NeverShowExt—When this setting is present, Windows Millennium suppresses the file's extension, even if extensions are turned on globally.

Undocumented
If you've edited the advanced settings for a file type, you can prevent other people from changing those settings by setting EditFlags to 8 (0x00000008). This disables the file type's Advanced button in the File Types dialog box.

I'll show you how to customize some of these settings in the "Some Unauthorized Shortcut Tricks" section a bit later in this chapter.

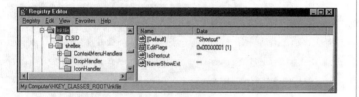

Figure 10.1
The lnkfile subkey contains various settings related to the shortcut file type.

I don't discuss DOS shortcut files much in this chapter, but it's worth noting that these files are a different kettle of fish entirely. They're called *program information files*, or PIFs, for short. These files contain special DOS-related data that governs how the program runs in DOS, what its DOS window looks like, and more. PIFs use the pif extension, which is associated in the Registry with the piffile file type:

```
\HKEY_CLASSES_ROOT\piffile
```

This subkey contains the same settings that I described earlier for Windows shortcuts.

Creating a Shortcut

Windows Millennium's genius (if that's the right word) for offering us too many ways to perform a task applies equally well with shortcuts. Following is the long list of methods you can

Watch Out!
Although batch
(.bat) files are
executable files,
Windows
Millennium does
not automatically
create a shortcut
when you drag and
drop one of these
files. To create a
shortcut for a
batch file, you
have to treat it as
a nonexecutable
file.

use to create a shortcut. I've arranged this list more or less with the easiest methods first:

- Drag an executable (.exe or .com) file and drop it on the destination.

- Right-drag any file or folder, drop it on the destination, and then click Create Shortcut(s) Here in the context menu that appears.

- Drag any file or folder, hold down both the Ctrl key and the Shift key, and drop it on the destination.

- Copy a file or folder, open the destination, and then select Edit, Paste Shortcut.

- In Windows Explorer or a folder window, select File, New, Shortcut. (You can also right-click and choose New, Shortcut in the context menu.) This launches the Create Shortcut Wizard, which takes you step-by-step through the process of selecting the shortcut's target, name, and icon.

- To create a PIF shortcut for a DOS executable file, either use any of the previous methods or make changes to the properties for the DOS executable.

Modifying Shortcut Properties

Shortcuts have a number of properties you can manipulate to customize them to your liking. To see the property sheet for a shortcut, either highlight the shortcut in Windows Explorer and select File, Properties, or right-click the shortcut and choose Properties in the context menu. Figure 10.2 shows the property sheet's Shortcut tab.

Here's a summary of the available controls:

Target—This text box tells you what the shortcut points to. If the shortcut points to a file, for example, this text box displays the file's full pathname (drive, folder, and filename). You should need to edit only this text box if the target gets moved or renamed.

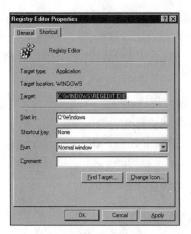

Figure 10.2
The Shortcut tab contains the controls you use to customize a Windows shortcut.

Shortcut
Another good reason to edit the Target text is to add parameters or switches that modify how the shortcut starts the target. For example, if the target is Windows Explorer, you could add any of the Explorer.exe command-line switches. (In Chapter 8, "Expert Windows Explorer Techniques," see "Using Windows Explorer's Command-Line Options," page 229.)

Start in—If the target is an application or document, this text box displays the folder in which the target resides. This will be the application's default folder (that is, the one that first appears when you display the Open or Save As dialog box). If you prefer to use a different default folder (such as My Documents), edit the path accordingly.

Shortcut key—When this text box is active and you press a key, Windows Millennium inserts a key combination of the form Ctrl+Alt+*character*, where *character* is the letter or number you pressed. You can then press this key combination to launch the shortcut. Here are some notes about this setting:

- Other key combinations are possible by holding down Ctrl+Shift, Alt+Shift, or Ctrl+Alt+Shift.

- If you don't use the numbers on your keyboard's numeric keypad, you can get a "one-key" shortcut key by pressing a number (make sure that Num Lock is turned on). For example, if you press 1, the Shortcut key field displays Num 1, which means you can invoke the shortcut just by pressing 1.

- The shortcut key works only if the shortcut resides in the Start menu hierarchy or on the desktop.

Shortcut
To help you remember which key combination applies to which shortcut, include the key combination in the shortcut's name.

Watch Out!
If you plan on making any adjustments to the Target text box, make sure you add quotation marks around any file or folder names that include spaces.

- For any shortcut, the key combination works while the target application is running. That is, pressing the key combination switches to the target application.

- Not all programs respond to the shortcut key.

- Windows Millennium doesn't give you any way to generate a list of the shortcut keys you've used, so consider keeping your own list to avoid using duplicate key combinations.

Run—For applications and documents, this list specifies how the application's window appears. You can select Normal window (for the application's default window), Minimized, or Maximized.

Comment—This text box holds a description of the shortcut. This description appears as a banner when you hover your mouse over the shortcut.

Find Target—Click this button to open the folder that contains the target.

Change Icon—Click this button to select a different icon for the shortcut, as explained in Chapter 17, "Customizing the Windows Millennium Interface."

→ **See Also** "Changing an Icon," **p. 387.**

Finding a Moved or Renamed Target

A shortcut points to an object, which is known in the Windows trade as the *target*. What happens if the target is moved, renamed, or even deleted? When you attempt to launch the shortcut, Windows Millennium will be unable to locate the target and it will then initiate a search for the object. While the search is in progress, Windows Millennium displays the Missing Shortcut dialog box, shown in Figure 10.3. (This dialog box is misnamed because it's the target that's missing, not the shortcut.) Click Browse to find the target yourself, or click Cancel to abandon the search (for example, if you know the target has been deleted).

Figure 10.3
If Windows
Millennium can't
find the target,
it starts looking
for it.

If Windows Millennium can't find a file with the same name, it looks for a file that has the same size, file type, and date and time stamp. If it finds a matching file, the shortcut is updated and the target loads. If Windows Millennium isn't sure, it displays a Problem with Shortcut dialog box similar to the one shown in Figure 10.4. If this is the correct target, click Fix it to update the shortcut. If you prefer to get rid of the shortcut, click the Delete it button, instead.

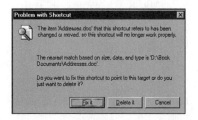

Figure 10.4
You see this dia-
log box if
Windows
Millennium isn't
quite sure that it
has found the file.

Some Unauthorized Shortcut Tricks

Shortcuts are relatively straightforward to work with, but there are still a few items in the "Unauthorized Bag of Tricks" that you might consider using. The next three sections show you how to view shortcut file extensions, tell Windows Millennium not to include Shortcut to in the shortcut filename, and tell Windows Millennium not to use the icon arrow.

Viewing Shortcut Extensions

You saw earlier that the Registry's shortcut file type key—HKEY_CLASSES_ROOT\lnkfile—contains a setting named NeverShowExt. The presence of this setting tells Windows Millennium not to display the extension for any Windows shortcut file, even if file extensions are activated globally.

If you want to see the lnk extension in a shortcut's filename, change the name of this setting to AlwaysShowExt. Note that this tells Windows Millennium to display the extension for any

Watch Out!
Windows
Millennium won't
find the file if you
moved it off your
hard disk (for
example, to a
removable drive or
a network drive).

Windows shortcut file, even if file extensions are hidden glob-ally.

Note, too, that if you want to see the pif extension for a DOS PIF shortcut, head for HKEY_CLASSES_ROOT\piffile and rename the NeverShowExt setting to AlwaysShowExt.

In both cases, you must exit and restart Windows Millennium to put the change into effect.

Disabling the Shortcut to Text

When you create a shortcut, Windows Millennium names the shortcut file Shortcut to *object*, where *object* is the name of the target. Many people prefer to delete the extraneous Shortcut to text. Rather than doing this every time, you can save some work by telling Windows Millennium not to add the Shortcut to text. You can do this either via the Registry or via Tweak UI.

Inside Scoop

When you view the link setting originally, it will likely have a value such as 16.00 00 00. The link set-ting is a hexadeci-mal value that tracks the Shortcut to text. When you create a shortcut, this value is incre-mented by 1; when you delete the Shortcut to text, this value is decremented by 5. When the value reaches 0, Windows Millennium auto-matically stops adding the Shortcut to text.

To do it in the Registry, load the Registry Editor and head for the following key:

```
HKEY_CURRENT_USER\Software\Microsoft\Windows\CurrentVersion
\Explorer
```

Change the value of the link setting to 00 00 00 00 and then exit and restart Windows Millennium. (Note that Windows Millennium doesn't create the link setting until you create your first shortcut. Therefore, if you don't see this setting, go ahead and create a new binary setting and give it a value of 0.)

To do the same thing with Tweak UI, follow these steps:

1. Open Tweak UI from the Control Panel.

2. Display the Explorer tab.

3. Deactivate the Prefix "Shortcut to" on new shortcuts check box.

4. Click OK.

Note that the Tweak UI doesn't require you to exit and restart Windows.

Customizing the Shortcut Icon Arrow

Besides adding the Shortcut to text to the filename, Windows Millennium also indicates a shortcut by overlaying a small arrow in the lower-left corner of the target's default icon. You can customize this arrow either by choosing a different overlay icon or by telling Windows Millennium not to use any overlay.

To specify a different icon, open the Registry Editor and select the following key:

```
HKEY_LOCAL_MACHINE\Software\Microsoft\Windows\CurrentVersion
\explorer\Shell Icons
```

You'll see in Chapter 17 that you change a system icon by creating a new setting in this key, and giving the setting the same name as the icon's position within `Shell32.dll`. The default shortcut icon overlay is the 29th icon in `Shell32.dll`, so create a new string value named `29`. Change this setting to the full pathname of the icon file you want to use, followed by the position of the icon within that file. Here's an example:

→ **See Also** "Customizing Windows Millennium's System Icons," **p. 396.**

```
c:\windows\system\shell32.dll,30
```

If you don't want Windows Millennium to use any overlay, open the Registry's shortcut file type keys— `HKEY_CLASSES_ROOT\lnkfile` for a Windows shortcut, and `HKEY_CLASSES_ROOT\piffile` for a DOS shortcut—and rename the `IsShortcut` setting.

Once again, Tweak UI can help with these customizations:

1. Open Tweak UI from the Control Panel.

2. Display the Explorer tab.

3. In the Shortcut overlay group, select one of the following options:

   Arrow—This is the default shortcut arrow.

   Light arrow—This is an alternative arrow overlay that comes with Tweak UI.

   None—Select this option to get rid of the overlay.

Remember
To put the new overlay icon into effect, you have to refresh the `ShellIconCache` file. See Chapter 17 to learn how to do this.

Custom—Select this option to display the Change Icon dialog box and select the new overlay.

4. Click OK. The new setting goes into effect immediately.

Getting the Most out of Shortcuts

So far, I've concentrated mostly on creating shortcuts to files—either application executables or documents. However, Windows Millennium supports shortcuts to all kinds of other objects, and you should be familiar with these techniques to wring the most out of your shortcuts. Here's a look at the other kinds of objects you can work with:

Document scraps—A *document scrap* is a shortcut to a section of text or an image. To create the scrap, highlight the data in the source application, drag the data, and then drop it where you want the scrap to appear. (If you can't drop the data, that means the application doesn't support scraps.) When you double-click the scrap, the source application opens and loads the data. Note that this works only for applications that support object linking and embedding.

Folders—You create shortcuts to folders just as you do any nonexecutable file. (That is, you must either hold down Ctrl+Shift while you drag the folder, or else right-drag the folder.)

Disk drives—You can create a shortcut for each disk drive on your system. This gives you quick access to the drive you want, and also enables you to perform some disk-related operations directly from the shortcut. For example, you can right-click a floppy disk drive shortcut and then click Format to format the disk that's currently in the drive. Note that the default drag operation for disk drives is to create a shortcut.

Network computers—You can create a shortcut for any computer that appears in the My Network Places folder. If you connect to your network remotely, launching the shortcut invokes Dial-Up Networking automatically. The default

Inside Scoop
By default, Windows Millennium displays folder shortcuts in the single-paned My Computer view. If you prefer the two-paned Windows Explorer view, open the folder shortcut's property sheet. In the Target text box, add `explorer.exe /e`, before the folder name (for example, `explorer. exe /e, "C:\My Documents"`).

drag operation for network computers is to create a shortcut.

Printers—If you create a shortcut to a printer, you can drag a document and drop it on the printer shortcut. Windows Millennium then prints the document without further prompting. The printer shortcut also gives you quick access to the printer's queue, which means you can easily double-click the shortcut to make changes to pending print jobs. The default drag operation for printers is to create a shortcut.

Dial-Up Networking connections—Creating a shortcut to a Dial-Up Networking connection means you can establish the connection by launching the shortcut, and thus avoiding the Dial-Up Networking folder. To create these shortcuts, you must either hold down Ctrl+Shift while you drag the connection, or else right-drag the connection.

Control panel icons—If you have some Control Panel icons you use regularly (such as Tweak UI), create a shortcut on the desktop or Start menu. The default drag operation for Control Panel icons is to create a shortcut. I showed you a few other methods for accessing Control Panel icons in Chapter 3, "An Insider's Guide to Four Crucial Configuration Tools."

➔ **See Also** "Controlling the Control Panel," **p. 84.**

Email recipients—If you have a few people to whom you regularly send email messages, creating a shortcut for each person enables you to send messages without having Outlook Express running. To set this up, create a new shortcut and use `mailto:address` as the command line, where `address` is the recipient's email address (for example, `mailto: paul@mcfedries.com`).

Web sites—Shortcuts to Web sites give you quick access to sites you visit often. To create a shortcut for the current page in Internet Explorer, either select File, Send, Shortcut to Desktop, or right-click the page and then click Create Shortcut. (You can also drag the URL icon shown in the

Address bar and drop it where you want the shortcut created.) To create a Web site shortcut from a link, drag the link and drop it on the destination.

Essential Information

- A shortcut is a pointer to a program, document, or other target that gets launched automatically when you open the shortcut.

- Windows shortcuts use the lnk extension, whereas DOS shortcuts are program information files (PIFs) that use the pif extension.

- Dragging and dropping an executable file (exe or com extension) automatically creates a shortcut.

- For nonexecutable files, either hold down Ctrl+Shift while dragging the file, or else right-drag the file.

- Right-click a shortcut file and then click Properties to customize the shortcut's icon or target, or to set up a shortcut key.

- You can create shortcuts to document scraps, folders, disk drives, network computers, printers, Web sites, and more.

PART IV

Windows Millennium Performance Tuning and Troubleshooting

Getting the Most out of Your Applications

Chapter 11

IT'S A RARE (and no doubt unproductive) user who does nothing but run Windows on her computer. After all, after Windows starts, it doesn't do much of anything. No, to get full value for your computing dollar, you have to run an application or two. As an operating system, it's Windows' job to help make it easier for you to run your programs. Whether it's loading them into memory, managing their resources, or printing their documents, Windows has plenty to do behind the scenes. Windows Millennium also comes with a few tools and techniques that you can use to make your applications run faster and more reliably. In this chapter, you'll learn how to install applications safely, how to launch applications, how to switch between running programs, and how to uninstall applications you no longer need.

Installing Applications Safely

Outside of hardware woes and user errors (see the Quote sidebar next to this paragraph), most computer problems are caused by improperly installing a program or installing a program that doesn't mesh correctly with your system. It could be that the installation makes unfortunate changes to your configuration files, or that the program replaces a crucial system file with an older version, or that the program just wasn't meant to operate on (or wasn't tested with) a machine with your configuration.

An Installation Safety Checklist

Whatever the reason, you can minimize these kinds of problems by following a few precautions before installing a new software package. Here's a checklist:

- **Have a bootable disk ready**—If a program installation creates a big enough mess, you might not be able to restart your computer. In that case, you'll be glad you have a bootable floppy disk that will give you control of your machine once again. See Chapter 15, "Preparing for Trouble."

→ **See Also** "Putting Together an Emergency Boot Disk," p. 347.

- **Examine `readme.txt` Text Files**—Most programmers hate to write, so if your application comes with a `readme.txt` file or some other "read me first" material, chances are it contains important information. For example, this kind of documentation often tells you what you need to do to prepare for the installation, what the program will alter on your system, program changes that went into effect after the manual was produced, and so on.

- **Back up your data files**—If the program is an upgrade, make backup copies of all your data files. Many upgrades include new file formats for documents created with the program. These upgrades are usually upward compatible (the upgrade can read documents that use an older file format), but rarely downward compatible (previous versions of the software can't work with the new file format). Having backup copies of files in the old format will ensure that you can still use your documents in the event that you uninstall the program.

- **Back up your configuration files**—Installation programs can cause all kinds of trouble by making imprudent changes to your system's configuration files. Therefore, always back up the Registry, Win.ini, and System.ini.

→ **See Also** "Using the Registry Checker," **p. 65.**

- **Check downloaded programs for viruses**—If the program you're about to install was downloaded from the Internet or an online service, use a virus checker to examine the installation files for viruses.

- **Always run "custom" installations**—Most install programs offer you both a "typical" installation and a "custom" installation. The typical option installs the program with just the default options and little interaction. The custom option usually enables you to control many aspects of the installation, including where the files are stored, which program options are installed, whether configuration files are updated automatically, and so on. The custom route is more work, but it's always better to have the extra control.

Another safe setup technique I recommend is to compare the contents of some folders before and after the installation. Windows programs like to add all kinds of files to the Windows and Windows\System folders. To troubleshoot problems, it helps to know which files were installed.

To figure this out, write directory listings for both folders to text files. The following two DOS statements use the DIR command to produce alphabetical listings of the Windows and Windows\System folders and redirect (using the > operator) these listings to text files:

```
dir c:\windows /a-d /on /-p > c:\windir.txt
dir c:\windows\system /a-d /on /-p > c:\sysdir.txt
```

After the installation is complete, run the following commands to save the new listings to a second set of text files:

```
dir c:\windows /a-d /on /-p > c:\windir2.txt
dir c:\windows\system /a-d /on /-p > c:\sysdir2.txt
```

The resulting text files are long, so comparing the before and after listings is time-consuming. To make this chore easier, use the DOS FC (File Compare) command. Here's the simplified syntax to use with text files:

Shortcut
The easiest way to back up all your configuration files is to use Windows Millennium's Registry Checker. I showed you how to use this utility in Chapter 3, "An Insider's Guide to Four Crucial Configuration Tools."

Remember
How you get to the DOS prompt has changed slightly in Windows Millennium. To get there, you now have to select Start, Programs, Accessories, MS-DOS Prompt. (In Windows 9x, the MS-DOS Prompt command was on the Programs menu.)

```
FC /L filename1 filename2
```

/L	Compares files as ASCII text.
filename1	The first file you want to compare.
filename2	The second file you want to compare.

For example, here's the command to run to compare the files sysdir.txt and sysdir2.txt that you created earlier:

```
fc /l c:\sysdir.txt c:\sysdir2.txt > fc-sys.txt
```

This statement redirects the FC command's output to a file named fc-sys.txt. Here's an example of the kind of data you'll see in this file when you open it in Notepad:

```
Comparing files sysdir.txt and sysdir2.txt
****** c:\sysdir.txt
FILESEC   VXD       21,449   03-14-00   8:29a FILESEC.VXD
FIOLOG    VXD       10,732   03-14-00   8:29a FIOLOG.VXD
****** c:\sysdir2.txt
FILESEC   VXD       21,449   03-14-00   8:29a FILESEC.VXD
FINDFAST  CPL       40,960   02-10-99  11:48a FINDFAST.CPL
FIOLOG    VXD       10,732   03-14-00   8:29a FIOLOG.VXD
******
```

In this case, you can see that a file named FINDFAST.CPL has been added between FILESEC.VXD and FIOLOG.VXD.

Installing the Application

After you've run through this checklist, you're ready to install the program. Here's a summary of the various methods you can use to install a program in Windows Millennium:

Add/Remove Programs wizard—This wizard is the standard Windows Millennium method for installing all types of applications, but it requires too many steps for it to be practical. To use this wizard, select Start, Settings, Control Panel and then open the Add/Remove Programs icon. In the Add/Remove Programs Properties dialog box, display the Install/Uninstall tab and then click Install. The wizard's dialog boxes lead you through finding the installation program and launching it. The wizard departs at this point and you follow the installation program's instructions.

AutoPlay install—If the program comes on a CD that supports AutoPlay, it's likely that the installation program will launch automatically after you insert the disc into the CD-ROM drive. To prevent the install program from launching automatically, hold down the Shift key while you insert the disc.

Run `setup.exe`—For most applications, the installed program is named `setup.exe` (sometimes it's `install.exe`). Use Windows Explorer to find the install program and then double-click it. Alternatively, select Start, Run, enter the path to the `setup.exe` file (such as `e:\setup`), and click OK.

Decompress downloaded files—If you downloaded an application from the Internet, the file you receive will either by an `.exe` file or a `.zip` file. Either way, you should always store the file in an empty folder just in case it needs to extract files. You then do one of the following:

- If it's an `.exe` file, double-click it; in most cases, the install program will launch; in other cases, the program will extract its files and you then launch `setup.exe` (or whatever).

- If it's a `.zip` file, double-click it and Windows Millennium will open a new *compressed folder* that shows the contents of the `.zip` file. If you see an installation program, double-click it. It's more likely, however, that you won't see an install program. Instead, the application is ready to go and all you have to do is extract the files to a folder and run the application from there.

Install from an INF file—Some applications (such as the Tweak UI utility discussed in Chapter 3) install via an information (`.inf`) file. To install these programs, select the Windows Setup tab in the Add/Remove Programs

Watch Out!
The wizard finds the installation program only if it exists in the CD's root folder. If the wizard fails to find the program, it may be because the program resides in a sub-folder (look for a subfolder named Setup or Install).

Shortcut
An easier way to install from an .inf file is to right-click the file and then click Install in the shortcut menu that appears.

Properties dialog box, and then click Have Disk. In the Install from Disk dialog box, enter the path of the folder containing the .inf file and click OK. You should now see a Have Disk dialog box with a list of components to install. Activate the check boxes for the components you need, and then click Install.

→ **See Also** "Installing and Running Tweak UI," **p. 82.**

Applications and the Registry

I mentioned in Chapter 3 that the Registry is perhaps Windows Millennium's most important component because it stores thousands of settings that Windows needs. The Registry is important for your applications, as well, because most Windows applications (particularly those designed for Windows 9x or Windows Millennium) use the Registry to store configuration data and other settings.

When you install an application, it typically makes a half dozen different Registry modifications:

- Program settings

- User settings

- File types

- Application-specific paths

- Shared DLLs

- Uninstall settings

Program Settings

Program settings are related to the application as a whole: where it was installed, the serial number, and so on. The program settings are placed in a new subkey of HKEY_LOCAL_MACHINE\Software:

HKEY_LOCAL_MACHINE\Software\Company\Product\Version

Here, `Company` is the name of the program vendor, `Product` is the name of the software, and `Version` is the version number of the program. Here's an example for Office 2000:

`HKEY_LOCAL_MACHINE\Software\Microsoft\Office\9.0`

User Settings

User settings are user-specific entries, such as the user's name, preferences and options the user has selected, and so on. The user   settings   are   stored   in   a   subkey   of `HKEY_CURRENT_USER\Software`:

`HKEY_CURRENT_USER\Software\Company\Product`

File Types

File types refers to the file extensions used by the program's documents. These extensions are associated with the program's executable file so that double-clicking a document loads the program and displays the document. The extensions and file types are stored as subkeys within `HKEY_CLASSES_ROOT`. (See Chapter 9, "Powerful Techniques for File Types," for details.)

If the application comes with OLE support, it will have a unique *class ID*, which will be stored as a subkey within `HKEY_CLASSES_ROOT\CLSID`.

Application-Specific Paths

In computing, a *path* is a listing of the folders that the operating system must traverse to get to a particular file. Windows Millennium uses a variation on this theme called *application-specific paths*. The idea is that if you enter only the primary name of a program's executable file in the Run dialog box (select Start, Run), Windows Millennium will find and run the program. For example, WordPad's executable file is `Wordpad.exe`, so you enter `wordpad` in the Run dialog box and WordPad opens.

Windows finds the program because the application's executable file is associated with the particular path to the folder in which the file resides. These application-specific paths are set up in the following key:

Remember
A file's *primary name* is the part of the filename to the left of the period (.). For example, the primary name of the file Excel.exe is excel.

Undocumented
It's possible to set up your own application-specific paths. Just add a new subkey to the AppPaths key, and name it whatever word you want to use to launch your application, followed by .exe. In this new subkey, open the Default setting and enter the full pathname of the executable file that runs the application.

`HKEY_LOCAL_MACHINE\Software\Microsoft\Windows\`
`CurrentVersion\AppPaths`

Each application that supports this feature adds a subkey that uses the name of the application's executable file (for example, `Wordpad.exe`). Within that subkey, the value of the `Default` setting is the full pathname (drive, folder, and filename) of the executable file. Note, too, that many applications also create a `Path` setting that specifies a default folder for the application.

Shared DLLs

It's common for multiple applications to share a common DLL (dynamic link library) file. Windows Millennium uses settings in the following key to keep track of how many applications are sharing a particular DLL:

`HKEY_LOCAL_MACHINE\Software\Microsoft\Windows\`
`CurrentVersion\SharedDLLs`

As you can see in Figure 11.1, the name of each setting is the full pathname of a DLL, and the value is the number of applications that share the file.

Figure 11.1
The SharedDLLs key keeps a running total of the number of applications that share a particular DLL file.

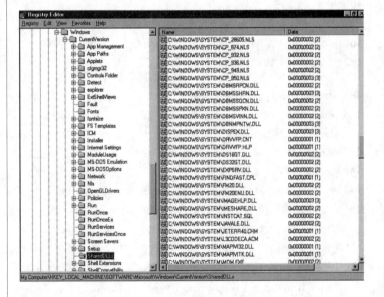

During the installation of most 32-bit applications, the setup program checks to see if any DLLs that it requires are already on the system. If so, it finds the appropriate settings within the SharedDLLs key and increases their values by 1.

Uninstall Settings

Most 32-bit applications also use the Registry to hold data related to uninstalling the application. To store this data, the setup program creates a subkey for the application within the following key:

HKEY_LOCAL_MACHINE\Software\Microsoft\Windows\
CurrentVersion\Uninstall

Launching Applications

Although you'd never know it from the documentation, Windows Millennium rarely gives you just one way to do anything. In fact, most operations have two or three routes you can take. This isn't just mere overkill on Windows' part, because one procedure is usually better than another under a given set of circumstances. For example, a keyboard technique (such as pressing a shortcut key) might be preferred over a mouse technique (such as right-clicking an object) if your fingers are already poised over the keyboard.

Launching applications is a classic example of a destination that has many roads leading to it. That makes sense because not only is launching applications one of the primary jobs of an operating system, but we also have to deal with many different types of applications. Here's a summary of the various Windows methods available for launching applications (you learn some ways to launch programs automatically in the next section):

- **Use the Start menu**—Click the Start button, open menus until you see the item you want, and then click the item.

- **Double-click the executable file**—Use Windows Explorer to find the application's executable file, and then double-click that file.

Undocumented
Theoretically, you could rid your system of unused DLL files by looking in the SharedDLLs key for items that have a value of 0. This is a bit dangerous because not every application supports the SharedDLLs key. However, what you can do is move the DLL files into a floppy disk and then see if any program misses them.

Most of the programs installed on your computer are available from one convenient location—the Programs section of the Start menu.
—*Microsoft*

Remember
If Web integration is activated, you have to only single-click the executable file.

Shortcut
If you have a keyboard with the Windows logo key([wl]), press [wl]+R to open the Run dialog box.

- **Double-click a shortcut**—If a shortcut points to a program's executable file, double-clicking the shortcut will launch the program.

- **Double-click a document**—If you can use the application to create documents (these include word processing files, spreadsheets, graphics, and so on), double-clicking one of those documents launches the program and loads the document automatically.

- **Use the Run dialog box**—Select Start, Run to display the Run dialog box shown in Figure 11.2. Use the Open text box to specify the application (click OK when you're done):

  - If the application resides within the Windows or Windows\Command folder, if it's in your DOS PATH statement, or if it has an application-specific path in the Registry, just type the primary name of the executable file.

  - For all other applications, enter the full pathname (drive, folder, and filename) for the executable file.

  - If you're not sure about the application's executable file, click Browse and then use the Browse dialog box to track down the file you need.

Figure 11.2
Use the Run dialog box to launch a program's executable file.

Run	? X
Type the name of a program, folder, document, or Internet resource, and Windows will open it for you.	
Open: regedit	
OK Cancel Browse...	

- **Use the Quick Launch toolbar**—Windows Millennium's Quick Launch toolbar (to the right of the Start button) offers one-click access for launching programs. I show you how to add your own programs to this toolbar in Chapter 17, "Customizing the Windows Millennium Interface."

→ **See Also** "Customizing the Quick Launch Toolbar," **p. 405.**

■ **Use the Scheduled Tasks folder**—The Scheduled Tasks folder can run programs automatically at a given date and time, or on a regular schedule. See Chapter 14, "Crucial System Maintenance Skills."

→ **See Also** "Automatic System Maintenance with the Scheduled Tasks Folder," **p. 333.**

■ **Enter the executable path at the DOS prompt**—At the DOS prompt, enter the full pathname of the executable file. Note that you need only use the file's primary name if the application resides within the current folder, the Windows folder, or Windows\Command folder, or if it's in your DOS PATH statement.

■ **Use the Start command at the DOS prompt**—To launch Windows applications from the DOS prompt, use the Start command:

START [/M] [/MAX] [/R] [/W] *program*

/M   Starts the application minimized.

/MAX   Starts the application maximized.

/R   Starts the application restored (neither minimized nor maximized); this is the default.

/W   Waits for the application to finish before you're returned to the DOS prompt. This is useful in batch files when you need an operation to complete before continuing with the rest of the batch file. For an example, see Chapter 2, "Understanding and Controlling the Windows Millennium Startup."

→ **See Also** "Controlling Startup Using Msdos.sys," **p. 50.**

program   The full pathname of the program's executable filename. If the application resides within the current folder, the Windows folder, or Windows\Command folder, if it's in your DOS PATH

Watch Out!
To avoid errors when working at the DOS prompt, either use a file's 8.3 filename or else surround the long filename with quotation marks.

Inside Scoop
It's possible to set up your machine to run only certain programs. In the System Policy Editor, open the Registry and then open Local User, Windows Millennium System, Restrictions. Activate Only run allowed Windows applications and then click Show to display the Show Contents dialog box. Click Add, enter the name of the program's executable file, and click OK.

statement, or if it has an application-specific path in the Registry, use the file's primary name only.

Launching Applications Automatically at Startup

Besides all those methods for launching applications by hand, Windows Millennium also offers several techniques for launching applications automatically at startup. The next few sections discuss three methods: the StartUp folder, the Registry, and Win.ini.

Using the StartUp Folder

The idea behind the StartUp folder is that any program or document (or more likely, a shortcut to a program or document) within this folder is launched automatically each time Windows Millennium starts. (If you've used Windows 3.x, you'll recognize the StartUp folder as being the Windows Millennium equivalent of the old StartUp group in Program Manager.)

To add a shortcut to the StartUp folder, follow these steps:

1. In Windows Explorer's Folders bar, display the following folder (see Figure 11.3):

   ```
   Windows\Start Menu\Programs\StartUp
   ```

Figure 11.3
To launch applications automatically at startup, create shortcuts in the StartUp folder.

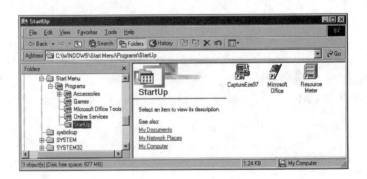

2. Locate the executable file or document you want to launch.

3. Right-drag the file (that is, hold down the right mouse button and drag the file) and drop it on the StartUp folder.

4. In the shortcut menu that appears, click Create Shortcut(s) Here.

Using the Registry

If you have quite a few items in your StartUp folder, you might find yourself often holding down Shift at startup to avoid loading programs from the Startup folder to get Windows Millennium up and running quicker. What do you do, however, if you have one or two items that you *always* need to be launched at startup? In this case, bypassing the StartUp folder is a hassle because it means you have to launch these items by hand. (One way to do this is to select Start, Programs, StartUp and then select the item you want to launch.)

An easier way is to remove those important items from the StartUp folder and put them into the Registry's Run key. Items in this key are also run automatically at startup, but they aren't bypassed when you hold down the Shift key.

Follow these steps:

1. In the Registry Editor, open the following key:

   ```
   HKEY_LOCAL_MACHINE\Software\Microsoft\Windows\
   CurrentVersion\Run
   ```

2. Select Edit, New, String Value.

3. Type a name for the new setting and press Enter. It doesn't matter what name you use, but something descriptive (such as the name of the program) is best.

4. Open this new setting and enter the full pathname of the executable file.

Note, too, that the Run key is also accessible via the System Policy Editor. After you've opened your Registry with System

Shortcut
If you can no longer see the StartUp folder, drag the file to the top of the Folders bar (to scroll the list down) or to the bottom of the list (to scroll up).

Remember
You can avoid loading the StartUp folder items by holding down the Shift key while Windows Millennium starts.

Inside Scoop
Below the Run key you'll see a key named RunOnce. If you place a program in the RunOnce key, it will run automatically the next time you start Windows, and it will then be removed from RunOnce.

Policy Editor, select Local Computer, Windows Millennium System, Programs to Run, Run. Click the Show button to display the Show Contents dialog box, which offers a list of the programs. You can use this dialog box to add and remove startup items.

→ **See Also** "Exporting a Key to a Registration (.reg) File," p. 75.

Using Win.ini

The third and final method for launching applications automatically at startup involves the Win.ini file. If you open this file (which you can do by selecting Start, Run, typing win.ini, and clicking OK), you'll see a line that begins run= near the top of the file. Use this line to add the full pathname of the executable file you want to launch. To include multiple entries, separate each path with a semicolon (;).

Note, however, that this method is obsolete because most applications use either the StartUp folder or the Registry's run key. However, it's good to know about the run= line in Win.ini just in case you're trying to track down a program that starts automatically on your system.

Switching Between Running Applications

I'm sure the vast majority of Windows users are into *multitasking*, which means having multiple programs open at the same time. Most of those users will typically have two or three programs running all the time. Having said that, I think it's also true that few Windows users regularly run more than four or five applications at a time. Windows Millennium's unfortunate resource limitations (discussed in Chapter 12, "Maximizing Your System's Memory") guarantee that you can't run a large number of applications at once for very long.

→ **See Also** "Tracking and Optimizing System Resources," p. 294.

Of course, multitasking is useful only as long as you can switch easily and quickly from one program to another. Windows Millennium offers four ways to do this:

- If you can see part of the window you want, use your mouse to click inside that window.

- Click the application's taskbar button.

- Hold down Alt and press the Tab key. Windows Millennium displays a box showing an icon for each running program. With each press of the Tab key, Windows Millennium highlights the next icon in the list. When the icon that represents the program you want is highlighted, release Alt.

- Hold down Alt and press the Esc key. This is the same as Alt+Tab, except in this case Windows Millennium cycles through the running applications by displaying each application's window. When you see the window you want, release Alt.

Uninstalling Applications

There's no law that says humans and software have to get along. You might end up with a program that doesn't do what you want, is too buggy or slow, or takes up too much hard disk real estate. In that case, the best approach is to uninstall the program and get on with your life.

Using Add/Remove Programs to Uninstall 32-Bit Applications

I mentioned earlier that most 32-bit programs add uninstall data to the Registry in the following key:

```
HKEY_LOCAL_MACHINE\Software\Microsoft\Windows\
CurrentVersion\Uninstall
```

Each application adds its own subkey that includes two settings: DisplayName—the name of the application—and UninstallString—the command that Windows Millennium must run to start the uninstall process.

All this means that you can remove these programs from your system by following this simple procedure:

1. Select Start, Settings, Control Panel to open the Control Panel folder.

Undocumented
When you attempt to uninstall an application, you might receive an error message that tells you the Uninstallation has been cancelled. This likely means that the program has already been uninstalled manually. Head for the Uninstall key in the Registry and then delete the subkey for the application. This removes the application from the uninstall list in Add/Remove Programs.

2. Launch the Add/Remove Programs icon. As you can see in Figure 11.4, the bottom part of the Install/Uninstall tab lists the programs and features that can be uninstalled (note that your system will almost certainly display a different list of programs than the one shown in Figure 11.4):

Delete Windows Millennium uninstall information—This item refers to the system files that you saved from your previous version of Windows or DOS. If you remove this item, you won't be able to run Windows Millennium's automatic uninstall feature.

Uninstall Windows Millennium—This item runs the Windows Millennium uninstall feature and will be present only if you upgraded to Windows Millennium.

All others—Everything else in the list is a program or component that can be uninstalled automatically.

Figure 11.4
The Install/
Uninstall tab lists
the programs that
you can uninstall
automatically.

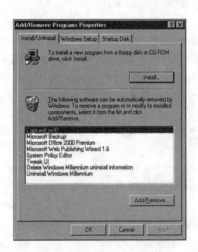

3. Highlight the item you want to uninstall, and then click Add/Remove. Windows Millennium launches the uninstall program.

4. Some applications (such as older versions of Microsoft Office) might ask that you insert their source CD at this point. Follow the instructions onscreen.

5. If the uninstall program asks if you're sure you want to remove the program, click Yes.

6. The uninstall program decrements the appropriate setting in the Registry's SharedDLLs key for each DLL used by the application. If the usage counter for a DLL is now 0, you'll see a dialog box asking if you want to remove the DLL file, as shown in Figure 11.5. If you're certain that the DLL was used only by the application you're removing, click Yes. If you're not sure, click No. (How can you be sure? The only way is if you compared the Windows and Windows\System folders before and after the install, as I described earlier.)

Figure 11.5
You'll see this dialog box if a DLL's usage is down to 0 in the SharedDLLs Registry key.

7. When the uninstall is complete, restart your computer. (This is not strictly necessary in most cases, but it's a good idea, particularly if device drivers and other system files were involved in the uninstall.)

Uninstalling 16-Bit Applications by Hand

16-bit Windows programs don't know about the Uninstall Registry key, so they can't be removed using Add/Remove programs. If the program doesn't come with its own uninstall tool, you have to remove the program from your system by hand.

The first step is to figure out which files to delete. If the program installed all its files into its own folder, then you need look no further. On the other hand, many 16-bit Windows programs add a number of support files to the Windows folder and the Windows\System folder.

Earlier I mentioned that you should save DIR command listings before and after installing an application. If you did that, then you know which files the program installed. Otherwise, you have to do some detective work.

Watch Out!
It's possible that a DLL with a usage counter of 0 could still be used by another program, particularly a 16-bit program that doesn't know about the SharedDLLs Registry key. A better approach would be to make a note of the DLL's filename, click No, and then move the DLL to another folder. If none of your programs misses the file after a while, it's safe to delete it.

One of the best ways to determine which files a program uses is the Quick View utility that came with Windows 9x. (It's not part of the Windows Millennium package, so it will be on your system only if you upgraded from Windows 9x.) This program is normally used to examine what's inside a document without having to open (or even install) the original application. However, it also works for executable files:

1. In Windows Explorer, find the program's executable file.

2. Highlight the executable file and select File, Quick View. (You can also right-click the file and click Quick View in the shortcut menu.)

3. Scroll down until you find a section called either `Imported-Name Table` or `Import Table`. This section provides a list of the DLLs that the program uses, as shown in Figure 11.6. (Note that, in some cases, just the file primary names are shown.)

Figure 11.6
Use Quick View to see a list of the DLLs that a program uses.

4. Make a note of the DLL filenames.

5. Only some of these DLLs will be specific to the program. Others will be common DLLs used by other applications. Here are three ways to tell the difference:

   - Check the Registry `SharedDLLs` key to see if any of the listed DLLs are being used by other applications.

- The files for most applications have a common date and time stamp. See if the listed DLLs use the same date and time stamp.

- The DLLs for some applications often have file-names that begin with the same two or three letters. For example, WordPerfect uses a number of DLLs that begin with the letters WP.

Again, if you're not certain whether you can safely delete a DLL, just move it to another folder for now.

If you don't have Quick View, there are other forms of detective work you can use to track down the application's files:

- Look for filenames that suggest the original application. For example, you can be reasonably confident that a file-name beginning with WP is probably a WordPerfect file.

- Display the application's main folder and check the files for a common date and time stamp (particularly the date and time stamp on the application's executable file). Then, use Windows Explorer's Search feature to find all other files with the same date.

- Look for specific filenames in the Win.ini and System.ini files. Many 16-bit applications modify these files, and these modifications often give hints about where certain files were stored.

Here are the steps to follow to delete a 16-bit Windows application by hand:

1. Just in case you decide to reinstall the application down the road, make backup copies of any data files you created using the program.

2. In Windows Explorer, highlight the application's folder in the All Folders list and select File, Delete. Click Yes when Windows Explorer asks you to confirm the deletion.

3. If the application added any submenus or shortcuts to the Start menu, open the Start menu and, for each item

Undocumented
One way to check if other programs use a particular DLL is to run a search for files that reference the DLL. Select Start, Find, Files or Folders to display the Find window. In the Containing text box, type the primary name of the DLL. In the Look in box, type c:\windows. Click Find Now to run the search.

Watch Out!
If you're just not sure about a particular file, especially one in your Windows or Windows\System folder, try moving it to another folder or to a removable disk instead of deleting it outright. That way, if Windows or some application displays an error message complaining about the missing file, you can easily restore it.

added by the application, right-click and then click Delete in the shortcut menu.

4. Use Notepad to open Win.ini and System.ini and remove any traces of the application.

5. The one part of the Registry that 16-bit Windows applications do use is HKEY_CLASSES_ROOT. In the Registry Editor, delete any keys and settings related to the program (file extension keys, file type keys, CLSID keys, and so on).

6. Restart your computer.

Essential Information

- To ensure a safe installation, back up configuration files, read readme.txt files, and perform other preparatory chores before launching an application's setup program.

- Windows Millennium offers quite a number of methods for launching programs, including the Start menu, the Run dialog box, double-clicking the executable file or a document, the Scheduled Tasks folder, and more.

- You have three methods for launching applications automatically at startup: the StartUp folder, the Registry's Run key, and the run= line in Win.ini.

- To switch to another running application, click the window, click the taskbar button, press Alt+Tab, or press Alt+Esc.

- Use Control Panel's Add/Remove Programs icon to uninstall 32-bit applications automatically.

GET THE SCOOP ON...
Understanding Memory Concepts ▪ Optimizing
Memory Configuration ▪ Working with the Windows
Millennium Swap File ▪ Getting the Most Out of
System Resources

Maximizing Your System's Memory

Chapter 12

A LTHOUGH THE FIVE CHAPTERS HERE IN PART IV, "Windows Millennium Performance Tuning and Troubleshooting," all offer valuable performance tips, this chapter covers the most important performance tuning technique: optimizing your system's *random access memory*, or RAM, for short. There are two main reasons why this topic is so crucial:

- When you open an application or a document, the underlying files are copied from the hard disk to RAM. So, in a sense, *everything* you do with a computer happens within RAM.

- Small improvements in RAM usage can lead to significant improvements in performance.

According to the authorized Microsoft party line, there isn't much you can do to improve how Windows Millennium uses memory. Although that's true in many cases, you can use a few "unauthorized" techniques to eke out maximum performance. This chapter gives you both sides of the story.

Memory: The Lifeblood of Your Computer

Why do computers need memory in the first place? Why not run programs and data directly from the hard disk? The answer is simple: *speed*. A typical hard disk has an access time of

> **“**
> Before you install Windows Millennium, make sure your computer meets the following minimum system require-ments:...32MB of RAM. (More memory improves performance.)
> —*Microsoft*
> **”**

285

Remember
The latest main memory chips boast access times as low as 10ns! There are even cache memory chips with access times as low as 2ns.

approximately 12 milliseconds, whereas a typical memory chip has an access time of roughly 60 nanoseconds (ns), or about *20,000 times* quicker! This enormous speed difference is the main reason RAM is such an important performance component.

Before discussing the specifics of Windows Millennium memory management, let's run through a few concepts that you need to know to get through the rest of the chapter.

The Address Space

The individual memory locations within a memory chip can hold a single byte of data. These locations are connected to the microprocessor via *address lines*, each of which carries a single bit: either a low current or a high current. This binary state is represented internally using, naturally enough, the binary number system: 0 for the low current state (off) and 1 for the high current state (on).

Therefore, the total number of possible memory locations— the *address space*—is a function of the number of address lines and these two states. In the simplest case, a machine with only one address line could deal with two memory locations: 0 (when the address line has low current) and 1 (when the address line has high current). Similarly, a system with two address lines could deal with four memory locations: 00 (both lines off), 01 (first line off and second line on), 10 (first line on and second line off), and 11 (both lines on). In general, the total amount of addressable memory is 2 to the power of the number of address lines.

The 8088 processor in the original IBM PC came with 20 address lines, meaning it had an address space of 1,048,576 bytes (2 to the power of 20), or 1MB. The 80386, 80486, and Pentium processor all use 32 address lines, which yields an address space of 4,294,967,296 bytes (2 to the power of 32), or 4GB.

Types of Memory

Your computer actually contains a number of different memory subsystems, all of which come into play when discussing memory optimization. Here's a quick summary of the various memory categories available on a typical system:

Main memory—This is RAM that your system uses for running programs and opening documents. On most systems, main memory consists of one or more *memory modules*, which are circuit boards that contain memory chips. These modules are packaged either as Single In-Line Memory Modules (SIMMs) with chips along one side of the circuit board, or as Dual In-Line Memory Modules (DIMMs) with chips along both sides of the circuit board. The boards plug in to special slots (*banks*) on your system's motherboard.

Disk cache—In computer parlance, a *cache* is a chunk of RAM that stores frequently used data for later use. The idea is that the cache is faster than the source from which the data normally comes, so keeping at least some data within the cache should improve performance. For example, rather than grabbing code and data from the hard disk as it's needed, modern systems make educated guesses about what data might be required in the future. This "popular" data is then stored in a separate section of main memory called the *disk cache*.

Level 1 (L1) cache—As fast as main memory is, it's still slower than the processor. For example, a 60ns access time is equivalent to approximately 16MHz, far slower than the 400MHz to 1GHz processors found on many modern systems. To help ease this bottleneck, most computers now incorporate a RAM cache directly into the processor. This Level 1 cache (L1, for short) uses super-fast (and super-expensive) Static RAM (SRAM) memory that runs as fast as the processor. This cache is used to hold processor instructions and data that would otherwise be accessed from main memory.

Remember
If you're looking to buy more main memory for your computer, make sure you buy the right memory modules. Check your system manual to learn the module size you need (30-pin, 72-pin, or 168-pin), the appropriate RAM access time (such as 70ns or 60ns), and whether you need parity, nonparity, or Error Correcting Code (ECC) modules.

Level 2 (L2) cache—The L2 cache is a secondary processor cache that sits outside the processor. Larger than
the L1 cache (128KB to 512KB versus 16KB to 32KB), the
L2 cache also runs a bit slower, with access times equivalent to the motherboard in which the cache resides (typically 15ns, which is equivalent to about 66MHz). Note,
however, that newer L2 caches reside within the processor
housing, so these models boast access times as low as 5ns
(equivalent to 200MHz).

Virtual memory—If your system has only 32MB or 64MB of
main memory, does that mean your computer's capability
to address up to 4GB of memory is mostly wasted? Not at
all. Your computer can still address memory beyond what
is physically installed. This nonphysical memory is called
virtual memory, and it's implemented by using a piece of
your hard disk that's set up to emulate physical memory.
This hard disk storage is actually a single file called a *swap
file* (or sometimes a *paging file*). When physical memory is
full, Windows Millennium makes room for new data by
taking some data that's currently in memory and swapping
it out to the hard disk.

Determining How Much Memory Is Installed

If you're not sure how much memory you have in your system,
Windows Millennium makes it easy to find out:

- Open the Control Panel's System icon (or right-click My
  Computer and then click Properties). The General tab of
  the System Properties dialog box shows you the number of
  megabytes of RAM on your system.

- Select Start, Programs, Accessories, System Tools, System
  Information to open the System Information utility. Make
  sure System Summary is highlighted at the top of the tree. As
  you can see in Figure 12.1, the right pane shows you the
  number of megabytes on your system.

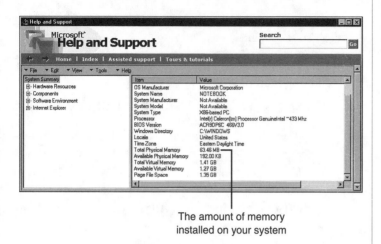

Figure 12.1
The System
Information utility
tells you how
much RAM you
have.

The amount of memory
installed on your system

Restricting Memory Usage

Whatever the amount of RAM you have installed, Windows
Millennium has a feature that enables you to restrict how
much memory is available to the system. Why would you want
to restrict memory usage? Here are three good reasons:

- In the next section, I tell you about some tests that I ran to
  determine whether Windows Millennium has a memory
  "sweet spot," beyond which performance increases only
  marginally no matter how much memory you have.
  Systematically restricting memory usage is a better way to
  test this than adding and removing memory circuit
  boards.

- A fault in physical memory might be causing Windows
  Millennium to throw fatal exception errors. If you restrict
  the amount of memory available to Windows Millennium
  and the problem goes away, then you know you have a
  defective memory chip.

- Many Pentium systems use Intel's 430TX or 430VX
  chipset. Unfortunately, the L2 cache on these chipsets can
  cache data only from the first 64MB of main memory.
  Anything beyond that isn't cached, so installing more than
  64MB of main memory in these systems can actually *reduce*
  performance. In this case, you want to restrict memory
  usage to the first 64MB.

Undocumented
The failure of the
TX and VX
chipsets to cache
memory beyond
64MB is particu-
larly hard on
Windows' perfor-
mance. The rea-
son is that
Windows loads its
files into the top
of memory, so on
a system with
more than 64MB,
the Windows files
don't ever hit the
L2 cache.

Here are the steps to follow to restrict the amount of memory used on your system:

1. Load the System Configuration Utility using either of the following methods:

    * Select Start, Run, type `msconfig`, and click OK.

    * Select Start, Programs, Accessories, System Tools, System Information. In the Help and Support window, select Tools, System Configuration Utility.

2. In the General tab, click Advanced to display the Advanced Troubleshooting Settings dialog box.

3. Activate the `Limit memory to` check box, as shown in Figure 12.2.

Figure 12.2
Use this dialog box to restrict the amount of memory used on your system.

Watch Out!
Even though the `Limit memory to` spinner can go as low as 4MB, Windows Millennium requires 32MB to operate. Therefore, never select a value less than 32MB.

![Advanced Troubleshooting Settings dialog box. It is recommended that only advanced users and system administrators change these settings. Settings: Disable System ROM Breakpoint, Disable Virtual HD IRQ, EMM Exclude A000-FFFF, Force Compatibility mode disk access, VGA 640 x 480 x 16, Enable Startup Menu, Disable Scandisk after bad shutdown, Limit memory to 64 MB (checked), Disable UDF file system. Standby feature is enabled. Hibernate feature is enabled. OK Cancel]

4. Use the spinner to select the maximum number of megabytes you want your system to use.

5. Click OK to return to the System Configuration Utility.

6. Click OK. Windows Millennium asks if you want to restart your computer.

7. Click Yes.

How Much Memory Is Enough?

The Windows documentation laconically states that "More memory improves performance." That seems like an obvious statement, but is it true? That is, if you just keep adding memory, will Windows Millennium's performance improve accordingly?

To test this hypothesis, I ran a series of application benchmark tests using various memory configurations: 32MB, 40MB, 48MB, 56MB, and 64MB. Figure 12.3 shows the results.

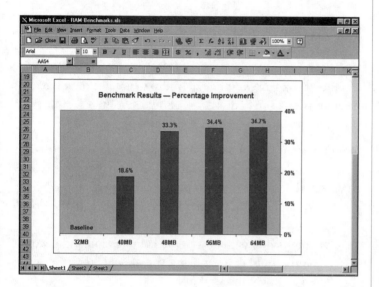

Figure 12.3
Benchmark results for various memory configurations.

As you can see, the answer to the previous questions is "Yes, to a point." That is, Windows Millennium seems to have a memory "sweet spot" that gives you the biggest bang for your memory dollar. Looking at the chart in Figure 12.3, you can see that Windows Millennium's performance improved dramatically by increasing memory from 32MB to 40MB and performance improved less dramatically but still significantly by moving to 48MB. Surprisingly, subsequent memory boosts actually had only a minor effect on performance.

Therefore, on my test system, the memory sweet spot seems to be around 48MB, and that's probably the case on most systems. However, the sweet spot will be higher if you deal with massive databases or immense graphics files that benefit from having access to large amounts of main memory.

Remember
If you want to try your own benchmark testing, Winstone 2000 is an excellent tool. It runs a series of tests using mainstream business applications such as Word, Excel, PowerPoint, WordPerfect, and CorelDRAW. You can find out more by visiting the Ziff-Davis Benchmark Operation at www.zdbop.com.

Managing the Windows Millennium Swap File

No matter how much main memory your system boasts, Windows Millennium still creates and uses a swap file for virtual memory. To maximize swap file performance, you should make sure that Windows Millennium is working with the swap file optimally. Here are some techniques that help you do just that:

Store the swap file on the hard disk that has the fastest access time—You see later in this section that you can tell Windows Millennium which hard disk to use for the swap file. If you have multiple hard disks (not just multiple partitions of a single disk), you should store the swap file on the disk that has the fastest access time.

Store the swap file on an uncompressed hard disk—Windows Millennium is happy to store the swap file on a compressed hard disk (assuming you're using a protected mode compression driver). However, as with all file operations on a compressed disk, the performance of swap file operations suffers thanks to the compression and decompression required. Therefore, you should store the swap file on an uncompressed disk.

Store the swap file on a defragmented hard disk—Windows Millennium can store the swap file in noncontiguous clusters, but the more fragmented the file is, the slower the swap file paging will be. Therefore, always keep the swap file drive defragmented.

Store the swap file on the hard disk that has the most free space—Windows Millennium expands and contracts the swap file dynamically, depending on the system's needs. To give Windows Millennium the most flexibility, make sure the swap file resides on a hard disk that has a lot of free space.

Watch the swap file size—Windows Millennium's System Monitor (choose Start, Programs, Accessories, System Tools, System Monitor) can track the size of the swap file. Select Edit, Add Item, highlight Memory Manager in the

Undocumented
Windows Millennium doesn't include the swap file in its usual defragment process. To defrag the swap file, you must first turn it off. To do so, activate the `Disable virtual memory` check box in the Virtual Memory dialog box (see Figure 12.4 later in this chapter). After you've defragmented the disk, return to the Virtual Memory dialog box and deactivate the check box.

Category list, highlight Swapfile size in the Item list, and then click OK. If you see that this value is approaching the amount of free space left on the disk, you might want to run the Disk Cleanup utility to free up some disk space.

The swap file is named Win386.swp, and it's usually stored in the Windows folder. Here's how to change the hard disk that Windows Millennium uses to store the swap file:

1. If necessary, defragment the hard disk that you'll be using for the swap file. See Chapter 13, "Optimizing Your Hard Disk."

→ **See Also** "Optimizing Disk Access Times with Disk Defragmenter," **p. 310.**

2. Open the Control Panel's System icon to display the System Properties dialog box.

3. Select the Performance tab.

4. Click the Virtual Memory button. Windows Millennium displays the Virtual memory dialog box.

5. Activate the Let me specify my own virtual memory settings option, as shown in Figure 12.4.

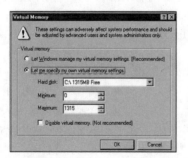

6. Use the Hard disk list to select the hard disk you want to use.

7. Click OK. Windows Millennium asks you to confirm the change.

8. Click Yes to return to the System Properties dialog box.

Inside Scoop
If you hear your hard disk working even when you're not using your computer, that's usually a sign that Windows Millennium is compacting the swap file. It usually leaves that chore until your computer has been idle for a while.

Figure 12.4
Use the Virtual Memory dialog box to select a different hard disk to store the swap file.

9. Click Close. Windows Millennium asks if you want to restart your computer.

10. Click Yes.

In Figure 12.4, you can see that activating the Let me specify my own virtual memory settings option also activates the Minimum and Maximum spinners. Should you bother with those? Some folks think you should. It has become almost conventional wisdom that you should set these two values to 2.5 times the amount of main memory on your system. (For example, on a 32MB system, set them to 80MB each.) The idea is that by doing this, you're telling Windows Millennium to use a fixed-size swap file. Theoretically, this prevents Windows Millennium from having to waste time resizing the file.

Practically, however, this just doesn't work. In my benchmark testing, I've found that doing this actually *decreases* overall performance, albeit slightly. I've found about a 1% performance decrease in a general application benchmark, and about a 3% decrease in a subsystem benchmark. So, this is one of those rare times when the official Windows way is also the right way.

Tracking and Optimizing System Resources

One of the ironies of Windows memory management is that, for many computers, certain small pieces of memory are more important than the entire memory system. These small pieces comprise the *system resources*. They're special memory areas called *heaps* that Windows Millennium uses to store data structures for windows, menus, toolbars, fonts, ports, and more. The irony lies in the frustrating fact that your computer can have megabytes of free memory, but if the system resource heaps reach their limits, your programs might crash and Windows might refuse to run.

The good news is that Windows Millennium's system resource management has been much improved over that of Windows 3.*x*. The latter used four 16-bit heaps that could hold a mere 64KB of data each. By contrast, Windows Millennium mostly uses a single 32-bit heap, which is capable of addressing 2GB.

(For compatibility reasons, Windows Millennium retains one of the old 16-bit heaps.) This enabled the Windows Millennium designers to greatly increase the system resource limits. For example, in Windows 3.*x* you could install no more than 250 or 300 fonts, but with Windows Millennium that number is closer to 1,000.

Besides increasing the heap size, Windows Millennium continues the system resource management improvements that were introduced in Windows 95:

- Windows Millennium monitors and, if necessary, cleans up after 32-bit applications. Windows Millennium examines the heap after a 32-bit program shuts down and then removes any allocated resources that remain on the heap.

- 16-bit applications often intentionally leave some resources allocated after shutdown so other processes can use those resources. This is efficient, so Windows Millennium waits until all 16-bit applications have been closed before it removes allocated resources from the heap.

Unfortunately, all this good news doesn't mean that you never have to worry about system resources. Windows Millennium's system resource limits might be larger and better managed, but they're still limits, nonetheless. On my main computer (which has 128MB of RAM), I still need to reboot every three or four days because Windows Millennium runs low on system resources.

Using the Resource Meter to Track System Resources

I discuss a few ways to keep system resources under control in the next section. For now, let's see how you track the current system resource levels to avoid getting into trouble. The tool to use is the Resource Meter (`Rsrcmtr.exe`), which you launch by selecting Start, Programs, Accessories, System Tools, Resource Meter. The first time you open the utility, a dialog box warns you that the Resource Meter itself uses up some system resources. To avoid being reminded of that obvious fact each

Remember
To get a quick read on the current level of free resources, right-click the desktop's My Computer icon, click Properties, and then display the Performance tab. You can also usually see the current free resources by selecting the Help, About command in most programs.

time you use this tool, activate the Don't display this message again check box, and then click OK.

The Resource Meter adds an icon to the taskbar's system tray. This icon offers a graphical view of the current resource level. The more green you see, the more system resources are available. To get an exact measure, use either of the following techniques:

- Position the mouse pointer over the Resource Meter icon. After a second or two, a banner displays the current resource percentages.

- Double-click the Resource Meter icon to display the dialog box shown in Figure 12.5, which displays the current levels.

In both cases, you see three values:

User—This is the percentage of system resources available in the User heap, which holds the data structures for things such as windows and menus.

GDI—This is the percentage of system resources available in the Graphical Device Interface heaps, which hold the data structures for things such as fonts, pens, and brushes (the latter two are objects the graphics system uses to draw lines and fill interiors).

System—This is the lower of the User and GDI values.

Figure 12.5
You get the current values for the system resources either by hovering over the Resource Meter icon, or by double-clicking the icon.

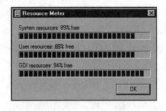

The color of the Resource Meter icon also gives you a clue to the current state of the system resources:

- When the Resource Meter icon is green, you have plenty of system resources available.

- When the Resource Meter icon is yellow, it means that the System value has dropped below about 34%. You should now be cautious about opening more applications and windows, and you might consider trying some of the resource-saving techniques that I discuss in the next section.

- When the Resource Meter icon is red, it means that the System value has dropped to 15% or less. It's time to quit some applications before the meter drops any further.

- If the System value drops to 10% or less, Windows Millennium displays the Low Resources dialog box shown in Figure 12.6. (This warning appears even if the Resource Meter isn't running.) Windows is in imminent danger of running out of resources, which means possible application lockups or a system crash. You should immediately save your work and shut down applications you don't need.

Watch Out!
Unfortunately, the system resources usually don't perform a nice, slow slide into the red territory. Instead, your system often appears stable in the yellow zone and then suddenly "falls off a cliff" and drops dangerously into the red.

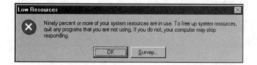

Figure 12.6
This dialog box appears when system resources drop to 10% or less.

Some Ways to Save System Resources

Although you can't prevent Windows Millennium from eventually running out of system resources, you can do some things to stave off the inevitable. Here's a rundown of a few methods that will save and recover system resources:

- Shut down any applications you're not using.

- Many programs use up system resources as you work, and the longer the program is open, the more unnecessary resources are allocated. You can rid the system of these unnecessary resources by exiting and restarting the application.

- Each open document window uses up some resources, so close any documents you don't need.

- Other application features—such as toolbars and status bars—use up resources, so shut down any of these features that you don't use.

- Some applications are huge system resource hogs. Internet Explorer, for example, seems to use an inordinate amount of resources, particularly if it's running for a long time. Keep an eye on your resources as you use your programs to determine which ones seem to use up large amounts of resources. Use those programs as sparingly as possible, and never leave them running for long periods of time.

- Eliminate any startup program or services that you don't need right away.

- Turn off the Active Desktop.

- Don't use wallpaper, animated cursors, or desktop themes.

- Run your DOS applications full-screen instead of in a window.

More Memory Management Techniques

Finding your memory sweet spot and keeping an eye on system resources are good starting points for proper Windows Millennium memory management. Here are a few other techniques to bear in mind:

Shut down unnecessary applications—This is probably the most obvious piece of advice, but it's one that people seem to constantly ignore. For example, many users leave Windows Explorer open all day long even though they might need it only a few times a day. It's much better to restructure the Windows Millennium interface—by, say, rearranging the Start menu and taking advantage of the Quick Launch toolbar—so programs can be launched quickly when you need them.

Don't load unnecessary programs and services at startup— Similarly, don't load up your Startup folder or Run Registry key with applications that run at startup. Use the System Configuration Utility to remove all unnecessary startup items (see Chapter 2, "Understanding and Controlling the Windows Millennium Startup").

→ **See Also** "Controlling Startup Using the System Configuration Utility," **p. 46.**

Keep the Clipboard's contents small—The Clipboard resides in main memory, so anything cut or copied to the Clipboard not only uses up some memory, but it remains in memory until the next time you cut or copy something. If the current Clipboard contains a large image or other object, having it sit there just wastes memory. To clear the Clipboard, either copy a small item (such as a single character), or select Start, Programs, Accessories, System Tools, Clipboard Viewer, and then select Edit, Delete to clear the Clipboard.

Use only minimal network services—If you're running Windows Millennium on a network, use only a single network client and use only the network protocols that you need for network access.

Essential Information

- Windows Millennium can address up to 4GB of memory.

- For memory needs beyond what is physically installed, Windows Millennium uses virtual memory: a hard disk swap file that emulates physical memory.

- Windows Millennium has a memory "sweet spot" that maximizes performance gains. If you add memory beyond that, performance improvements are only marginal.

Undocumented
Exiting a program doesn't always return the system resources to the level they were before you launched the program. That's because Windows Millennium defers initializing some resources (such as fonts) until programs request them. These resources remain allocated after you exit the program. (Remember, too, that resources allocated by 16-bit programs are not freed until you exit all 16-bit programs.)

Undocumented
Another possible waste of system resources occurs when you launch a program and then quit it before it has had time to finish its loading routine. This means that the resources already allocated will usually not be freed. To avoid this, always let a program finish its loading sequence before shutting it down.

- For best virtual memory performance, move the swap file to an uncompressed, defragmented drive that has the fastest access time and the most free space.

- To make the most of Windows Millennium's limited system resources, use the Resource Meter to track the current levels; close applications you don't need; close documents you're not using; turn off toolbars, status bars, wallpaper, and animated cursors; and run DOS programs full screen.

Optimizing Your Hard Disk

I N THE PREVIOUS CHAPTER, you learned that optimizing
Windows Millennium's memory management is crucial
because all your work happens within the confines of memory and you need to take full advantage of the approximately
20,000-fold access time difference between memory and the
hard disk.

However, that's not to say that you should ignore the hard disk
in your quest for maximum performance. The opposite, in
fact, is true:

- All your work may be done in memory, but all that work
  has to be read from the hard disk at some point, and then
  written back to the disk when you're done.

- As explained in the previous chapter, if you run out of
  physical memory, Windows Millennium uses a part of your
  hard disk as virtual memory.

- What hard disks lack in speed (at least compared to RAM),
  they make up for in their capability to act as a permanent
  storage medium for programs and data.

All this means that there are four different optimization categories for your hard disk: speed, reliability, storage capacity,
and storage efficiency. This chapter takes you through several
Windows Millennium techniques for improving hard disk performance in all four categories.

Chapter 13

Examining Hard Disk Properties

A disk drive is an object in Windows Millennium, so it comes with various properties you can examine. These include the disk label, the total capacity of the disk, and the free space on the disk. Windows Millennium offers several methods for examining these properties:

Undocumented
To quickly examine the properties of multiple drives, open the My Computer folder and then select each drive by holding down Ctrl and clicking the drive icons. Then right-click any selected drive and click Properties. The dialog box that appears has a property sheet tab for each drive.

- In Windows Explorer, the Folders list displays the hard disks using their labels followed by the drive letter, such as Boot (C:). If a partition doesn't have a label, Windows Millennium displays Local Disk.

- If you highlight a hard disk in the Folders list, Windows Explorer displays the disk's free space in the status bar.

- If you select My Computer in the Folders list and then highlight a hard disk in the Contents list, the information panel displays the disk's capacity as well as its used and free space, along with a pie chart for the latter two values. (The free space and capacity appear in the status bar, as well.)

- If you right-click a hard disk and then click Properties, Windows Millennium displays the property sheet shown in Figure 13.1. This dialog box shows the disk Label in an editable text box, as well as the disk type, the file system, the used and free space, and the disk capacity. Note, too, that you can click Disk Cleanup to launch the Disk Cleanup utility (see "Using Disk Cleanup to Remove Unnecessary Files," later in this chapter).

Figure 13.1
The property sheet for a hard disk supplies you with disk data such as the label, capacity, and free space.

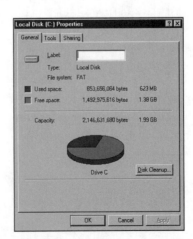

The Tools tab gives you access to two hard disk utilities in the following groups:

Error-checking status—This group deals with ScanDisk. It tells you when you last ran ScanDisk on the hard disk and offers the Check Now button to launch ScanDisk. See "Detecting and Repairing Hard Disk Errors with ScanDisk," later in this chapter.

Defragmentation status—This group deals with the Disk Defragmenter utility. It shows you when you last used the program on the hard disk and offers the Defragment Now button to start the program. See "Optimizing Disk Access Times with Disk Defragmenter," later in this chapter.

Using Disk Cleanup to Remove Unnecessary Files

The easiest form of hard disk maintenance is to delete any file and folder detritus that has accumulated over the years. This frees up disk space, makes your system easier to navigate, and slightly improves hard disk performance.

Windows Millennium comes with a Disk Cleanup utility that enables you to remove certain types of files quickly and easily. Before discussing this utility, let's look at a few methods you can use to perform a spring cleaning on your hard disk by hand:

Uninstall programs you don't use—With the Internet and online services only a modem call away, it's easier than ever to download new software for a trial run. Unfortunately, that also means it's easier than ever to have unused programs cluttering your hard disk. Chapter 11, "Getting the Most out of Your Applications," showed you how to uninstall these and other rejected applications.

→ **See Also** "Uninstalling Applications," **p. 279.**

Delete downloaded program archives—Speaking of program downloads, your hard disk is also probably littered with Zip files or other downloaded archives. For those programs you use, you should consider moving the archive files to a removable medium for storage. For programs you don't use, you should delete the archive files.

Remove Windows components that you don't use—If you don't use some Windows Millennium components, use the Control Panel's Add/Remove Programs icon to remove those components from your system.

Delete application backup files—Applications often create backup copies of existing files and name the backups using either the bak or old extension. Use the Search utility to locate these files and delete them (see Chapter 8, "Expert Windows Explorer Techniques").

➔ **See Also** "Powerful Search Techniques for Finding Files," **p. 219**.

Delete empty files—Your system often accumulates empty files that just take up directory entries unnecessarily. Again, you can use Search to locate these files (click Search Options, activate the Size check box, and set the controls to at most 0KB).

Watch Out!
The Windows Millennium uninstall data is actually spread across multiple files. The best way to remove all this data safely is to run the Control Panel's Add/Remove Programs icon and then select the Delete Windows Millennium uninstall information item.

Delete the Windows Millennium uninstall data—If you upgraded directly from an earlier version of Windows and elected to save your system files during the Windows Millennium installation, Setup stores those files in a hidden file called Winundo.dat in your hard disk's root folder. This file could be over 120MB, so if you're sure you want to stick with Windows Millennium, you should delete the uninstall data.

Before Windows 98, the preceding techniques were the only methods available for cleaning out a hard disk, short of what third-party programs offered. Windows 98 fixed that by offering the Disk Cleanup utility, which can automatically remove some of the preceding categories, as well as several other types of files. It's not the most powerful tool in the world, but it's not bad. Here's how it works:

1. Select Start, Programs, Accessories, System Tools, Disk Cleanup. The Select Drive dialog box appears.

2. Choose the disk drive you want to work with and then click OK. Disk Cleanup scans the drive to see which files can be deleted, and then displays a window similar to the one shown in Figure 13.2.

3. In the `Files to delete` list, activate the check box beside each category of file you want to remove (note that for most of these items you can click View Files to see what you'll be deleting):

> **Temporary Internet Files**—A collection of HTML files, images, and other Web page data that Internet Explorer stores just in case you revisit a Web site. These files are from the `Windows\Temporary Internet Files` folder.

> **Offline Web Pages**—The files that Internet Explorer stores on your system (in the `Windows\Offline Web Pages` folder) if you set up one or more pages as offline favorites. Removing these files prevents you from viewing the pages offline and requires you to resynchronize the pages.

Shortcut
Windows Millennium offers two methods for bypassing the Select Drive dialog box. One is to click the Disk Cleanup button in a disk drive's property sheet (refer to Figure 13.1). The other is to select Start, Run, and enter `cleanmgr /ddrive`, where *drive* is the letter of the drive you want to work with (for example, `cleanmgr /dc`).

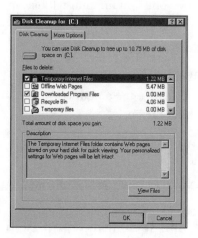

Figure 13.2
Disk Cleanup can automatically and safely remove certain types of files from a disk drive.

> **Downloaded Program Files**—A collection of Java applets and ActiveX controls that were used by some of the Web sites you've visited. These files are from the `Windows\Downloaded Program Files` folder.

Recycle Bin—The collection of deleted files in the drive's Recycle Bin.

Temporary Files—The collection of files in Windows Millennium's `Temp` folder, which is usually `Windows\Temp`. Windows Millennium and most Windows applications use this folder to store working files that they need temporarily. These files are usually deleted either when you shut down the application or exit Windows. Activating this check box only deletes old temporary files that are not currently being used.

Temporary PC Health files—Temporary files created by the various PC Health features, including System Restore and System File Protection (discussed in Chapter 14, "Crucial System Maintenance Skills"). These are usually backup files created during program installations, but the files that get deleted are only those backups that the system no longer needs.

➔ **See Also** "Understanding Windows Millennium's PC Health Features," **p. 337.**

Delete Windows uninstall information—This item represents the Windows Millennium uninstall files mentioned previously.

4. The buttons on the More Options tab enable you to remove Windows Millennium components, uninstall programs, and reduce the amount of disk space used by the System Restore feature.

5. Click OK. Disk Cleanup asks if you're sure you want to delete the files.

6. Click Yes. Disk Cleanup deletes the selected files.

Detecting and Repairing Hard Disk Errors with ScanDisk

Hard disk errors and crashes are unfortunate facts of computing life. Not only can events such as a power surge or an improper shutdown wreak havoc on a hard disk's file system, but most hard disks simply wear out after a few years, the victims of deterioration and the daily grind of constant disk accesses. Here's a rundown of just a few of the maladies that can befall the modern hard disk:

Lost file fragments—The File Allocation Table (FAT, for short; see "Understanding the FAT," later in this chapter) tracks which hard disk clusters belong to which file. If a cluster has a nonzero entry in the FAT, it indicates that the cluster is part of a file. However, if one of those non-zero clusters isn't part of any file's cluster chain, the result is a *lost file fragment* (sometimes called a *lost cluster*).

Cross-linked files—This error occurs when the FAT assigns the same cluster either to two different files or twice to the same file.

Invalid filenames—This error occurs when a filename contains an invalid character.

Invalid dates and times—This error occurs when a file has a date and time stamp that uses an illegal date or time (such as 31/31/00).

Duplicate filenames—This rare error occurs when two or more files in the same folder have the same name.

Invalid DOS name length—This error occurs when the full DOS 8.3 path and name for a file exceeds 66 characters. This is never a problem in a Windows DOS session, but it can lead to errors if you boot to DOS using a floppy disk.

Fortunately, Windows Millennium's ScanDisk utility can check for and fix all these errors. It can also examine the surface of the hard disk to make sure there are no flaws—called *bad sectors*—that could render a file unreadable. If ScanDisk does find such a bad sector, it updates the FAT to mark the flaw so that no file uses the sector for storage.

Here are the steps to follow to run ScanDisk:

1. Select Start, Programs, Accessories, System Tools, ScanDisk. Figure 13.3 shows the ScanDisk window that appears.

Remember
The following characters are illegal in Windows Millennium's long filenames:
~ ' ! @ # $ % ^
& ( ) _ - + = [
] ; ' ,

Actual list is:
\ / : * ? "
< > |

Figure 13.3
Use ScanDisk to
check for and
repair hard disk
errors.

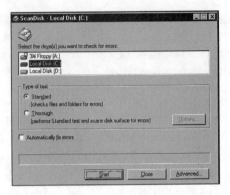

2. Pick out the drive you want to check by highlighting it in
   the Select the drive(s) you want to check for errors list.
   You can select multiple drives, if necessary.

3. Select the Standard option to check just the disk's files and
   folders. If you also want ScanDisk to check the disk surface, activate the Thorough option.

4. If you chose the Thorough scan, the Options button
   becomes available. Clicking this button displays the
   Surface Scan Options dialog box with the following settings (click OK when you're done):

   Areas of the disk to scan—These options tell ScanDisk
   which part of the disk to scan. The *system area* is the
   disk location that stores the master boot record and
   other data structures used by the file system. The *data
   area* is the disk location that stores the files and folders. I recommend activating the System and data areas
   option.

Watch Out!
ScanDisk usually
won't be able to
fix bad sectors in
the system area.
However, it's still
worthwhile to
check this area
because errors
here are indica-
tions that hard
disk failure might
be imminent.

   Do not perform write-testing—To ensure data
   integrity, the surface scan reads whatever data a sector
   contains and then writes it back to the disk. This is a
   good idea, but it can slow down the surface scan. For
   a faster scan, activate this check box. I recommend
   leaving this check box deactivated.

   Do not repair bad sectors in hidden and system files—
   If ScanDisk finds a bad sector where a file is stored, it
   "repairs" the file by moving it to a different location
   on the disk. This can be a problem for some hidden

or system files because applications often expect these files to be in specific disk locations. To avoid these kinds of problems, activate this check box. Note, however, that only very old programs expect system files to be in specific locations, so I recommend leaving this check box deactivated.

5. Click the Advanced button to display the ScanDisk Advanced Options dialog box, which contains the following groups (click OK when you're done):

Display summary—Use these options to determine whether ScanDisk displays a summary of disk statistics and problems repaired at the end of the check.

Log file—These options determine whether and how ScanDisk creates a log that summarizes the errors found and fixed during the check. (The log file is named Scandisk.log, and it's stored in the drive's root folder.)

Cross-linked files—These options specify what ScanDisk does if it comes across any cross-linked files. Note that Make copies is probably your best option because at least one of the files involved probably will remain valid.

Lost file fragments—These options specify the action ScanDisk takes when it discovers a lost file fragment. Select Free to allow other files to use the cluster, or select Convert to files to convert the fragments to files.

Check files for—These check boxes control whether ScanDisk performs the indicated checks.

Check host drive first—If you have a compressed drive on your system, errors on this drive are almost always caused by errors on the uncompressed host drive. Leave this check box activated to have ScanDisk check the host drive before checking the compressed drive.

Report MS-DOS mode name length errors—Activate this check box to have ScanDisk look for DOS names that are too long.

Inside Scoop
If you're running ScanDisk unattended while checking multiple drives, be sure to select Never in the Display summary group. Otherwise, ScanDisk will display the summary after checking the first drive and won't continue until you dismiss the dialog box.

Inside Scoop
The files created from the lost fragments are root folder files with names like File0000.chk and File0001.chk. The latter are almost always unusable, so freeing up the affected cluster is usually the best approach.

6. If you activate the Automatically fix errors check box, ScanDisk repairs any errors it finds by using the options outlined in step 5. This is useful if you'll be running ScanDisk unattended. Otherwise, you should leave this check box deactivated.

7. Click Start to begin the check.

8. If ScanDisk detects a problem, it displays a dialog box to let you know. For example, Figure 13.4 shows the dialog box that appears if ScanDisk finds lost file fragments. Choose the repair option you want and then click OK.

Figure 13.4
ScanDisk displays a dialog box such as this when it comes across an error.

9. When the check is complete, ScanDisk displays a summary. Click OK.

10. Click Close to exit ScanDisk.

Optimizing Disk Access Times with Disk Defragmenter

Undocumented
Fragmented files not only slow disk access, but they also make the disk cache less effective. The cache uses a *read-ahead* technology that assumes the next cluster in the FAT is the one that is most likely to be accessed. This is less likely to be true when files are fragmented.

Except for very small files, most of the files on your hard disk are stored in multiple clusters (called a *cluster chain*), and everything is tracked by the FAT. When you delete a file, the FAT marks that file's clusters as free, and after several deletions, you end up with gaps throughout the FAT. When you save new files (or install a program), the FAT uses these gaps to store the files.

This is an efficient way to work, but it results in *file fragmentation*: files whose clusters are scattered throughout the hard disk. This can drastically reduce disk performance because although it probably takes only about 2ms to read a 4KB cluster, the seek time to another, noncontiguous cluster could take 10- or 12ms.

To optimize disk access, you need to *defragment* your hard disk so that all the files reside in contiguous clusters. Windows Millennium's Disk Defragmenter tool does this by physically rearranging each file's clusters so they're contiguous (and adjusting the FAT accordingly).

Running Disk Defragmenter *Cannot defragment compressed drives.*

Depending on the size and type of hard disk, Disk Defragmenter can take up to several hours to complete its chores, so you should wait until you won't be using your computer for a while before running the optimization. I usually run it overnight. Here are the steps to follow to use Disk Defragmenter:

1. Select Start, Programs, Accessories, System Tools, Disk Defragmenter. The Select Drive dialog box appears.

2. Choose the drive you want to work with by highlighting it within the `Which drive do you want to defragment?` list. To defragment all hard disks, select All Hard Drives at the bottom of the list.

3. To set some Disk Defragmenter options, click Settings to display the dialog box shown in Figure 13.5. You have the following options (click OK when you're done):

   Rearrange program files so my programs start faster—When this setting is activated, Disk Defragmenter arranges the clusters of some application startup files so that they are more easily accessed on the disk. See the following "Understanding the Intel Application Launch Accelerator" section, for details.

   Check the drive for errors—When this setting is activated, Disk Defragmenter runs ScanDisk behind the scenes before it defragments the disk.

   I want to use these options—Use these settings to tell Disk Defragmenter when you want to use the options you've selected.

Shortcut
One way to avoid the Select Drive dialog box is to display the property sheet for the drive you want to defragment, select the Tools tab, and then click Defragment Now. Another way is to select Start, Run, enter `defrag d:` (where *d* is the letter of the drive you want to work with), and then click OK.

Figure 13.5
Use this dialog
box to work with
some Disk
Defragmenter
settings.

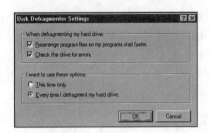

Undocumented
During the defrag-
menting, the Disk
Defragmenter win-
dow displays the
percentage of the
operation that
has been com-
pleted. It might
appear that the
operation is
stalled at 10%.
However, that's
the part
where Disk
Defragmenter
optimizes your
program startup
files, so it's really
not a problem.
After that's done,
the operation pro-
ceeds normally.

4. Click OK. Disk Defragmenter runs ScanDisk (assuming you left the Check the drive for errors setting activated) and then starts defragmenting the drive. If you want to watch the clusters as they're rearranged, click Show Details.

5. When the defragmenting is complete, the program asks if you want to exit. Click Yes to exit, or else click No to optimize another drive.

Understanding the Intel Application Launch Accelerator

When you launch an application, you're running an executable file—generally an .exe or .com file. However, most large applications hoist themselves into memory by also calling a number of other support files, mostly .dll files. Not only that, but programs typically load part of one file, then call another file, load more of the first file, and so on. For example, Word 97 begins by loading winword.exe, which then loads wwint132.dll, then mso97.dll, then mso7enu.dll, then Normal.dot, then more of mso97.dll, and so on.

In other words, defragmenting an application's startup files probably won't produce the fastest load times. For optimal startup performance, it would be better to take all the files that an application uses at startup and then arrange the clusters sequentially—that is, in the order in which they load when you start the application.

That's the premise behind the Intel Application Launch Accelerator (IALA) technology included in Windows Millennium. Each time you start Windows Millennium, a small (28KB) program called Task Monitor (Windows\Taskmon.exe) is loaded into memory automatically via the TaskMonitor setting in the following Registry key:

```
HKEY_LOCAL_MACHINE\Software\Microsoft\Windows\CurrentVersion
\Run
```

Task Monitor runs in the background and watches out for application launches. When it detects an application loading, it monitors the progress of the startup at the cluster level. It then writes the entire launch process to a log file in the hidden Windows\Applog folder. The bulk of the log is stored in a text file with the lgc extension (for example, Winword.lgc), although other files are used as well. Note, too, that Task Monitor also tracks how many times you run each program.

When you run Disk Defragmenter (and assuming you have the Rearrange program files so my programs start faster setting activated), the program examines the Task Monitor's log files and then uses IALA to optimally arrange the clusters of the startup files. Also, programs you launch most often are placed closer to the start of the disk for fastest access.

When the optimization is complete, Disk Defragmenter creates a text file named Optlog.txt in the Applog folder. This file is divided into five sections:

- **Programs Eligible for Optimization**—This section lists all the programs that were optimized. The programs are arranged with the most used at the top, and you get the number of uses, the last time you launched the program, the path of the program's executable file, and more.

- **Maximum Number of Programs Eligible for Optimization Reached**—IALA optimizes only the 50 most-launched programs. All other programs are listed in this section.

- **Programs Ineligible for Optimization**—This section lists the programs that, for one reason or another, could not be optimized. The Flag column displays one or more letter codes that tell you why the program was not optimized.

- **Control parameters**—This section tells you some of the settings that IALA uses:

> **❝**
> The IALA-enabled PC launched all three Microsoft Office applications—Microsoft Word, Microsoft Excel and Microsoft PowerPoint—in approximately 3.2 seconds, compared to 12.3 seconds required to launch the same applications on the PC without IALA technology. —*Rick Coulson, Intel Platform Architecture Lab*
> **❞**

Use app profile—When this is Yes, IALA uses the Task Monitor log to optimize the program.

Minimum log size—This is the minimum size, in bytes, that a log file must be for IALA to optimize the program. The idea here is that a program with a small log file must be loading only a few files at startup, and so wouldn't benefit from optimization. The default value is 1000.

Maximum no use days—This setting is the maximum number of days a program can go unused before it's no longer eli-gible for optimization. The default value is 90.

Maximum apps—This is the maximum number of applica-tions that IALA will optimize. The default value is 50.

- **Flags for Ineligible Programs**—This section gives you a key to the letter codes used in the Flags column of the Programs Ineligible for Optimization section.

Making the Move to FAT32

One of the hidden surprises in the Windows Millennium pack-age is the lack of hard disk support in the DriveSpace disk compression program. The Windows Millennium version com-presses only removable drives.

So, if you want to eke out a bit more disk space on a hard disk partition (and if you've already deleted unnecessary files and programs), your only choice is to turn to the FAT32 file system. As you'll see in this section, FAT32 enables your hard disk to store files more efficiently. This means your existing files take up less room on the disk, thus effectively increasing your disk space. And because the files themselves aren't altered, there's no performance hit. True, FAT32 doesn't net you as much extra disk real estate as DriveSpace did, but FAT32 also brings a few other improvements to the file allocation table, includ-ing support for very large hard disks. The rest of this chapter discusses these advantages and a few disadvantages, and shows you how to convert a hard disk to FAT32.

Understanding the FAT

You don't need to understand how FAT32 works to use it successfully. However, a bit of background on the underlying technology will help you make the decision on whether to convert a disk to FAT32. The next two sections guide you through the inner mysteries of this file system.

When a hard disk is partitioned using the FDISK command, a number of data structures are written to the disk, including the Master Boot Record. When you then format the disk, more data structures are created, including the root directory and the file allocation table (FAT). Besides these *system area* structures, the format also creates a *data area*, which consists of (usually) thousands of *clusters* (the exact number depends on the capacity of the disk).

To keep track of everything on the disk, the file system uses two structures:

- A file directory

- The FAT

A *file directory* is a list of all the files and subfolders within a folder. Each file directory entry is a 32-byte value that tracks the data shown in Table 13.1.

Remember

Clusters (or *file allocation units* as they're often called) aren't the fundamental storage unit on the disk. That honor belongs to the *sectors*, which are 512-byte divisions of the disk's magnetic medium. Because a typical disk has so many sectors (2 million per gigabyte), the file system groups them into clusters, which range in size from 2,048 bytes (four sectors) to 32,768 bytes (64 sectors).

TABLE 13.1: THE DATA TRACKED BY EACH FILE DIRECTORY ENTRY

Data	Size
Primary name	8 bytes
Extension	3 bytes
Attributes (hidden, read-only, and so on)	1 byte
Reserved for future use	6 bytes
Date the file was last modified	2 bytes
Exclusive access handle	2 bytes
Time the file was created	2 bytes
Date the file was created	2 bytes
Starting cluster number in the FAT	2 bytes
File size in bytes	4 bytes

The *FAT* is a database of all the disk's clusters. It contains 16-bit values that track what's in each cluster:

- If the value is 0, it means that no file is using the cluster.

- If the value is nonzero, it means a file is using the cluster. The FAT value is a hexadecimal number that points to the cluster that stores the next part of the file.

- If the value is a special EOF marker, it means the cluster represents the end of a file.

Inside Scoop
The FAT also uses a special value (FFF7 in hexadecimal) to indicate that a cluster has at least one bad sector. Clusters marked with this value are not used to store data.

From all this, you can now deduce how the file system tracks an individual file:

1. The file is located in the file directory.

2. The file's starting cluster number is read from the file directory (see Table 13.1).

3. The cluster number is found in the FAT.

4. If the FAT entry points to another cluster number, repeat step 3.

5. Stop when the FAT entry contains the EOF marker.

The FAT and Cluster Size

The key thing about the FAT is its "16-bitness." 16 bits can be arranged in up to 65,536 ways, which means that no hard disk can have more than 65,536 clusters. How does this jibe with the fact that hard disk partitions capacities range from a few dozen megabytes to a couple of gigabytes? The relationship is simple: The larger the partition, the larger the cluster size, as shown in Table 13.2.

Inside Scoop
Floppy disks and other disks with partitions less than 16MB use a 12-bit FAT with 4,096-byte cluster sizes.

TABLE 13.2: CLUSTER SIZES FOR VARIOUS PARTITION SIZES

Partition Size	Cluster Size
16MB–127MB	2,048 bytes
128MB–255MB	4,096 bytes
256MB–511MB	8,192 bytes
512MB–1,023MB	16,384 bytes
1,024MB–2,047MB	32,768 bytes

Calculating Cluster Slack

Earlier I told you that the FAT maps out a disk at the cluster level, so finer divisions aren't possible. This means that even the smallest file takes up an entire cluster. Similarly, if a file spans multiple clusters, the end of the file could be just a tiny piece that uses up a whole cluster. For example, suppose a partition uses 2,048-byte clusters and you have a 2,049-byte file. The first 2,048 bytes take up one cluster, but that last byte doesn't fit, so it takes up its own 2,048-byte cluster. The difference between the size of a cluster and the amount of data stored in the cluster is called the *cluster slack* (or sometimes the *cluster overhang*).

To see cluster slack in action, open a DOS session and run the following command in any folder:

```
dir /a /ogn /v
```

The /a switch displays hidden and system files, the /ogn switch sorts the listing by name with directories first, and the /v switch initiates verbose mode, which tells you, among other things, the number of bytes allocated to each file. Listing 13.1 shows a partial directory listing for a 2GB partition that uses 32,768-bytes clusters (the last two columns have been deleted to fit the listing on the page).

LISTING 13.1: A DIRECTORY LISTING SHOWING THE CLUSTER SLACK

```
Volume in drive C has no label
 Volume Serial Number is 101B-18F7
 Directory of C:\
File Name        Size        Allocated      Modified

MYDOCU~1      <DIR>                        09-11-00   6:18p
PROGRA~1      <DIR>                        09-11-00   5:53p
RECYCLED      <DIR>                        09-21-00   4:24p
WINDOWS       <DIR>                        09-11-00   5:42p
AUTOEXEC DOS           162      32,768     09-11-00   5:46p
AUTOEXEC BAT           195      32,768     10-14-00  10:47p
COMMAND  DOS        54,645      65,536     05-31-94   6:22a
COMMAND  COM        93,880      98,304     05-11-00   8:01p
```

LISTING 13.1: CONTINUED

```
CONFIG   DOS           177      32,768  09-11-00  5:46p
CONFIG   SYS           230      32,768  10-14-00  3:52p
IO       DOS        40,774      65,536  05-31-94  6:22a
IO       SYS       222,390     229,376  05-11-00  8:01p
MSDOS    DOS        38,138      65,536  05-31-94  6:22a
MSDOS    SYS         1,694      32,768  09-30-00  9:16a
SETUPLOG TXT       121,824     131,072  09-11-00  6:15p
SUHDLOG  DAT         7,798      32,768  09-11-00  6:03p
SYSTEM   1ST       544,800     557,056  09-11-00  6:03p
USBLOG   TXT           120      32,768  10-05-00  8:58a
WINUNDO  DAT     5,407,171   5,439,488  09-11-00  5:53p
WINUNDO  INI       298,320     327,680  09-11-00  5:53p
        16 file(s)      6,832,318 bytes
         4 dir(s)       7,208,960 bytes allocated
                    1,729,495,040 bytes free
                    2,146,631,680 bytes total disk space,
                    19% in use
```

Note, in particular, the difference between the values in the Size and Allocated columns. For example, the AUTOEXEC.DOS file is a mere 162 bytes, but it takes up an entire 32,768-byte cluster, resulting in cluster slack of 32,606 bytes! This means that about 99.5% of that cluster is wasted. On the other hand, the WINUNDO.DAT file is 5,407,171 bytes and is allocated 5,439,488 bytes (166 clusters). The slack is 32,317 bytes. This is nearly an entire cluster, but that represents a mere 0.6% of the total allocated space.

These two extreme examples demonstrate the reality of file storage on FAT partitions: Very small files waste large amounts of space, although very large files waste only small amounts of space. But what about the overall slack on your disk? Here's how to find out this crucial value:

1. In Windows Explorer's Folders list, click the drive you want to work with.

2. Either run the Edit, Select All command, or press Ctrl+A. Windows Explorer selects every object in the Contents list.

3. Right-click any selected object, and then click Properties. Windows Explorer takes a few seconds to perform some calculations and then displays both the size of selected files and the number of bytes they use on the disk. In Figure 13.6, for example, you can see the files in this partition constitute 570,681,764 bytes, but the total number of bytes allocated in clusters is 739,147,776.

Figure 13.6
The property sheet for the selected objects shows you the total size of the objects and the number of bytes allocated in clusters.

4. Subtract the size from the bytes allocated to get the total cluster slack.

5. Divide the slack by the total bytes allocated to get the percentage of wasted space.

In the example shown in Figure 13.6, the slack is a whopping 168,466,012 bytes, or about 160MB! (To get the number of megabytes, divide the value by 1,048,576.) This means that a little more than 23% of the used disk space in this partition is wasted.

In one sense, this is a worst-case scenario because of the 32,768-byte clusters used on this partition. However, the worst case is quickly becoming the most common case because gigabyte-sized partitions (the ones that use 32,768-byte clusters) are becoming the norm. Most multigigabyte hard disks arrive now with multiple 1GB–2GB partitions, so cluster slack is automatically a problem for most people.

Watch Out!
To get a true slack value, make sure Windows Explorer is displaying hidden and system files. Select Tools, Folder Options, display the View tab, and then activate the Show hidden files and folders option and deactivate the Hide protected operating system files check box.

What can be done about this waste? Until recently, your only recourse was to use the DOS command FDISK to divide a drive into smaller partitions that use smaller clusters. However, Windows Millennium offers a much more attractive alternative: FAT32. The next section shows you how FAT32 can help overcome the problem of cluster slack.

What Is FAT32?

Besides wastefully large cluster sizes, the FAT file system has a few other drawbacks:

- The capacity of a FAT partition is limited to 2GB. That limit is derived by multiplying the maximum number of clusters (65,536) by the maximum cluster size (32,768 bytes).

- When you format a disk, the root directory is created in a fixed location. If a bad sector appears within this area, the root directory could be trashed.

- The root directory's fixed location also means the root has a fixed size. For a hard disk, this means the root can't contain more than 512 entries.

FAT32 solves all these FAT16 (as the old file architecture is now called) problems:

Support for partitions larger than 2GB—The "32" in FAT32 tells you that this architecture uses 32-bit values. Six of those bits are reserved for future use, so that leaves 26 bits, or 67,108,864 possible cluster values (2 to the power of 26). Multiplying this by the 32,768-byte cluster limit gives a maximum partition size of 2,199,023,255,552 bytes. This is 2,048GB or 2TB (terabytes).

Dynamic partitioning—Under FAT32, the root folder no longer has a fixed location or a fixed size. This means that it's possible to convert a partition to FAT32 without losing data. Theoretically, it also means you can resize a partition on-the-fly, again without losing data.

Better reliability—The fact that the root directory no longer has a fixed location means that it can be moved to avoid bad sectors. Also, FAT32 maintains backup copies of the FAT and a few other data structures.

What about cluster slack? That's probably the biggest advantage of all because FAT32 has dramatically improved storage efficiency, as attested by Table 13.3.

TABLE 13.3: CLUSTER SIZES FOR VARIOUS PARTITION SIZES IN FAT32

Partition Size	Cluster Size
512MB to 8GB	4,096 bytes
8GB–16GB	8,192 bytes
16GB–32GB	16,384 bytes
Over 32GB	32,768 bytes

As you can see, partitions up to 8GB now use only 4,096-byte clusters, a vast improvement over the 32,768-byte clusters that FAT16 uses in gigabyte-sized partitions.

FAT32 sounds like the cat's pajamas of file systems, but it does have some caveats and disadvantages you should be aware of:

- Other file systems—such as FAT16, NTFS, and HPFS—aren't compatible with FAT32. That is, if you boot to a partition or floppy disk that uses one of these file systems, you won't be able to see any FAT32 partitions on your computer.

- The latter also implies that you can't dual-boot with another operating system if you convert your boot partition to FAT32.

- FAT32 works only on 512MB or larger partitions. (This implies that you can't convert Zip or floppy disks to FAT32.)

- FAT32 works only on uncompressed partitions. If you've compressed a partition using DriveSpace, you won't be able to convert the partition to FAT32.

Remember
Windows 2000 has built-in support for FAT32 partitions.

- After you convert a partition to FAT32, Windows Millennium offers no method for converting it back to FAT16.

- FAT32 slightly changes the structure of the file directory entries shown earlier in Table 13.1. Specifically, the size of the "Starting cluster number in the FAT" entry has been increased from 2 bytes (16 bits) to 4 bytes (32 bits) to allow for the new 32-bit cluster numbers. (To compensate, the number of bytes "reserved for future use" has dropped from 6 to 4.) This means that file system utilities that expect to use the old file directory structure will not work under FAT32.

How Much Disk Space Will You Save?

For most people, the main issue when deciding whether to convert a partition to FAT32 is how much disk space they'll save in the process. That's a tricky question because it depends on the composition of your files. If your system has many large files, you save less space because large files consist mostly of full clusters. If you have many small files, however, you save more disk space because small files create all that wasted space inside relatively large clusters.

These distinctions are crucial when deciding whether to convert your partitions to FAT32. To help take some of the guesswork out of this decision, Microsoft has a small (87KB) program called the FAT32 Conversion Information utility that scans a partition and lets you know how much space you'll gain by converting.

To get this program, you have two choices

- Insert the Windows 98 CD, open the \tools\reskit\ config\ folder, and launch the file named fat32win.exe.

- Download fat32win.exe from the Windows 98 Resource Kit Web site:

  http://resourcelink.mspress.microsoft.com/reslink/win98
  /toolbox/default.asp

Inside Scoop
Many of these FAT32 problems have been solved by third-party partitioning utilities. The best of these utilities is Partition Magic, by PowerQuest Corporation (www.powerquest. com).

Here are the steps to follow to use this program:

1. In the FAT32 Conversion Information window that appears, highlight the drive you want to work with.

2. Select Scan. The program checks the drive and then reports how much disk space you'll save.

3. Click OK. This returns you to the FAT32 Conversion Information window, which shows various disk statistics, including the amount of additional space you'll get.

Converting a Partition to FAT32

If you decide to take the FAT32 plunge, Windows Millennium offers a couple of different methods for performing the conversion. The next two sections discuss those methods.

Using FDISK

FDISK is the command-line partitioning program that has been around since the earliest days of DOS. It's used to set up primary and extended partitions, specify the boot partition, and to set the size of each partition.

Fortunately, the version of FDISK that comes with Windows Millennium has been updated to include FAT32 support. Unfortunately, FDISK is still as destructive as ever. That is, if you use FDISK to repartition your hard disk, you lose all the information on the disk. (In fact, each partition has to be reformatted.) Therefore, go the FDISK route only if you plan on wiping out your disk anyway.

Boot to the DOS prompt, and then type fdisk and press Enter. When FDISK loads, you'll probably see a long message followed by a prompt:

```
Do you wish to enable large disk support (Y/N)..........?
```

This message and prompt appear only if your hard disk's capacity is 512MB or more. If you press **y** and Enter at this prompt, FDISK automatically converts all partitions larger than or equal to 512MB to FAT32.

Shortcut
Before attempting to convert a drive to FAT32, you should check to see if the drive is FAT16 by opening the drive's property sheet.

Using the FAT to FAT32 Converter

If you want to keep your data intact during the conversion to FAT32, you need to use the FAT to FAT32 Converter utility that comes with Windows Millennium. This utility is easy to use and takes only a few minutes.

Although Windows 98 came with both a Windows version and a real mode version of the Converter, Windows Millennium comes with only the real mode version. Therefore, because Windows Millennium no longer supports real mode, you can run only the Converter by using a floppy disk to boot to DOS. Follow these steps to run the conversion:

1. Use your emergency boot disk to boot to the DOS prompt.

2. Assuming Windows Millennium is installed in `c:\Windows`, enter the following two commands:

   ```
   c:
   cd\windows\command
   ```

3. Enter the command cvt *d:*, where *d* is the letter of the drive you want to convert. Windows Millennium displays a warning that older versions of DOS or Windows won't be able to access the drive.

4. Select Continue. The Converter runs through the conversion process. When the conversion is complete, the program displays a dialog box that tells you the conversion was successful.

5. Select OK. Another dialog box tells you that the Converter will reboot your computer.

6. Remove the bootable floppy disk and select OK.

Watch Out!
Although I have never heard of a user losing data during the conversion to FAT32, you should probably assume the worst. Therefore, you should back up the drive before converting it.

Essential Information

- The property sheet for a disk drive tells you the disk's label, the amount of free and used space, and the total capacity of the disk. It also provides shortcuts to Disk Cleanup, ScanDisk, and Disk Defragmenter.

- The Disk Cleanup utility offers an easy method for ridding your system of temporary local files, temporary Internet files, downloaded controls and applets, Recycle Bin files, and more.

- To ensure the good health of your hard disk, run ScanDisk regularly to look for lost file fragments, cross-linked files, bad sectors, and other disk errors.

- Disk Defragmenter improves hard disk access times by rearranging file clusters so that they're contiguous.

- The file allocation table (FAT) is a database of all the clusters on a disk. From the FAT's perspective, a cluster is the smallest unit of storage on the disk, so files that don't fill in an entire cluster create wasted space called cluster slack. The larger the partition, the larger the cluster size, and the greater the amount of cluster slack.

- FAT32 reduces cluster slack by using 4,096-byte clusters on partitions up to 8GB. FAT32 also supports partitions up to 2TB and improves the reliability and flexibility of the root directory.

Undocumented
Iomega Jaz drives come in 1GB and 2GB sizes, so they're candidates for FAT32. To run the conversion, however, you must make sure that the drive supports *Interrupt 13* BIOS calls. In the Control Panel, launch the System icon and then select the Device Manager tab. Open the Disk drives branch, highlight the Jaz drive, and then click Properties. In the Settings tab, make sure the Int 13 unit check box is activated.

GET THE SCOOP ON...
Getting In-Depth Information About the Hardware and
Software Components on Your System ▪ Checking for System
Files That Have Been Corrupted, Changed, or Deleted ▪
Making Your System More Robust by Resolving System File
Conflicts ▪ Protecting Your Computer from Viruses

Crucial System Maintenance Skills

Chapter 14

W HEN YOU ATTEND MICROSOFT-RELATED conferences
and trade shows, the official Windows world view is
a pleasant one where systems are up "24/7" and bad
things never happen. However, this "don't worry, be happy"
attitude is belied by the fact that Windows Millennium ships
with over two dozen maintenance, information, and troubleshooting tools.

It's a good thing Windows Millennium has all those tools, too,
because in the real world, bad things can and do happen.
Luckily, a few of those Windows Millennium system tools
enable you to perform important maintenance tasks that can at
least help you stave off trouble. This chapter discusses the
System Information and File Information utilities, the
Scheduled Tasks folder, System File Protection, and System
Restore. You'll also learn about the Windows Update Web site
and Windows Millennium's new AutoUpdate feature.

Getting the Big Picture: Windows Millennium Information Utilities

Let's begin by looking at a couple of programs—System
Information and File Information—that aren't maintenance
tools, per se. Instead, they're information tools that provide
you with data that's useful for troubleshooting problems or
understanding the information provided by other programs.

The System Information Utility

Troubleshooting problems is often a matter of having a good supply of information about your system's hardware and software components. To its credit, Windows Millennium is willing to provide power users with a generous supply of system data. The biggest repository of system info is the Registry, which, as you learned in Chapter 3, "An Insider's Guide to Four Crucial Configuration Tools," is Windows Millennium's central storehouse for hardware and software settings.

→ **See Also** "An Insider's Guide to the Registry," **p. 62.**

Another good source of hardware data is Device Manager. As you'll see in Chapter 21, "Taking the Mystery Out of Hardware," Device Manager presents a list of the hardware on your system, as well as the drivers, settings, and resources used by each device.

→ **See Also** "Dealing with Device Manager," **p. 479.**

But probably the most comprehensive source of system data is the System Information utility. There are two methods you can use to load this program:

- Select Start, Programs, Accessories, System Tools, System Information.

- Select Start, Run, type `msinfo32`, and click OK.

Figure 14.1 shows the window that appears.

Figure 14.1
The System Information program gives you a comprehensive picture of what's on your system.

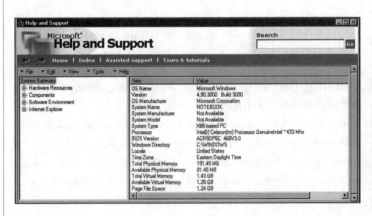

The tree on the left contains various information categories, while the pane on the right displays data for the currently selected category. In the opening view, the left pane shows four main categories:

System Summary—This top-level category displays general information about your system, including the Windows Millennium version number, the amount of RAM installed, the size of the swap file, and more.

Hardware Resources—This section contains six categories that show you the resources used by the devices on your system. Of particular note is the Conflicts/Sharing category, which tells you if any devices on your system use conflicting resources. (If your system supports IRQ steering, this category shows you the resources that are shared between devices.) To learn about IRQs, DMA channels, and other hardware concepts, see Chapter 21.

→ **See Also** "IRQ Lines, I/O Ports, and Other Device Settings," p. 464.

Components—This section contains a long list of categories that represent the various hardware components on your system. For each category, you see the resources allocated to the device, the drivers used by the device, and much more.

Software Environment—This section contains various categories that tell you about the software running on your system, including the device drivers loaded, the 16-bit and 32-bit executables loaded, the background tasks currently running, the programs that run at startup (and where they run from), and much more.

Besides these categories, there is also a category for Internet Explorer that offers information on the program's version, cache settings, installed certificates, and more. This is an example of an application-specific category. As you install programs within Windows Millennium, you may find that they create their own System Information categories.

Remember
The component categories also show color-coded messages if any hardware problems are detected. For example, if the device isn't working properly, you see This Device Has a Problem in red type, followed by a description of the problem. Similarly, if a device driver isn't installed, the message Driver Not Installed appears in blue type. Take a look at the Problem Devices category as well.

Within the categories, System Information also offers two different views (these are commands on the View menu):

Basic—This is the default view and it shows you the information that Microsoft thinks is interesting or useful for the
curious user.

Advanced—This view gives you everything in the Basic view as
well as quite a few extra bits of information (such as Plug
and Play data), most of which is of interest only to support
professionals.

System Information also offers two different views of the categories as a whole (again, these are View menu commands):

Current System Information—When you select this view (the
default), each category shows the current system data.

History—When you select this view, the categories display a
chronological account of the updates that have occurred
within each section. For example, if you're suddenly having problems with a device, check its history to see what
changes were made.

The File Information Utility

When maintaining or troubleshooting Windows, you'll often
find yourself dealing with arcane Windows Millennium system
files of every persuasion from DLLs to VXDs. If you find yourself scratching your head about what a particular file does, you
can get at least a bit more information about the file by using
the File Information utility that came on the Windows 98 CD's
Resource Kit Sampler.

You can't run this program from the Windows 98 CD. To get it
on your hard disk, you have two choices:

- Explore the CD and open the `tools\reskit\diagnose`
  folder. Copy the files `fileinfo.exe` and `win98.mfi` to your
  hard disk. When that's done, right-click `win98.mfi` and
  then click Properties. In the property sheet, deactivate the

Read-only check box and then click OK. In this case, you run the program by launching the `fileinfo.exe` file.

- Install the Resource Kit Sampler by launching `setup.exe` from the CD's `tools\reskit` folder. After that's done, you launch the program by first selecting Start, Programs, Windows Millennium Resource Kit, Tools Management Console. Now double-click Tools A to Z, highlight D to O, and then double-click Microsoft File Information.

You can also download this program from the Windows 98 Resource Kit Web site:

```
http://resourcelink.mspress.microsoft.com/reslink/win98/
toolbox/default.asp
```

Follow these steps to use this program to get information about a Windows Millennium file:

1. Select the File Information tab, shown in Figure 14.2.

Watch Out!
The File Information program requires that some support files be present on your system. If the program refuses to run after you copy `fileinfo.exe` and `win98.mfi` to your hard disk, you need to install the Resource Kit Sampler to get the proper support files onto your system.

Figure 14.2
Use the File Information tab to pick out the file you want to work with.

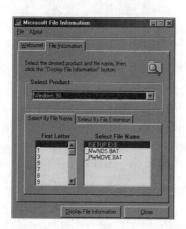

2. Choose the file you want to work with by using one of the following tabs:

   Select By File Name—Use the First Letter column select the first letter of the filename, and then use the Select File Name column to highlight the file.

   Select By File Extension—Use the File Extension column to select the extension used by the file, and then use the Select File Name column to highlight the file.

3. Click the Display File Information button. The File Information dialog box appears. Figure 14.3 shows the dialog box for `Kernel32.dll`. Notice how you get the file size, its installed location, its location on the Windows Millennium CD and floppy disks, the date stamp, and a description of the file. (Not all files will display a description.)

Figure 14.3
The File Information dialog box displays all kinds of useful data about Windows Millennium's files.

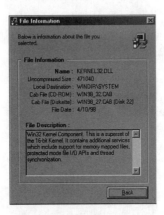

4. Click Back to close the dialog box.

Finding the Version Number of a File

System files and support files are always stamped with a version number to differentiate the various incarnations that the files have gone through. In general, the higher the version number, the newer the file (although, frustratingly, this isn't universally true).

Still, if you're faced with two copies of a single system file and are trying to decide which one to keep, comparing version numbers often helps. Here's one way to determine the version number of a file:

1. In Windows Explorer, highlight the file you want to check.

2. Select File, Properties to display the property sheet for the file.

3. Display the Version tab. As you can see in Figure 14.4, the `File version` line tells you the version number.

4. Click OK.

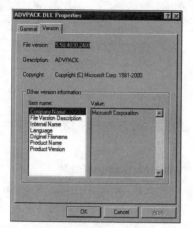

Figure 14.4
In a file's property
sheet, the Version
tab tells you the
file's version
number.

Automatic System Maintenance with the Scheduled Tasks Folder

The key to keeping your system in fine fettle is to run your maintenance programs—ScanDisk, Disk Defragmenter, or whatever—regularly. Placing shortcuts for these programs in your Windows Millennium Startup folder is one way to ensure regularity. However, performing a "Thorough" ScanDisk check or a file defragment, might not be the most productive way to start your day.

Fortunately, Windows Millennium comes with a great little program called Scheduled Tasks that schedules these chores not only to run at regular intervals, but also to run in the evening or overnight when you won't be using your machine.

Displaying the Scheduled Tasks Folder

To see what Scheduled Tasks is all about, display its window by selecting Start, Programs, Accessories, System Tools, Scheduled Tasks. Figure 14.5 shows the window that appears. The five columns give you the name of the scheduled task, the time it's scheduled to run, the last time it started and ended, and the status of the last result.

Figure 14.5
Use the
Scheduled Tasks
folder to run main-
tenance utilities
and other pro-
grams regularly.

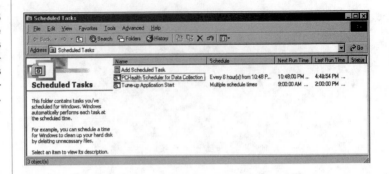

Adding a New Scheduled Task

Although you use it most for system maintenance utilities,
you're free to schedule Windows applications, macros, DOS
programs, or even batch files. To create a new scheduled task,
follow these steps:

1. Launch the Add Scheduled Task item. This runs the Add
   Scheduled Task Wizard.

2. The first dialog box just presents an overview, so click Next
   to proceed.

3. The wizard scours your Start menu and displays a list of all
   the programs. Click the program that you want to schedule. If the item you want to schedule isn't in this list, click
   Browse, use the Select Program to Schedule dialog box to
   choose the program, and then click Open. When you're
   ready to move on, click Next.

4. Now the wizard prompts you for a name and to choose the
   frequency with which this task is to be run. Enter a name,
   select a schedule option, and then click Next.

5. You use the next dialog box to set up a schedule for the
   task. (The layout of the dialog box depends on the schedule you chose for your task in step 4.) Specify the schedule
   you want and then click Next.

6. The last wizard dialog box has a check box named Open
   advanced properties for the task when I click Finish. If you

activate this check box and click Finish, the wizard opens the properties sheet for the task. See "Modifying a Scheduled Task's Properties," later in this chapter.

Working with Scheduled Tasks

Here are a few techniques you can use to work with scheduled tasks:

- If you prefer to run the scheduled task right away, either highlight the task and select File, Run, or right-click the task and select Run from the shortcut menu.

- If a task is running, you can stop it by selecting File, End Scheduled Task.

- To remove a task, either highlight it and select File, Delete, or right-click it and select Delete from the shortcut menu. When Scheduled Tasks asks you to confirm, click Yes.

- To suspend all the scheduled tasks, select Advanced, Pause Task Scheduler. To resume operations, select Advanced, Continue Task Scheduler.

- If you no longer want to use Scheduled Tasks at all, select Advanced, Stop Using Task Scheduler. To enable Scheduled Tasks again, select Advanced, Start Using Task Scheduler.

Modifying a Scheduled Task's Properties

Each scheduled task has various properties that control the program's executable file, how it runs, which folder it runs in, and more. To view and modify these properties, either highlight a task in the Scheduled Tasks window and select File, Properties, or right-click the task name and click Properties from the shortcut menu.

In the property sheet that appears, use the Task tab to control the task's executable file and default folder, and use the Schedule tab to adjust the task's schedule.

Remember
You can toggle a task on and off by toggling the Task tab's Enabled check box on and off.

Here's a quick look at the controls on the Settings tab, shown in Figure 14.6:

Delete the task if it is not scheduled to run again—If you set up your task to run only a limited number of times, activate this check box to have Scheduled Tasks delete the task after its final run.

Stop the task if it runs for *x* hour(s) *y* minute(s)—Use these controls to set an upper limit on the amount of time the task can run.

Only start the task if computer has been idle for at least—If you activate this check box, Scheduled Tasks won't run the task if you're still using your computer. Use the spinner to set the number of minutes your machine must be idle before the task begins.

If computer has not been idle that long, retry for up to—Use this spinner to set the number of minutes Scheduled Tasks waits for idle time.

Stop the task if the computer ceases to be idle—If you activate this check box, Scheduled Tasks shuts down the task if you start using your computer while the task is running.

Don't start the task if the computer is running on batteries—When this option is turned on, Scheduled Tasks checks to see whether your notebook is on battery power and, if so, it won't run the task.

Stop the task if battery mode begins—When this check box is on, Scheduled Tasks shuts down a running task if your notebook switches from AC to batteries.

Wake the computer to run this task—If you activate this check box, Scheduled Tasks wakes a computer that is currently in sleep mode to run the task.

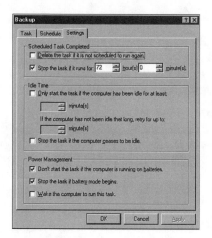

Figure 14.6
Use the Settings tab to control how the task runs.

Understanding Windows Millennium's PC Health Features

One of Microsoft's slogans for Windows Millennium is "It Just Works." I predict the world's wags will have a field day rewriting this dubious slogan to more accurately reflect the true nature of Windows Millennium's reliability ("It Just Barely Works," "It Just Sucks," and on and on). Cynicism aside, is there *any* substance behind the marketing?

Actually, there is. It's all based on the *PC Health* initiative that's designed to make systems that are "self-repairing" and easy to troubleshoot. In Windows Millennium, Microsoft implemented *PC Health* in four separate features: Help and Support, System File Protection, System Restore, and AutoUpdate.

Help and Support

Help and Support is a revamped Help system and you get there by selecting Start, Help. Like the Windows 98 Help system, Help and Support is HTML-based and appears within a special Web browser. The home "page" lists various topics (see Figure 14.7) and you click links to drill down into each topic. There's also a Search feature and an Index page for finding topic keywords. Besides these Help features, there are also Support features such as Troubleshooters that lead you step-by-step through problem-solving techniques and an Assisted Support page that gives you access to Web-based forums and message boards.

Figure 14.7
The home page of
Windows
Millennium's new
Help and Support
feature.

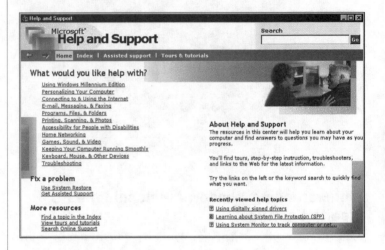

System File Protection

Like most programs, Windows Millennium comes with support files that provide various services. There are .dll files (dynamic link libraries), .ocx files (ActiveX controls), .vxd and .drv files (device drivers), and of course a lot of .exe files (applications). Together, these constitute the Windows Millennium system files, and there are well over 1,000 of them located in the Windows and Windows\System folders.

It is by no means a stretch to say that the health of Windows Millennium as a whole is dependent on the health of these system files. If one of these files becomes corrupted, gets deleted, or gets overwritten by an older version, you could experience program crashes, at best, or system lockups, at worst. Unfortunately, in previous versions of Windows system files were constantly under siege by setup programs that insisted upon installing their own versions of system files.

With Windows Millennium, however, Microsoft is finally fighting back against this system file onslaught with a new PC

Health feature called System File Protection. The idea is simple and its implementation is ruthless. Windows Millennium maintains a list of the most vital system files and watches over them like a hawk. If any application (or user) attempts to delete, modify, or overwrite any of these files, Windows Millennium immediately restores the original file, no questions asked.

System File Protection sounds great in theory, but what it means in practice only time will tell. However, two things seem likely:

- Windows Millennium should be far more stable than previous versions. The majority of stability problems in older versions of Windows were directly attributable to system file damage and replacement. So, with Windows Millennium rabidly protecting these files, this should knock out a huge category of system problems.

- Some applications will become less stable. A program usually replaces system files for a good reason: The updated files contain code that the application requires to function properly. When the system file is restored and that code disappears, the application isn't likely to respond well. However, Microsoft has warned vendors of potential System File Protection problems and has asked them to tweak their programs accordingly. Users will be wise to look for programs that are Windows Millennium-compatible.

Wondering which files are protected by System File Protection? To find out, display the Windows\System\sfp folder and open the file named sfpdb.sfp. (It's a text file, so use Notepad or WordPad.)

Unfortunately, if you want to keep track of what System File Protection is doing, Windows Millennium isn't much help because it doesn't warn you when a program attempts to mess with a system file. The only choice you have is to examine the System File Protection log file. It's a text file named sfplog.txt and it's in the Windows\System\sfp folder.

Inside Scoop
Why did Windows allow installation programs to overwrite crucial system files in the first place? It all began back when Windows 3.1 was released. It included handy features such as common dialog boxes that could be used by all applications, and these features were implemented as new or updated .dll files. To ensure that applications taking advantage of these features would run under Windows 3.0, Microsoft allowed developers to install the appropriate .dll files.

System Restore

Trashed system files were certainly the biggest cause of system instabilities in previous versions of Windows. The second biggest cause was newly installed programs that just didn't get along with Windows. It could be an executable file that didn't mesh with the Windows system or a Registry change that caused havoc on other programs or on Windows itself. Similarly, hardware installs often caused problems by adding faulty device drivers to the system or by corrupting the Registry.

To help guard against software or hardware installations that bring down the system, Windows Millennium introduces a PC Health feature called System Restore. It's job is straightforward, yet clever: To take periodic snapshots—called *system checkpoints* or *restore points*—of your system, each of which includes the currently installed program files and Registry settings. The idea is that if a program or device installation causes problems on your system, you use System Restore to revert your system to the most recent checkpoint before the installation.

System Restore creates checkpoints using three methods:

Shortcut
If you have the System Information utility open, you can also run System Restore by selecting the Tools, System Restore command. Also, in the home page of Help and Support, click the Use System Restore link.

- Automatically using the PC Health Scheduler. This program is set up as a task in the Scheduled Tasks folder (described earlier in this chapter). See the item named PCHealth Scheduler for Data Collection. It creates a checkpoint every six hours, as long as your computer has been idle for at least five minutes.

- Automatically before installing certain applications. Some newer applications—notably Office 2000—are aware of System Restore and ask it to create a checkpoint prior to installation.

- Manually using the System Restore user interface.

To create a checkpoint manually, follow these steps:

1. Select Start, Programs, Accessories, System Tools, System Restore. The System Restore window appears.

2. Activate the Create a restore point option and click Next.

3. Use the Restore point description text box to enter a description for the new checkpoint, and then click Next. System Restore creates the checkpoint and displays the Confirm New Restore Point window.

4. Click OK.

If you ever need to restore a checkpoint, follow these steps:

1. Select Start, Programs, Accessories, System Tools, System Restore.

2. Make sure the Restore my computer to an earlier time option is activated and click Next. The Choose a Restore Point window appears, as shown in Figure 14.8.

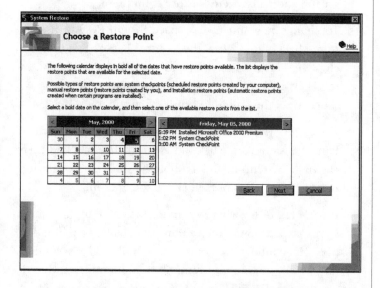

Figure 14.8
Use the System Restore window to choose the checkpoint you want to revert to.

3. Use the calendar to click the date on which the checkpoint was made. System Restore displays that day's checkpoints in a box to the right of the calendar.

4. Click the checkpoint you want to restore. (Note that the System Checkpoint items are the checkpoints created automatically via the PC Health Scheduler.)

5. Click Next. System Restore asks you to close all open programs and warns you not to do anything with your computer until the restore is done.

6. Click OK to get to the Confirm Restore Point Selection window.

7. Click Next. System Restore begins restoring the checkpoint. When it's done, it restarts your computer and displays the Restoration Complete window.

8. Click OK.

Here are a few System Restore details to keep in mind:

- System Restore is available in safe mode. So, if Windows Millennium won't start properly, perform a safe mode startup and run System Restore from there.

- To change how much disk space System Restore uses to store checkpoints, open the Control Panel's System icon, click the Performance tab, and then click File System. In the Hard Disk tab, use the System Restore disk space use slider to set the amount of disk space you want.

- To toggle System Restore on and off, open the Control Panel's System icon, click the Performance tab, and then click File System. In the Troubleshooting tab, toggle the Disable System Restore check box on and off.

- If you want to see what System Restore is up to, first make sure that Windows Millennium isn't showing any hidden files. (In Windows Explorer, select Tools, Folder Options, display the View tab, activate Show hidden files and folders and deactivate Hide protected operating system files.) Then display drive C's _RESTORE folder (there's one on each drive partition). The ARCHIVE subfolder contains various .cab files that contain the backed-up program files and Registry files.

Inside Scoop
System Restore requires a minimum of 200MB of free disk space. If your hard disk dips below that number, Windows Millennium automatically turns System Restore off.

AutoUpdate

Windows 98 introduced the world to the Windows Update Web site (`windowsupdate.microsoft.com`), the purpose of which was to provide a convenient place to download security patches, updated accessories, fonts, themes, and more. It's a nice idea, particularly when compared to the Windows 95 situation, which was a mess of OEM service releases and updates scattered around the Microsoft Web site. However, Windows Update suffered from a couple of problems that reduced its usefulness:

- There wasn't a proper notification service, so you had to remember to check out the site from time to time. (Windows Update did offer the Critical Update Notification service, but it was so buggy that it was practically unusable.)

- It usually wasn't easy to uninstall an update, so you had to hope the new code wouldn't wreck your system.

In an attempt to solve these problems, Windows Millennium augments Windows Update with a new feature called Automatic Updates, or just AutoUpdate for short. This is a service that runs in the background and, while you're connected to the Internet, checks for the availability of "critical" updates on the Windows Update site. (A critical update is one that directly affects Windows Millennium's functionality—that is, a bug fix—or its security.) If such an update is present, AutoUpdate downloads and installs it behind the scenes.

Getting Started with AutoUpdate

When Windows Millennium detects an Internet connection for the first time, it adds a new AutoUpdate icon to the taskbar's system tray. You eventually see a banner appear above this icon telling you to click the icon to set up Automatic Updates. Click the AutoUpdate icon and the Updates Wizard appears so you can set things up. You have three choices at this point, each of which has a button in the first wizard dialog box:

Settings—Click this button to adjust some AutoUpdate settings. See the next section, "Setting Some AutoUpdate Options."

Remind Me Later—Click this button if you don't want AutoUpdate turned on just yet. Use the Remind Me Later dialog box to select when you want to be reminded, and then click OK.

Next—Click this button to turn on AutoUpdate. Follow the prompts in the dialog boxes until the setup is complete.

Setting Some AutoUpdate Options

AutoUpdate doesn't have many settings, but the ones it does have are important. To see them, select Start, Settings, Control Panel, Automatic Updates. (Remember, too, that you can also click Settings in the initial Updates Wizard dialog box.) In the Automatic Updates dialog box, the Options group offers three choices:

Automatically download updates and notify me when they are ready to be installed—This is the default option and it means that AutoUpdate downloads any available updates without asking for permission. When the download is done, AutoUpdate asks if you want to install the update.

Notify me before downloading any updates and notify me again when they are ready to be installed—Activate this option if you want AutoUpdate to ask your permission before downloading any updates. This is the best option because it gives you total control over the update procedure while still automating the notification process.

Turn off automatic updating. I will update my computer manually—Activate this option to bypass AutoUpdate and use the Windows Update Web site to perform all updates.

If AutoUpdate downloads an update but you reject the installation, the update remains on your computer as a hidden file. You can install the update later by clicking the Restore Hidden Items button in the Automatic Updates dialog box.

How AutoUpdate Works

After AutoUpdate is configured, it immediately begins monitoring the Windows Update Web site whenever you're connected to the Internet. If it detects that an update is available, the AutoUpdate icon appears in the taskbar's system tray. How you proceed depends on whether AutoUpdate prompts you to download:

- If you didn't ask AutoUpdate to prompt you, the download begins automatically.

- If you told AutoUpdate to prompt you before downloading, you see a banner telling you that an update is available. Click the AutoUpdate icon to see a list of the available updates. Each update has a check box beside it, so if you don't want to install an update, deactivate its check box. When you're done, click Start Download.

To check the progress of the download, move your mouse pointer over the icon. After a second or two, a banner appears that reads `Downloading Updates` *x*`% Complete`.

When the download finishes, the icon sprouts another banner that reads `New updates are ready to be installed. Click here.` as shown in Figure 14.9.

The Auto
Update icon

Figure 14.9
AutoUpdate notifies you when it has downloaded a new Windows Millennium update.

Click the icon to return to the Updates Wizard. Again, you have three buttons to choose from:

Details—Click this button to see a list of the updates that will be installed, each of which has a check box beside it. If you don't want an update installed, deactivate its check box.

Remind Me Later—Click this button to have AutoUpdate remind you to install the update later.

Install—Click this button to install the update. Note that you may need to restart your computer when the installation is complete.

Reversing an Update

If you install an update and decide you don't want it after all or if it has messed up your system, you can reverse the update. The secret here is that each time you install an update, AutoUpdate creates a System Restore checkpoint. Therefore, you reverse the update by loading System Restore, choosing the Restore my computer to an earlier time, and clicking the Windows Automatic Update Install checkpoint. (See the "System Restore" section, earlier in this chapter.)

If the update was a program, you may be able to uninstall it by opening the Control Panel's Add/Remove Programs icon, highlighting the update in the Install/Uninstall tab's list, and then clicking Add/Remove.

Essential Information

- The System Information utility (Start, Programs, Accessories, System Tools, System Information) provides an extensive look at the hardware and software resources on your system, while the File Information utility offers useful details on Windows Millennium system files.

- To get the version number of a file, right-click the file, click Properties, and then select the Version tab.

- Use the Scheduled Tasks folder (Start, Programs, Accessories, System Tools, Scheduled Tasks) to run programs and utilities on a schedule.

- Windows Millennium's new PC Health initiative is an attempt to give users more troubleshooting options and to make PCs "self-healing." Its core components are Help and Support, System File Protection, System Restore, and AutoUpdate.

Preparing for Trouble

Chapter 15

T HE PAST FEW CHAPTERS have run through many of Windows Millennium's system tools and other features that are designed to keep your computer running smoothly. Regular application of those tools and techniques should keep Windows Millennium humming along quite nicely. However, despite your best maintenance efforts, your system may give up the ghost thanks to a hardware failure, virus, power surge, rogue application, or incorrect Windows configuration.

Anyone who has used a computer for more than a couple of years will tell you that it's not *if* these kinds of problems will occur, but *when*. In fact, the savviest of users assume their systems are going to fail and take steps to ensure they're prepared when the fateful day arrives. To help you prepare for the inevitable, this chapter runs through a few techniques that will not only get you ready for a crash, but will help you recover gracefully when (not if) it happens.

Putting Together an Emergency Boot Disk

If you do nothing else to prepare your system for trouble, at the very least you should create a bootable floppy disk. That way, if your hard disk goes down for the count, you can boot to drive A and thus regain some control over your recalcitrant machine.

Inside Scoop
The bootable disk works because once the POST is complete, the BIOS code checks for a floppy disk in drive A. If no disk is present, the BIOS boots from the hard disk's active partition. However, if drive A does contain a bootable disk, the BIOS ignores the hard disk and loads the operating system (DOS) from the floppy. You should check your computer's BIOS settings to make sure that it's set up to check drive A before the hard disk.

Remember
Unlike previous version of Windows, the Windows Millennium startup disk recognizes FAT32 partitions.

Of course, regaining control is one thing, but actually doing something useful after you have control is another. Therefore, the ideal boot disk will contain an extensive collection of utilities and programs for troubleshooting and repairing problems. Such a disk then becomes a full-fledged *emergency boot disk*. (Note, too, that because the emergency boot disk loads DOS, a working knowledge of basic DOS commands and techniques is useful.)

Creating a Windows Millennium Startup Disk

In previous versions of Windows, you could create an emergency boot disk by formatting a floppy disk with the Windows system files. Unfortunately, Windows Millennium's format feature no longer comes with a Copy system files option, and the DOS FORMAT command no longer supports the /s switch for copying system files to a floppy. The only way to create a bootable disk in Windows Millennium is to create a *startup disk*. Here's how it's done:

1. In the Control Panel, open the Add/Remove Programs icon to display the Add/Remove Programs Properties dialog box.

2. Display the Startup Disk tab.

3. Click Create Disk. Windows Millennium gathers the files it needs and then prompts you to insert a disk in drive A.

4. Insert the disk. (Make sure this disk doesn't contain valuable data. Windows Millennium formats the disk, so all the existing data is lost.)

5. Click OK. Windows Millennium formats the disk and copies a number of files.

6. When the disk is done, click OK to close the Add/Remove Programs Properties dialog box.

7. Write-protect the disk.

Table 15.1 shows you the names and descriptions of the two dozen files that are copied to the startup disk.

TABLE 15.1: THE FILES THAT ARE COPIED TO THE WINDOWS MILLENNIUM STARTUP DISK

Filename	Description
ASPI2DOS.SYS	Device driver for Adaptec SCSI adapter models AIC-6260/6360/6370.
ASPI4DOS.SYS	Device driver for Adaptec SCSI adapter models AHA-154X/1640.
ASPI8DOS.SYS	Device driver for Adaptec SCSI adapter models AIC-75XX/78XX.
ASPI8U2.SYS	Device driver for Adaptec SCSI adapter models AIC-789X.
ASPICD.SYS	Device driver for an Adaptec SCSI CD-ROM drive.
AUTOEXEC.BAT	Startup batch file.
BTCDROM.SYS	Device driver for a Mylex/BusLogic SCSI CD-ROM drive.
BTDOSM.SYS	Device driver for a Mylex/BusLogic SCSI adapter.
CHECKSR.BAT	Checks whether a System Restore restoration was the last action performed on the system.
COMMAND.COM	DOS command interpreter.
CONFIG.SYS	Startup configuration file.
EBD.CAB	Cabinet archive file containing several DOS utilities.
EBD.SYS	Emergency book disk system file.
EBDUNDO.EXE	Reverses the most recent System Restore restoration.
EXTRACT.EXE	Extracts files from a .cab file.
FDISK.EXE	Partitions the hard disk.
FINDRAMD.EXE	Finds a RAM drive.
FIXIT.BAT	Displays a message after the startup disk loads.
FLASHPT.SYS	Device driver for a BusLogic FlashPoint SCSI adapter.
HIBINV.EXE	Detects whether the system was in hibernate mode when it was shut down.
HIMEM.SYS	Extended memory manager.
IO.SYS	Windows Millennium startup system file.
MSDOS.SYS	Windows Millennium startup system file.
OAKCDROM.SYS	Device driver for an IDE CD-ROM drive.
RAMDRIVE.SYS	Creates a temporary disk drive in RAM.
README.TXT	Text file containing information about the startup disk.
SETRAMD.BAT	Sets the letter used by the RAM drive.

Inside Scoop
To write-protect a 3 1/2-inch floppy, turn it over and look for a small, movable, plastic tab in one of the corners. Move that tab toward the edge of the disk until it snaps into place and a hole appears where the tab used to be.

Undocumented
The startup disk has over 400KB of free space, so you can include other files on it. To create a startup disk and have Windows Millennium automatically include other files, first copy those files to the Windows\Command\Ebd folder. Then, switch to the Windows\Command folder and run the command **bootdisk a:**. Unlike the Add/Remove Programs method (which gathers the startup disk files from the Windows Millennium .cab files), this method gathers the files from the Ebd folder.

Watch Out!
The startup disk
doesn't include
Uninstal.exe, the
program that unin-
stalls Windows
Millennium. I sug-
gest you copy this
file from the
Windows\Command
folder to the
startup disk,
just in case you
need it.

Test Driving the Startup Disk

After you create your startup disk, you should test it out right away to make sure it works properly. Insert the disk in drive A (if it's not in there already), select Start, Shut Down, choose the Restart option, and then click OK.

When your computer reboots, the version of Io.sys on the floppy disk takes over the boot process after the POST is complete. The following menu appears:

```
Microsoft Windows Millennium Startup Menu
===================================

1. Help
2. Start computer with CD-ROM support.
3. Start computer without CD-ROM support.
4. Minimal Boot

Enter a choice:
```

The startup disk's CONFIG.SYS file—shown in Figure 15.1—is configured to display this menu and process your selection.

Figure 15.1
The startup disk's
CONFIG.SYS file.

CONFIG.SYS is divided into five sections:

The [menu] section sets up the menu that you see on-screen. Each menu command is created by a menuitem line:

menuitem=*block*, [*text*]

In each line, block is the name of another configuration block (such as [CD]) within Config.sys), and the optional text parameter is the command that you see when the menu is displayed (such as Start computer with CD-ROM support). The [menu] block also contains two other features:

- The menudefault line specifies the command that will be selected automatically and the number of seconds after which that command will be selected.

- The menucolor line sets the menu's foreground (the first value) and background (the second value) colors, as given by the values in Table 15.2.

TABLE 15.2: COLOR VALUES TO USE WITH THE MENUCOLOR STATEMENT

Value	Color	Value	Color
0	Black	8	Gray
1	Blue	9	Bright blue
2	Green	10	Bright green
3	Cyan	11	Bright cyan
4	Red	12	Bright red
5	Magenta	13	Bright magenta
6	Brown	14	Yellow
7	White	15	Bright white

The [HELP] configuration block is processed if you select the first menu item (Help). The block runs through a list of device lines that try all the IDE, SCSI adapter, and SCSI CD-ROM drivers on the disk.

All those device lines in the [HELP] block are unnecessary and only serve to slow down the floppy boot sequence. There are two ways you can customize this section:

- Comment out each `device` line that's not required by your system. You comment out a line by placing REM and a space at the beginning of the line. This tells DOS not to process the line. Remember that SCSI CD-ROMs need both the SCSI adapter driver and the SCSI CD-ROM driver. If you're not sure, do a step-by-step boot (by pressing Shift+F8) to see which lines load successfully.

- If none of these lines is appropriate for your system, comment out all of them and add the appropriate `device` statement (or statements) for your CD-ROM drive.

The [HELP] block also runs the following statement:

```
devicehigh=ramdrive.sys /E 2048
```

This statement carves out a 2,048KB piece of RAM to use as a disk drive. (The /E switch creates the drive in extended memory.) A bit later, I'll explain why this RAM disk is needed.

The [CD] block is processed if you select the second menu item (Start computer with CD-ROM support). It contains the same sequence of commands as the [HELP] block.

The [NOCD] block is processed if you select the third menu command (Start computer without CD-ROM support). It loads only ramdrive.sys to create the RAM drive.

The [QUICK] block is processed if you select the fourth menu command (Minimal Boot). This block is empty, which means this command doesn't set up CD-ROM support or a RAM drive.

The [COMMON] block is processed no matter what menu command you select. These statements set up the DOS environment.

After you select a menu command (by pressing the command's number and then pressing Enter), IO.SYS processes CONFIG.SYS and then runs the AUTOEXEC.BAT batch file. Figure 15.2 shows most of this file.

1.—
2.—
3.—
4.—
5.—
6.—
7.—
8.—

Figure 15.2
The startup disk's
AUTOEXEC.BAT file.

Inside Scoop
The %config%
environment vari-
able holds the
name of the con-
figuration block
that was selected
in CONFIG.SYS. For
example, the
AUTOEXEC.BAT line
that begins IF
"%config%"=="QUI
CK" is checking to
see if the QUICK
block was
choosen (that is,
the Minimal Boot
command in the
Startup menu).

Here's what happens:

1. The path is set, hibernation is checked (hibinv.exe), and the system determines if a System Restore restoration was the last task performed (checksr.bat).

2. Several environment variables are set.

3. The setramd.bat batch file is run. This batch file calls the Findramd.exe program to determine the drive letter being used by the RAM drive. The batch file then sets the RAMD environment variable to that letter.

4. The path is adjusted to include the RAM drive, and then command.com is set up to run from the RAM drive.

5. Extract.exe and Readme.txt are copied to the RAM drive.

6. If the file ebd.cab exists, skip to the EXT label (step 7).

7. Extract all the files from ebd.cab and store them on the RAM drive.

8. If one of the non-CD menu options was selected, skip to the appropriate label. Otherwise, run Mscdex.exe to initialize the CD-ROM drive and set its drive letter.

9. Process the rest of the file (not shown in Figure 15.2).

After Autoexec.bat is processed, you're dropped off at the A:\ prompt. Table 15.3 lists the files in Ebd.cab that get copied to the RAM drive.

TABLE 15.3: FILES STORED IN EBD.CAB

Filename	Description
ATTRIB.EXE	Sets and removes file attributes.
CHKDSK.EXE	Checks a disk for errors; can repair some errors.
COMMAND.COM	DOS command interpreter.
DEBUG.EXE	Tests, edits, and debugs binary files.
EDIT.COM	Text editor that's useful for editing configuration files.
EXT.EXE	Extracts files from a .cab archive; uses an interactive command line.
EXTRACT.EXE	Extracts files from a .cab archive.
FORMAT.COM	Formats a disk.
HELP.BAT	Displays the Readme.txt file.
MSCDEX.EXE	Initializes the CD-ROM drive.
README.TXT	Displays help text.
SCANDISK.EXE	Scans and repairs a disk.
SCANDISK.INI	Contains configuration options for ScanDisk.
SYS.COM	Transfers Windows Millennium system files to a disk.

Backing Up Your Files

I'd like to have a megabyte of memory for every computer book and computer magazine article that has regaled the reader with stories of hard disk crashes, office fires, and stolen computers as a way to underline the importance of backups. (I've been the author of quite a few of those finger-waggings, myself.)

You'll be happy to know that you'll be getting no such lectures from me this time. As a savvy Windows Millennium user, you *know* the importance of backups and you don't need me or anyone else nagging you about it. What you probably *do* need are a few techniques for making backups less of a chore. After all, the more inconvenient it is to back up, the less likely you are to do it regularly. This section shows you how to take control of the backup process and how to streamline it to make it as painless as possible.

The first thing you should know is that the Backup utility in Windows Millennium is unchanged from the one in Windows 98, which is still a big improvement over its Windows 95 predecessor. That is, it has wizards for common tasks, a wider variety of options—including the welcome ability to include the Registry in any backup job—and it supports a much wider range of backup hardware, including SCSI, IDE/ATAPI, and parallel port units, and the following media:

- 8 millimeter tapes

- DAT (DDS1 and DDS2) tapes

- DC 6000 tapes

- Digital line tapes (DLTs)

- QIC-80, 80 Wide, 3010, 3010 Wide, 3020, and 3020 Wide tapes

- Travan TR1, TR2, TR3, TR4 tapes

- Removable media such as floppy disks, Zip disks, Jaz disks, and SyQuest cartridges

Of course, you can also use a second hard disk or a shared network folder as the backup destination.

Installing Microsoft Backup

The only thing that *is* different between the Windows 98 and Windows Millennium versions of Backup is the latter is nowhere to be seen during the Windows Millennium installation. In fact, even if you run Control Panel's Add/Remove Programs icon, you'll see that Backup is AWOL from the list of Windows Millennium components. Backup still exists, but Microsoft chose to hide it on the Windows Millennium CD. What gives?

Remember
The Windows Millennium version of Microsoft Backup does not support QIC-40 tapes.

I honestly wish I had a good answer to that question. Why Microsoft would deliberately make it difficult for even experienced users to install Backup—arguably the most important of the system tools—is truly unfathomable.

All that aside, here are the steps to follow to install Backup:

1. Insert your Windows Millennium CD.

2. Using My Computer or Windows Explorer, display the CD's add-ons\MSBackup folder.

3. Double-click the msbexp.exe file.

4. When prompted to restart your computer, click Yes.

Starting Microsoft Backup

To launch Microsoft Backup, select Start, Programs, Accessories, System Tools, Backup. The first time you launch Backup, it checks to see if you have a backup tape device attached to your machine. If you don't, a dialog box asks if you want to run the Add New Hardware Wizard to look for the device. If you do have a backup device that Windows Millennium hasn't yet recognized, click Yes. Otherwise, click No to continue.

You now see a dialog box that welcomes you to Microsoft Backup. This dialog box appears each time you start Backup, and it offers the following options:

Create a new backup job—This option runs the Backup Wizard, which leads you through the steps required to create a backup job.

Open an existing backup job—This option displays a dialog box from which you can open an existing backup job.

Restore backed up files—This option runs the Restore Wizard, which takes you step-by-step through the process of restoring files from a backup.

It's my goal in this section to show you the nuts and bolts of Backup, so I won't discuss these options, which are in any case aimed at beginning users. Click Close to remove the dialog box and get to the Microsoft Backup window, shown in Figure 15.3.

Setting Up a Backup Job

A *backup job* consists of the files you want backed up, the options you want to use for the backup, and the destination for the backup file. Here are the steps to follow to create a backup job:

1. Select the drives, folders, and files you want to include in the backup. The two panes in the middle of the Microsoft Backup window work much like the Folders bar and the Contents list in Windows Explorer. In this case, each drive, folder, and file has a check box beside it. To include an object in the backup job, activate its check box.

Shortcut
If you'd prefer that Backup not show this initial dialog box at startup, select Tools, Preferences, deactivate the Show startup dialog when Microsoft Backup is started check box, and click OK.

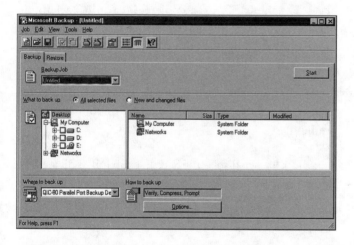

Figure 15.3
You use the Microsoft Backup window to define and work with your backup jobs.

2. Use the Where to back up list to select a backup device or File. If you select the latter, a text box appears so you can enter the path and filename for the backup.

3. Click Options to display the Backup Job Options dialog box shown in Figure 15.4. Here's a summary of the tabs in this dialog box:

Figure 15.4
Use this dialog box to set options for your backup job.

General—The Compare original and backup files... check box toggles backup verification on and off (although it's slower, it's best to leave this on). You can also set the compression used and what Backup does if the media already contains a backup.

Password—Use this tab to protect the backup file with a password.

Type—This tab determines how Backup treats the selected files. If you activate All selected files, every file is included in the backup job. Otherwise, activate New and changed files only and then select either Differential backup type or Incremental backup type.

Exclude—Use this tab to exclude certain file types from the backup job.

Report—After the backup is complete, Microsoft Backup displays a report that summarizes the backup operation. Use the check boxes in this tab to customize the contents of that report.

Advanced—Activate the Back up Windows Registry check box to include the Registry files in the backup job (highly recommended).

4. Select Job, Save to display the Save Backup Job As dialog box. Enter a name in the Job Name text box, and then click Save.

5. Click Start to launch the backup.

Notes Toward Easier Backup Jobs

I think the main reason most people don't back up is that it's often a difficult or inconvenient process. However, there are a few things you can do to make backing up easier. Here are some notes:

Forget floppies, if possible—Backing up to floppy disks ranks just above "root canal" on the Top Ten Most Unpleasant Chores list. The reason, of course, is that a standard 3 1/2-inch floppy disk holds a mere 1.39MB (*not* 1.44MB) of data. If your hard disk contains hundreds of megabytes, you'll have to back up to hundreds of floppy disks, which hurts just to think about it.

Try a tape drive—Tape drives are the de facto backup standard, and come in many different capacities. You can back up several hundred megabytes for an extremely low cost.

Other backup media—The big downfall for tape drives is their relatively slow access times. Fortunately, there are much faster media available. These include floppy-compatible drives such as the SuperDisk (120MB) and the HiFD (200MB); removable media such as Iomega's Zip (100MB and 250MB) and Jaz (1GB and 2GB) drives; a second hard disk (*not* a second partition on the same hard disk!); and a network folder.

Consider online backups—Some companies offer remote backups over the Internet where you pay for a certain amount of storage space. Some of the companies that offer this service are @Backup (www.atbackup.com), Driveway (www.driveway.com), and Connected (www.connected.com).

Back up data, not programs—Although you see in the next section that a full system backup can come in handy, it isn't strictly necessary. The only irreplaceable files on your system are those you created yourself, so they're the ones you should spend the most time protecting.

Shortcut
If you want to know the size of the backup job, run the View, Selection Information command.

Remember
One thing that would make your backup life easier would be the ability to schedule unattended backups. Unfortunately, Microsoft Backup offers no such feature, an inexplicable oversight that has left many a Windows Millennium user scratching their head and saying "Gee, I thought those folks at Microsoft were supposed to be *smart*."

Keep data together—You save an immense amount of backup time if you store all your data files in one place. It could be the My Documents folder, a separate partition, or a separate hard disk. In each case, you can select all the data files for backup simply by activating a single folder or drive check box.

Back up downloaded archives—If space is at a premium, you can leave program files out of your backup job because they can always be reinstalled from their source disks. The exceptions to this are downloaded programs. To avoid having to find and download these files again, make backup copies of the archives.

Don't always run the full backup—You can speed up your backup times by running differential and incremental backups. You might consider running an incremental backup each day, a differential backup each week, and a full backup each month.

Restoring a Backup Job

Backup's Restore component is one of those features that you hope is just a waste of disk space that you'll never have to use. If disaster does strike, however, Restore will be a most welcome tool. (Note that Restore doesn't have a real mode component, so if your system fails, you need to reinstall Windows Millennium and then run the restore operation.)

If you like the step-by-step approach, you can run the Restore Wizard by selecting the Tools, Restore Wizard command. Alternatively, you can run the restore by hand by following these steps:

1. In the Microsoft Backup window, select the Restore tab.

2. If Backup asks if you want to refresh the current view, click Yes and then skip to step 6.

3. In the Restore from list, select the backup source you want to work with.

4. Click Refresh. Backup asks if you want to refresh the current view.

5. Click Yes. Backup accesses the media and displays a list of backup jobs.

6. Select a backup job and then click OK. The backup job's drives, folders, and files appear in the What to restore panes.

7. Use the check boxes to select the drives, folders, and files you want to restore.

8. In the Where to restore list, select a destination for the restored files—either Original Location or Alternate Location. If you select the latter, a text box appears below the Where to restore list. Use this text box to set the new destination for the restored files.

9. Click Options to display the Restore Options dialog box shown in Figure 15.5. Here's a summary of the tabs in this dialog box:

   General—These options determine what Backup does if a filethat it's trying to restore already exists in the destination folder. You can leave the existing file, replace the existing file.

   Report—When the restore operation is done, Backup displays a report. Use the check boxes in this tab to customize the contents of that report.

   Advanced—Activate the Restore Windows Registry check box to include the Registry files in the restore.

10. Click Start to launch the restoration.

11. If Backup displays the Media Required dialog box, insert the backup media containing the backup job, and then click OK.

12. If your backup job included the Registry, Backup will ask if you want to replace the existing Registry. Click Yes to replace it, or click No to leave the existing Registry files.

13. If your backup job included the Registry, Backup will ask if you want to restore the Registry's hardware and software settings. Again, click Yes or No, as appropriate.

Figure 15.5
Use this dialog box to set options for restoring the backup job.

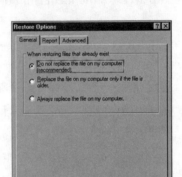

Gathering Troubleshooting Information

One of the keys to recovering gracefully from a problem is having information about the state of your system at the time the problem occurred, as well as data about the problem itself. Luckily, Windows Millennium has many tools for gathering this type of data. Here are the two most useful ones:

Print out system information—The System Information utility (see Chapter 14, "Crucial System Maintenance Skills") contains an exhaustive inventory of the current hardware and software configuration. Printing out this data will provide you with detailed configuration information, and should be useful for a tech-support engineer. Note, however, that this printout will be at least 75 pages.

→ **See Also** "The System Information Utility," **p. 328.**

Run Dr. Watson—If you have programs that are causing general protection faults, exception errors, or other problems, try loading the Dr. Watson utility into memory. Dr. Watson monitors the system and traps application errors. It then takes a snapshot of the system, records data about the application and the error, and writes everything to a log file in the Windows\Drwatson folder. This data will be useful for a tech-support engineer to diagnose your system. To run Dr. Watson, use either of the following techniques:

Inside Scoop
Rather than printing out the System Information data, print it to a .prn file and then save that file to a floppy. You can then print out the data (or email it to a tech-support rep) when and if you need it. (To print a .prn file, type *filename*.prn > lpt1, where *filename*.prn is the name of the file.) To print to a file, add a new printer and, when prompted for the port, select FILE.

- Select Start, Run, type `drwatson.exe`, and click OK.

- Select Start, Programs, Accessories, System Tools, System Information, and then run the Tools, Dr. Watson command.

Essential Information

- A Windows Millennium startup disk is an essential component of any troubleshooting and recovery toolkit.

- You should customize the startup disk to suit your SCSI and (if necessary) CD-ROM setup and to add other troubleshooting tools.

- To make backing up easier, bypass floppy disks in favor of tape, higher-capacity removable media, or another hard disk; and put most of your energy into protecting your data files.

- Use the System Information utility and Dr. Watson to gather information that's useful for troubleshooting problems.

Advanced Windows Millennium Customizing

PART V

GET THE SCOOP ON...
Web Integration and the Windows Millennium
Interface ▪ Turning Web Integration On and Off ▪
Specifying Custom Web Integration Settings ▪
Understanding and Customizing the Web Integration
Templates ▪ Working with the Active Desktop

An In-Depth Look at Web Integration

ONE OF WINDOWS 98'S MOST TALKED ABOUT (and most controversial) innovations was the integration of Internet technologies within the operating system. In particular, Windows 98 incorporated many of the technologies and techniques used on the World Wide Web—hence the name *Web integration* for these innovations.

Web integration wasn't the sea change that many pundits (and Microsoft marketers) made it out to be. Overall, it represented a relatively minor update to the existing user interface. That's not to say that Web integration should be ignored, far from it. This may have been a minor interface course correction, but the new direction was a definite improvement over the tired desktop metaphor that had dominated the Windows interface ever since version 3.0.

To get excited about Web integration, and to truly appreciate this new direction, you have to go "under the hood" and take an in-depth look at how Web integration works. Once you understand the inner workings of this technology, you can use it in powerful new ways that go well beyond the "authorized" uses prescribed by Microsoft. This chapter shows you everything you need to know.

Chapter 16

The Integration Interface I: Opening and Selecting Objects

Here's a summary of the changes Web integration brings to opening and selecting objects:

Clickable Windows objects look like Web page links—In most Web pages, links have the following characteristics:

- The link text appears underlined.

- When you position the mouse over a link, the mouse pointer changes into a small hand with a pointing finger.

You get the same effect with Web integration: Icon titles and filenames are underlined, and the mouse pointer changes into a hand when positioned over an icon or filename.

You single-click to launch icons and programs—Web page links require just a single click to activate them, and Web integration brings the same idea to Windows Millennium. That is, you can launch icons and files by single-clicking them instead of the usual double-clicking required in the classic Windows interface.

You select objects by hovering the mouse over them—As you saw in Chapter 8, "Expert Windows Explorer Techniques," you normally select an object by clicking it. With Web integration turned on, you select an object by positioning the mouse pointer over the object for a second or two (this is called *hovering* over the object). To select multiple objects, hover over the first object to select it, and then hold down Ctrl and hover over each of the rest of the objects. If the objects are contiguous, hover over the first object, and then hold down Shift and hover over the last object.

→ **See Also** "Selecting Files and Folders," **p. 205.**

To control these settings, first display the Folder Options dialog box (see Figure 16.1) by using either of the following techniques:

Watch Out!
Until you get used to the new single-click metaphor (which doesn't take long), you'll occasionally lapse into the old ways and try to select an object by clicking it. This, of course, launches the object, which can have disastrous consequences. For example, if you accidentally launch a registration (.reg) file, it will update the Windows Millennium Registry, which could lead to problems.

- Select Start, Settings, Control Panel, Folder Options.

- In any folder window (such as Windows Explorer or Control Panel), select Tools, Folder Options.

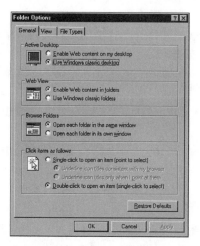

Figure 16.1
You use the Folder Options dialog box to toggle various Web integration settings on and off.

The options in the General tab's `Click items as follows` group determine how you launch and select icons and files:

Single-click to open an item (point to select)—If you activate this option, Windows Millennium accepts single-clicks to launch objects, and hovering to select objects. You also get two ways to determine how Windows Millennium underlines objects:

> **Underline icon titles consistent with my browser settings**—If you activate this option, Windows Millennium underlines icon and file links the same way that Internet Explorer is set up to underline Web page links. I tell you how to control Internet Explorer underlining in Chapter 5, "Expert Internet Explorer Techniques."

→ **See Also** "Internet Explorer's Advanced Options," **p. 146**.

> **Underline icon titles only when I point at them**—If you activate this option, Windows Millennium only underlines an object when you point at it.

Inside Scoop
I suggest that you
select the
Underline icon
titles consistent
with my browser
settings option.
This will give you
a strong visual
clue that single-
clicking is acti-
vated, so you'll be
less likely to
launch icons and
files accidentally.

Double-click to open an item (single-click to select)—If you activate this option, Windows Millennium reverts to the traditional double-click launching and single-click selecting.

The Integration Interface II: Viewing Folders As Web Pages

Web Integration also comes with a *Web view* that displays folder contents within a Web page structure. Note that, unlike Windows 98, this view is turned on by default in Windows Millennium.

The Web view creates a margin to the left of the contents and, when you select an object, this margin displays some information about the object. As you can see in Figure 16.2, this *information panel* also displays a thumbnail image for certain files, particularly graphics, HTML documents, and some Microsoft Office documents. (Figure 16.2 also points out a few other features of the information panel that you'll be dealing with later in this section.)

Figure 16.2
A folder viewed
as a Web page.

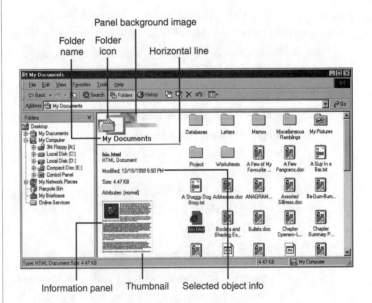

Panel background image

Folder
name

Folder
icon

Horizontal line

Information panel   Thumbnail   Selected object info

To toggle the Web view on and off, return to the General tab of the Folder Options dialog box and activate one of the following option buttons:

Enable Web content in folders—Activate this option to turn on the Web view.

Use Windows classic folders—Activate this option to turn off the Web view.

If you used Windows 98, note that you can no longer toggle Web view on and off for specific folders (via Windows Explorer's View, as Web Page command). In Windows Millennium, Web view is either on or off for *all* folders.

Creating a Custom Web View Background

One of the "authorized" ways that Windows Millennium gives you for customizing the Web view involves modifying the background image and text colors. Here are some things to keep in mind:

- When you set a background for a folder's Web view, all the icons and filenames are displayed on this background.

- The background and text colors affect only the Contents list. They don't change the background of the information panel that runs down the left side of the Web view.

- If your background image is smaller than the Contents list, Windows Millennium tiles the image so that it covers the entire list.

- Using the default Windows Millennium method, you can specify the background and colors for only one folder at a time.

Here's how it works:

1. Open the folder you want to work with.

2. Select View, Customize this Folder. The Customize this Folder wizard appears.

3. The initial dialog box just provides an introduction, so click Next.

Shortcut
You can also launch the Customize this Folder Wizard by right-clicking an empty section of the folder and then clicking Customize This Folder.

4. Activate the Modify background picture and filename appearance check box, deactivate any other active check boxes (I talk about the other check boxes later), and then click Next.

5. In the dialog box that appears, select the image you want to use as the background by using either of the following methods:

   • Highlight an item in the Select a background picture... list (see Figure 16.3).

   • Click Browse and use the Open dialog box to choose the image file you want to use. Note that you can select an image file on a network folder.

Figure 16.3
Select the image you want to use as the folder background.

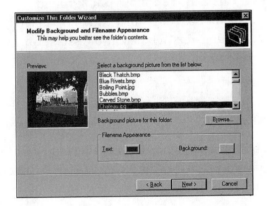

6. To change the color of the folder text, click the Text button, choose a color in the Color dialog box, and then click OK.

7. To change the color of the text background, click the Background button, select a color in the Color dialog box, and then click OK.

8. Click Finish. Windows Millennium applies the background and colors to the folder.

Windows Millennium keeps track of the background image and text colors by means of a hidden file named Desktop.ini, which is stored within the folder.

The background is specified by an `IconArea_Image` line, as in this example:

```
IconArea_Image=Folder Settings\Background.jpg
```

What this tells you is that Windows Millennium created a new subfolder named `Folder Settings` within the customized folder. It copied the selected background image into `Folder Settings` and renamed it to `Background.jpg`.

The text foreground and background colors are specified by the `IconArea_Text` and `IconArea_TextBackground` lines:

```
IconArea_Text=0x00bbggrr
IconArea_TextBackground=0x00bbggrr
```

For each value, *bbggrr* is a color code where *bb* (the blue component), *gg* (the green component), and *rr* (the red component) are two-digit hexadecimal values between 00 and FF.

To remove the formatting from a folder, you have two choices:

- Select View, Customize this Folder, click Next, activate the Remove customizations option, and then click Next again. This displays the Remove Customizations dialog box, which offers check boxes for each removable customization. Activate the check boxes for the customizations you want removed, click Next, and then click Finish.

- Delete the `Desktop.ini` file.

Adding a Folder Comment

When no object is selected, the Web view's information panel displays just the name of the folder, the message `Select an item to view its description`, and links for My Documents, My Network Places, and My Computer. You can your add own text to this display by inserting a *folder comment* that gets above the links when no file or folder is selected. Here are the steps to follow:

1. Open the folder you want to work with.

2. Select View, Customize This Folder to get the Customize This Folder Wizard going, and then click Next.

Watch Out!
Make sure the image you select doesn't hamper the readability of the folder text. For example, a dark image may make it impossible to read black file-names or icon titles. Note, however, that you can also change the color of the text (see step 5).

Undocumented
To create a solid-color background, use Paint to create a small image consisting only of the background color you want. Save this image into the My Pictures folder, and it will appear in the list of backgrounds displayed by the Customize This Folder Wizard.

Remember
You need to be familiar with HTML in order to get the most out of Web integration. If you're looking for an HTML tutorial, may I humbly suggest my book *The Complete Idiot's Guide to Creating a Web Page* (ISBN: 0-7897-2256-9). You can find out more about the book from my Web site (www.mcfedries.com/books/cightml/).

3. Activate the Add folder comment check box, deactivate any other active check boxes, and click Next. The Add folder comment dialog box appears.

4. Use the large text box to enter the text you want to display. Figure 16.4 shows both the Add folder comment dialog box and the customized folder. Here are some notes to bear in mind:

   - If you know HTML, you can add tags (such as <B> for bold) to format your text.

   - To start a new line, be sure to add the
 (line break) tag, as shown in Figure 16.4.

   - If you have Internet access, you can add links to Web pages. The general format to use is <A HREF="*address*">Link text</A>. Here, *address* is the full address of the page, and *Link text* is the text you'll click on.

   - You can create links that point to folders on your hard disk or on your network. You use the same format, except use the folder location as the address. Here's an example: <A HREF="C:\My Documents">Go to My Documents</A>.

Figure 16.4
Use this wizard dialog box to add a comment—text and HTML tags—to display in the information area.

The comment appears here

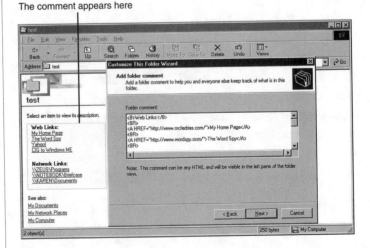

5. When you're done, click Next.

6. Click Finish.

Understanding Web View Templates

The customizations you've seen so far are a step up from what you could do in Windows 95, but they're not particularly exciting. The real meat of the Web view matter comes when you work with the underlying structure of the Web view. This structure comes in the form of *hypertext template* files, which use the htt extension. This is a text file that contains references to special ActiveX controls for displaying folder-specific items such as the contents, the folder icon, and data about the highlighted object. The rest of the file is pure HTML and JavaScript, just like you'd see in a Web page. The beauty of this is that you can easily modify the template with your own tags and text to create a customized Web view.

There are three ways to go about this:

- Use Notepad to modify the hidden Windows\Web\Folder .htt file. This is the default template that Windows Millennium uses to display the Web view in most folders. If you modify this file, you customize the Web view for all of those folders at once.

- Modify one of the folder-specific templates that comes with Windows Millennium. There are more than two dozen of these files. Here's a list of the most important ones:

Program Files\folder.htt—The Web view template for the Program Files folder.

Windows\folder.htt—The Web view template for the Windows folder.

Windows\System\folder.htt—The Web view template for the Windows\System folder.

Windows\Web\controlp.htt—The Web view template for the Control Panel folder.

Windows\Web\dialup.htt—The Web view template for the
Dial-Up Networking folder.

Windows\Web\nethood.htt—The Web view template for the
Network Neighborhood folder.

Windows\Web\printers.htt—The Web view template for the
Printers folder.

Windows\Web\recycle.htt—The Web view template for the
Recycle Bin folder.

Windows\Web\safemode.htt—The Web view template
displayed by the Active Desktop if an error occurs.

Windows\Web\schedule.htt—The Web view template for the
Scheduled Tasks folder.

- Use the Customize this Folder command, as described
  next.

Here are the steps to follow to modify a folder's template using
the Customize This Folder command:

1. Open the folder you want to work with.

2. Select View, Customize This Folder and click Next when
   the wizard appears.

3. Activate the Choose or edit an HTML template for this
   folder check box, deactivate all other active check boxes,
   and then click Next. The wizard displays the Change
   Folder Template dialog box shown in Figure 16.5.

Figure 16.5
Use this wizard
dialog box to
choose the folder
template you
want to use.

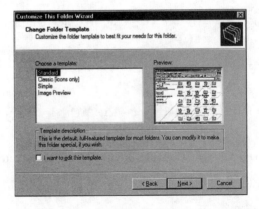

4. Use the Choose a template list to select the hypertext template file you want to use. (The Preview box shows you what the general template layout looks like.)

5. If you know HTML, you can edit the template in Notepad by activating the I want to edit this template check box.

6. Click Next.

7. If you asked to edit the template, the wizard displays it in Notepad. Make your changes (see the next section for details), save your work, and then exit Notepad.

8. In the final wizard dialog box, click Finish.

What happens here is that Windows Millennium takes your chosen (or edited) template, copies it to the folder's Folder Settings subfolder, and renames the template as Folder.htt (it's a hidden file). This copy overrides the default template to create a custom Web view for the folder.

The Registry keeps track of the name of the folder where the default Web view is stored. Rather than modifying Folder.htt, you could create your own custom template file and then modify the Registry to point to your file.

Under the Hood: The Structure of a Web View Template

To get the most out of the Web view, you need to edit the hypertext templates directly. To help, this section gives you an overview of how the standard template (the Folder.htt file that's copied to the Folder Settings subfolder) is structured.

This template, like all Web pages, is divided into two main areas:

The header—The first part of the template contains support data for displaying the Web view. This support data includes various styles that determine how the folder appears, and various JavaScript functions that are executed under different circumstances. It's unlikely that you'll want or need to modify anything in this section, so I don't cover it here.

The body—The rest of the template—that is, the section between and including the `<body>` and `</body>` tags—contains the text, ActiveX control references, and HTML tags that govern what you see when the folder is in Web view. The rest of this section looks at the body structure in detail.

To get to the body, scroll down until you see the following line:

```
<body scroll=no onload="Load()">
```

Figure 16.6 shows the first part of the body and points out a few interesting landmarks. Note that these correspond to the Web view features that I pointed out earlier in Figure 16.2.

Figure 16.6
The first part of the body section of the Folder.htt template.

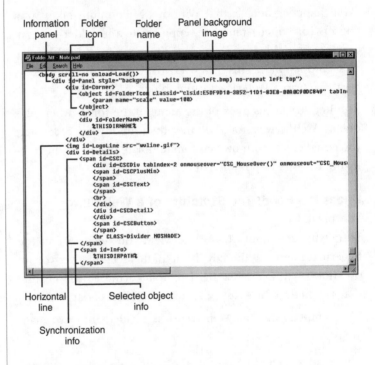

(Top labels: Information panel · Folder icon · Folder name · Panel background image)

(Bottom labels: Horizontal line · Synchronization info · Selected object info)

Here's a brief explanation of each part:

Information panel—This is the information panel that appears in the left margin. It's encompassed by a set of `<div>` and `</div>` tags named Panel (id=Panel).

Panel background image—This is the URL value specified in the panel's `<div>` tag.

Folder icon—This <object> tag (id=FolderIcon) is used to display the folder icon. You can eke out a bit more room in the information panel by either deleting the entire <object></object> construct, or preferably, by commenting it out.

Folder name—This section (id=FolderName) uses the %THISDIRNAME% environment variable to display the folder name.

Horizontal line—This <img> tag (id=LogoLine) defines the horizontal line that appears below the folder name.

Synchronization info—This <span> and </span> set (id=CSC) defines the area where synchronization data appears if the folder contains objects set up for offline viewing. (Note that these objects must be created by a program that supports Windows Millennium's Synchronization Manager.)

Selected object into—This <span> and </span> set (id=Info) marks the spot where the data on the currently selected object appears.

Figure 16.7 shows the rest of the template body.

Inside Scoop
Not all the templates display the JavaScript code within the header. Instead, you see a <script src=> line that references a file named WebView.js. This is a JavaScript file (it's a text file) that contains the Web view functions and code.

Thumbnail

Media preview

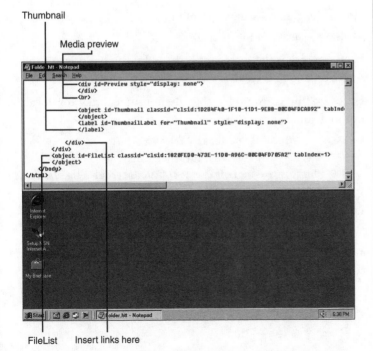

Figure 16.7
The rest of the body section of the Folder.htt template.

FileList   Insert links here

Inside Scoop
In the `<body>`
tag, the
`onload="Load()"`
part means that
Windows
Millennium runs a
JavaScript func-
tion named `Load()`
whenever you
open a folder. If
you're curious,
you can find this
function in the
template header.

Undocumented
You can set up a
custom back-
ground for the
information panel
by changing the
URL value to the
name of another
file. You can enter
just the filename
if you copy the
file to the folder's
`Folder Settings`
subfolder.
Otherwise, use
the full path to
the image you
want to use. If
you want the
image to be tiled
to cover the
entire panel,
delete the `no-
repeat` attribute.

Once again, let's run through the particulars:

Media preview—This `<div>` tag (`id=Preview`) displays the Media Player control, which can be used to play movies, sound files, and other media supported by Media Player. Note that this feature is turned off by default.

Thumbnail—This `<object>` tag (`id=Thumbnail`) represents the Thumbnail Viewer ActiveX control that displays thumb-nails for images, Web pages, and other documents.

Inserting your own links—You can insert links to local and remote resources here. See "Inserting Links to Local, Intranet, and Internet Resources," later in this chapter.

FileList—This `<object>` tag (`id=FileList`) displays the FileList ActiveX control, which displays the contents of the folder.

Inserting Links to Local, Intranet, and Internet Resources

One of the most useful ways to customize a Web view template is to add links that appear within the information panel. You can enter links to other folders (local), network resources (intranet), or even the Internet.

Here's the general syntax for a link:

```
<A HREF="address">Link text</A>
```

Here, *address* is the local, network, or Internet address of the resource, and *Link text* is the text that you click.

Here are three examples that demonstrate links for local, intranet, and Internet resources:

```
<A HREF="C:\Windows\">A local link</A>
<A HREF="\\SERVER\Data\">An intranet link</A>
<A HREF="http://www.mcfedries.com/">An Internet link</A>
```

Note, too, that the standard template that Windows Millennium copies in the `Folder Settings` subfolder doesn't include the usual links for My Documents, My Network Places, and My Computer. To include these links, add the following code to the template:

```
<a href="file:///::{450D8FBA-AD25-11D0-98A8-
0800361B1103}">My Documents</a>
<br>
<a href="file:///::{20D04FE0-3AEA-1069-A2D8-
08002B30309D}">My Computer</a>
<br>
<a href="file:///::{208D2C60-3AEA-1069-A2D7-
08002B30309D}">My Network Places</a>
```

Remember
To comment out a section of HTML code, place <!-- at the beginning and -->
at the end.

The Integration Interface III: Web Content on the Desktop

The idea behind Windows Millennium's Active Desktop is to get away from the static, do-nothing desktop of Windows 95. In its place, the Active Desktop offers a three-tiered replacement:

- The top level contains the regular desktop icons, such as My Computer and the Recycle Bin.

- The middle level is the *desktop items layer*. You use this layer to display dynamic content on the desktop. Possible items include Web pages, images, Java applets, ActiveX controls, and more.

- The bottom level is the *HTML desktop background layer*. This level replaces the wallpaper with an HTML document that can display anything that would normally be available in a Web page.

This all sounds interesting, but it requires that your desktop be visible. However, most users—power users in particular—cover their desktop either with multiple open windows or with maximized windows. (In its defense, Microsoft did give users an easy route to the desktop by including the Show Desktop icon in the Quick Launch toolbar.) Not only that, but the Active Desktop tends to eat a lot of system resources, and, at least in my experience, isn't particularly robust. (Hence, as mentioned earlier, the need for the safe mode folder template—Safemode.htt—that displays if the Active Desktop crashes.)

That's not to say that the Active Desktop should be written off completely. It does have a few interesting technical aspects, it runs well on systems with lots of memory (at least 64MB), and keeping an eye on the desktop might not be a problem for

66

Active Desktop was supposed to be one of the coolest and widely used new features of Internet Explorer 4.0 and Windows 98. But today, almost nobody uses it.
—*Mike Elgan, Windows Magazine*

99

users who are running multiple monitors or who have a large monitor running at high resolution. If you fall into any of these categories, the rest of this chapter shows you how to get the most out of the Active Desktop.

Shortcut
You can jump directly to the Web tab by right-clicking the desktop, and then clicking Active Desktop, Customize my Desktop.

Turning the Active Desktop On and Off

The Active Desktop is off by default after you install Windows Millennium. Here are the techniques to use to toggle the Active Desktop on and off:

- Right-click the desktop, and then click Active Desktop, Show Web Content.

- Open Control Panel's Display icon, select the Web tab, and then toggle the Show Web content on my Active Desktop check box.

Working with Desktop Items

The desktop items layer is actually a stripped-down Web browser. (Technically, it's an ActiveX control called *WebBrowser*.) This means that you can set up the desktop items layer with all manners of Web page content. Here's how to get started:

1. Open the Display Properties dialog box, head for the Web tab, and make sure the Show Web content on my Active Desktop check box is activated.

2. Click New. Windows Millennium displays the New Active Desktop Item dialog box. (A faster way to display this dialog box is to right-click the desktop and then click Active Desktop, New Desktop Item.)

3. You now have three choices:

    - To choose from a collection of desktop items, click Visit Gallery. In this case, Windows Millennium starts Internet Explorer and displays the Active Desktop Gallery Web site. After you've found an item you want, click the Add to Active Desktop link. In the confirmation dialog box that appears, click Yes.

- To add a Web page to the Active Desktop, use the Location text box to enter the page address, and then click OK. If the page is set up as a favorite, click Browse, highlight the URL shortcut in the Favorites folder, and then click Open.

- To specify a local or network HTML file or image, either enter the file's path in the Location text box or click Browse, use the Browse dialog box to highlight the file, and then click Open.

4. If you added remote content, you next see the Add item to Active Desktop dialog box. This dialog box lets you know that Windows Millennium treats each remote desktop item as an offline favorite (see Chapter 5, "Expert Internet Explorer Techniques"). If you want to schedule the synchronization and enter a login username and password, click Customize. When you're done, click OK.

→ **See Also** "Reading Pages Offline," **p. 138**.

The items you add are displayed in the Web tab of the Display Properties dialog box, as shown in Figure 16.8. Use the following techniques to work with these items:

- Use the check boxes to toggle the items on and off the Active Desktop. Alternatively, right-click the desktop and then click Active Desktop in the shortcut menu. The submenu that appears lists the available desktop items at the bottom. Click an item to toggle it on and off.

- To delete an item, highlight it and click Delete.

- To change the synchronization of a remote item, highlight the item and click Properties.

You can also work with the desktop items directly. When you position the mouse pointer over a desktop item, a border appears around the item. When you move the mouse pointer to the top of the item, a larger bar appears on top of the item, as shown in Figure 16.9.

Undocumented
If you want to add a Java applet to the Active Desktop, place the appropriate <APPLET> tag inside an HTML document (you don't need anything else inside this file). Then, use the New Active Desktop Item dialog box to choose that document.

Cover desktop   Split desktop with icons

Given this, you can use the following techniques to work with the item:

- To resize the item, drag its border.

- To move the item, drag the top bar.

- To display the item's Control menu, click the arrow that appears on the left side of the top bar.

- To expand the item so that it covers the entire desktop, click the Cover Desktop button (see Figure 16.9).

- To expand the item so that it covers the empty part of the desktop (that is, the part without any icons), click the Split Desktop With Icons (see Figure 16.9).

- To remove the item from the desktop, click the Close button that appears on the right side of the top bar.

- If you don't want your desktop items moved or changed in any way, right-click the desktop and then activate the Active Desktop, Lock Desktop Items command.

Turning the Active Desktop into a Web Page

As I mentioned earlier, the HTML desktop background layer enables you to convert the desktop into a Web page. Here's how it's done:

1. Right-click the desktop and then click Properties to get the Display Properties dialog box onscreen.

2. Make sure the Background tab is selected.

3. In the Wallpaper list, select Windows Me.

4. Click OK. If the Active Desktop is not currently activated, Windows Millennium asks if you want to enable it.

5. Click Yes.

The "wallpaper" you selected is actually an HTML document named `Windows Me.htm`, which you'll find in the `Windows\Web\Wallpaper` folder. Feel free to edit the document to customize the default Active Desktop wallpaper.

Alternatively, you may prefer to create your own HTML document and use it as your Active Desktop wallpaper. Here are a few things to keep in mind when designing your wallpaper:

- Make sure any elements in your HTML document won't be hidden behind the regular desktop icons.

- You can't scroll the wallpaper, so make sure the layout of the HTML document fits inside your desktop. (If the page is too big, Windows crops the excess.)

Remember
If you have the item covering the desktop or split with the icons, you display the item's button bar again by moving the mouse pointer to the top of the screen and pressing Alt.

Inside Scoop
Rather than working around the regular desktop icons, you may prefer to turn them off while the desktop is displayed as a Web page. To do this, right-click the desktop, and then deactivate the Active Desktop, Show Desktop Icons command.

- Your HTML document must reside either on your hard disk or on a network drive. You can't use Internet pages.

- When specifying images and other elements, use items either on your hard disk or on your network. Again, Internet-based items are not allowed.

Once your page is ready, follow these steps to set it as your Active Desktop wallpaper:

Shortcut
You'll be able to select your HTML document directly from the Wallpaper list if you place the file in the Windows\Web\ Wallpaper folder.

1. Right-click the desktop and then click Properties to get the Display Properties dialog box onscreen.

2. Make sure the Background tab is selected.

3. Click Browse to display the Browse dialog box.

4. Select your HTML document and then click Open.

5. Click OK. If the Active Desktop is not currently activated, Windows Millennium asks if you want to enable it.

6. Click Yes.

Essential Information

- Web integration displays objects as links, and it enables you to launch objects by single-clicking and select objects by hovering.

- To turn on Web integration, select Start, Settings, Folder Options and activate the Web style option.

- Select View, As Web Page to display a folder in Web view.

- Customize the htt folder template files to set up Web view to your liking.

- Right-click the desktop and then select Active Desktop, View As Web Page to turn on the Active Desktop.

Customizing the Windows Millennium Interface

Chapter 17

M ICROSOFT READILY ADMITS a sense of "ownership" when it comes to the look and feel of the Windows Millennium interface, which explains why they refuse to let computer manufacturers implement custom desktops on the machines they sell. This sense of ownership probably also explains why Microsoft doesn't supply users with all that much information about customizing.

What's weird about this is that Microsoft loaded Windows Millennium with a large number of customization features. Whether you want to customize the desktop, the Start menu, the taskbar, or the look of everything from window menu bars to icon title text, Windows Millennium has what you need to get the job done. And if you dig a little deeper, tools such as the Registry, the System Policy Editor, and Tweak UI enable you to customize system icons and other "built-in" components. This chapter introduces you to Windows Millennium's basic customizing features, and then pulls out the heavy artillery for some truly "unauthorized" customizing.

Changing an Icon

In several places in this chapter, and in other places throughout this book, you customize an object by changing its icon. (For example, right-click any shortcut, click Properties, and then click Change Icon.) So, I begin this chapter by showing you the generic steps for selecting a different icon.

How you get started depends on the object you're working with. However, in all cases you eventually end up at the Change Icon dialog box shown in Figure 17.1.

Here are some notes about working with this dialog box:

- In Windows Millennium, icons are usually stored in groups within executable files, particularly exe and dll files. Files with the ico extension are pure icon files.

- If the icon you want isn't displayed in the Change Icon dialog box, use the File name text box to enter the name of an icon file and then press Tab. Here are a few suggestions:

```
C:\Windows\System\Shell32.dll
C:\Windows\System\Pifmgr.dll
C:\Windows\System\User.exe
C:\Windows\Explorer.exe
C:\Windows\Moricons.dll
C:\Windows\Progman.exe
```

- If you're not sure about which file to try, click the Browse button and choose a file in the dialog box that appears.

Click the icon you want to use and then click OK.

In some cases, especially when you're working within the Registry, you need to know the *icon number* that an icon uses within an executable or icon file. To figure this out, use the Change Icon dialog box to open the executable or icon file.

Now count the icons, as follows:

- The first icon (the one in the upper-left corner) is 0.

- If the file contains more than four icons, they're displayed in columns. Be sure to count down each column and then work your way across to the next column. For example, the first icon in the second column is icon 4.

More Than Just Wallpaper: Customizing the Desktop

Let's now examine a few methods for customizing the desktop. Most of the standard Windows Millennium methods for touching up the desktop are straightforward, so I'll only include brief descriptions of them so that I can concentrate on more powerful methods.

A Quick Look at Windows Millennium's Display Settings

Most of Windows Millennium's basic desktop customizing happens within the Display Properties dialog box, shown in Figure 17.2. (Note that some video adapter drivers add extra tabs to this dialog box, so yours may have a different configuration than the one shown in Figure 17.2.) To get this dialog box onscreen, open the Control Panel and then launch the Display icon.

Inside Scoop
Rather than making do with Windows Millennium's built-in icons, you might prefer to use your own, either by editing existing icons or by creating icons from scratch. There are a number of decent icon-creation programs available. The ones I like are IconEdit Pro, IconForge, and Icon Easel (all available from www.zdnet.com/downloads).

Figure 17.2
Use the various tabs in the Display Properties dialog box to customize the desktop and a few other Windows Millennium interface features.

Shortcut
An often faster method for getting to the Display Properties dialog box is to right-click an empty section of the desktop and then click Properties.

Watch Out!
Almost every video-related problem I've had with every version of Windows I've ever worked with has been screen saver–related. Something about the mode switch required to activate the screen saver causes a machine to lock up. Therefore, I always recommend that users *not* activate any screen saver.

Here's a brief summary of the kinds of customizations you can perform with each tab:

Background

Use the Select a background picture... list to select a wallpaper pattern to sit on the desktop. Note that most wallpaper files are only small squares, so to cover the entire desktop you need to select Tile in the Display list. For a larger image that doesn't quite fit the desktop, try selecting Stretch in the Display list.

As an alternative to wallpaper, click Pattern to cover the desktop with a pattern.

Screen Saver

Use the Screen Saver list to select an animated screen saver pattern that will appear after your system has been idle for a specified amount of time. After you've chosen a screen saver, the following controls become active:

- **Settings**—Click this button to customize the screen saver.

- **Preview**—Click this button to get a full-screen preview of the screen saver.

- **Password protected**—If you activate this check box, the screen saver won't exit to the desktop unless you enter the correct password. Click Change to set the password.

- **Wait**—Use this spin box to set the number of minutes your computer must be idle (no keyboard or mouse input) before the screen saver kicks in.

Your Screen Saver tab may also have a group named Energy saving features of monitor. I discuss power management for monitors in Chapter 22, "Maximizing Multimedia Hardware."

→ **See Also** "Using Your Monitor's Power Management Features," **p. 494**.

Appearance

Use this tab to customize the colors and fonts that Windows Millennium uses. You have two ways to proceed:

- To use one of Windows Millennium's predefined color schemes, select an item from the Scheme list.

- To create your own scheme, select objects from the Item list and use the rest of the controls to set the size, color, and font of the object.

Effects

Use the Desktop icons group to pick out a new icon for several desktop stalwarts, including My Computer, My Documents, My Network Places, and Recycle Bin in its full and empty states. This tab also offers the following check boxes:

Use transition effects for menus and tooltips—This check box is activated by default, and it tells Windows Millennium to use animation when displaying or hiding certain items. Specifically, windows "slide" down to the taskbar when minimized, and menus and lists "scroll" onto the screen when opened. These objects show up marginally faster if you deactivate this feature.

Smooth edges of screen fonts—Activate this option to have Windows Millennium smooth the jagged edges that appear when you use a large font. Unless you use a large font regularly, leave this option deactivated for better performance.

Use large icons—Activate this check box to increase the size of every icon from 32 pixels per side to 48 pixels per side.

Show icons using all possible colors—When this check box is activated, Windows Millennium uses every available color to render the icons, thus giving them extra detail. You should deactivate this check box only if you have a graphics card that doesn't display the icons properly.

Remember
Full-window drag is a useful setting to activate. However, some older video cards may not have enough horsepower to handle this feature. Most newer cards can handle this, as can older cards that have plenty of video memory.

Show window contents while dragging—When this check box is deactivated, Windows Millennium displays just an outline when you use your mouse to drag a window. If you activate this check box, Windows Millennium leaves the window intact while you drag it (this is called *full-window drag*), which usually makes it easier to position windows.

Web

As you saw in the previous chapter, this tab is used to work with the Active Desktop.

➜ **See Also** "Working with Desktop Items," **p. 382**.

Settings

This tab offers a number of controls for working with your video card and monitor. See Chapter 22 for details.

➜ **See Also** "Configuring the Color Depth and Resolution," **p. 488** and "Working with Windows Millennium's Monitor Features," **p. 492**.

Modifying the Desktop Items

This section looks at a few methods for customizing the desktop items ("item" meaning an icon and its text). You learn how to select different icons, hide items, and work with specific items such as My Documents and Recycle Bin.

Changing the Desktop Icons

You saw earlier that the Effects tab in the Display Properties dialog box enables you to choose a different icon for some of the desktop items. For the rest, the Registry is required.

All the desktop items have their own subkeys within the following Registry key:

```
HKEY_CLASSES_ROOT\CLSID
```

The subkeys in this branch are all 32-digit (16-byte) hexadecimal class ID values. Table 17.1 lists the class IDs for most of the desktop icons.

TABLE 17.1: CLASS IDS FOR THE DESKTOP ITEMS

Desktop Item	Class ID
My Documents	{450D8FBA-AD25-11D0-98A8-0800361B1103}
My Computer	{20D04FE0-3AEA-1069-A2D8-08002B30309D}
My Network Places	{208D2C60-3AEA-1069-A2D7-08002B30309D}
Recycle Bin	{645FF040-5081-101B-9F08-00AA002F954E}
Internet Explorer	{3DC7A020-0ACD-11CF-A9BB-00AA004AE837}
Setup MSN Internet Access	{88667D10-10F0-11D01-8150-00AA00BF8457}
My Briefcase	{85BBD920-42A0-1069-A2E4-08002B30309D}

Watch Out!
To ensure that you can recover your default desktop at any time, export the HKEY_CLASSES_ROOT \CLSID key (as described in Chapter 3) before performing any of the customizations mentioned in the next few sections.

When you examine these branches, you usually see a subkey named DefaultIcon. The Default setting in this subkey uses the following general format:

```
IconFile,IconNumber
```

IconFile   This string is the full pathname of the file that contains the icon used by the desktop item.

IconNumber   This number specifies the icon position within IconFile (recall that the first icon is 0).

For example, here's the setting used by the My Network Places item:

```
c:\windows\system\shell32.dll,17
```

To specify a different icon, you have two choices:

- Change the icon number to another in the same file.

- Specify a different icon file and select an icon number within that file.

Editing the Desktop Item InfoTips

When you hover your mouse pointer over most desktop items, a banner appears with a brief description of what the item does. This banner is called an InfoTip, and most of them can be changed by editing the Registry.

To try this, select the class ID of the desktop item you want to work with. Figure 17.3 shows the class ID for the My Computer item. As you can see, the item's class ID key has an InfoTip setting that stores the banner text. Edit this string value to modify the InfoTip text.

Hiding Desktop Items

In the previous chapter, I showed you how to hide desktop items when viewing Web content on the Active Desktop. Windows Millennium also enables you to hide the desktop items even when you're not using the Active Desktop. Here's how:

1. Open the System Policy Editor.

2. Select File, Open Registry to load the local Registry.

3. Launch the Local User icon and then select Windows 98 System, Shell, Restrictions.

4. Activate the Hide all items on Desktop check box.

5. Click OK.

6. Select File, Save to write the change to the Registry.

7. Exit and restart Windows.

Working with the My Documents Icon

One of the easiest ways to make backing up files easier is to store all your documents in one place, such as a folder or hard drive partition. This saves you from the time-consuming chore of having to track down documents that may be scattered throughout the drive. Windows Millennium encourages this sensible approach by providing a folder named My Documents, which is located on the same drive that you used to install Windows Millennium (the likely path is C:\My Documents).

Windows Millennium also creates a handy shortcut to this folder: the My Documents icon on the desktop. This is no ordinary shortcut, however. The My Documents icon is known as a *shell extension shortcut* because it's a shortcut that's also part of the Windows Millennium shell. One consequence of this is that it's easy to change the target of the My Documents shortcut:

1. Right-click My Documents and then click Properties. The My Documents Properties dialog box appears.

2. You now have two choices:

   • To use a different folder target, use the Target text box to enter the full path for the folder you want to use.

   • To move the contents of the existing My Documents folder to another folder, click Move, choose the folder using the Browse For Folder dialog box, and click OK.

3. Click OK.

4. If you elected to move the folder, Windows Millennium asks if you want to move all the folder contents to the new location. If so, click Yes.

Renaming the Recycle Bin

You can rename most of the desktop items by right-clicking them and then clicking Rename in the shortcut menu. This doesn't work for the Recycle Bin, unfortunately. To rename this item, first find its class ID subkey in the Registry:

```
HKEY_CLASSES_ROOT\CLSID\{645FF040-5081-101B-9F08-
00AA002F954E}
```

To rename the item, edit just the `Recycle Bin` part of the `LocalizedString` setting. (That is, the name of the Recycle Bin is given by whatever text you enter after the last comma in this setting.) To put the new name into effect, click the desktop and then press F5 to refresh it.

Setting Up Custom Shell Folders

Windows Millennium defines a number of *shell folders*—special folders used by Windows Millennium and its applications. These shell folders define what's included on the desktop, the Send To menu, the Fonts folder, and various Start menu folders (including the Start menu itself). You can use the Registry to set up alternative locations for these shell folders that contain the icons you want to work with.

The various shell folders are defined in the following key:

```
\HKEY_CURRENT_USER\Software\Microsoft\Windows\
CurrentVersion\Explorer\Shell Folders
```

Most of the settings in this key are straightforward. For example, the location of the Send To menu's folder is given by the SendTo setting. Note, however, that the My Documents shortcut's current target is stored in the Registry as the Personal setting.

Undocumented
Many of these custom shell folders may be more easily defined using the System Policy Editor. To see how, open the Local User icon and then select Windows Millennium System, Shell, Custom Folders. This branch contains six check boxes that enable you to specify custom shell folders for the desktop, the Start menu, and more.

The Desktop setting also requires a bit more explanation. Most of the desktop items are built in to the Windows Millennium desktop. However, some of the items—including My Briefcase and Online Services—appear on the desktop only by virtue of being located in the Windows\Desktop folder (or whatever is specified in the Desktop setting in the Shell Folders key). Therefore, specifying another folder for the desktop only replaces some of the desktop items.

Customizing Windows Millennium's System Icons

The *system icons* are the icons Windows Millennium uses for file types, folders, drives, Start menu items, and more. Most system icons can be customized with just a simple Registry tweak.

To see how, refer back to Figure 17.1, which shows the icons contained in \Windows\System\Shell32.dll. This file is where most of the Windows Millennium system icons are stored. As you can see, the first icon (which is, you'll remember, icon 0) is the system icon for an unregistered file type, the second icon (icon 1) is below it, and it's the system icon for a WordPad document.

To specify custom icons, first head for the following Registry key:

```
HKEY_LOCAL_MACHINE\SOFTWARE\Microsoft\Windows\
CurrentVersion\explorer\Shell Icons
```

The idea is that, for each system icon you want to customize, you create a new string setting in this key, and give the setting the same name as the position in Shell32.dll of the icon you want to work with. For example, the "unregistered file type" icon is in position 0, so to customize this icon you create a new string setting named 0. Similarly, to customize the WordPad icon (icon 1), create a new string setting named 1.

After you've done that, edit this new setting and give it the following value:

```
shell32.dll,IconNumber
```

IconNumber   The icon position within Shell32.dll of the icon you want to use.

For example, the following value specifies the "globe" icon (icon 13):

```
shell32.dll,13
```

Renovating the Start Menu

Messing around with icons and colors is fine for rugged individualists who enjoy fritterware. If you're more into boosting your productivity, spending a few minutes now to reconstruct your Start menu will pay off handsomely over time. Why? Simply because the default Windows Millennium Start menus are a model of poor design. Features that you might use only rarely (such as the Log Off command) are easily accessible, whereas crucial features (such as Backup and ScanDisk) are buried four menus deep.

The next few sections show you how to customize the Start menu. Using these techniques, you can perform the following Start menu productivity boosts:

- Move important features closer to the beginning of the Start menu hierarchy.

- Remove features you don't use.

- Add new commands for features not currently available on the Start menu (such as the Registry Editor).

Undocumented
The system icons are stored in a hidden file named ShellIconCache in the Windows folder. To put your new system icons into effect, you have to force Windows Millennium to refresh this file. The easiest way is to right-click the desktop, click Properties, and select the Appearance tab. In the Item list, select Icon, modify the Size value, and then click Apply. Return Icon to its original value, and then click OK.

66

fritterware, *noun*
Feature-laden software that seduces people into spending inordinate amounts of time tweaking various options for only marginal gains in productivity.
—*The Word Spy*
(www.wordspy.com)

99

I also show you a few tricks for making it easier to select Start menu commands.

Adding and Removing Start Menu Shortcuts

On the main Start menu (the one that appears when you click the Start button), the commands from Programs on down are built into the Windows Millennium system. This means the following:

- Everything else on the Start menu and its submenus is a shortcut that points to a program or document.

- You can't add new shortcuts to the area that contains the built-in commands. You can add shortcuts above Programs, or you can add shortcuts to the Programs menu (or any of its submenus).

- You can't hide the built-in commands directly, although it *is* possible to hide some of these commands indirectly (see "Some Start Menu Properties," later in this chapter).

Windows Millennium offers four methods for adding and removing Start menu shortcuts, and I explain each of them in the next four sections.

Using the Create Shortcut Wizard

The Create Shortcut Wizard is available by selecting Start, Settings, Taskbar and Start Menu to display the Taskbar Properties dialog box. Select the Advanced tab and you see three buttons in the Start menu group:

Add—Click this button to launch the Create Shortcut Wizard. This is a cumbersome method, and I recommend it only for novices.

Remove—Click this button to display the Remove Shortcuts/ Folders dialog box, from which you can delete a Start menu shortcut.

Advanced—Click this button to open Windows Explorer and display the Start Menu folder, which I describe a bit later in "Working with the Start Menu Folder."

Watch Out!
Clicking the Advanced button displays Windows Explorer with the Start Menu folder as the root. This means you can't access the other folders and drives on your system, which is inconvenient if you want to add new shortcuts. Click the Advanced button only if you need to rename or delete Start menu shortcuts.

Dragging and Dropping onto the Start Button

The quickest way to add a shortcut is to drag an executable file from Windows Explorer and then do either of the following:

- Drop it on the Start button. This creates a shortcut on the main Start menu, above the Programs command.

- Hover over the Start button. After a second or two, the main Start menu appears. Now drag the file into the Start menu and drop it where you want the shortcut to appear.

Working with the Start Menu *Folder*

All the Start menu shortcuts are stored in the Windows\Start Menu folder, as shown in Figure 17.4. As you can see, this folder contains only the Programs menus, its submenus, and any shortcuts displayed above the Programs menu.

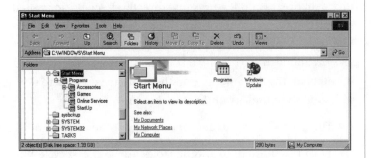

By working with this folder, you get the most control over not only where your Start menu shortcuts appear, but also the names of those shortcuts. Here's a summary of the techniques you can use:

- You can drag existing Start menu shortcuts from one folder to another.

- To create a new shortcut, drag the executable file and drop it inside the folder you want to use. (Remember that if you want to create a shortcut for a document or other nonexecutable file, right-drag the file and then select Create Shortcut(s) Here when you drop the file.)

Remember
If you drag the file to the Programs command, the Programs submenu opens, and you can then continue dragging within that submenu. Repeat as necessary.

Figure 17.4
The Start menu shortcuts are stored in the Start Menu folder.

Shortcut
A quick way to get to the Start Menu folder is to right-click the Start button and then click Explore.

Inside Scoop
If you have user profiles enabled on your system, each user will have her own Start Menu folder, which will be located at Windows\Profiles\ User\Start Menu (where User is the person's user-name).

Watch Out!
If you change any of a program's Start menu short-cuts, it's unlikely that those short-cuts will be deleted if you uninstall the pro-gram. You'll proba-bly have to delete the shortcuts by hand.

Shortcut
A quicker way to get to the Taskbar Properties dialog box is to right-click an empty section of the taskbar and then click Properties in the context menu.

- To make a shortcut appear on the main Start menu (above the Programs command), create the shortcut in the Start Menu folder.

- You can create your own folders within the Start Menu folder hierarchy and they'll appear as submenus within the Start menu.

- You rename a Start menu shortcut the same way you rename any file.

- You delete a Start menu shortcut the same way you delete any file.

Working with Start Menu Shortcuts Directly

When I'm examining a new version of Windows, I generally ignore the headline-grabbing "big" features. Instead, I look for the small tweaks and features that directly affect efficiency and productivity, because those are the ones that save time in the long run. A perfect example of such a feature was Windows 98's capability to work with Start menu shortcuts directly. That is, you open the Start menu, find the shortcut you want to work with, and then use any of these techniques:

- Drag the shortcut to another section of the Start menu.

- Drag the shortcut to another folder or to the Recycle Bin.

- Right-click the shortcut and then select a command (such as Delete) from the context menu.

Some Start Menu Properties

The Start menu also offers a number of properties that enable you to toggle commands on and off, expand folders into sub-menus, and much more. To work with these settings, first dis-play the Taskbar and Start Menu Properties dialog box by selecting Start, Settings, Taskbar and Start Menu.

The General tab has two Start menu-related check boxes:

Show small icons in Start menu—If you activate this check box, Windows Millennium removes the Windows Me Millennium Edition banner along the side of the main Start menu and uses slightly smaller icons within all the Start menus. This enables you to get more shortcuts onto each menu. However, these smaller icons are difficult to see if you're running at a high-video resolution.

Use personalized menus—Deactivating this check box tell Windows Millennium not to use its new personalized menus feature.

There are more Start menu options in the Advanced tab, shown in Figure 17.5.

Figure 17.5
The Advanced tab contains a number of Start menu settings.

The Start menu and Taskbar group contains a list of check boxes that toggle various Start menu features on and off. Here's a quick summary:

- **Display Favorites**—Activate this check box to add the Favorites submenu onto the main Start menu.

- **Display Logoff**—Deactivate this check box to remove the Log Off *User* command from the main Start menu (where *User* is the name of the user who's currently logged on).

- **Display Run**—Deactivate this check box to remove the Run command from the main Start menu.

- **Enable dragging and dropping**—When this check box is activated, it means you can drag and drop most of the Start menu items as described earlier (see "Working with Start Menu Shortcuts Directly").

- **Expand Control Panel**—Activate this check box to display all the Control Panel icons in a submenu when you select Start, Settings, Control Panel. I highly recommend activating this feature because it gives you a much quicker route to all the Control Panel icons.

- **Expand Dial-Up Networking**—Activate this check box to display a submenu listing your Dial-Up Networking connection icons when you select Start, Settings, Dial-Up Networking.

- **Expand My Documents**—Activate this check box to display a submenu containing your My Documents files when you select Start, Documents, My Documents.

- **Expand My Pictures**—Activate this check box to display a submenu containing your My Pictures files when you select Start, Documents, My Pictures.

- **Expand Printers**—Activate this check box to display a menu of your installed printers when you select Start, Settings, Printers.

- **Scroll Programs**—This setting determines what Windows Millennium does if the Programs menu contains so many items that the entire menu can't fit into the height of the screen. When this setting is off, Windows Millennium displays Programs as a two-column menu. When this setting is on, Windows Millennium displays Programs as a single menu with up and down arrows on the top and bottom, respectively. You click these arrows to scroll through the menu.

To put the new settings into effect, click OK or Apply.

Creating Accelerator Keys for Start Menu Shortcuts

When you open the main Start menu, notice that the built-in commands each have an accelerator key. This means you can select one of these commands quickly by pressing the letter of its accelerator key. For example, press **p** to select Programs.

All the other Start menu shortcuts have an implied accelerator key, which is the first character of the shortcut name. If multiple shortcuts share the same first character, pressing the character repeatedly will select each item in turn. In the Accessories menu, for example, press **c** to select the Communications menu, and press **c** again to select Calculator.

You can take advantage of this behavior to create custom accelerator keys that are quick to press and are unique. The secret? Rename the shortcuts so that each one begins with a different single-digit number. For example, if you have a shortcut named "Registry Editor," renaming this to "1. Registry Editor" means that you can select this shortcut by pressing 1.

Redoing the Taskbar

Fixing the Start menu is a great way to streamline your Windows work. Another way to enhance efficiency is to customize the taskbar. Windows Millennium gives you quite a few ways to do this, and I discuss them all in the next few sections.

Setting Taskbar Properties

Let's begin by looking at a few properties that enable you to customize the look of the taskbar. To see these properties, select Start, Settings, Taskbar and Start Menu. In the Taskbar and Start Menu Properties dialog box that appears, the General tab contains the following taskbar-related check boxes:

- **Always on top**—If you deactivate this check box, open windows—particularly maximized windows—can cover the taskbar. This is useful when you need some extra screen real estate.

Inside Scoop
If you deactivate Always on top and then maximize a window, the taskbar disappears. To see it again, press Ctrl+Esc or the Windows logo key ( ).

- **Auto hide**—If you activate this check box, Windows Millennium shrinks the taskbar down to a thin gray strip at the bottom of the screen. To display the full taskbar, move your mouse to the bottom edge of the screen. (Many experienced users dislike this setting because it's too easy to accidentally display the taskbar when they move their mouse near the bottom of a program window.)

- **Show clock**—This check box toggles the system tray's Clock on and off.

In the Advanced tab (refer to Figure 17.5), the Start menu and Taskbar list has a branch named Taskbar that contains two check boxes:

Display shortcut menu on right-click—If you deactivate this check box, Windows Millennium disables right-click functionality for the taskbar and all its toolbars. You learn more about this right-click functionality in the next section. See also "Displaying Other Taskbar Toolbars," later in this chapter.

Enable moving and resizing—If you deactivate this check box, Windows Millennium prevents you from changing the size of the taskbar and moving the taskbar to a different edge of the screen. (See "Moving and Sizing the Taskbar," later in this chapter.) Many novices get themselves into trouble by accidentally moving or resizing the taskbar, so consider deactivating this check box if you're configuring Windows Millennium for a new user.

Using the Taskbar to Control Open Windows

The taskbar's shortcut menu also offers a few commands for working with open windows. Right-click an empty part of the taskbar to see the following commands:

- **Cascade Windows**—Select this command to arrange the nonminimized windows in an overlapping, diagonal pattern.

- **Tile Windows Horizontally**—Select this command to arrange the nonminimized windows into horizontal strips that cover the desktop.

- **Tile Windows Vertically**—Select this command to arrange the nonminimized windows into vertical strips that cover the desktop.

- **Minimize All Windows**—Select this command to clear the desktop by minimizing each open window.

Moving and Sizing the Taskbar

Somewhat surprisingly, the position and size of the taskbar are not set in stone. Here are the techniques you can use:

To move the taskbar—You can move the taskbar to any edge of the screen. To try this, position the mouse pointer over an empty section of the taskbar, drag the taskbar to a screen edge, and then drop the taskbar.

To size the taskbar horizontally—The Windows Millennium taskbar can be sized horizontally, which is useful if you need more room to display other taskbar toolbars. To size the taskbar, drag the left edge of the taskbar to the left or right.

To size the taskbar vertically—The default taskbar uses a single row to display the icons of your open windows. If you often have half a dozen or more programs running, the taskbar can appear crowded. To remedy this, you can add more rows by dragging the top edge of the taskbar up.

Customizing the Quick Launch Toolbar

Windows Millennium's taskbar includes a Quick Launch toolbar on the left. These icons offer one-click access to some Windows Millennium features:

- **Show Desktop**—Minimizes all open windows.

- **Launch Internet Explorer Browser**—Runs Internet Explorer.

Shortcut
If you have the Microsoft Natural Keyboard or its equivalent, you can minimize all windows by pressing ⊞+D. Alternatively, click the Show Desktop icon in the Quick Launch toolbar.

Undocumented
The maximum number of taskbar rows depends on the current screen resolution. If you're running at 640×480, the taskbar can have 9 rows. If you're running at 1,280×1,024, you can create up to 20 rows.

- **Launch Outlook Express**—Runs Outlook Express.

- **Windows Media Player**—Runs Media Player.

These icons are a good start, but that one-click access is too good to leave just to these four features. The good news is that you can populate the Quick Launch toolbar with your own shortcuts, just as you can the Start menu. The secret is that the Quick Launch icons all reside in the following folder:

```
Windows\Application   Data\Microsoft\Internet   Explorer\
Quick Launch
```

Any shortcuts you add to this folder are automatically displayed in the Quick Launch toolbar.

After you start adding icons to the Quick Launch toolbar, you'll probably run out of room, so you may need to resize the taskbar to compensate. Alternatively, create two taskbar rows and display the Quick Launch toolbar on its own row. If you have a large number of icons, consider dragging the Quick Launch toolbar off the taskbar and positioning it on another edge of the screen.

Shortcut
You can also create Quick Launch shortcuts by dragging an executable file and dropping it inside the Quick Launch toolbar. (For nonexecutable files, remember to right-drag, drop the file, and then click Create Shortcut(s) Here.) Make sure you drop the file between one of the existing icons.

Displaying Other Taskbar Toolbars

Windows Millennium's taskbar is happy to share some screen space with other toolbars. The Quick Launch toolbar, discussed in the previous section, is but one example. To see the others, follow these steps:

1. Right-click the taskbar to display its shortcut menu, and then click Toolbars to see a list of the available toolbars:

   Links—This is the Links bar that appears in Internet Explorer.

   Address—This is the same Address bar that appears in Windows Explorer, folder windows, and Internet Explorer. You can use it to enter local addresses (folder paths), network addresses (UNC paths), or Internet addresses (URLs).

   Desktop—This toolbar displays the desktop icons, which is handy if you usually run applications maximized and so don't see the desktop.

Quick Launch—This command toggles the Quick Launch toolbar on and off.

New Toolbar—Use this command to display another folder as a toolbar.

2. Click the command you want.

3. If you clicked New Toolbar, the New Toolbar dialog box appears. Use this dialog box to select the folder you want to use, and then click OK.

You can customize a toolbar by right-clicking the left edge of the toolbar to display its shortcut menu. You can then click one of the following commands:

- **View**—Use this command to set the size of the toolbar icons. When you click View, a submenu appears with two options: Large and Small.

- **Show Text**—Click this command to turn the icon titles on and off.

- **Refresh**—Click this command to refresh the toolbar's contents.

- **Show Title**—Click this command to turn the toolbar title on and off. (The title is displayed on the left side of the toolbar.)

Essential Information

- The Registry offers some powerful desktop customization methods that go well beyond the standard wallpaper and color customizations.

- Rearranging the shortcuts on your Start menu is an excellent way to improve your day-to-day productivity. In particular, be sure to move commonly used shortcuts closer to the beginning of the Start menu hierarchy.

- For maximum flexibility, work with the Start Menu folder when customizing the Start menu.

Inside Scoop
Toolbars can be dragged off the taskbar and dropped on the desktop to get a floating "palette." If you want this palette to always appear on top of your other windows, right-click an empty section of the palette and then click Always on Top.

- You can access some Start menu operations by right-clicking a shortcut.

- The taskbar can be moved, sized, shrunk to a line, or displayed behind windows.

- The Quick Launch toolbar's one-click icon launching makes it an excellent place to store shortcuts for frequently used programs and documents.

Windows Millennium Networking Skills

PART VI

GET THE SCOOP ON...
Peer-to-Peer Networks Versus Client/Server Networks ▪
Network Interface Cards and Network Cables ▪ Hubs,
Routers, and Other Network Hardware ▪ The Star Topology
Versus the Bus Topology ▪ Networking Protocols: TCP/IP,
IPX/SPX, and NetBEUI

Understanding Networking

Chapter 18

A FEW YEARS AGO, any discussion of networking required a preamble that justified why a network was necessary: You can share a printer or other peripheral with multiple machines; you can easily transfer files between machines; you can share disk drives and folders among machines; and you can easily back up files to another computer.

Nowadays, these and other networking benefits are well known, so the burning networking question is no longer "Why?," but "How?" The chapters here in Part VI, "Windows Millennium Networking Skills," are designed to answer that question. My focus is on setting up a local area network (LAN) suitable for a small office or home. This chapter gets you started by running through some crucial networking concepts such as network types, network hardware and topology, and the various protocols that are available. Chapter 19, "Setting Up Your Own Local Area Network," gets practical by showing you how to set up workgroups and accounts, and gives you a step-by-step procedure for setting up each network client. Chapter 20, "Windows Millennium Networking Features," takes you through some Windows Millennium networking techniques, including logging on, accessing the Network Neighborhood, sharing resources, mapping resources, and network printing.

> **"**
> **basement area network,** *noun* A home-based local area network.
> —*The Word Spy* (*www.wordspy.com*)
> **"**

Network Types: Client/Server Versus Peer to Peer

When designing your network, the first decision you have to make is what network type you want to use. You have two choices: client/server or peer to peer.

A *client/server* model is one that divides the network into two types of computers:

Clients—These are computers that require access to services such as printing, file storage, or security. To access those services, each computer must have *networking client* software installed.

Servers—These are computers that provide services such as a shared printer, shared disk drives or folders, and password authentication. Network servers typically run *network operating system* software such as Windows 2000 Server or Novell NetWare.

In a traditional client/server setup, a number of client machines connect to a single server. When deciding whether to implement this model, you have to ask yourself whether your network requires a dedicated server running a network operating system. The answer depends on whether your network has any server-specific needs. For example, although the Windows Millennium networking model enables you to set up password protection for shared resources, it's a bit cumbersome to use. *User-level security* is a much better system, but it requires a dedicated server. Similarly, if you want your network to implement an email server or Web server, most such software requires a true server.

A *peer-to-peer* model makes no distinction between the computers attached to the network. In other words, every machine can act as both a client and a (very basic) server. For example, computer A can act as a server by sharing a printer, and computer B can act as a client by using that shared printer. Conversely, computer B can act as a server by sharing a CD-ROM drive, and computer A can act as a client by accessing files on that drive.

This type of network doesn't implement a dedicated server running a network operating system. And because it's usually the server that adds the bulk of the complexity to any network setup, the peer-to-peer model is easier to set up and maintain than the client/server model. Note, too, that peer-to-peer is usually cheaper than client/server because network operating systems tend to be expensive, and they require a substantially greater hardware investment (a lot of memory, for example).

Network Hardware: NICs, Cables, and More

A network is essentially a physical connection between two or more computers. That connection can be extremely simple. For example, Chapter 23, "The Ins and Outs of Windows Millennium Notebook Features," you see how running a humble null-modem cable between two machines is enough to establish a bare-bones network using Direct Cable Connection. To establish a *real* network—one that's substantially faster and more reliable than the Direct Cable Connection variety—you need to bump up the hardware. This section runs through the hardware you need to set up your small LAN.

The Connection Point: The Network Interface Card

Your network hardware considerations should always begin with what is almost certainly the most important component: the *network interface card* (NIC). The NIC is, for most machines, a circuit board that slips into a bus slot inside the computer. (For notebook computers, PC Card NICs are common.) The NIC's backplate contains one or more ports into which you plug the network cables, so the NIC acts as the network connection point for each node. Not only that, but the NIC brings some intelligence to that connection. Depending on the underlying network architecture, the NIC can detect whether data is being sent over the network. This helps to avoid data collisions and increase the overall reliability of the network.

When purchasing NICs, keep the following points in mind:

- For the easiest possible installation, look for a NIC that is Plug and Play-compatible.

■ To avoid system bottlenecks, get 16-bit or even 32-bit NICs.

■ For the best performance, look for PCI-based NICs that support bus mastering. (I explain bus mastering in a sidebar in Chapter 21, "Taking the Mystery out of Hardware.")

→ **See Also** "Direct Memory Access Channels," **p. 467.**

66
Ethernet technology is ubiquitous. More than 83 percent of all installed network connections were Ethernet by the end of 1996 according to IDC.—*Gigabit Ethernet Alliance (www.gigabit-ethernet.org)*
99

The final consideration when planning NIC purchases is perhaps the most crucial one: the network architecture. Each NIC is designed to work with a specific architecture, and that in turn determines the throughput of the network and the specific methodology used to avoid data collisions. Although many such architectures exist, the most popular architecture by far (and the only one you should consider for your LAN) is called *Ethernet*. It actually comes in several flavors, but only two are relevant for small LANs:

Ethernet—The majority of the world's networks use standard Ethernet, which offers 10Mbps throughput. You have a choice of cables to use, as well as a choice of topologies (see "Network Topology: Star Versus Bus," later in this chapter).

Fast Ethernet—The majority of new and upgraded networks probably use Fast Ethernet, which offers 100Mbps throughput. This architecture requires Category 5 twisted-pair cable, a hub, and the star topology. (I discuss all of these concepts later in this chapter.) Note that many NICs can support both Ethernet and Fast Ethernet, and can automatically switch between the two, depending on the network architecture. These are often called "10/100" NICs.

The Connection: The Network Cable

After you've decided on the NICs you want to use for your LAN, your next consideration is what kind of network cable to use. The cable connects all the network nodes, so in one sense the cable *is* the network.

The two decisions actually go hand in hand because the type of cable you use affects the specific NICs you must purchase.

The cable attaches to a port on the NIC's backplate. However, as you'll see in a bit, the two main types of cable require completely different ports. Therefore, you must get NICs with ports that match the cable. Note, too, that the cable decision is affected by the type of network topology you want to use. (I discuss network topologies a bit later in this chapter.)

The two primary network cable types are *twisted-pair* and *coaxial*:

Twisted-pair—This type of cable consists of a pair of copper wires twisted together and surrounded by shielding. It uses RJ-45 jacks (similar to, but a bit larger than, the RJ-11 jacks used with telephone cables) that plug into complementary RJ-45 ports in a NIC's backplate (see Figure 18.1). Twisted-pair cable comes in various categories that determine the maximum bandwidth for data transmission along the cable. If you'll be setting up an Ethernet network, use Category 3 twisted-pair cable, which is rated at 10Mbps. For a Fast Ethernet network, use Category 5 cable, which is rated at 100Mbps. (Actually, to make a possible upgrade easier down the road, you should get Category 5 cable no matter what type of network you're setting up. The cost difference between the two types is negligible.) This cable is most often used with the star network topology. The maximum length for a twisted-pair cable is 100 meters.

Coaxial—This type of cable consists of multiple, stranded copper wires at the core, surrounded by various insulating layers. There are two types available: *thinnet* and *thicknet*. Thinnet—also called *10BASE-2*—is 0.2 inch in diameter and has a maximum length of 185 feet; thicknet—also called *10BASE-5*—is 0.4 inch in diameter and has a maximum length of 500 feet. Both are rated for 10Mbps transmission. Figure 18.2 shows the connections used with coaxial cable. The NIC must have a BNC port on its backplate. To that you attach a T-connector that has a bayonet-style connector and two BNC ports. To those two ports you connect your coaxial cables. This type of cable is most often used with the bus network topology.

Shortcut
If you think you may change cables down the road (for example, it's common to start with coaxial cable and then switch to twisted-pair cable when your LAN gets a bit larger), purchase NICs that have multiple ports for the different cable types. For easiest configuration, get NICs that can automatically detect what kind of cable is attached.

Watch Out!
You can't use coaxial cable to connect computers in a "circle." Instead, the first and last computers in the network must use a special *terminator* (see Figure 18.2) to close the circuit created by the cables. See Figure 18.4 for a diagram of how this works.

Figure 18.1
The RJ-45 jack used by twisted-pair network cable attaches to the RJ-45 connector in the back-plate of the NIC.

Figure 18.2
To connect a coaxial cable, attach a T-connector to the NIC's BNC port, and then attach the cable to the T-connector.

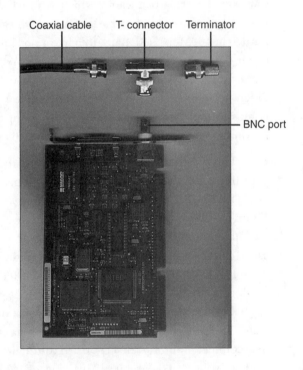

Here are a few cabling tips to bear in mind when laying your cables:

- Don't run cables under carpet (they might get stepped on).

- To avoid disruption, don't run twisted-pair cable near phone lines, and avoid electromagnetic sources.

- If you're laying coaxial cable, make sure the connections are secure. The bayonet-style connectors are a bit tricky to use at first, and they can be easily installed incorrectly.

- Try not to leave excess cable lying in loops or coils that could generate an electrical field that disrupts transmissions.

- Don't pinch the cable. In particular, if the back of the computer is near a wall, make sure the machine isn't right against the wall or the cable could get pinched at the connection.

Other Network Hardware

A network can be as simple or as complex as you want to make it. In the simplest case, you can use coaxial cable to connect two computers. Here's what you need:

- Two NICs with BNC connectors

- A single coaxial cable long enough to reach both computers

- Two T-connectors

- Two terminators

From this humble beginning you can branch out to all kinds of configurations and layouts. Depending on the number of clients in the LAN, the type of topology used, and the extra features you require (such as a direct Internet connection), you may need some extra equipment. A complete list of the extra networking goodies available would fill an entire book. However, because we're just talking about a small LAN, there

Inside Scoop
Actually, there's a network setup that's even simpler: two computers connected by a single twisted-pair cable. Note, however, that the wiring of a standard twisted-pair cable prevents you from using it to connect computers directly. Instead, you must use a special *crossover cable,* which crosses the sending wire on one end to the receiving wire on the other end (and vice versa).

are only a few network knickknacks that you'll ever have to consider. Here's a summary:

Hub—Also known as a *concentrator*, this device is a box that consists of four or more RJ-45 ports. When you're running twisted-pair cable, you use the hub as a central connection point for each client. That is, each twisted-pair cable is attached to the client's NIC at one end and to the hub at the other end. The hub serves only to pass along the network data, so each client can "see" the others that are attached to the hub. See Figure 18.3, later in this chapter, for a diagram that shows how a hub is used in a star topology network. Here are two things to bear in mind when looking for a hub:

- If you think you might need to add a second hub down the road, make sure you purchase hubs that each have an *uplink* port that can be used to attach the two hubs. Ideally, the uplink port should handle the crossover to the second hub automatically (that is, without requiring a crossover cable).

- Get a hub that supports the network type you'll be using. If you plan on using Fast Ethernet, for example, get a hub that supports 100Mbps transmissions. If you'll be using Ethernet, a 10/100 hub that supports both 10Mbps and 100Mbps (and can automatically detect the transmission speed) gives you the most upgrade flexibility.

- Look for a hub that has LEDs that tell you when a workstation is on the network and that can signal data collisions.

Repeater—Earlier, I mentioned that each type of cable has a maximum length. Although you're unlikely to exceed those lengths in a small network, it might happen. In that case, you need to use a repeater to boost the signal. For example, if you're using twisted-pair cable, you need to add a repeater every 100 meters. Note, that many hubs (called *active hubs*) act as repeaters.

Bridge—This device connects two LANs. As your network grows, you'll likely find that the overall performance on the network drops. When that happens, split the network into two separate LANs and then use a bridge to enable the two networks to see each other. (If you have a server, you can create a de facto bridge by adding a second NIC to the server.)

Router—This is a box that routes network data by examining the address information contained in each network packet. (Most routers can also be used as simple *firewalls* that protect your network from Internet intrusions.) If you'll be setting up a direct Internet connection (using, say, an ISDN or DSL line), then you need a router so that incoming and outgoing data is sent to the correct IP address. Figure 18.3, later in this chapter, shows a network setup that includes a router for a direct Internet connection.

Remember
There's a great deal of emphasis on small-office and home networking these days, so many companies are coming out with affordable networking equipment that combines multiple devices into a single package. For example, ZyXEL (www.zyxel.com) has a product called the Prestige 100MH, which combines a V.90 (56Kbps) modem with a four-port Ethernet hub and a router, all for about U.S. $300.

Network Topology: Star Versus Bus

The final hardware aspect to consider is the layout of the network, or its *topology*. This describes how the network nodes are connected, and also affects the type of cabling you use and the other equipment you need. Although a number of topologies are available, only two are relevant to the small LAN:

Star topology—In this topology, each workstation is connected to a hub. By far the most common setup is to run twisted-pair cables from each workstation to the hub. The main advantages of this kind of setup are that it's easy to add nodes (just run another cable to the hub) and the entire network stays up if one node goes down. The main disadvantages are the expense of the hub and the inability to add new nodes if you run out of hub ports (although, as I mentioned earlier, it's possible to expand by connecting a second hub to the first one). The diagram in Figure 18.3 shows a typical star topology.

Figure 18.3
In a typical star
topology, network
workstations and
other devices
(such as a router)
are connected to
a central hub.

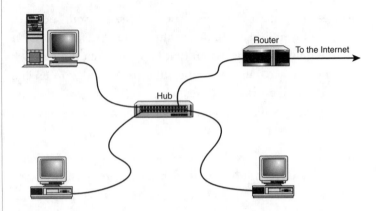

Inside Scoop
A *barrel connector*
is a small compo-
nent that consists
of two BNC ports.
(Think of a T-con-
nector without the
BNC connector.)
As shown in
Figure 18.4, you
use a barrel con-
nector to connect
two coaxial
cables.

Bus topology—In this topology, each workstation is usually connected to a main cable, which is known as a *bus* or a *backbone*. On a smaller LAN, that bus is usually formed by the various coaxial cables connecting each workstation. The main advantage of the bus topology is that it's inexpensive (no extra equipment is required). On the downside, if a single network node goes down, the entire network goes down. The diagram in Figure 18.4 shows a small-network bus topology using coaxial cables.

Figure 18.4
In a small-network
bus topology,
each network
workstation is
attached to a
series of con-
nected coaxial
cables. Note the
use of terminators
in the first and
last NICs.

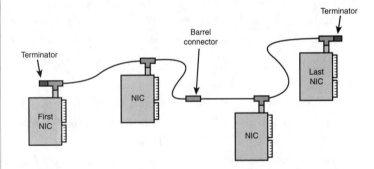

Network Protocols: NetBEUI, IPX/SPX, and TCP/IP

The final networking component to consider is software-based: the *network protocol.* The idea behind the protocol is to establish a common structure for the *packets* of data sent along the network. These packets contain information on the source (the computer from which the data was sent) and the destination (the computer to which the data is being sent), as well as the actual data. The protocol also defines procedures to take if a packet doesn't arrive at the destination, if it arrives damaged, if a multipacket transmission arrives out of order and needs to be reassembled, and much more.

The key thing about network protocols is that it really doesn't matter which one you use. However, all the clients must have *at least one* protocol in common. A number of protocols are available, but three are the most common:

NetBEUI—This is the NetBIOS Extended User Interface protocol, and it's supported by all Microsoft networks. It uses a simple and efficient structure that requires little or no configuration. Overall, it's ideally suited to small networks.

IPX/SPX—This is the Internet Packet eXchange/Sequenced Packet eXchange protocol. It's most often used on Novell NetWare networks, but it's fully supported by Microsoft networks.

TCP/IP—This is the Transmission Control Protocol/Internet Protocol. It's the protocol used on the Internet, but many companies are also implementing it on LANs because it's reliable, routable, and scalable. TCP/IP is a must if you plan on using your network as an intranet, or if you'll have a direct connection to the Internet and you want each workstation to be able to access the Internet via that connection. Note, however, that TCP/IP requires more effort to configure than either NetBEUI or IPX/SPX. See Chapter 4, "Getting on the Internet."

➜ **See Also** "Installing and Configuring the TCP/IP Protocol," **p. 122**.

Essential Information

- In a client/server network type, clients (also known as a workstations or nodes) that require access to network services—such as file storage, printing, or security—interact with a server running a network operating system and providing access to network services.

- In a peer-to-peer network type, each computer can share resources with the network (that is, act as a server) and can access resources shared by other computers on the network (that is, act as a client).

- The network interface card (NIC) is an internal circuit board or PC Card that provides ports for connecting network cables.

- Two types of network architecture are commonly used with small LANs: Ethernet (10Mbps throughput) and Fast Ethernet (100Mbps throughput).

- For network cabling, use either twisted-pair (Category 5 is best) or coaxial (thinnet is the most common).

- The star topology normally uses twisted-pair cables attached to a central hub, while the bus topology uses a series of connected coaxial cables with terminators at both ends.

- You can use any protocol on your network—NetBEUI, IPX/SPX, or TCP/IP—but just make sure that all the nodes have at least one protocol in common.

GET THE SCOOP ON...
Performing a Few Preliminary Setup Chores ▪
Installing Various Networking Components ▪ Choosing
Between Share-Level and User-Level Access Control ▪
Sharing an Internet Connection Between Clients ▪
Running the New Home Networking Wizard

Setting Up Your Own Local Area Network

Chapter 19

I N THE PREVIOUS CHAPTER, I hope I showed you that, at least at the small LAN level, networking is not all that complicated or expensive. (Networking doesn't become complex until you hit the enterprise level, and then the level of complexity rises exponentially.) Although I've been critical of many Windows Millennium features in this book, small-LAN networking isn't one of them. Windows has been a decent small network client ever since Windows for Workgroups, and Windows Millennium is the best client yet. This is particularly true if you have Plug-and-Play NICs combined with a Plug-and-Play BIOS. In this case, Windows Millennium sets up everything for you automatically, although tweaks are still required because Windows Millennium's networking defaults include a few bad configuration decisions. Even if you don't have Plug-and-Play hardware, it's still not that difficult to get your small network up and running. And if you don't feel like getting your hands dirty with *any* network configuration chores, there's also Windows Millennium's new Home Networking Wizard that sets up each client step-by-step. This chapter tells you everything you need to know.

Some Preparatory Chores

Before getting to the heart of this chapter—setting up a computer as a network client—let's take a second and go through a few tasks that you might need to run to get your network ready:

Decide on the peer-to-peer servers—If you'll be running a peer-to-peer setup, you need to decide which clients will share which resources. This applies not so much to folders and hard disks, but to your Internet connection and to devices such as printers, CD-ROM drives, and scanners. For example, it doesn't make sense to attach any of these devices to a notebook computer that might be disconnected from the network from time to time.

Establish workgroups—A *workgroup* is a network subset that consists of a collection of related computers. On larger networks, workgroups usually comprise departments, floors, divisions, or some other logical or physical grouping. If your network consists of just a few computers, there's no need to create more than one workgroup. However, if you're administering a dozen or more machines, or if there's a logical way that the clients should be grouped, workgroups may be the way to go. Fortunately, it's trivial to set up workgroups in Windows Millennium. All you do is, for the related computers, provide the same workgroup name when entering the network identification for each machine. See "Step 5: Identifying the Computer," later in this chapter.

Remember
A good place to get all the NOS information you need is from Que's *The Complete Idiot's Guide to Networking, Second Edition.*

Create server accounts—If you decided on a client/server network setup, you'll need to install the network operating system (NOS) and perform other server setup chores. The details of this depend on the NOS and are in any case beyond the scope of this book. However, one of the basic tasks you'll have to perform on any network server is to create accounts for each user. These accounts are used not only for logon purposes, but also for user-level security.

Create an LMHOSTS file—If you have IP addresses for each client (unlikely on a small LAN) and if you'll be running TCP/IP as a common protocol on a peer-to-peer network, you have to map each computer's network name (also known as its NetBIOS name) to its assigned IP address. To do this, create a text file named LMHOSTS (no extension) and, for each machine, enter the IP address and the network name on a single line. This file must be copied to the Windows folder of each client. Here's an example:

```
127.0.0.1 localhost
123.45.67.89 nessman
123.45.67.90 tarlek
```

Enable WINS resolution on the server—WINS—the Windows Internet Name Service—runs on Windows NT Server or Windows 2000 Server and maps each computer's network name to an IP address. If you plan on using TCP/IP as a common network protocol, and you're using Windows NT/2000 Server on a client/server network, then you must enable WINS on the server and use the WINS Manager to set up a mapping for each name/IP address combination.

A Seven-Step Guide to Setting Up a Network Client

With all the theory and decision-making out of the way, it's time to get to the meat of the matter by configuring the network clients. I'm assuming here that you've installed the network interface card (or PC Card, if you're working with a notebook), and that you (or Windows Millennium) have installed the appropriate device driver for the card.

I've divided the client setup into a simple seven-step procedure. All the configuring takes place inside the Network dialog box, which you get onscreen by opening the Control Panel's Network icon. Figure 19.1 shows a typical example of this dialog box.

Remember
Windows Millennium ships with a file named LMHOSTS.SAM (it's in the Windows folder) that acts as a sample LMHOSTS file. Note, too, that the 127.0.0.1 localhost entry in my example file refers to the client on which the LMHOSTS file resides. If you're running TCP/IP and you're having network problems, try pinging 127.0.0.1 to see if TCP/IP is configured properly on your machine.

Remember
In Windows 9x, you installed a NIC driver by hand by using the Control Panel's Network icon. You can't do that in Windows Millennium. Instead, you have to use the Control Panel's Add New Hardware icon.

Figure 19.1
All your network client configuration chores take place in the Network dialog box.

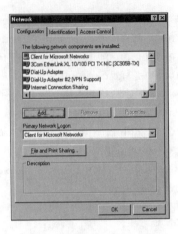

Shortcut
Another way to get to the Network dialog box is by right-clicking desktop's My Network Places icon and then clicking Properties in the shortcut menu.

The list in the Configuration tab shows you which networking components are currently installed. Here are some points to bear in mind when working with this list:

- As you see a bit later, many of the network components are bound to each other. For example, to use a particular protocol, you bind it to your NIC. If a particular item is bound to multiple components, the list of components signifies this by listing all components separated by an arrow (->).

- To add a new component to the list, click the Add button.

- To remove a component, highlight it and click Remove.

- To configure a component, double-click it (or highlight it and click Properties).

The next eight sections run through the steps required to use this dialog box to configure a network client. Remember, however, that if you don't feel like getting into this level of detail, consider using Windows Millennium's Home Networking Wizard. See "Running the New Home Networking Wizard," later in this chapter.

Step 1: Installing a Network Client Driver

The network client driver handles the network logon, viewing computers in the My Network Places folder (formerly the Network Neighborhood), accessing shared resources, and more. Although Windows Millennium comes with several clients, the best one to use with your small LAN is the Client for Microsoft Networks. This client should be installed automatically after your NIC is installed. If not, follow these steps:

1. In the Network dialog box, click Add to display the Select Network Component Type dialog box shown in Figure 19.2.

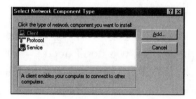

Figure 19.2
Use the Select Network Component Type dialog box to choose what type of networking component you want to install.

2. Highlight Client and click Add to display the Select Network Client dialog box.

3. In the Manufacturers list, highlight Microsoft (this will likely be the only item in this list).

4. In the Network Clients list, highlight Client for Microsoft Networks.

5. Click OK. The client is added to the list of installed components.

I discuss the properties associated with the Client for Microsoft Networks a bit later (see "Step 7: Specifying the Network Logon").

Step 2: Installing Network Protocols

I mentioned in the previous chapter that you must install at least one common protocol on all the network clients. TCP/IP should be installed by default. Here's how to install other protocols:

1. In the Network dialog box, click Add to display the Select Network Component Type dialog box.

2. Highlight Protocol and click Add. Windows Millennium displays the Select Network Protocol dialog box.

3. In the Manufacturers list, highlight Microsoft (again, this may be the only item in the list).

4. In the Network Protocols list, highlight the protocol you want to install (use either IPX/SPX-compatible Protocol, NetBEUI, or TCP/IP).

5. Click OK. The protocol is added to the list of installed components.

Although the NetBEUI and IPX/SPX protocols have a few configurable properties, you don't need to worry about them. For details on the TCP/IP protocol's properties, see Chapter 4, "Getting on the Internet."

➜ **See Also** "Installing and Configuring the TCP/IP Protocol," **p. 122**.

For a simple TCP/IP-based peer-to-peer network with no shared Internet connection, let's see how you set up TCP/IP on the clients. First, one machine acts as a DHCP "server," which means it supplies IP addresses to the other clients automatically as they need them. It's best to choose a machine that's on the network full time. Here's how to set up TCP/IP on that machine:

- In the list of network components, highlight the TCP/IP component that's bound to the NIC and then click Properties. In the TCP/IP Properties dialog box, display the IP Address tab, activate the Specify an IP address option, and enter the following:

  IP Address: `198.168.0.1`

  Subnet Mask: `255.255.255.0`

- In the TCP/IP Properties dialog box, display the WINS Configuration tab and make sure the Disable WINS Resolution option is activated.

- Don't specify a gateway and don't specify any DNS information.

Here's how to set up all the other machines:

- In the list of network components, highlight the TCP/IP component that's bound to the NIC and then click Properties. Display the IP Address tab, and make sure the Obtain an IP address automatically option is activated. Note the other client IP addresses will be 198.168.0.x, where x is a number between 2 and 254.

- Display the WINS Configuration tab and make sure the Use DHCP for WINS Resolution option is activated.

- Don't specify a gateway and don't specify any DNS information.

Step 3: Installing Network Services

Most of the network services you'll need are provided by the Client for Microsoft Networks driver. However, another vital service—file and printer sharing—isn't installed by default. To install this or a different service, follow these steps:

1. In the Network dialog box, click Add to display the Select Network Component Type dialog box.

2. Highlight Service and click Add. Windows Millennium displays the Select Network Service dialog box.

3. In the Models list, highlight File and printer sharing for Microsoft Networks.

4. Click OK. The service is added to the list of installed components.

Step 4: Setting Up File and Print Sharing

The file and printer sharing service enables the workstation to share resources—such as a disk drive, folder, or printer—with the rest of the network. If you installed the service, you must now tell Windows Millennium what in general you want to share:

1. In the Network dialog box, click File and Print Sharing. Windows Millennium displays the File and Print Sharing dialog box, shown in Figure 19.3.

Figure 19.3
Use the File and
Print Sharing dia-
log box to acti-
vate sharing for
files and printers.

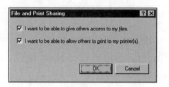

2. To share drives and folders, activate the I want to be able to give others access to my files check box.

3. To share a printer, activate the I want to be able to allow others to print to my printer(s) check box.

4. Click OK.

Step 5: Identifying the Computer

Each computer on the network must have a unique identity within a workgroup. Identifying the computer is handled by the Identification tab, shown in Figure 19.4. This tab offers three text boxes:

Computer name—Use this text box to enter a unique name for the client. (This is the NetBIOS name that I mentioned earlier in the context of the LMHOSTS file and WINS.) The name must be 15 characters or less, and you can use any alphanumeric character along with the following symbols (spaces aren't allowed):

~ ! @ # $ % ^ & ( ) _ - { } ' .

Workgroup—Use this text box to enter the name of the workgroup for this client. (Use the same naming rules that I mentioned for the computer name.) All clients that use the same workgroup name will appear together in the My Network Places folders. If you're running a client/server setup with Windows NT Server or Windows 2000 Server, use this text box to enter the name of the client's domain.

Computer Description—Use this text box to describe the client. This description will be visible to other network clients if they configure the My Network Places folder to use the Details view. You can enter up to 48 characters.

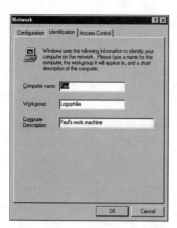

Figure 19.4
Use the
Identification tab
to enter the
client's name and
description, as
well as its work-
group name.

Step 6: Specifying Access Control

When you share resources with the network, you probably
don't want the entire network to have complete access to those
resources. Instead, you may want to allow full access to only a
few users, allow read-only access to some other users, and deny
access to the rest.

To enable this, Windows Millennium offers two types of access
control:

Share-level access control—This is a resource-by-resource
method. For each shared resource on your system, you
assign two passwords: one for full access and another for
read-only access. (Windows Millennium is flexible about
this: You can assign the same password to both, assign only
one of the passwords, or assign neither of them.)

User-level access control—This is a user-by-user method. For
each shared resource on your system, you specify one or
more users in three access categories: full, read-only, and
custom. For this to work, you must have a Windows NT or
Windows 2000 server on your network and you must be
running the Client for Microsoft Networks. When a user
attempts to access a shared resource on the client, the person's username is sent to the server for validation. If they
pass muster on the server, access is granted at the specified
level.

To choose the access control method you want, display the Access Control tab, shown in Figure 19.5. Select either Share-level access control or User-level access control. For the latter, use the Obtain list of users and groups from list to enter your Windows NT/2000 domain or the name of the server.

Figure 19.5
Use the Access Control tab to choose between share-level and user-level access control.

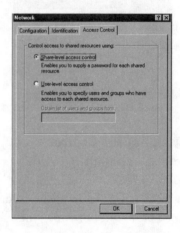

Watch Out!
Because you're probably not actually on the network just yet, Windows Millennium may tell you that it can't find the "security provider" you entered after activating User-level access control. If that happens, click Yes and then, in the Authenticator Type dialog box, select the type of object you specified: Windows NT domain or Windows NT server.

Step 7: Specifying the Network Logon

Your final task for setting up the network client is to specify the logon options. This involves just two steps:

1. In the Configuration tab, use the Primary Network Logon list to select Client for Microsoft Networks. This will log you on to the network at startup.

2. In the list of installed components, highlight Client for Microsoft Networks and then click Properties. This displays the dialog box shown in Figure 19.6. There are two groups:

Logon validation—If you have a network server and you'll be logging on to an Windows NT/2000 domain, activate the Log on to Windows NT domain check box, and then enter the name of the domain in the Windows NT domain text box.

Network logon options—These options determine how you're logged on to the network. Selecting Quick logon doesn't reconnect network resources at startup, which makes

Windows Millennium load faster. Selecting Logon and restore network connections takes a bit of extra time to reconnect all network resources, but that makes them available for use immediately.

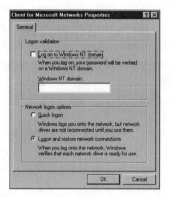

Figure 19.6
Use this property sheet to specify some network logon options for the Microsoft Networks client.

Finishing Up

With the client setup complete, click OK to close the Network dialog box. Windows Millennium installs the software and then asks whether you want to restart your computer. Click Yes. I discuss logging on to the network, sharing resources, and other network techniques in Chapter 20, "Windows Millennium Networking Features."

Sharing a Dial-Up Connection Between Network Clients

I look at networks as just big "sharing machines." The whole point of any network is to be able to share both information (for example, files and email) and devices (for example, printers and disk drives). This sharing machine gets extended even further when the Internet is involved. Two scenarios are common:

■ You have a direct connection to the Internet using an ISDN line or some other technology, and each client has a permanent IP address. In this case, you need to include a router on your network and configure each machine's TCP/IP protocol for Internet access (see Chapter 4).

→ **See Also** "Installing and Configuring the TCP/IP Protocol," p. 122.

Inside Scoop
One other client setup chore you may want to run through involves the various bindings set up by Windows Millennium. As I mentioned earlier, each protocol is bound to each NIC, as well as to the Dial-Up Adapter (used by Dial-Up Networking), if it's installed. Also, the client software and the network services are bound to each protocol. To turn these bindings on and off, open the component's property sheet and select the Bindings tab. You'll see a check box for each binding.

- You have a dial-up account or broadband (cable or DSL) connection without a permanent IP address, and you want each machine to be able to access the Internet using that account. You *could* supply each machine with its own modem and split the phone line, but that's both costly and inconvenient. A better solution would be to share a single modem connection among all users. The machine that shares the connection is called the *gateway*.

For the latter, Windows Millennium offers a feature called Internet Connection Sharing (ICS). The easiest way to configure ICS is to run the new Home Networking Wizard, as described in the next section.

Running the New Home Networking Wizard

Creating a network client setup by hand isn't hard, but it's finicky stuff. If you don't feel like wrestling with all those dialog boxes and options, Windows Millennium's new Home Networking Wizard might be a better way to go.

Here's how it works.

1. Double-click the desktop's My Network Places icon and then double-click the Home Networking Wizard icon. (Alternatively, select Start, Programs, Accessories, Communications, Home Networking Wizard.) Windows Millennium launches the Home Networking Wizard.

2. The first dialog box just provides an overview, so click Next.

3. The wizard asks if this computer connects to the Internet. If not, activate No, this computer does not use the Internet, click Next, and then skip to step 6. Otherwise, activate Yes, the computer uses the following and proceed to step 4.

4. If you chose Yes in step 3, the wizard enables two option buttons:

- **A connection to another computer on my home network...**—Choose this option if you're setting up a machine that will use a shared Internet connection from a gateway computer. Click Next and skip to step 6.

- **A direct connection to my ISP using the following device**—Choose this option if you're configuring the gateway machine. Use the list to select the Internet connection "device" the machine uses. If the machine uses a dial-up connection, select the Dial-Up Networking item; if the machine uses a broad-band connection, select the network adapter associated with that connection. Click Next.

5. If you chose A direct connection to my ISP using the following device in step 4, the wizard now asks if you want to share that Internet connection with the network. You have two choices (click Next when you're done):

- If you're setting up the gateway computer, activate Yes. Then use the list to select the NIC that the computer uses to connect to the network.

- If you don't want to share the connection with other computers on your network, activate No, I do not want to share my Internet connection.

6. In the next wizard dialog box, enter the Computer Name. To specify a workgroup name, activate the Use this work-group name option and then type in the new name. Click Next.

7. You use the next wizard dialog box to share some folders and printers, as shown in Figure 19.7. For files and folders, activate the My Documents folder and all folders in it check box. You then need to protect this folder with a password by clicking the Password button beside the check box, entering the password (twice), and clicking OK.

Inside Scoop

After Internet Connection Sharing is set up and running, a new ICS icon appears in the gateway machine's system tray. Right-click this icon to see a shortcut menu with four commands: Status (tells you how many people are using the connection); Options (displays a dialog box of ICS settings); Disable Internet Connection Sharing (turns off ICS); and Hide Taskbar Icon.

Watch Out!

If you want to share an Internet connection, be sure to run the Home Networking Wizard on the gateway machine first.

Figure 19.7
Use this dialog
box to share
some folders and
your printer.

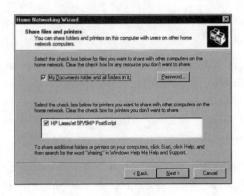

8. If you have a printer installed and you want to share it, make sure the check box beside it is activated. When you're done with this dialog box, click Next.

9. The next wizard chore covers the possibility that there are Windows 95 or Windows 98 computers on your network. If so, you need to create a Home Networking Setup disk that you then use to configure the Windows 9x clients. You have two choices (click Next after you pick one):

   • **Yes, create a Home Networking Setup disk**—Activate this option if you have Windows 9x clients on your network. See "Setting Up Windows 9x Clients," later in this chapter.

   • **No, do not create a Home Networking Setup disk**—Activate this option if your workgroup has only Windows Millennium machines. Skip to step 11.

10. If you elected to create the disk, insert a disk and click Next.

11. The wizard lets you know that it has finished and is ready to make your machine network ready. Remove the Home Networking Setup disk (if you created one) and click Finish.

12. When the wizard asks if you want to restart your computer, click Yes.

Two things to note at this point:

- After running the wizard, the Network dialog box renames a couple of the TCP/IP components. The one bound to the NIC (for your network connection) is renamed TCP/IP (Home) and the one bound to the Dial-Up Adapter (for your Internet connection) is renamed TCP/IP (Shared). These names are governed by each component's DriverDesc setting in the Registry. To see these settings, locate the appropriate protocol subkeys in the following Registry key:

  ```
  HKEY_LOCAL_MACHINE\System\CurrentControlSet\Services\
  Class\NetTrans\
  ```

- The wizard leaves the TCP/IP (Shared) -> Dial-Up Adapter component bound to file and printer sharing, which is dangerous. To fix this, highlight the component, click Properties, go to the Bindings tab, and deactivate the check box for File and printer sharing for Microsoft Networks.

Setting Up Windows 9x Clients

If you want to set up networking on a Windows 9x machine, follow these steps:

1. Insert the Home Networking Setup disk, created in the previous section, into the Windows 9x client.

2. In Windows Explorer, display the floppy drive and launch the setup.exe file. The Home Networking Wizard appears.

3. Follow the steps from the previous section.

Setting Up the Shared Internet Connection

After you set up the gateway host computer, you need to configure the other clients to use the shared connection:

1. Double-click the Connect to the Internet icon if it's still on the desktop. If it's not, select Start, Programs, Accessories, Communications, Internet Connection Wizard.

2. In the first wizard dialog box, activate the I want to set up my Internet connection manually... option and click Next.

3. Activate the I connect through a local area network (LAN) option and click Next.

4. Make sure the Automatic discovery of proxy server (recommended) check box is activated, and then click Next.

5. Follow the rest of the Internet Connection Wizard's prompts.

Essential Information

- Before configuring the network clients, decide which of the machines will be peer-to-peer servers, select your workgroups (if more than one is needed), and set up either an LMHOSTS file or WINS resolution.

- To configure a network client, open the Control Panel's Network icon (or right-click the My Network Places icon and then click Properties).

- To add a new client driver, protocol, or service, open the Network dialog box, click Add, select the component type you want to add, and then select the component from the dialog box that appears.

- To establish a workgroup, supply each computer in the workgroup with the same workgroup name.

- Share-level access control is a resource-by-resource method that assigns passwords to each shared resource, whereas user-level access control is a user-by-user method that gives individual users specific permissions for each resource.

- To run the new Home Networking Wizard, double-click the desktop's My Network Places icon and then double-click the Home Networking Wizard icon. (Alternatively, select Start, Programs, Accessories, Communications, Home Networking Wizard.)

GET THE SCOOP ON...
Options for Logging On to the Network ▪ Sharing
Drives, Folders, and Printers ▪ Mapping Shared
Network Drives and Folders ▪ Setting Up a Network
Printer ▪ Configuring a Client As a Dial-Up Server

Windows Millennium Networking Features

W ITH YOUR NETWORK PLANNED, installed, and configured, you're ready to put it to good use. This chapter gets you started by showing you how to log on to the network and access the My Network Places folder. From there, I show you how to share your resources with the network, work with resources shared by others on the network, set up a network printer, monitor other computers remotely, and configure a machine as a dial-up server.

Accessing the Network

You first need to get a handle on the basics of logging on to the network and then you'll take a look around the My Network Places folder. Along the way, you learn how to set up automatic logons and how to use the Universal Naming Convention to refer to network resources.

Logging On to the Network

After Windows Millennium is set up for networking, you're prompted to log on to the network each time you start or reboot your computer. The logon dialog box you see depends on the type of network you're using:

Chapter 20

Peer-to-peer network logon—In this case, you see the dialog box shown in Figure 20.1. Your User name should be filled in for you automatically, so enter your Password and click OK.

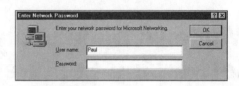

Client/server network logon—If, as described in the previous chapter, you adjusted the properties of the Client for Microsoft Networks to log on to a Windows NT (or Windows 2000) domain, you see the dialog box shown in Figure 20.2. Your User name and Domain should be filled in for you automatically, so enter your Password and click OK.

➜ **See Also** "Step 7: Specifying the Network Logon," **p. 432**.

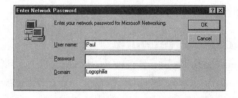

Logging On to Windows and the Network at the Same Time

If you have a Windows password set up, then you may be forced to negotiate both the Enter Network Password dialog box and the Welcome to Windows dialog box at startup. You can unify the logon so that a single dialog box logs you on to both the network and Windows Millennium. To do this, you need to set the same password for both logons. Here are the steps to follow:

1. Open the Control Panel's Passwords icon to display the Passwords Properties dialog box.

2. In the Change Passwords tab, click Change Windows Password.

3. If you log on to a Windows NT/2000 domain, a dialog box asks if you also want to change the password for Microsoft Networking. Leave the check box deactivated and click OK.

4. In the Change Windows Password dialog box, enter your existing password in the Old password dialog box, and then enter your network password in both the New password and Confirm new password text boxes. Click OK.

5. When Windows Millennium confirms that your password was changed, click OK to return to the Passwords Properties dialog box.

6. Click Close.

Setting Up an Automatic Logon

Because you're dealing with small networks, there's a good chance that security isn't a huge issue for you. In that case, it's possible to set up Windows Millennium to log you on to the network automatically. The following method applies to both peer-to-peer and client/server networks:

1. Open the Control Panel's Tweak UI icon.

2. Display the Logon tab.

3. Activate the Log on automatically at system startup check box.

4. Enter your User name and Password.

5. Click OK.

Watch Out!
Before leaving Tweak UI, display the Paranoia tab and make sure the Clear Last User at logon check box is deactivated. If it's not, the automatic logon feature won't work.

You may have noticed that Tweak UI's Network tab warns you that any user with access to Regedit can view or modify your password. What does this mean? To find out, open the Registry Editor and display the following key:

```
HKEY_LOCAL_MACHINE\Software\Microsoft\Windows\
CurrentVersion\Winlogon
```

Inside Scoop
The Windows Millennium password list is actually a .pwl file. The name of this file is *user*.pwl, where *user* is your username. Look for this file in the Windows folder.

Your username appears in the DefaultUserName setting, and your password appears in the DefaultPassword setting. The kicker is that the password appears as plain text, so anyone can read it or change it.

If you're on a client/server network where you log on to a Windows NT domain, and you're not comfortable having your network password in plain view, here's a workaround that stores your network password in the encrypted Windows Millennium password list:

1. Follow the steps outlined earlier to change your Windows password. (Again, don't change your Microsoft Networking password.) In this case, leave both the New password and Confirm new password text boxes blank. Click OK until you're back in the Control Panel.

2. Open the Control Panel's Network icon.

3. In the Primary Network Logon list, select Windows Logon. (While you're in this dialog box, double-click Client for Microsoft Networks and make sure you're set up to log on to a Windows NT domain.)

4. Click OK.

5. When Windows Millennium asks if you want to restart your computer, click Yes.

6. When the Enter Network Password dialog box appears, enter your Password, make sure that the Save this password in your password list check box is activated, and then click OK.

How to Access the My Network Places folder

Most of your network chores occur within the friendly confines of Windows Millennium's new My Network Places folder. This is a special folder that gives you access to the workgroups (or domains) and computers on your network.

If you upgraded from Windows 9x, My Network Places is the replacement for the Network Neighborhood. As you'll see, My Network Places offers several new features that make it much easier to work with the computers and shared resources in your workgroup.

To get to the My Network Places folder, Windows Millennium offers three routes:

Windows Explorer—Open My Network Places in the Folders bar (see Figure 20.3).

My Computer—Click the My Network Places link.

The desktop—Open the My Network Places icon.

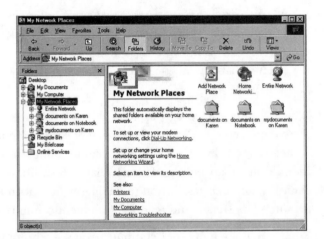

Figure 20.3
Windows Millennium's new My Network Places folder.

Here are some notes about the My Network Places folder's landmarks:

Add Network Place—Use this icon to populate the folder with *network places*. In Windows Millennium, a network place is an icon for a shared drive or folder. See "Adding a Network Place," later in this chapter.

Home Networking Wizard—Use this icon to launch the Home Networking Wizard and edit your network setup.

Entire Network—Use this icon to access all the workgroups and computers on your network. If you're in Windows Explorer, this icon also appears as a subfolder of My Network Places in the Folders bar (see Figure 20.3).

Shortcut
My Network Places is also available in the standard Windows Millennium file dialog boxes. In the Open dialog box, select My Network Places in the Look in list; in the Save As dialog box, use the Save in list. Note, too, that many 16-bit dialog boxes have a Network button that you can use to map a shared network drive.

Shortcut
My Network
Places is also
available in the
standard Windows
Millennium file dia-
log boxes. In the
Open dialog box,
select My
Network Places in
the Look in list; in
the Save As dialog
box, use the Save
in list. Note, too,
that many 16-bit
dialog boxes have
a Network button
that you can use
to map a shared
network drive.

Network places—The rest of the icons represent folders that have been shared by other members of your workgroup. Seeing an icon named documents on Karen, for example, means that the user of the machine named Karen has shared a folder with the name documents. In Windows Explorer, these icons appear as subfolders of My Network Places (see Figure 20.3).

Here are some notes about navigating the Entire Network folder:

- When you open Entire Network, you first see a list of the workgroups in your network. (If you double-click the Entire Network icon, you then have to click the View the entire contents of this folder link to see the work-group icons.)

- When you open a workgroup icon, you then see a list of the computers in the group. The name of each computer is determined by the Computer name value in the Identification tab of the Network dialog box. To see a client's Computer description value, highlight its icon (or activate View, Details and read the Comment column).

- When you open a network computer, you see a list of the resources that it's sharing with the network. In Figure 20.4, for example, you can see that the computer named Karen is sharing a folder and a printer.

Figure 20.4
Select a com-
puter to view its
shared resources.

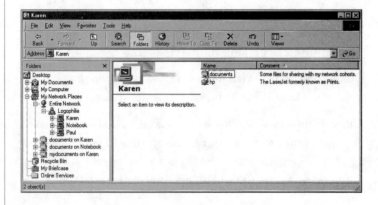

- It's unlikely that you'll have trouble finding a computer on your small network. Just in case, however, Windows Millennium offers a feature that can search the network for a particular machine. In the My Network Places folder, click the Search button, use the Computer Name text box to enter all or part of the computer name you want to find, and then click Search Now.

- You use a network place in much the same way that you use a local drive or folder. That is, you open the resource and then manipulate the files. Note, however, that you may need to enter a password to access a shared resource.

Remember
What you can do with the remote files depends on the access rights you have. For example, if you have just read-only access, you won't be able to delete or add files.

Understanding the Universal Naming Convention

When working with network resources, you often need to specify the address of the resource directly. To do that, you use a syntax called the Universal Naming Convention (UNC) for network addresses. UNC addresses use the following general format:

`\\computername\sharename\path\file`

`computername`	The name of the network computer
`sharename`	The name of the shared resource
`path`	A folder path within the shared resource
`file`	A filename within the folder indicated by `path`

For example, consider the following UNC address:

`\\Karen\documents\memos\fiat19.doc`

This address points to the shared resource named documents on the Karen computer, and refers to the fiat19.doc file within the memos folder.

Here are some notes about working with UNC paths within Windows Millennium:

- If the shared resource is a folder or disk drive, you can open it in a folder window by selecting Start, Run, entering the UNC path, and clicking OK.

Inside Scoop
If you're working at the DOS prompt, you can open a shared folder or drive by typing **start** by the UNC address (for example, start \\Karen\ documents).

- You can use UNC addresses in DOS commands. For example, the following command copies the file fiat19.doc into the current directory:

```
copy \\Karen\documents\memos\fiat19.doc
```

- In Windows Millennium's standard Open and Save As dialog boxes, you can use UNC addresses in the File name text box.

Adding a Network Place

New network shares in your workgroup are added to the My Network Places folder automatically. (To make sure you're seeing all the workgroup shares, open My Network Places and press F5 or select View, Refresh.) If you want to add icons for shared resources in other workgroups, or from Web folders or FTP sites, you need to follow these steps:

Shortcut
Type two back-slashes (\\) followed by the computer name, followed by another backslash (\), and the wizard displays a list of the available shares on that computer.

1. In the My Network Places folder, launch the Add Network Place icon. The Add Network Place Wizard appears.

2. Use either of the following methods to specify the resource you want to work with:

    - Use the text box to enter the UNC path of the shared resource, or the address of the Internet resource.

    - Click Browse to display the Browse For Folder dialog box, highlight the computer that has the resource, and click OK.

3. The last of the wizard's dialog boxes suggests a name for the new network place, which takes the form *Share Name* on *Computer Name*. Edit the name, if necessary, and then click Finish.

4. If the resource is protected by a password, the Access Denied dialog box appears. Enter the Password and click OK.

Windows Millennium opens a window for the resource and adds a new icon in My Network Places.

Sharing Your Resources on the Network

You've seen how My Network Places displays the resources shared by other computers. To be a good network citizen, you should share some resources of your own. The next couple of sections show you how to share drives, folders, and printers using both share-level access and user-level access, as discussed in Chapter 19, "Setting Up Your Own Local Area Network."

→ **See Also** "Step 6: Specifying Access Control," **p. 431**.

Working with Share-Level Access

Peer-to-peer networks use share-level access control to share resources and set up individual passwords for each resource. (Nodes on a client/server network can also use share-level access, but they're usually better off with user-level access control, discussed in the next section.) To set up sharing, display the property sheet for the object you want to share and then display the Sharing tab. Figure 20.5 shows a completed Sharing tab.

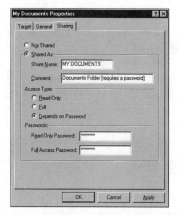

Shortcut
A quick way to the Sharing tab is to right-click the object you want to share, and then click Sharing.

Figure 20.5
With share-level access control, the Sharing tab appears as shown here.

Here are the steps to follow to set up sharing for a disk drive or folder:

1. Activate the Shared As option.

2. Edit the Share Name, if necessary. This is the name that appears when other people open your computer in the My Network Places folder. Names can be up to 12 characters long and can include spaces, all alphanumeric characters, and the following symbols: ~ ! @ # $ % ^ & ( ) _ - { } ' .

3. Enter a 48-characters-or-less description of the resource in the Comment text box. This description appears in My Network Places when remote users open your computer in Details view.

4. Use the Access Type options to select the access rights assigned to remote users:

    Read-Only—Allows users to view the resource contents, but does not let them modify those contents. In a folder or disk drive, for example, users can open a file and save it locally. However, they can't delete or rename a file or folder, edit a file and then save it, or create a new file or folder.

    Full—Gives users complete access to view and modify the resource contents.

    Depends on Password—If you activate this option, the access rights assigned to the user depends on the password they enter when they attempt to work with the object.

5. If you activated either Read-Only or Depends on Password, enter the access password in the Read-Only Password text box.

6. If you activated either Full or Depends on Password, enter the access password in the Full-Access Password text box.

7. Click OK. If you entered a password, the Password Confirmation dialog box appears.

8. Re-enter the password and click OK.

Note that, for every resource you share, Windows Millennium adds a small hand icon underneath the object's regular icon.

To share a printer, you follow a similar set of steps:

1. Activate the Shared As option.

2. Edit the Share Name, if necessary.

3. Enter a description in the Comment text box.

4. Enter an optional password in the Password text box.

5. Click OK.

6. Confirm the password, if prompted, and then click OK.

Working with User-Level Access

Share-level access control works well enough, but it's a bit cumbersome to use because you have to assign passwords to every shared resource and you have to distribute those passwords to the affected network users. This isn't a big deal if you have a small peer-to-peer network because your use of passwords will probably be limited. If you're on a client/server network, however, you have a more powerful alternative: user-level access control. In this case, the server maintains a list of the network users, and you use that list to select which users get access to each shared resource. After a user logs on to the network (a logon that is verified by the server), she can access any resource for which she is listed without having to worry about passwords. Note, too, that user-level access also gives you much finer control over the access rights granted to each user.

Watch Out!
If you've shared your resources using passwords (or if you decide to change your passwords later on), don't forget to distribute those passwords to the appropriate users.

As before, you get started by opening the property sheet for the object you want to share, and then displaying the Sharing tab. As you can see in the completed tab shown in Figure 20.6, the layout is a bit different.

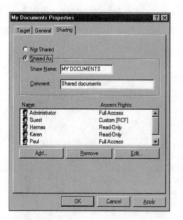

Figure 20.6
The layout of the Sharing tab with user-level access control.

Here's how to set up user-level sharing for a disk drive, folder, or printer:

1. Activate the Shared As option and edit the Share Name and Comment text boxes as required. (Use the same rules outlined earlier for share-level access.)

Watch Out!
The "user" named
World refers to
everyone who has
access to the
network, so use
this name with
caution.

2. Click Add to display the Add Users dialog box.

3. If your network has multiple domains, select the domain you want to use from the Obtain List From drop-down list.

4. In the Name list, highlight the user or users you want to add.

5. Click one of the following buttons:

   Read Only—The selected users can view the resource contents, but they can't modify those contents.

   Full Access—The selected users have complete access to view and modify the resource contents. Note that this is the only button available if you're sharing a printer.

   Custom—The selected users have only specific rights within the resource. See step 8.

6. Repeat steps 4 and 5 until you've added all the users.

7. Click OK.

8. If you added a user with custom access rights, the Change Access Rights dialog box appears, as shown in Figure 20.7. Use the check boxes to spell out the specific rights this user has, and then click OK.

Figure 20.7
Use the Change
Access Rights
dialog box to set
up custom access
rights for a user.

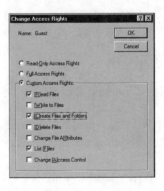

9. To remove a user, highlight his name in the Sharing tab and then click Remove.

10. To change the access rights for a user, highlight his name and click Edit. Use the Change Access Rights dialog box to modify the user's access rights.

11. Click OK.

Mapping a Shared Resource As a Local Disk Drive

So far, you've seen two ways to access shared network resources: the network places in the My Network Places folder and the UNC address. These methods have some drawbacks, however:

- You often have to drill down a number of levels in My Network Places to find the resource you want.

- UNC addresses can get complex and unwieldy.

- Many CD-ROM or DVD-ROM programs won't run from a network share.

- Many older applications don't support either My Network Places or UNC addresses.

You can solve all these problems by *mapping* a remote shared resource as a local disk drive. That is, you can take any shared disk drive or folder and have it show up on your system as a local disk drive. For example, if your system currently uses drives A through E, you can map a shared drive or folder so that it appears on your system as drive F. This gives you quick access to the resource; it avoids UNC addresses; many disk-based programs will run because they see the mapped drive as a local drive; and it appears as a local resource to older programs.

Mapping a Resource

Here are the steps to follow to map a shared network resource to a local disk drive on your system:

1. (Optional) Use the Entire Network folder to highlight the shared resource you want to map. (Note that you can't do this with a network place. You have to go through the Entire Network.)

Shortcut
Windows
Explorer's toolbar
can be cus-
tomized to display
two extra but-
tons: Map Drive
and Disconnect.
Select View,
Toolbars,
Customize to get
to the Customize
toolbar dialog
box. Highlight
Map Drive and
click Add, high-
light Disconnect
and click Add,
and then
click OK.

Watch Out!
If you attempt to
disconnect a
mapped resource
while you have
open files from
that resource,
Windows
Millennium dis-
plays a warning.
To avoid losing
data, cancel the
disconnect, close
the files, and then
attempt the dis-
connect again.

2. Select File, Map Network Drive. The Map Network Drive dialog box appears.

3. Use the Drive list to select the local drive letter to use for the selected resource.

4. If you didn't highlight the resource in step 1, use the Path text box to enter the UNC path for the resource. If it's a hidden resource, don't forget to add the dollar sign ($) at the end.

5. To map the resource automatically each time you start Windows Millennium, activate the Reconnect at logon check box.

6. Click OK.

7. If the resource is protected by a password, the Enter Network Password dialog box appears. Type the appropriate password and click OK.

Disconnecting a Mapped Resource

When you no longer require a shared resource to be mapped to a local drive, use any of the following techniques to disconnect the share:

- Highlight the local drive that's mapped to the resource and then select File, Disconnect. (You can also right-click the resource and then click Disconnect.)

- In Windows Explorer, select Tools, Disconnect Network Drive, highlight the drive in the dialog box that appears, and then click OK.

Printing over the Network

If someone on your network has shared a printer, you can "install" that printer on your system and then print to it as if it were a local printer attached directly to your computer. Windows Millennium offers two methods for installing a network printer: the Add Printer Wizard and Point and Print.

Note, however, that you may not have to bother with these steps. If a computer is sharing a printer within your workgroup, Windows Millennium automatically recognizes it and sets it up on your system. To make sure, select Start, Settings, Printers and see if an icon exists for the shared printer.

If not, or if you want to install a network printer from a different workgroup, follow these steps to use the Add Printer Wizard:

1. Select Start, Settings, Printers. Windows Millennium opens the Printers folder.

2. Launch the Add Printer icon to load the Add Printer Wizard, and then click Next in the first dialog box.

3. Activate the Network printer option and click Next. The wizard prompts you for the location of the network printer.

4. In the Network path or queue name text box, enter the UNC address of the printer, or click Browse and choose the printer from the Browse for Printer dialog box.

5. From here, you follow the same steps that you would for a local printer.

The Point and Print method enables you to install a network printer directly, which means you skip the first four steps of the Add New Printer Wizard. If the network printer is attached to a Windows 9x or Windows Millennium machine, Point and Print also installs the remote printer driver and configures the printer using the remote computer's settings. Windows Millennium offers a number of Point and Print methods:

- In My Network Places, highlight the remote printer and select File, Connect. (You can also right-click the printer and then click Connect.)

- In the My Network Places folder, drag the remote printer and drop it inside your Printers folder. (Note that you must drop it inside the open Printers folder window; you can't drop it on Printers in the Folders bar.)

Undocumented
If you have trouble printing to a network printer, try "capturing" the remote printer port so that it appears to be a physical port on your system. To do this, highlight the remote printer in My Network Places and then select File, Capture Printer Port. In the dialog box that appears, select the port you want to use (such as LPT2) and click OK.

- Select Start, Run, enter the UNC address of the remote printer, and click OK. When Windows Millennium asks if you want to set up the printer, click Yes.

- Drag a document that you want to print and drop it on the remote printer. Again, click Yes when you're asked if you want to set up the printer.

In all cases, a shorter version of the Add Printer Wizard leads you through the driver installation.

Dialing In to Your Network

Back in Chapter 4, "Getting on the Internet," I showed you how to create a Dial-Up Networking connection to the Internet. You can also use Dial-Up Networking to make a remote connection to your network, and I show you how it's done in this section. You'll see that the process is similar, but there are a few things you have to do differently when connecting to a LAN. If you're running a peer-to-peer network, this section begins by showing you how to configure a Windows Millennium machine as a dial-up server.

➜ **See Also** "Using Dial-Up Networking," **p. 108**.

Setting Up Windows Millennium As a Dial-Up Server

Dial-Up Networking assumes you have a dial-up server to connect to. On a client/server network, this will usually mean a Windows NT/2000 Server machine running the Remote Access Service (RAS). What do you do if you're just running a humble peer-to-peer network? In this case, you can configure one of the Windows Millennium machines as a dial-up server. You won't get all the features of a RAS dial-up, but it's an easy (and inexpensive!) way to establish a remote connection.

Setting Up the Dial-Up Server

The Dial-Up Server is a kind of network resource, so you must "share" it so that remote users can dial in. In this case, however, "sharing" just means setting up the Dial-Up Server to allow callers. As with the sharing of network resources, how you do this depends on whether you're using share-level or user-level access control.

To get started, open the `Dial-Up Networking` folder and then select the Connections, Dial-Up Server command. Windows Millennium displays the Dial-Up Server dialog box shown in Figure 20.8.

Figure 20.8
This version of the Dial-Up Server dialog box appears if you're using share-level access control.

Here are the steps to follow to configure the Dial-Up Server:

1. If you have multiple modems installed, the Dial-Up Server dialog box shows a tab for each modem. Display the tab you want to use with Dial-Up Server.

2. Activate the Allow caller access option.

3. If you want to protect the dial-up server with a password (a good idea), click the Change Password button and use the Dial-Up Networking Password dialog box to specify the password.

4. Use the Comment text box to add a description or other text related to the Dial-Up Server.

5. Click the Server Type button. Dial-Up Server displays the Server Types dialog box.

6. Make your choices from the following options and then click OK:

   Type of Dial-Up Server—If the incoming calls will be strictly from Windows 9x and Windows Millennium machines, select the PPP: Internet, Windows 2000/NT, Windows ME item. If there will also be Windows for Workgroups or Windows NT 3.51 dial-ups, select Default to let the Dial-Up Server figure out the correct type.

Remember
You see a slightly different Dial-Up Server dialog box if your machine is set up for user-level access. Instead of a Password button, you specify individual users. To do so, click Add, use the Add Users dialog box to select the users who are allowed to dial up the server, and click OK.

Enable software compression—When this check box is activated, the server and the remote machine use software compression to exchange data.

Require encrypted password—When this check box is activated, Dial-Up Server requires that the remote machine send its passwords in encrypted form (instead of plain text).

7. Click Apply. Dial-Up Networking adds the Dial-Up Server icon to the system tray and begins monitoring the modem for incoming calls.

Monitoring the Connected User

With the Dial-Up Server configured, the Status box displays Monitoring to indicate that it's looking for incoming calls. When a call comes in, the Status line tells you who it is and when the user connected, as shown in Figure 20.9. You can disconnect the user at any time by clicking the Disconnect User button.

Figure 20.9
When a user is connected, the Status box tells you who it is and when he connected.

Creating and Configuring a Network Connection

As I mentioned before, creating a Dial-Up Networking connection for a remote network server isn't all that much different from creating one for the Internet. Let's run through the basic steps:

1. Select Start, Settings, Dial-Up Networking.

2. The next step depends on how Dial-Up Networking started:

- If this is the first time you've launched Dial-Up Networking, the Welcome to Dial-Up Networking dialog box appears. In this case, click Next.

- Each subsequent time you launch Dial-Up Networking, the Dial-Up Networking folder appears. In this case, open the Make New Connection icon.

3. Enter a name for your connection and, if you have multiple modems, choose the modem you want to use from the Select a device list. Click Next.

4. Enter the dial-up server's Area code, Telephone number, and Country code, and then click Next.

5. Click Finish. An icon for your new connection appears in the Dial-Up Networking folder.

Now let's configure the new connection. Highlight the icon and then select File, Properties to open the connection's property sheet. (You can also right-click the icon and then click Properties.) Display the Networking tab and configure it as follows:

- I'm assuming here that you're dialing in to either a Windows NT/2000 Server machine, or to a Windows Millennium machine configured as a dial-up server (as explained in the previous section). Therefore, make sure the Type of Dial-Up Server list shows PPP: Internet, Windows 2000/NT, Windows ME.

- Activate the other check boxes in the Advanced options group, depending on the configuration of the dial-up server.

- In the Allowed network protocols group, activate the check boxes for the networking protocols you need to communicate with the server. If you're using TCP/IP, click the TCP/IP Settings button and fill in your TCP/IP details (including your network's primary and secondary WINS servers, if any).

Remember
Dial-Up Server only uses software compression and encrypted passwords if both the server and the remote machine have these options enabled. For the remote computer, open the Dial-Up Networking connection icon, display the Server Types tab, and then activate the Enable software compression and Require encrypted password check boxes.

Watch Out!
The Dial-Up Server always answers incoming calls on the first ring, and there's no way to change that. Therefore, the Dial-Up Server will interfere with other communications software that answers incoming calls (such as Microsoft Fax).

When you're done, click OK to return to the Dial-Up Networking folder.

Making the Connection

After your Dial-Up Networking connection is configured, connecting to the network isn't much different than connecting to the Internet. Here are the steps to follow:

Shortcut

There are some other routes you can take to the Connect To dialog box. You can double-click the icon, highlight the icon, and then click the toolbar's Dial button, or you can right-click the icon and then click Connect.

1. In the Dial-Up Networking folder, highlight the connection icon and then select Connections, Connect. The Connect To dialog box appears.

2. Make sure the User name text box shows your network username.

3. Enter your network password in the Password text box. You also have two check boxes to work with:

   Save password—Activate this check box to have Dial-Up Networking remember your password the next time you connect.

   Connect automatically—Activate this check box to bypass the Connect To dialog box when you launch the icon. If you never change settings in this dialog box, deactivating this check box will save you an extra step when connecting.

4. If necessary, use the Dialing from list or the Dial Properties button to adjust the dialing location.

→ **See Also** "Setting Dialing Properties," **p. 100**.

5. Click Connect. Dial-Up Networking connects to the dial-up server and establishes a network connection.

6. Log on to the network in the usual manner. The Connection Established dialog box appears, and the system tray gets a new Dial-Up Networking icon.

7. Click Close.

To disconnect from the network, use any of the following procedures:

- Double-click the taskbar's Dial-Up Networking icon and then click Disconnect.

- Right-click the taskbar's Dial-Up Networking icon and then click Disconnect.

- In the `Dial-Up Networking` folder, right-click the icon and then click Disconnect.

Essential Information

- You can access the `My Network Places` folder either via Windows Explorer, by opening the desktop's My Network Places icon, or within the standard Windows Millennium Open and Save As dialog boxes.

- The Universal Naming Convention (UNC) specifies remote addresses using the form `\\computername\sharename\path\file`.

- To share a resource, open its property sheet, select the Sharing tab, activate the Shared As option, and then set up either a password or a list of users.

- To map a shared folder as a local disk drive, highlight the folder in My Network Places and then select File, Map Network Drive.

- To use a network printer, either run the Add New Hardware Wizard and choose the Network printer option, or else use Point and Print to install the remote printer directly.

- To configure the Dial-Up Server, run Dial-Up Networking and select Connections, Dial-Up Server.

- To start your Dial-Up Networking connection, open the `Dial-Up Networking` folder and launch the Make New Connection icon.

Undocumented
You can launch a Dial-Up Networking connection in the Run dialog box or a batch file by using the following syntax:

`rundll rnaui.dll, RnaDial` *connection*

Replace *connection* with the name of the Dial-Up Networking icon you want to use. Note that this command is case sensitive.

- To connect to the dial-up server, highlight the connection icon in the Dial-Up Networking folder and select Connections, Connect.

High-Powered Hardware Techniques

PART VII

GET THE SCOOP ON...

Device Drivers, IRQ Lines, I/O Ports, DMA Channels, and Other Hardware Settings ▪ Making Plug and Play Work Properly ▪ Installing Device Drivers Automatically and by Hand ▪ Using the Signature Verification Tool ▪ Using Device Manager to Adjust Device Properties, Settings, and Resources

Taking the Mystery out of Hardware

Chapter 21

ALTHOUGH I'VE BEEN A PROGRAMMER for over 25 years (ouch!), I've always enjoyed working with hardware. When writing a book such as this, for example, I relish the idea of prying open the cases of my test computers to see how Windows Millennium reacts to different configurations: internal modems, SCSI controllers, network interface cards, graphics adapters, memory chips, and so on. Until recently, however, the part I truly disliked about these "machine-ations" was the endless tweaking and configuring required to get the devices to cooperate with each other. Now, thanks to Plug and Play and other automatic hardware configuration technologies, all that fiddling is a thing of the past.

In this chapter, my goal isn't so much to get you to "relish" the idea of working with hardware. (That would be asking a lot, I know.) Instead, I aim only to remove some of the mystery surrounding hardware, and to help you configure your own system. If you have an older machine or if you have legacy devices, you learn how to avoid the conflicts that can cause hardware to fail. If you have a newer system and Plug-and-Play devices, you see how easy Windows Millennium makes it to create a problem-free setup.

Crucial Hardware Concepts

That hardware seems a mysterious and arcane subject is probably because the underlying concepts are, at first blush, confusing and obscure. However, the good news is that these concepts are not unexplainable. The next few sections take you through some hardware basics that will serve you well not only through the rest of this chapter, but also in the next two chapters where I discuss specific devices.

IRQ Lines, I/O Ports, and Other Device Settings

One of Windows Millennium's core responsibilities is to coordinate the interaction of hardware and software. In general, that means sending signals from software to hardware (such as printing instructions) and relaying signals from hardware to software (such as displaying characters in response to keystrokes). All these signals going back and forth need some sort of communication channels, and most devices use one or more of the following: interrupt request lines, input/output ports, Direct Memory Access channels, and memory addresses.

Interrupt Request Lines

An *interrupt request line* (IRQ) is a wire built in to the computer's motherboard or a device slot. It's used by the processor and a device to send signals to each other. In other words, the device uses the wire to send a "request" to the processor to "interrupt" whatever the processor is doing (and vice versa).

For example, most serial ports incorporate a special chip called a Universal Asynchronous Receiver/Transmitter (UART). Its job is to convert bits coming in from the modem into bytes that can be processed by the computer. (The UART also converts the computer's outgoing bytes into serial bits for transmission via the modem across the phone line.) Most UARTs use special buffers to hold these incoming bytes. When a specified numbers of those buffers are full, the UART uses an IRQ line to send a signal to the processor that there are bytes to take care of. The processor then goes through the following (greatly simplified) steps:

1. The processor saves its current state in a special memory area called a *stack*.

2. The processor accesses the *interrupt vector table*, which contains a list of memory locations that correspond to each IRQ line. In particular, the processor uses the table to determine the memory location of the device driver that works with whatever device initiated the interrupt request.

Inside Scoop
A stack is a memory location that stores data in a last-in, first-out (LIFO) format.

3. The processor gets the device driver to handle the interrupt request.

4. The original contents of the processor are restored off the stack and the processor continues what it was doing prior to the interrupt.

The crucial step here is when the processor uses the interrupt vector table to look up the required device driver. This works because, in a typical system, a single IRQ line is assigned to each device that requires one. Table 21.1 lists the IRQ line assignments in a typical PC.

TABLE 21.1: IRQ LINE ASSIGNMENTS IN A TYPICAL PC

IRQ Line	Device
0	System timer
1	Keyboard
2	Programmable interrupt controller
3	Serial port 2 (COM2)
4	Serial port 1 (COM1)
5	Available, sound card, or parallel port 2 (LPT2)
6	Floppy disk controller
7	Parallel port 1 (LPT1)
8	Real-time clock
9	Available
10	Available
11	Available
12	Available or PS/2 mouse port
13	Math coprocessor
14	Primary IDE controller
15	Available or secondary IDE controller

Inside Scoop
The *programmable interrupt controller* on IRQ 2 is a second IRQ controller chip. The main IRQ controller chip takes care of IRQ lines 0 through 7, which were the only ones available in the original IBM PC. For the IBM AT, a second IRQ controller chip was added to bring the total number of IRQ lines to 16 (8 through 15). The main chip has IRQ 2 available, so that line is used to coordinate the two chips.

As you can see, as many as six and as few as three IRQ lines are available on just a bare-bones system configuration. Therein lies the rub because so many other devices require IRQ lines: graphics adapters, network interface cards, SCSI controllers, PC card controllers, infrared ports, and more. For older devices that aren't compatible with Plug and Play (discussed later in this chapter), the IRQ line number used by a device is configured usually either by adjusting a jumper or DIP switch, or by running a setup program.

All this leads to three possible IRQ problems:

- Two devices configured to use the same IRQ line.

- An interrupt vector table that doesn't correctly match an IRQ line with the IRQ line used by a device.

- No available IRQ lines for a new device.

These are among the most common PC hardware headaches and are the source of many system lockups and bizarre device behavior. As you'll see throughout the rest of this chapter, Windows Millennium not only gives you tools to properly configure IRQs, but it also supports a number of new technologies that aim to eliminate IRQ conflicts. Perhaps the most important of these is *IRQ steering*. This technology enables Windows Millennium to manage some of the available IRQ lines to enable multiple devices to share a single IRQ line. This enables you to install more devices than you have IRQ lines.

Input/Output Ports

An *Input/Output port* (or I/O port) is a small block of memory (typically 8 bytes, 16 bytes, or 32 bytes) that acts as a communications channel between a device and the processor or a device driver. Each I/O port address is expressed as a range of hexadecimal numbers. For example, the first I/O port on most systems is used by the Direct Memory Access controller, and its address is the 16-byte range 0000 - 000F.

Most devices "listen in on" (or *poll*) their I/O port looking for new data, and then process that data when it's found. The processor, too, polls the used I/O ports looking for incoming data from a device. For a high-speed device such as a SCSI controller, IRQ lines and I/O ports are used together to avoid the inherent inefficiency of polling.

Almost all devices use an I/O port, but there are 65,536 bytes of memory available for these ports, so there is no danger of ever running out of ports. As with IRQ lines, however, an I/O port conflict in which two devices are configured to use the same I/O port can lead to problems.

Direct Memory Access Channels

In the previous section, you saw how the processor and a device pass data back and forth by using an I/O port. However, if there is a large amount of data to exchange, the relatively tiny size of the I/O port forces the processor and the device to interact frequently, thus slowing system performance. Some devices overcome this by using a *Direct Memory Access channel* (DMA channel). This is a connection maintained by a DMA controller chip that enables a device to transfer data directly to and from memory. The processor tells the DMA controller chip what device to work with and what data is needed. The DMA controller chip then uses the channel to perform the complete data transfer without involving the processor.

Like IRQ lines, modern computers come with only a limited number of DMA channels, as outlined in Table 21.2.

TABLE 21.2: DMA CHANNEL ASSIGNMENTS IN A TYPICAL PC

DMA Channel	Device
0	Available
1	Available
2	Floppy disk controller
3	Available
4	DMA controller chip
5	Available
6	Available
7	Available

Remember
PCI systems also implement a technique that's similar to DMA: *bus mastering*. In this case, the processor delegates I/O control over the PCI bus to the PCI controller. (That is, the PCI controller becomes the "master" of the bus.) This enables the PCI controller to work directly with I/O devices (such as a PCI SCSI controller).

Some of the available channels are usually taken up by devices such as a sound card, an ISA SCSI controller, or an ECP printer port. DMA channel conflicts can cause problems, but it's a rare machine that uses up all eight available channels.

Memory Addresses

The final medium for device communication is system memory, including the 384KB of upper memory that resides between conventional memory (up to 640KB) and extended memory (1MB and beyond). This memory is used by a variety of devices for a variety of uses:

- Graphics adapter video RAM—the pixel values that appear on your monitor

- Graphics adapter BIOS code

- BIOS code for other adapters (such as a PCI SCSI adapter)

- Motherboard BIOS code

Again, no two devices can use the same memory block.

Understanding Device Drivers

A *device driver* is a small software program that acts as a kind of digital equivalent to the proverbial one-trick pony: All it does is act as a go-between for a device and other programs (including Windows). The device driver is intimately "familiar" with the instructions and code required to make a device perform a specific task. When a program needs the device to perform that task, it tells the device driver what needs to be done and the driver handles everything from there.

Other than obtaining and installing the correct driver for a device (see "Installing Device Drivers," later in this chapter), the most important concept to bear in mind is that Windows Millennium no longer supports real-mode device drivers. (Real-mode drivers are 16-bit programs that used to be loaded via either CONFIG.SYS or AUTOEXEC.BAT.) Instead, you must use only virtual device drivers (32-bit programs that run in Windows Millennium's native protected mode).

One of the innovations introduced back in Windows 95 was the *universal driver/mini-driver architecture* for device drivers. (This idea actually began with the printer support in Windows 3.*x*, but it was extended to all device classes in Windows 95). There are two components:

Universal driver—This is a driver that contains all the code needed for any device in a particular class of devices to work with the appropriate subsystem of the operating system. For example, the universal printer driver enables any printer to interact with the Windows Millennium printing subsystem.

Mini-driver—This is a smaller driver that contains the code required to implement the unique functionality of a specific device.

How to Make Plug and Play Work (Most of the Time)

As you could tell even from my simplified explanations of IRQ lines, I/O ports, DMA channels, and memory addresses given earlier, configuring a device to avoid conflicts is a tricky operation. This untenable situation existed for many years until three companies—Compaq, Intel, and Phoenix Technologies—decided to do something about it. The result was an industry standard called *Plug and Play* with a simple, yet tantalizing, premise: to define a system in which *all* device configuration occurred automatically and without any user intervention.

Plug and Play (PnP) was introduced in 1995, and, despite all the promise (and all the hype), it immediately flopped. Why? Well, it wasn't because it was an imperfect standard, to be sure. No, Plug and Play got off to a bad start because it was just ahead of the technology curve and, therefore, ahead of its time. You see, for Plug and Play to work, it requires hardware and software (an operating system) that meet certain rigid restrictions. Back in 1995, the operating system existed (Windows 95), but the requisite hardware didn't exist in the mainstream. Most users had only *legacy devices* (as non-PnP hardware is now called), so the full Plug and Play equation wasn't satisfied.

Remember
If you purchased your computer within the last couple of years, it will almost certainly have a PnP BIOS. If you're not sure, check with your manufacturer. If you don't have the correct BIOS, your manufacturer should be able to supply you with either a new BIOS chip or a program that upgrades the BIOS code.

Shortcut
The following devices are automatically PnP-compatible: PCI devices, USB devices, and IEEE 1394 (FireWire) devices.

Three things are required for PnP to work:

A Plug and Play BIOS—This BIOS adds a few extra steps to the Power-On Self Test (POST) code that runs at system startup. Specifically, the code enumerates all the PnP-compliant devices installed on the system and interrogates each device to determine its resource requirements. The code then checks for and resolves conflicts automatically.

Windows Millennium (or some other PnP-compatible operating system)—Windows Millennium's Configuration Manager component gathers all the data on the system's Plug and Play devices and stores everything in the Registry. (Configuration Manager either uses the data gleaned by the Plug and Play BIOS or, if no such BIOS is present, it enumerates and configures the Plug and Play devices directly.) It also monitors the system to watch for *hot swapping*—Plug and Play devices (such as PC Cards or USB hardware) added and removed while the system is running. In this case, Windows Millennium automatically reconfigures the system, reallocates resources, and alerts running applications of the hardware change.

Plug and Play devices—These are the key to the entire Plug and Play exercise. If you don't use Plug and Play devices, neither a Plug and Play BIOS nor Windows Millennium will be able to do much in the way of automatic configuration. When purchasing a device, always check to see whether it's PnP-compatible.

Installing Device Drivers

As I mentioned earlier, for whatever device you install on your system, you must also install a device driver so that Windows Millennium can work with the device. This isn't something you have to worry about if the device is PnP-compatible. In this case, Windows Millennium reacts in one of two ways:

- If you *hot-swapped* a device such as a PC Card or a printer, Windows Millennium recognizes the device immediately and installs the driver for it.

- If you turned your computer off to install the device, Windows Millennium recognizes it the next time you start the machine, and installs the appropriate driver.

Note, too, that if Windows Millennium doesn't have a driver of its own, it might ask you to install a driver from the manufacturer's disk (or from a downloaded driver file).

The next couple of sections show you how to install a driver for legacy devices and for those few Plug and Play devices not immediately recognized by Windows Millennium.

Using Automatic Hardware Detection

Windows Millennium has a Detection Manager component that checks ports, buses, SCSI controllers, and other hardware nooks for clues that a new device is present. The Detection Manager is usually pretty good at ferreting out new hardware. However, even if the Detection Manager fails to find a new device, you can always install the appropriate driver by hand. I discuss the latter in the next section. For now, here are the steps to follow to have Windows Millennium check for new devices:

1. Open the Control Panel's Add New Hardware icon. (This icon isn't in the default Control Panel view, so you might first need to click the View all control panel options link.) This launches the Add New Hardware Wizard.

2. Click Next. The wizard lets you know that it will now look for Plug and Play devices.

3. Click Next. Windows Millennium runs the Configuration Manager to check for Plug and Play devices. If it finds any, it displays the New Hardware Found dialog box while it's installing the required drivers.

4. When the Plug and Play phase is complete, the wizard displays a dialog box with a list of the devices that were installed, if any. (If no devices were found, skip to step 6.) The wizard wonders whether your devices were installed:

Yes, I am finished installing devices—If Windows Millennium found your new device, activate this option, click Next, and then click Finish to exit the Add New Hardware Wizard.

No, I want to install other devices—If Windows Millennium didn't find your device, activate this option and click Next. The remaining steps assume you chose this option.

5. If you have any devices that have a problem, the wizard displays a list of those devices and offers two options:

No, the device isn't in the list—If your device isn't in the list, activate this option and click Next.

Yes, the device is in the list—If your device is listed, highlight it and click Next. In this case, the wizard will likely tell you that the device has a problem. Click Finish to display the device's property sheet, which will explain the problem and (probably) offer an Update Driver button that you click to continue.

6. The wizard now asks whether you want Windows Millennium to search for legacy hardware:

Yes (Recommended)—Activate this option and click Next to have the Detection Manager scour your system for the new device. The remaining steps assume you chose this option.

No, I want to select the hardware from a list—Activate this option and click Next to install a driver by hand (see "Installing a Driver by Hand," next).

7. The wizard displays a dialog box that explains the detection process. Click Next. The wizard now displays a Detection progress meter that shows you how much of the hardware detection is complete. Note that this process takes a few minutes.

Watch Out!
If the Detection progress meter doesn't change for several minutes, it's likely that the Detection Manager is stuck. Shut down your computer and leave it off for several seconds to give all your devices time to spin down and stop completely. Then, turn your computer back on and try again. If the detection fails again, make sure you installed the hardware properly and that it's turned on (if applicable).

8. When the detection phase is complete, the wizard lets you know whether it found any new devices. (If it did, you can click the Details button to see a list of the installed devices.) Click Finish.

9. At this point, you might need to run through a configuration process for the new device.

10. If Windows Millennium asks whether you want to restart your computer, click Yes.

Installing a Driver by Hand

As you saw in the previous section, the Add New Hardware Wizard offers an option for installing a device driver by hand if Windows Millennium couldn't find your device or doesn't have a driver for it. You can also opt to install the driver by hand if you have a manufacturer's disk or a downloaded file that includes the appropriate driver.

To get started, you usually have two choices:

- If the manufacturer's disk or downloaded file has a setup program, run that program to install the driver.

- Use the Add New Hardware Wizard, as described in the previous section. When you get to step 6, activate the No, I want to select the hardware from a list option and click Next.

If you choose the latter route, here are the steps to follow from here:

1. The Add New Hardware Wizard displays a list of various hardware classes. Use the Hardware types list to highlight the appropriate class for your device, and then click Next.

2. Depending on the hardware class you selected, a new wizard might appear. (For example, if you chose the Modem class, the Install New Modem Wizard appears.) In this case, follow the wizard's dialog boxes. Otherwise, the Select Device dialog box appears. Figure 21.1 shows the Select Device dialog box for network adapters.

Inside Scoop
Most large hardware manufacturers have an extensive collection of device drivers on their Web sites. In most cases, look for a link to either the "Technical Support" or "Downloads" area. You can also get drivers from the Windows Update Web site (click Product Updates and then click Device Drivers) and the Windows Hardware Compatibility List (`www.microsoft.com/hwtest/hcl/`).

Figure 21.1
Use the Select
Device dialog box
to install a device
driver manually.

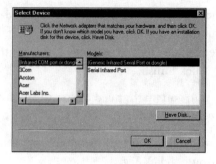

Watch Out!
Although
Windows
Millennium was
designed to work
with a wide vari-
ety of hardware,
you'll almost
always have an
easier installation
if you purchase
devices designed
for Windows
Millennium, or
that meet the
guidelines for the
PC 99 or
PC 2001
standards (see
www.microsoft.
com/hwdev/). You
should also check
the Windows
Hardware
Compatibility List
at www.microsoft.
com/hwtest/hcl/.

3. If you have a manufacturer's disk or downloaded file, click Have Disk, enter the appropriate path and filename in the Install From Disk dialog box, and click OK.

4. Highlight your device. (In the default Select Device dialog box, first highlight the device's manufacturer in the Manufacturers list and then highlight the name of the device in the Models list.)

5. Click OK.

6. If prompted, run through a configuration process for the new device.

7. If Windows Millennium asks whether you want to restart your computer, click Yes.

Working with the Signature Verification Tool

To ensure that device drivers work properly with Windows Millennium, Microsoft runs a Windows Hardware Quality Lab (WHQL); you can find it at: http://whql.microsoft.com/hwtest/.

Vendors submit their devices to the WHQL for testing. If a device passes, the vendor gets the following benefits bestowed upon them:

- A license to use the "Designed for Windows Millennium" logo on the device packaging.

- A listing for the device in the Hardware Compatibility list.

- Distribution of the device's drivers via the Hardware Compatibility list.

- A Microsoft digital signature that certifies the driver meets the WHQL standards and has not been altered in any way since the testing.

Most reputable manufacturers offer high-quality drivers. After all, if their drivers didn't work properly, people would stop buying their products. However, you can be sure you're getting a safe, high-quality, Windows Millennium-compatible driver if it has been digitally signed by Microsoft. How do you know? Well, if you download the driver from the Hardware Compatibility list or Windows Update, then you know automatically that you're installing a driver with a Microsoft digital signature. For all other drivers, you can set up Windows Millennium to warn you of nonsigned drivers, or to block their installation altogether.

To do this, follow these steps:

1. In the System Policy Editor, select File, Open Registry.

2. Open the Local Computer icon.

3. Select Windows Millennium System, Install Device Drivers, Digital Signature Check.

4. Select one of the following levels:

   Allow installation of all drivers—Select this level to disable the checking of digital signatures.

   Block installation of non-Microsoft signed drivers—Select this level to tell Windows Millennium not to install any driver that doesn't come with a Microsoft digital signature.

   Warn installation of non-Microsoft signed drivers—Select this option to tell Windows Millennium to warn you if you're about to install a driver that doesn't come with a Microsoft digital signature.

5. Click OK.

6. Select File, Save to put the option into effect.

Undocumented
If you don't have the System Policy Editor, you can do this by hand within the following Registry key: HKEY_LOCAL_ MACHINE\Software\ Microsoft\Driver Signing. Create a new DWORD value named Policy and assign it the value 1 for the "Allow" level, 2 for the "Warn" level, or 3 for the "Block" level.

What about drivers you've already installed? To see if they come with a Microsoft digital signature, you can use the new Signature Verification Tool to check your existing drivers. Here are the steps to run through:

1. To start the utility, use either of the following techniques:

   - Select Start, Run, type **sigverif**, and click OK.

   - Select Start, Programs, Accessories, System Tools, System Information, and then select Tools, Signature Verification Tool.

2. In the File Signature Verification window, click **Advanced** to display the Advanced File Signature Verification Settings dialog box.

3. You have two options in the Search tab:

   Notify me if any system files are not signed—Activate this option to have the program check only Windows system files.

   Look for other files that are not digitally signed—Activate this option to have the program check files that you specify. This also enables the controls in the Search options group, as shown in Figure 21.2. Use these controls to specify the file type and location you want to check.

Shortcut
If you don't restrict the type of file or the location, the Signature Verification Tool will find many Windows Millennium files that don't have (and don't need) a signature. For more useful results, use a specific folder that contains only a few files (such as some driver files you've downloaded).

Figure 21.2
Use this dialog box to specify which files should be checked for signature verification.

4. The options in the Logging tab control how the program logs the signature verification results. You can turn logging on and off, choose whether to append or overwrite the file, and change the name and location of the file.

5. Click OK to return to the File Signature Verification window.

6. Click Start to begin the verification. When the process is complete, the Signature Verification Results window appears with a list of the unsigned files.

7. When you've finished examining the results, click Close. The program writes the results to the log file and you're returned to the File Signature Verification window.

8. Click Close.

Using Automatic Skip Driver Agent to Bypass Troublesome Drivers

Windows Millennium loads a large number of virtual device drivers at startup. Many of these drivers, although still important for device functionality, are not considered critical to the operation of Windows Millennium. Critical drivers are those that, if they fail, will prevent Windows Millennium from starting.

Windows Millennium has a feature called Automatic Skip Driver Agent that monitors the startup procedure and flags any device driver that causes Windows Millennium to hang. The Automatic Skip Driver Agent then disables that driver so that it gets bypassed at the next restart.

To see a list of the drivers that have been disabled (if any), run Automatic Skip Driver Agent by using either of the following methods:

- Select Start, Run, type **asd**, and click OK.

- Select Start, Programs, Accessories, System Tools, System Information, and then select Tools, Automatic Skip Driver Agent.

If no critical failures have occurred on your machine, Automatic Skip Driver Agent displays a dialog box to let you know. Otherwise, the Automatic Skip Driver Agent window appears and displays a list of the drivers that failed to load.

Undocumented

When Automatic
Skip Driver Agent
disables a driver,
it records what it
did in the text file
Windows\Asd.log.

After you've solved the problem (usually by reinstalling the troublesome driver), use Automatic Skip Driver Agent to enable the disabled driver.

Getting Device Information

If you need data about the devices on your system—whether it's configuration information, device errors, or the drivers used by a device—Windows Millennium offers a number of tools to get the job done. Here's a summary:

Device Manager—Organizes devices by hardware class. Displays device problems and driver information, and enables you to change drivers and resources (such as IRQ lines and I/O ports). You get there by opening the Control Panel's System icon (see the next section for a more detailed look at this tool).

System Information—Contains a Hardware Resources branch that details the resources used by devices, as well as a Components branch that lists the hardware installed in various categories. The items in the latter branch display driver details, associated Registry locations, and current driver problems. Also contains a System History view (select the View, System History command) that outlines the history of the system's device changes. See Chapter 14, "Crucial System Maintenance Skills."

➜ **See Also** "The System Information Utility," **p. 328.**

Hardware Diagnostic Tool—Displays data on each device's Registry key, allocated resources, and drivers using a color-coded system (see Figure 21.3). To start this utility, select Start, Run, type **hwinfo /ui**, and click OK. The color codes used are as follows:

- **Green**—Registry data

- **Pink**—Driver file data

- **Dark red**—Configuration Manager (resource usage) data

- **Red**—Device errors

- **Blue**—Device warnings

Figure 21.3
The Hardware
Diagnostic Tool
provides color-
coded data about
your installed
devices.

Dealing with Device Manager

Of the three hardware information utilities listed in the previous section, the most important is Device Manager because
not only does it provide comprehensive data about each
device, but it also enables you to update device drivers, change
resource settings, enable and disable devices, and more.

To view Device Manager, open the Control Panel's System icon
and then display the Device Manager tab. As you can see in
Figure 21.4, Device Manager displays a tree-like hierarchy of
hardware classes. Opening a branch displays a list of the
installed devices within that branch.

Shortcut
You can also get
to Device
Manager by right-
clicking the desk-
top's My
Computer icon,
clicking
Properties, and
then displaying
the Device
Manager tab.

Figure 21.4
Device Manager
displays a list of
the hardware
classes installed
on your system.

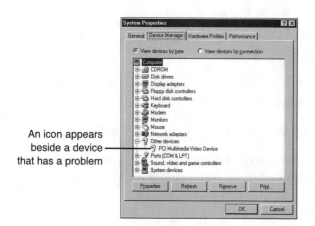

An icon appears
beside a device
that has a problem

Note, too, that you can also activate the View devices by connection option to display the devices according to how they're
connected within your system. If your computer has a Plug and
Play BIOS, for example, you can use this option to see the list
of devices enumerated by the BIOS at startup.

Undocumented
For a SCSI device to be enumerated properly at startup, the device must be turned on. If you forgot to turn on a SCSI device, you can let Device Manager know that it's now available by highlighting Computer at the top of the list and then clicking Refresh. This trick also works if you add a new SCSI device; clicking Refresh should force Windows to recognize the device without having to reboot.

Inside Scoop
The following Microsoft Knowledge Base article contains a description of the error codes used by Device Manager:
http://support .microsoft.com /support/kb/ articles/Q125/ 1/74.asp

Below the list of devices, you see four command buttons:

- **Properties**—Displays a property sheet for the highlighted device (see "Working with Device Properties," later in this chapter).

- **Refresh**—Updates the Device Manager display.

- **Remove**—Removes the highlighted device from the Device Manager list. Use this button to tell Windows Millennium when you're about to physically remove a legacy device from your system.

- **Print**—Prints some or all the Device Manager data. If you want to print the data only for a particular hardware class or device, select it before clicking this button. In the Print dialog box that appears, select System summary (resource usage only), Selected class or device (driver and resource usage for the highlighted hardware class or device), or All devices and system summary (driver and resource usage for all devices).

Device Manager is also useful as a troubleshooting tool. As pointed out earlier in Figure 21.4, Device Manager displays an icon beside the device name:

- A yellow icon with a black exclamation mark means the device has a problem.

- A white icon with a blue i means a device's resources have been configured manually.

- A red X means the device is missing or disabled.

Highlight the device in question and then click Properties to see a description of the problem.

Viewing Devices by Resource

If your system isn't fully PnP-compatible, you'll occasionally need to manipulate a device's IRQ lines, I/O ports, and other resources. To avoid conflicts with existing devices, it helps to get an overall view of the resources that are currently allocated on your machine. To do this in Device Manager, make sure My

Computer is highlighted at the top of the Device Manager list, and then click Properties. Figure 21.5 shows the Computer Properties dialog box that appears. If a setting is missing in the list (such as IRQ 5 in Figure 21.5), it means that resource is available. The default view is Interrupt request (IRQ). You can also view the devices by Input/Output (I/O), Direct memory access (DMA), and Memory.

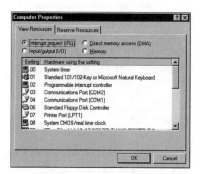

Figure 21.5
Use this dialog box to view devices by IRQ line, I/O port, DMA channel, and memory address.

Working with Device Properties

Each device on your system has a number of properties that you can view and, in some cases, manipulate. To view the property sheet for a device, highlight it and then click Properties. (You can also double-click the device.) The dialog box that appears will have two or more of the following tabs:

- **General**—Gives you basic data about the device, such as the manufacturer's name and the hardware version. The Device status group tells you whether the device is working properly or, if it's not, what the problem is. The check boxes in the Device usage group are used for enabling and disabling devices in a hardware profile.

- **Settings**—Displays one or more controls for working with device settings.

- **Driver**—Click Driver File Details to see a list of the driver files used by the device. To change the driver, click Update Driver.

■ **Resources**—Displays a list of the resources used by the device, as shown in Figure 21.6. To change a resource, deactivate the Use automatic settings check box and then use either of the following techniques:

Select a different configuration from the Setting based on list. Highlight the setting you want to change and then click Change Setting.

Figure 21.6
Use the
Resources tab to
view and change
a device's
resources.

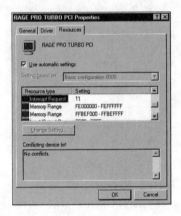

Essential Information

■ To enable communication between a device and the processor or a device driver, four hardware features are used: interrupt request (IRQ) lines, input/output (I/O) ports, Direct Memory Access (DMA) channels, and memory addresses.

Watch Out!
Make sure you
don't select a
resource that
conflicts with an
existing device.
Keep your eye on
the Conflicting
device list area to
watch for con-
flicts.

■ A device driver is a small software program that implements the code necessary for Windows Millennium to operate a device.

■ For Plug and Play to work properly, your system must have a Plug and Play BIOS, Windows Millennium (or some other PnP-compatible operating system), and PnP-compatible devices.

■ Run the Control Panel's Add New Hardware icon to install a device driver either via the automatic Detection Manager or by hand.

- The Signature Verification Tool can tell you whether a device driver has been digitally signed by Microsoft.

- Open the Control Panel's System icon to get to the Device Manager, which enables you to view your installed devices, their resource allocation, and the properties for each device.

GET THE SCOOP ON...

■ Installing a Driver for Your Graphics Adapter ■
Adjusting the Number of Colors Used by Your Display ■
Setting the Screen Resolution ■ Working with Power
Management and Other Monitor Features ■ Expanding
the Windows Millennium Desktop to Two or More
Monitors ■ Using Sound in Windows Millennium

Maximizing Multimedia Hardware

Chapter 22

THIS CHAPTER CONTINUES TO LOOK at specific hardware devices, this time in the multimedia category. I spend the bulk of the chapter discussing devices related to what you *see* on your computer. First, you learn about graphics adapters and how to install the appropriate driver. You also learn the important concepts of color depth and screen resolution and how to configure these settings. From there, you move to monitors and discover how to configure a monitor and work with your monitor's power management features, as well as how to put together a multiple-monitor setup. The final stop on the tour of visual hardware shows you how to work with scanners and digital cameras.

The rest of the chapter focuses on what you can *hear* with your computer, including setting up a sound card, assigning sounds to system events, and recording and editing sound files.

Installing and Configuring a Graphics Adapter

The *graphics adapter* (sometimes called a *video adapter*) is a system component that usually comes in the form of a circuit board that plugs into a bus slot inside the computer. (Therefore, the graphics adapter is also called a *graphics board,* a *graphics card,* and a *video card.* Note, too, that some graphics adapters are part of the computer's motherboard.) Its job is to enable software to display text or an image on the monitor. The basic process works something like this:

1. The software alerts the CPU to let it know that the program has something to display on the monitor.

2. The CPU contacts the graphics adapter's device driver and passes along the instructions:

   • For older adapters, the CPU passes along specific instructions about not only *what* to display, but *how* to display it.

   • The vast majority of modern graphics adapters are *accelerated,* which means they have their own processor that can handle the specifics of displaying graphics primitives (lines, boxes, and so on) onscreen. In this case, the CPU only has to send instructions about what to display.

3. The driver uses an IRQ to contact the adapter and uses the system bus to pass along the instructions from the CPU. (I explained IRQ lines in Chapter 21, "Taking the Mystery out of Hardware.")

➜ **See Also** "IRQ Lines, I/O Ports, and Other Device Settings," **p. 464**.

4. The adapter builds the new screen image and stores it in a *frame buffer:* a piece of the adapter's on-board memory.

5. The adapter uses a *RAMDAC—random access memory digital-to-analog converter*—to convert the digital data in the frame buffer to analog data that the monitor can understand.

6. The monitor displays the screen image by converting the incoming signal into the colors that get displayed using individual screen pixels.

Based on these steps, you can see that there are three crucial components to consider if you want to optimize video performance:

- **Make sure you get an accelerated graphics adapter**—The graphics coprocessor on this type of board shoulders much of the graphics burden that would otherwise fall to the CPU, thus improving overall system performance.

- **Get an adapter with as much video memory as you can afford**—As you'll see a bit later when I discuss color depth and resolution, the higher these values are, the larger the frame buffer that's required. The more video memory you have, the larger the frame buffer can be and the more memory the adapter's processor has for performing calculations and other video procedures.

- **Get an adapter that operates on a speedy bus**—If your system has an *Accelerated Graphics Port* (AGP) bus and a free AGP slot, then an AGP-based adapter is your best bet. (If you have an older system with a PCI bus, a PCI adapter will work well.)

Changing the Adapter Driver

On all but a tiny portion of the systems I've tested, Windows Millennium has correctly determined the graphics adapter (even for non-Plug and Play cards) and installed the appropriate driver. So, chances are your system will have the required driver installed and you won't have to worry about it. However, Windows Millennium does occasionally miss an adapter and will, instead, install just a generic driver. Here's how to change the driver:

1. Open Control Panel and launch the Display icon. The Display Properties dialog box appears.

2. Display the Settings tab and click the Advanced button to get the adapter's property sheet onscreen.

3. Display the Adapter tab and click Change. Windows Millennium launches the Update Device Driver Wizard.

4. Activate the Specify the location of the driver option and click Next.

5. Activate the Display a list of all the drivers... option and click Next.

Remember
The AGP enables the graphics adapter to come off the PCI bus, thus reducing bottlenecks that occur when several devices contend for the bus. AGP not only enables the CPU and the adapter to talk directly to each other, but it also gives the adapter access to system memory as a way of augmenting the existing memory on the adapter. The original spec (called AGP 2X) delivered over 500MB/sec bandwidth, but the newest spec (AGP 4x) provides over 1GB/sec.

Shortcut
Another way to get to the Display Properties dialog box is to right-click an empty section of the desktop and then click Properties.

Inside Scoop
Adapter manufacturers often release updated drivers that offer better video performance and bug fixes. You should check the manufacturer's Web site regularly to see if a new driver is available.

6. Activate Show all hardware, and then use the Manufacturers and Models lists to highlight your adapter. (Alternatively, if you have a disk from the manufacturer, click Have Disk and follow the dialog boxes to display a list of the disk's drivers.)

7. Click Next and follow the wizard's remaining dialog boxes to install the driver files.

Configuring the Color Depth and Resolution

How images appear on your monitor is a function of two measurements: the color depth and the resolution. This section explains these concepts and shows you how to manipulate them in Windows Millennium.

The *color depth* is a measure of the number of colors available to display images on the screen. In general, the greater the number of colors, the sharper your screen image will appear (and the more processing power that will be required to display those colors). Color depth is always expressed in either bits or total colors. For example, a 4-bit display can handle up to 16 colors (because 2 to the power of 4 equals 16). Table 22.1 lists the bit values for the most common color depths.

Inside Scoop
The 32-bit color depth yields the same number of colors as the 24-bit depth because the extra 8 bits are used for an alpha channel, which can hold transparency information. This information is used in some graphics and video applications to "mask out" a particular color and let some underlying images show through.

TABLE 22.1: BIT VALUES FOR SOME STANDARD COLOR DEPTHS

Bits	Colors
4	16
8	256
15	32,268
16	65,536
24	16,777,216
32	16,777,216

The *resolution* is a measure of the density of the pixels used to display the screen image. The pixels are arranged in a row-and-column format, so the resolution is expressed as *rows by columns*, where *rows* is the number of pixel rows and *columns* is the number of pixel columns. For example, a 640×480 resolution means screen images are displayed using 640 rows of pixels and 480 columns of pixels. The higher the resolution, the sharper your images appear. Individual screen items—such as icons and dialog boxes—also get smaller at higher resolutions because these items tend to have a fixed height and width, expressed in pixels. For example, a dialog box that's 320 pixels wide will appear half as wide as the screen at 640×480. However, it will appear to be only one quarter of the screen width at 1,280×1,024 (a common resolution for larger monitors).

The key thing to bear in mind about all this is that there's usually a trade-off between color depth and resolution. That is, depending on how much video memory is installed on your graphics adapter, you might have to trade off higher color depth with lower resolution, or vice versa.

Why does the amount of video memory matter? As I mentioned earlier, each screen image is stored in a frame buffer. The size of that buffer is a function of the total number of pixels used in the resolution and the number of bits required to "light" each pixel. For example, a resolution of 640×480 means there are a total of 307,200 pixels. If each pixel uses a color depth of 16 bits, then a total of 4,915,200 bits are required to hold the entire screen image, or 614,400 bytes (600KB). If you bump up the resolution to 1,024×768, the total number of bits involved leaps to 12,582,912, or 1,572,864 bytes (1,536KB). If your graphics adapter contains only 1MB of video memory, you won't be able to select the 1,024×768 resolution unless you drop the color depth down to 8 bits (bringing the total number of bytes required to 786,432).

In general, you use the following formula to calculate the number of bytes required to display a screen:

rows * columns * bits / 8

rows	The number of rows in the resolution.
columns	The number of columns in the resolution.
bits	The number of bits in the color depth.

Remember
A *pixel* is a tiny element that displays the individual dots that make up the screen image ("pixel" is short for "picture element"). Each pixel consists of three components—red, green, and blue—that are manipulated to produce a specific color.

Table 22.2 lists the most common resolutions and color depth values, and calculates the number of bytes required. When purchasing a graphics adapter, make sure you populate it with enough video memory to handle the resolution and color depth you want to work with. (This is less of a concern these days because most adapters come with 8MB, 16MB or even 32MB of video memory. If money is tight and you're just running business applications, go for an 8MB adapter because that's enough memory to handle any resolution and color depth.)

TABLE 22.2: TRANSLATING RESOLUTION AND COLOR DEPTH INTO MEMORY REQUIRED

Resolution	Color Depth	Bytes
640×480	4 bits	153,600
640×480	8 bits	307,200
640×480	16 bits	614,400
640×480	24 bits	921,600
800×600	4 bits	240,000
800×600	8 bits	480,000
800×600	16 bits	960,000
800×600	24 bits	1,440,000
1024×768	4 bits	393,216
1024×768	8 bits	786,432
1024×768	16 bits	1,572,864
1024×768	24 bits	2,359,296
1280×1024	4 bits	655,360
1280×1024	8 bits	1,310,720
1280×1024	16 bits	2,621,440
1280×1024	24 bits	3,932,160
1600×1200	4 bits	960,000
1600×1200	8 bits	1,920,000
1600×1200	16 bits	3,840,000
1600×1200	24 bits	7,680,000

To change the color depth, follow these steps:

1. Open the Control Panel's Display icon to get the Display Properties dialog box onscreen.

2. Display the Settings tab, as shown in Figure 22.1.

Figure 22.1
Use the Settings
tab to set the res-
olution and color
depth.

3. Select the color depth you want to use from the Colors drop-down list.

4. Click OK. The Compatibility Warning dialog box appears. Windows Millennium can perform color depth changes on-the-fly (this feature was introduced in Windows 98). However, some graphics applications might hang when you do this, so Windows Millennium asks if you want to restart your computer before implementing the change.

5. Select the option you want (note that it's rare to have to restart), and click OK.

To change the resolution, follow these steps:

1. Open the Display Properties dialog box and select the Settings tab again.

2. Drag the Screen area slider left or right.

3. Click OK. A dialog box tells you that Windows Millennium will now resize the desktop.

4. Click OK. If you went ahead with the resolution change, Windows Millennium performs the adjustment and then displays a dialog box asking if you want to keep the new setting.

Inside Scoop
Rather than being prompted about restarting each time you change the color depth, you can define a default response. In the Settings tab, click Advanced to display the adapter's property sheet. In the General tab, select a default option from the Compatibility group.

Shortcut
If you plan on changing the color depth and/or resolution frequently, there's a way to do it without opening the Display Properties dialog box. In the Settings tab, click Advanced to display the adapter's property sheet, activate the Show settings on task bar check box, and click OK twice. This adds a "monitor" icon to the system tray. Click this icon to display a list of all the possible resolution and color depth combinations, and then click the combo you want.

5. Click Yes. (If your graphics adapter or monitor can't handle the new resolution, you'll end up with a garbled display. In this case, just wait for 15 seconds and Windows Millennium will restore the resolution to its original setting.)

Working with Windows Millennium's Monitor Features

As I explained earlier, your monitor shows the result of all the pixels pushed around by the graphics adapter. Having a high-end adapter with loads of video RAM won't do you a lick of good if your monitor can't handle what the adapter sends it. Not only that, a cheap monitor is uncomfortable to look at and hard on the eyes in the long run. If you're in the market for a monitor, here are a few things to bear in mind:

- Get a monitor that's PnP-compatible for easiest setup.

- To save energy, get a monitor that supports the Energy Star standard for power management. See "Using Your Monitor's Power Management Features," later in this chapter.

- Check that the monitor supports a *refresh rate* of 75Hz or higher for the resolution that you use most often. The refresh rate measures the number of times per second that the screen is refreshed. If this rate is too low, the screen will flicker and the display will be hard on your eyes.

- Check that the monitor supports the same maximum display resolution as the graphics adapter. For example, if your graphics adapter supports 1,280×1,024 resolution, make sure your monitor supports that resolution as well.

- Look for a *noninterlaced* monitor. *Interlacing* means that the electron beam that generates the screen image uses two passes: first the odd lines and then the even lines. (The refresh rate determines the frequency of these passes.) Unfortunately, these separate passes can cause a slight flicker that makes the display hard on the eyes. To prevent this flicker, get a noninterlaced monitor that paints the entire screen during each pass.

- Look for a monitor with a *dot pitch* value of .28mm or less. The screen image is generated by the electron beam activating phosphors behind the monitor glass. The distance between each phosphor is the dot pitch. The smaller the dot pitch, the sharper the image.

- If your budget allows it, consider moving up to a flat-panel monitor. This type uses an LCD (liquid crystal display) rather than a CRT (cathode-ray tube), so the picture is glare-free and amazingly sharp. It is pricey, however; expect to pay hundreds of dollars more for it than for the equivalent CRT monitor. Note, too, that the newer digital flat-panel monitors require a special connector on the video adapter, so make sure your adapter is compatible with an LCD display.

Changing the Monitor Type

Windows Millennium is pretty good at detecting PnP-compatible monitors. In this case, all you need to do is plug in and connect the new monitor, turn it on, and then restart your computer. However, Windows Millennium will occasionally fail to recognize such a monitor and will end up listing it as Unknown Monitor. Here's how to fix this:

1. Open the Display Properties dialog box, select the Settings tab, and then click Advanced.

2. Display the Monitor tab.

3. Activate the Automatically detect Plug & Play monitors check box.

4. Click OK twice to return to the desktop.

5. Restart your computer to give Windows Millennium a chance to redetect your monitor.

For non-PnP monitors, you have to follow these steps to specify the monitor type:

Remember
If you don't see your monitor listed and you don't have a driver from the manufacturer, select {Standard monitor types} in the Manufacturers list and then choose a generic item from the Models list (such as Super VGA 1024×768).

Shortcut
If you already have the Display Properties dialog box open, you can get to the Power Management Properties dialog box by displaying the Screen Saver tab and clicking the Settings button in the Energy saving features of monitor group.

1. Open the Display Properties dialog box, select the Settings tab, click Advanced, and then display the Monitor tab.

2. Click Change. Windows Millennium displays the Select Device dialog box.

3. Use the Manufacturers and Models lists to highlight your monitor. (If you have a disk from the manufacturer, click Have Disk and follow the dialog boxes to display a list of the disk's drivers.)

4. Click OK to install the driver files.

Using Your Monitor's Power Management Features

If your monitor supports the VESA Display Power Management Signaling (DPMS) specification (or if it's Energy Star compliant), and if your graphics adapter driver supports the Advanced Power Management BIOS, then you can take advantage of certain monitor power management features. Specifically, you can make the graphics adapter driver turn off the monitor after a specified interval.

First off, you should make sure that your monitor's power management features are activated. To do this, open the Display Properties dialog box, select the Settings tab, click Advanced, and then display the Monitor tab. Activate the Monitor is Energy Star compliant check box, if necessary, and then click OK twice to return to the desktop.

With that done, Windows Millennium will manage the monitor's power and turn it off after a defined interval. Unfortunately, that defined interval is maddeningly short: only 15 minutes. To change this, follow these steps:

1. Open the Control Panel's Power Management icon to display the Power Management Properties dialog box.

2. Use the Turn off monitor drop-down list to select the interval you want.

3. Click OK.

Setting Up Multiple Monitors

Windows' capability to multitask is indispensable, of course, but multitasking inevitably leads to a problem: screen overcrowding. For years, I struggled with having word processor, email, Web browser, and dictionary/thesaurus programs vying for space on my monitor. Because I always run my word processor maximized, I had to constantly switch from one window to another, a process that grew tiresome even when using the quick Alt+Tab switching method.

When Windows 98 arrived on the scene, people asked me if it had any truly compelling new features. I told them that, for me, there was only one: multiple-monitor support. Running Windows with a two-monitor setup made my life so much easier and resulted in a significant productivity boost. I could keep my word processor open on my main monitor, and my email client open on the second monitor. If I'm doing research, I open the Web browser or CD program on the second monitor for easy referral.

Multiple-monitor support means that you insert two or more graphics adapters into your computer and then attach a monitor to each card. The result? An expanded desktop that enables you to move windows from one monitor to the other, display the taskbar in either window, and much more. Windows Millennium supports up to nine adapter/monitor combinations.

For a multiple-monitor setup to work, you have to use the appropriate graphics adapters:

- For the primary adapter, you can use just about any PCI adapter.

- For the secondary adapter(s), Microsoft maintains a list of PCI and AGP adapters that are compatible with this feature. These include many adapters from ATI, Number Nine, STB, and Diamond, as well as adapters that use the S3 ViRGE chipset. See the following Web page for the complete list:

```
http://support.microsoft.com/support/kb/articles/Q182/7
/08.asp
```

> 66
>
> With Windows 98, you can connect up to nine monitors to your computer. You can set up these monitors like one large desktop, or you can set them up to show a different program on each monitor. For example, you could have a financial report open in Word on one monitor, have a quarterly budget spreadsheet open in Microsoft Excel on another monitor, and refer to the budget while you write the report.
> —*From the Windows 98 "Getting Started" booklet*
> 99

■ You must use the graphics adapter device driver that comes with Windows Millennium.

Note, too, that the order of the adapters on the bus usually determines which is the main adapter and which is the secondary. Systems vary, but it's usually the case that the adapter closest to the motherboard (for example, on a tower system, the adapter in the higher slot) is considered to be the main adapter.

After you've inserted the second adapter and connected the monitor, Windows Millennium should recognize the new hardware and then display the following message on the second monitor at startup (you might need to restart your computer before you see this message):

```
If you can read this message, Windows has successfully ini-
tialized this display adapter.
```

```
To use this adapter as part of your Windows desktop, open
the Display option in the Control Panel and adjust the set-
tings on the Settings tab.
```

You might also need to go through a driver setup procedure for the new monitor. After Windows Millennium loads, follow these steps to enable the new adapter/monitor combination:

1. Open the Control Panel's Display icon.

2. Select the Settings tab. As you can see in Figure 22.2, this tab now has a new look. Monitor 1 represents your primary adapter/monitor and monitor 2 is the secondary adapter/monitor.

3. Click monitor 2. Windows Millennium asks if you want to enable this monitor.

4. Click Yes.

5. Click Apply. The second monitor activates and displays the extended desktop.

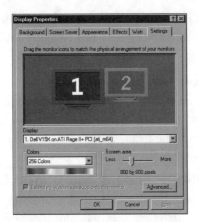

Figure 22.2
The Settings tab takes on a new look when you have multiple adapter/monitor combinations.

To work with an adapter/monitor combination, use either of the following techniques:

- Click the icon of the monitor you want to work with.

- Select the combination from the Display list.

After that's done, you can adjust the color depth, resolution, and advanced settings separately for each adapter/monitor combination.

Multiple-monitor support does have a few quirks that you need to be aware of:

- You can run full-screen DOS programs only on the primary monitor.

- When you run a DOS program full-screen (instead of in a window), you can't use your mouse on the secondary monitor.

- Some programs display dialog boxes and shortcut menus only on the primary monitor. This can be a bit disconcerting if the programs are running on the secondary monitor.

- When you use Alt+Tab to switch, the icon window appears on whatever monitor contains the active program.

- A few programs (graphics programs, mostly) just don't get along with multiple monitors at all. If you try to drag the program's window into the second monitor, the program

Inside Scoop
You can also change the relative positions of the two monitors by dragging the monitor icons.

hangs, and can even take the system down with it. For example, I've experienced this problem with QuickTime for Windows.

- If you move a program window to the secondary monitor, that program will likely open in the secondary monitor the next time you launch it. The newer the program, the more likely this is to be true.

Working with Scanners and Digital Cameras

Windows Millennium comes with built-in support for still-image devices, including scanners and digital cameras. This still-image architecture enables you to install a device and then have that device available to any TWAIN-compatible application, including the Paint and Imaging for Windows programs that come with Windows Millennium. (TWAIN is an industry-standard protocol and applications programming interface for enabling graphics programs to interact with graphics hardware and acquire digital images. TWAIN stands for Technology Without Any Interesting Name.)

Installing a Still-Image Device

To install a still-image device, you have two choices:

- If the device is PnP-compatible, just connect the device and turn it on. Windows Millennium should recognize the device and install the appropriate drivers the next time you boot.

- Launch the Control Panel's Scanners and Cameras icon, and then double-click the Add Device icon. This starts the Scanner and Camera Installation Wizard, which you can use to install either one of the supported Windows Millennium models or a driver from the manufacturer's disk.

After your still-image device is installed, you can test it using these steps:

1. Open the Control Panel's Scanners and Cameras icon.

2. Double-click the device to open its property sheet.

3. Display the General tab.

4. Click the "Test" button (the name of which varies depending on the device).

Capturing Images

Windows Millennium doesn't differentiate between digital cameras and image scanners. Both are "still-image devices" or simply "scanners." However Windows Millennium *does* differentiate between scanners that have drivers that are made for Windows Millennium and those that are made for earlier versions of Windows:

- If the device has a Windows Millennium driver, you use the new Scanner and Camera Wizard to acquire images from the device.

- If the device uses an older driver, you use the device's native TWAIN capture module to acquire images.

Using the Scanner and Camera Wizard

For a device with a Windows Millennium driver, use any of the following techniques to get started:

- Select Start, Programs, Accessories, Scanner and Camera Wizard.

- Run Paint (Start, Programs, Accessories, Paint) and select the File, From Scanner or Camera command.

- Run Imaging (Start, Programs, Accessories, Imaging) and select the File, Scan New command.

If you have multiple scanners, a dialog box will ask you which device you want to use. Highlight the device and click OK. You now see the Scanner and Camera Wizard with an interface tailored to the specific device. For example, Figure 22.3 shows the wizard layout for a Hewlett-Packard image scanner.

Undocumented
Depending on the device, the property sheet might contain one or more other tabs with options you can manipulate. For example, many scanners now support "push" scanning in which you press a button on the scanner and the scanning software loads and scans the current image automatically. If your scanner supports this feature, you should be able to specify the scanning application within the property sheet's Events tab.

Remember
Another way to run the Scanner and Camera Wizard is to open the Control Panel's Scanners and Camera icon, right-click the scanner, and then click Use Wizard.

Figure 22.3
The controls in
the Scanner and
Camera Wizard
are tailored to the
specific device.

Figure 22.3
The controls in
the Scanner and
Camera Wizard
are tailored to the
specific device.

Using the Scanner's TWAIN Module

For a device with an older driver, the Scanner and Camera Wizard isn't available. Instead, you need to follow these steps to initiate image capture using Windows Millennium's Imaging for Windows program:

1. Select Start, Programs, Accessories, Imaging. Windows Millennium launches the Imaging for Windows application.

2. If you have multiple still-image devices installed, choose the one you want to use by running File, Select Scanner, highlighting the device you want to use in the Select Scanner dialog box, and then clicking OK.

3. Select the File, Scan New command (or click the Scan New toolbar button).

Windows Millennium now loads the image capture software that was installed with the device. From here, use the software to capture the image.

Wiring Windows for Sound

Windows Millennium comes with drivers for hundreds of sound cards. If you install a PnP-compatible sound card, Windows Millennium should recognize it at startup and install the appropriate driver. For other cards, you need to run the Add New Hardware Wizard.

Assigning Sounds to Windows Millennium Events

Windows Millennium continuously monitors your system and then plays sounds when certain events occur. For example, one sound accompanies the appearance of a warning dialog box, another sound plays when a new email message arrives, and yet another sound is played when you start Windows. All of Windows Millennium's event-driven sounds are customizable, and there are even dozens of other events to which you can assign a sound. Windows Millennium even defines a few different *sound schemes* for making wholesale changes to event-related sounds.

To work with these sounds, follow these steps:

1. Open the Control Panel's Sounds and Multimedia icon to get to the dialog box shown in Figure 22.4.

2. In the Events list, highlight the event you want to work with.

3. Use the Name list to select the sound file to play when the highlighted event occurs. Alternatively, click Browse to select the file from a dialog box. To hear the sound, click the Play button beside the Name list.

4. To save your changes as a sound scheme, click Save As, enter a name for the scheme, and click OK.

Inside Scoop
Most of the events are straightforward. However, there are a few events that might seem strange at first blush, including Asterisk, Critical Stop, Exclamation, and Question. These are all dialog box–related events and the sounds are played when these types of dialog boxes are displayed by Windows Millennium or an application.

Figure 22.4
Use this dialog box to adjust Windows Millennium's event-related sounds.

Rather than work with individual events and sounds, you can use the Schemes list to select one of Windows Millennium's predefined sound schemes. (If you see only No Sounds and Windows Default in this list, then it means you didn't install the Multimedia Sound Schemes component when you installed Windows Millennium. Run the Control Panel's Add/Remove Programs icon to install the schemes, which are part of the Multimedia component.)

If you examine the Events list, you see that it includes application-related events for Windows Explorer, Sound Recorder, Media Player, and NetMeeting. You can expand this list to include other applications by editing the Registry. Here's how it works:

1. Launch the Registry Editor and highlight the following key:

   `HKEY_CURRENT_USER\AppEvents\Schemes\Apps`

2. Select the Edit, New, Key command to create a new subkey.

3. Type the name of the application's executable file, without the extension, and press Enter.

4. Highlight the new subkey and then open its `Default` setting. Enter the name of the application (this text will appear as a heading in the Events list) and click OK.

5. Create new subkeys within this key for the events to which you want to define sounds. You have eight choices for the names of these subkeys:

   `Close`—Closing the application.

   `Maximize`—Maximizing the application.

   `MenuCommand`—Selecting a menu command in the application.

   `MenuPopup`—Pulling down a menu in the application.

   `Minimize`—Minimizing the application.

   `Open`—Opening the application.

RestoreDown—Restoring the application after it has been maximized.

RestoreUp—Restoring the application after it has been minimized.

6. Exit the Registry Editor.

To assign sounds to these events, open the Sounds Properties dialog box again, find your new events, and then follow the previous procedure.

Recording a WAV File

Most modern sound cards are capable of recording sounds, and most come with a microphone to enable you to record voice messages and other sounds. Here's how you do it:

1. Select Start, Programs, Accessories, Entertainment, Sound Recorder.

2. Sound Recorder starts with an empty sound file ready to record. If you prefer to add your recording to an existing file, open the file (using the File, Open command) and then use the slider to choose the position within the sound file where you want your recording to begin.

3. To set the quality level of the new sound file, select Edit, Audio Properties and then click Advanced in the Sound Recording group to display the Advanced Audio Properties dialog box. Use the Sample Rate Conversion Quality slider to set the quality level. Click OK until you're back in Sound Recorder.

4. To change the sound format, select File, Properties to display the Properties for Sound dialog box. In the Choose from list, select Recording formats and click Convert Now to get to the Sound Selection dialog box. From here, the easiest way to set the format is to select a predefined format—CD Quality, Radio Quality, or Telephone Quality—from the Name list. Click OK until you return to Sound Recorder.

Inside Scoop
If you have trouble recording the file, the problem might lie in the sound card's hardware acceleration. Open the Advanced Audio Properties dialog box and use the Hardware acceleration slider to reduce the acceleration.

5. Click the Record button and then use the sound card's microphone to make the recording.

6. When your recording is complete, click the Stop button.

7. Select File, Save and use the Save As dialog box to save the file.

Editing a WAV File

Sound Recorder doesn't hold a candle to professional sound-editing software, but it does have a few bells and whistles for editing your bells and whistles.

For starters, the Edit menu offers the following commands:

- **Copy**—Copies the current sound file to the Clipboard.

- **Paste Insert**—Pastes a sound file from the Clipboard to the current position in the open sound file. (The existing file is expanded to include the pasted file.)

- **Paste Mix**—Takes a sound file from the Clipboard and mixes it with the open sound file so that the two sounds play together.

- **Insert File**—Inserts another sound file at the current position within the open sound file. (The existing file is expanded to include the inserted file.)

- **Mix with File**—Combines another sound file with the open sound file so that the two sounds play at the same time.

- **Delete Before Current Position**—Deletes everything from the current position to the beginning of the sound file.

- **Delete After Current Position**—Deletes everything from the current position to the end of the sound file.

The Effects menu also offers a few interesting techniques:

- **Increase Volume (by 25%)**—Makes the sound's volume louder by 25%.

- **Decrease Volume**—Makes the sound's volume quieter by 25%.

- **Increase Speed (by 100%)**—Doubles the speed of the sound.

- **Decrease Speed**—Halves the speed of the sound.

- **Add Echo**—Creates an echo effect.

- **Reverse**—Plays the sound backward.

Essential Information

- For maximum video performance, get an accelerated graphics adapter (that is, one with a built-in processor) that has as much video RAM as you can afford and that runs either on the PCI bus or the Accelerated Graphics Port (AGP).

- Color depth is a bit value that determines the maximum number of colors displayed, whereas resolution is a measure of the number of rows and columns of pixels used on the screen.

- When buying a monitor, look for a noninterlaced, PnP-compatible monitor that supports the same resolution as your graphics adapter, has a refresh rate of at least 75Hz, has a dot pitch of .28mm or less, and supports the Energy Star standard.

- To use Windows Millennium's multiple-monitor support, you need two graphics adapters, one of which can be any PCI adapter and the second of which must be on Microsoft's list of supported adapters.

- Use the Sounds Control Panel icon to assign sounds to system events.

- To set up application-specific events, add subkeys to the `HKEY_CURRENT_USER\AppEvents\Schemes\Apps` Registry key.

- Use the Sound Recorder program to play, record, and edit WAV files.

GET THE SCOOP ON...
Using Windows Millennium Power Management Features to
Extend Battery Life ▪ Using Windows Millennium New
Hibernate Feature ▪ Inserting, Removing, and Configuring PC
Card Devices ▪ Transferring Files Between Your Notebook
and a Desktop Computer ▪ Using a Briefcase to Synchronize
File Sharing Between a Notebook and a Desktop Computer

The Ins and Outs of Windows Millennium Notebook Features

Chapter 23

THE PRICES OF NOTEBOOK COMPUTERS remain stubbornly high compared to similarly equipped desktop machines. Yet notebooks are more popular than ever. Why? The reason can be summed up in one word: mobility. For many of today's professional and managerial workers, it isn't enough to have a desktop computer at work. These employees also take work home, run presentations at client sites, and travel to distant cities and countries. To do their jobs properly, mobile workers must also make their work mobile, which means packing a notebook case along with their briefcase or suitcase.

This trend was recognized long ago by Microsoft, so they included many new notebook features in Windows 95. Those features have been carried over into Windows Millennium with few changes. This chapter takes you through four of the most important notebook niceties in Windows Millennium: power management, PC Card devices, Direct Cable Connection, and Briefcase.

Power Management for Notebook Users

Power management support in Windows Millennium is a confusing mess of acronyms, standards, and tugs of war involving the operating system and the hardware. In an ideal world, notebook power management would be completely controlled by the operating system. In the *OnNow Design Initiative* (see www.microsoft.com/hwdev/onnow.htm), every aspect of the machine—from the devices, to the buses, to the device drivers—is involved in the power management process. An OnNow-compliant machine would be immediately available for use when it was turned on, it would turn itself off when not in use, it would respond to "wakeup events" such as an incoming fax, and it would offer precise control over the power state of every component. The last feature is provided by the Advanced Configuration and Power Interface (ACPI) BIOS standard, which provides a hardware interface for power management (among other things).

Unfortunately, in the real world support for OnNow and ACPI is spotty, at best. The vast majority of legacy notebook computers don't fully support OnNow. Notebooks manufactured since 1998 have a better chance of at least shipping with an ACPI BIOS, and most major vendors offer ACPI BIOS upgrades. How can you tell whether your machine has an ACPI BIOS? The easiest method is to launch Control Panel's System icon, select the Device Manager tab, and then open the System devices branch. If your notebook supports ACPI, you should see a number of related devices, such as ACPI Battery, ACPI Embedded Controller, and ACPI Sleep Button.

If you don't see any ACPI devices, then you most likely will see a few Advanced Power Management (APM) devices. Most notebooks support this earlier and less-powerful standard. Windows Millennium supports APM 1.2, which enables Windows to turn off some machine features (such as the display and hard disk), place the computer in *standby mode* (which shuts down the computer but preserves the operating system's current state), monitor battery life, and more. Muddying the APM waters is the fact that some older notebooks support only APM 1.0 and APM 1.1.

To complicate matters even further, most notebooks also support some kind of power management at the BIOS level. This

Even if you upgrade your notebook's BIOS to make it compliant with ACPI, Windows Millennium won't detect the change. To force it to detect ACPI, open the Registry Editor and head for `HKEY_LOCAL_MACHINE\Software\Microsoft\Windows\CurrentVersion\Detect`. Add a new string value named `ACPIOption` and set its value to 1. After that's done, launch the Add New Hardware Wizard and have it detect the devices on your system.

often leads to conflicts in which the operating system and the BIOS compete for power management supremacy.

The situation is a mess. Fortunately, power management is relatively straightforward for those systems that support either APM 1.2 or OnNow. For all other systems, Windows Millennium offers a few workarounds to help prevent crashes and other undesirable behavior. I discuss these workarounds throughout the rest of this section.

Putting the System into Standby Mode

If your notebook supports APM, you can put it into the low-power standby mode. Windows Millennium offers four ways to put the system into standby mode:

- Select Start, Shut Down, choose the Stand by option, and click OK.

- Set up a power scheme to place the system into standby mode after a preset interval of idle time. See "Setting Up a Power Scheme," later in this chapter.

- Set up a battery alarm that places the system into standby mode when the battery level falls to a certain percentage. See "Monitoring the Battery," later in this chapter.

- Configure your notebook's features—such as the power button or closing the lid—to put the system into standby mode. This is an ACPI-only option (see "Configuring Your Notebook's Power Buttons," later in this chapter).

Inside Scoop

One of the things you can do to make power management more manageable is to prevent Windows Millennium and the notebook's BIOS from competing with each other. To do this, access the notebook's BIOS settings at startup and turn off all the power management features. If there is no way to disable these features, set the time intervals higher than those you use in your Windows Millennium power scheme (see "Setting Up a Power Scheme," later in this chapter).

Putting the System into Hibernate Mode

Standby mode is great for preserving battery life, but it doesn't help your notebook start any faster. For the latter, Windows Millennium now supports a feature called *hibernate*, which not only shuts down your notebook, but also "preserves state." This means that you don't have to close your open documents and programs. Instead, Windows Millennium saves the entire contents of memory to a special system file (called a *hiberfile*), which is usually C:\hiberfil.sys. When you next start the notebook, the machine runs through the usual Power-On Self Test.

Watch Out!
If your notebook hangs when entering or leaving standby mode, the likely culprit is the BIOS not implementing APM correctly. You can often resolve this problem by opening the Control Panel's System icon, displaying the Device Manager tab, opening the System devices branch, and then double-clicking Advanced Power Management support. In the Settings tab, activate the Force APM 1.0 mode check box.

Then Windows Millennium reads the contents of the hiberfile and launches almost immediately with the programs and documents intact and ready for work.

Activating Hibernate Support

Follow these steps to enable hibernate:

1. Open Control Panel and launch the Power Options icon.

2. Display the Hibernate tab.

3. Activate the Enable hibernate support check box.

4. Click OK.

Hibernating the Computer

As with standby mode, Windows Millennium offers four ways to put the system into hibernate mode:

- Select Start, Shut Down, choose the Hibernate option, and click OK.

- Set up a power scheme (see "Setting Up a Power Scheme," next).

- Set up a battery alarm (see "Monitoring the Battery," later in this chapter).

- Set up your notebook's power buttons (see "Configuring Your Notebook's Power Buttons," later in this chapter).

Resuming from Standby Mode or Hibernate Mode

To resume from standby or hibernate, press the notebook's power button or reset button. If you want Windows Millennium to prompt you for your Windows password before resuming, follow these steps:

1. Open the Control Panel's Power Options icon.

2. Select the Advanced tab.

3. Activate the Prompt for password when computer goes off standby and hibernate check box.

4. Click OK.

Setting Up a Power Scheme

A *power scheme* is a collection of time intervals that control how Windows Millennium works with the power state of several components:

Monitor—Windows Millennium can blank the notebook screen. (This also works for desktop systems using Energy Star-compliant monitors.)

Hard disk—Windows Millennium can spin down the hard disk.

System standby—Windows Millennium can put the system into standby mode.

Hibernate—Windows Millennium can put the system into hibernation.

To choose a predefined power scheme, follow these steps:

1. Open the Control Panel's Power Options icon.

2. Select the Power Schemes tab in the dialog box that appears (see Figure 23.1). Note that the layout of the tab varies depending on your system's power management support.

3. Select an item from the Power schemes list.

4. Click OK.

To create your own power scheme, follow these steps:

1. Display the Power Schemes tab in the Power Options Properties dialog box.

2. Select Turn off monitor intervals for when the notebook is Plugged in and Running on batteries.

3. Select Turn off hard disks intervals for when the notebook is Plugged in and Running on batteries.

4. Select System standby intervals for when the notebook is Plugged in and Running on batteries.

Inside Scoop
Note all notebooks support the hibernate feature. To have it available, your machine must be using Windows Driver Model (WDM) drivers for audio and the modem, as well as a power management-capable network device driver. It must not have a SCSI controller or a legacy video-capture device, WebTV must not be installed, and the machine must not be set up as an Internet Connection Sharing host.

Shortcut
Another way to get to the Power Schemes tab is to right-click the power meter icon in the system tray (see Figure 23.2 later in this chapter), and then click Adjust Power Properties.

Figure 23.1
Use the Power
Schemes tab to
set up a power
scheme for your
notebook.

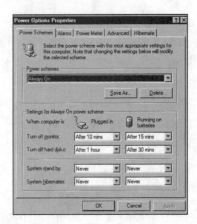

Shortcut
To select a power
scheme without
bothering with the
Power Schemes
tab, click the sys-
tem tray's power
meter icon (see
Figure 23.2 later)
and then click a
power scheme in
the menu that
appears.

5. Select System hibernates intervals for when the notebook is Plugged in and Running on batteries.

6. Click Save As, type a name for the new scheme, and click OK.

7. Click OK.

Monitoring the Battery

If you're forced to run your notebook without AC (on an air-plane, for example), maximizing battery life is crucial. That's why ACPI and APM power schemes support different time intervals for when the notebook is plugged in and when it's on batteries. It's equally important to monitor the current state of the battery to avoid a shutdown while you're working.

To help you monitor battery life, Windows Millennium dis-plays a power meter in the system tray, as shown in Figure 23.2. When you're on batteries, the power meter is a blue battery icon. As your notebook uses up battery power, the amount of blue decreases accordingly. To see the exact level of battery power remaining, you have two choices:

- Double-click the power meter icon. Windows Millennium displays the Power Meter dialog box, which shows the per-centage of battery life still available.

- Hover the mouse pointer over the power meter icon. After a second or two, Windows Millennium displays a banner that tells you the percentage of battery life available.

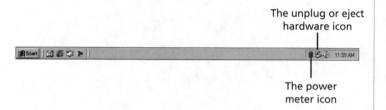

The unplug or eject
hardware icon

The power
meter icon

Figure 23.2
Windows
Millennium dis-
plays the power
meter as a bat-
tery icon when
you run your note-
book on batteries.

Besides monitoring the battery level by hand, Windows Millennium also enables you to set up alarms that are triggered when the battery level reaches specified percentages. Here's how to customize these alarms:

1. Open the Control Panel's Power Options icon.

2. Select the Alarms tab, shown in Figure 23.3.

3. In the Low battery alarm group, use the check box to toggle the alarm on and off.

4. Use the slider to set the percentage at which the alarm is triggered.

5. To customize the alarm, click Alarm Action. The dialog box that appears contains the following options:

   Sound alarm—When activated, beeps the notebook's speaker when the alarm is triggered.

   Display message—When activated, displays a warning message when the alarm is triggered.

   When the alarm goes off, the computer will—When activated, performs the action selected in the accompanying list (Standby, Hibernate, or Power Off) when the alarm is triggered.

6. Repeat steps 3–5 for the Critical battery alarm group.

7. Click OK.

Inside Scoop
If your notebook
has trouble enter-
ing or leaving
standby mode, the
Power
Management
Troubleshooter
tool can help. This
file is available
online at www.
microsoft.com/
downloads/search.
asp. After you
install the tool, it
runs automatically
at startup.
Suspend and
resume your
machine and, if
you encounter a
problem, examine
the tool's readout
(problems are
shown in red
text). Uninstall
the tool when
you're finished
with it.

Figure 23.3
Use the Alarms tab to customize the alarms that sound when your battery level gets low.

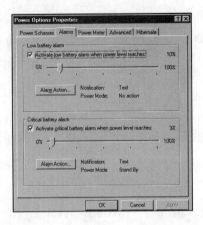

Remember
On some notebooks, there is no separate sleep button. Instead, you tap the on/off button quickly.

Configuring Your Notebook's Power Buttons

If your notebook supports ACPI, it will also enable you to configure three "power buttons": closing the lid, the sleep button, and the on/off button. When these buttons are activated, they put your system into standby or hibernate mode, or turn it off altogether.

Follow these steps to configure these buttons for power management:

1. Open the Control Panel's Power Options icon.

2. Select the Advanced tab, shown in Figure 23.4.

Figure 23.4
On ACPI systems, use the Advanced tab to configure your notebook's power buttons.

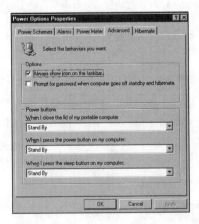

3. Use the three lists in the Power buttons group to set a power management option (Stand By, Hibernate, or

Power Off) for closing the lid, pressing the on/off (power) button, or pressing the sleep button.

4. Click OK.

Windows Millennium PC Card Support

The small footprint of a notebook computer means it doesn't have the expandability of a desktop machine. To get around this, small credit card–size modules called *PC Cards* (formerly PCMCIA cards) are used for a wide range of devices, including network interface cards, modems, hard disks, and SCSI controllers. These cards are inserted into special PC Card sockets, and most notebooks have one or two of these sockets.

If Windows Millennium Setup recognizes a PC Card controller during installation, it launches the PC Card (PCMCIA) Wizard to configure the controller. When you start Windows Millennium, you see the Unplug or Eject Hardware icon in the system tray, as shown earlier in Figure 23.2.

PC Card devices are *hot swappable,* which means you can insert them while Windows Millennium is running. The first time you do this, Windows Millennium recognizes the new device and automatically installs the appropriate driver.

Note, however, that although PC Card devices are hot swappable, you should never just yank a card from its socket. (If you do, Windows Millennium displays a warning message.) To give Windows Millennium a chance to reallocate the device's resources properly, stop the device before removing it. You have two choices:

- Click the Unplug or Eject Hardware icon, and then click the device you want to stop.

- Open the Control Panel's PC Card (PCMCIA) icon to display the PC Card (PCMCIA) Properties dialog box. In the Socket Status tab, highlight the device you want to remove and then click Stop.

Transferring Files Between Computers Using Direct Cable Connection

A common conundrum faced by notebook users involves transferring files between the notebook and another computer, usually a desktop system. For years the only solution was to toss some files from one computer onto a floppy disk, insert the disk into the other computer, and then copy the files. The disadvantages of this method are obvious: It's slow, cumbersome, and limited by the relatively small capacity of the floppy disk. (Although the recent popularity of the 100MB and 250MB Zip disk formats has solved the capacity problem to a certain extent.)

A more practical solution to this problem involved running a cable between the two machines and using that connection to transfer the files. Years ago, a program called LapLink got this idea off the ground by providing a cable and a decent interface for the file transfer. Microsoft got on board by including the forgettable InterLink program in DOS. InterLink was jettisoned when Windows 95 debuted, and it was replaced by the Direct Cable Connection accessory. The idea behind Direct Cable Connection is relatively simple: Establish the connection between the two machines as a kind of one-way mini-network. This enables one machine—called the *guest*—to browse folders and other resources that have been shared by the other machine—called the *host.*

To use Direct Cable Connection, you must have a cable to connect the two computers, and you must use the same type of port on each machine. The port can be serial, parallel, or infrared. The type of cable you use depends on the type of port you use:

Serial port—In this case, you use a *null-modem cable.* You can't use a regular serial cable because the wires aren't set up properly for these kinds of direct data transfers. For example, on a regular serial cable, data enters the cable via the port's Transmit Data pin and stays on that wire for the entire journey through the cable. This means the receiving port gets the data on the Transmit Data pin, which

> **❝**
> **sneakernet,** *noun*
> The transfer of files from one computer to another using a floppy disk or other removable medium. —*The Word Spy (www.wordspy.com)*
> **❞**

won't work. (At this point, a modem would normally reroute the data to the Receive Data wire.) A null-modem cable accepts data from the Transmit Data pin, but then makes sure it arrives at the receiving end on the Receive Data pin. Serial port transfers have a theoretical bandwidth limit of 115,200bps, or about 14Kbps.

4-bit parallel port—This type of parallel port is found on older computers and is designed for one-way communications between the port and a printer. It requires a *parallel LapLink cable* or a *parallel InterLink cable* instead of the standard parallel printer cable. Output uses all 8 of the port's bits, resulting in a throughput of 80Kbs to 120Kbps, but input is limited to 4 bits, for a throughput of 40Kbs to 60Kbps.

8-bit parallel port—This has been the standard parallel port on computers for the past few years. It uses 8 bits for both input and output, for a throughput of 80Kbs to 120Kbps. Again, you need a parallel LapLink cable.

Enhanced Parallel Port (EPP)—This type of port was popular on notebook computers in the mid-nineties. It offers throughput of approximately 300Kbps using a parallel LapLink cable.

Extended Capabilities Port (ECP)—This is similar to the EPP, but it uses a DMA channel for improved multitasking. It offers throughput of about 300Kbps with a parallel LapLink cable, and up to about 500Kbps with an ECP-compliant cable. This type of port is now standard on most new desktops and notebooks.

With your cable and port considerations resolved and the cable strung between the two machines, it's time to set up Direct Cable Connection. Your first consideration is to decide which machine is to be the host and which machine is to be the guest. Remember that the guest machine works with the shared resources on the host machine, but the host machine can't work with the guest computer's resources. (However,

Inside Scoop
To maximize serial port throughput, set up the port to transfer data at 115,200bps. To do this, open the Control Panel's System icon, display the Device Manager tab, open the Ports (COM & LPT) branch, and then double-click the serial port you'll be using— usually Communications Port (COM1). In the Port Settings tab, select 115200 in the Bits per second list.

Remember
To get the most out of your ECP, you should get an ECP-compliant cable. To ensure compatibility with your ECP, look for a *Universal Cable Module (UCM)* cable. For example, Parallel Technologies offers the Universal FAST Cable that boasts throughput up to 500Kbps. See http://www.lpt. com/.

later I'll show you an undocumented workaround that enables the host to peruse the guest under certain circumstances.) If one of the computers is already connected to a network, it makes sense to use it as the host because presumably it's already sharing resources.

To configure the host computer:

1. Select Start, Programs, Accessories, Communications, Direct Cable Connection. This launches a wizard that takes you through most of the configuration process.

2. Activate the Host option and click Next.

3. If this is the first communications program you've configured, Windows Millennium displays the Location information dialog box. Select your country, enter your area code and the number to dial for an outside line, activate Tone dialing or Pulse dialing, and click Close.

4. The wizard displays a list of ports. Highlight the port you want to use and click Next.

5. If your computer isn't already sharing resources, the wizard lets you know. In this case, click File and Print Sharing to display the Network dialog box. If you already have file and print sharing set up, skip to step 11.

6. In the Network dialog box, click File and Print Sharing to display the File and Print Sharing dialog box.

7. Activate the two check boxes, and click OK to return to the Network dialog box.

8. Click OK and when Windows Millennium asks if you want to restart, click Yes.

9. Share one or more folders for the guest computer to access, as explained in Chapter 20, "Windows Millennium Networking Features."

→ **See Also** "Sharing Your Resources on the Network," **p. 447.**

10. Start Direct Cable Connection again and run through steps 2–4.

11. The wizard asks if you want the guest user to enter a pass-word before accessing the host. If so, activate the Use pass-word protection check box. To enter the password, click Set Password, type the password twice, and click OK.

12. Click Finish. Direct Cable Connection initializes and then waits for the guest. Click Close.

Next, you have to configure the guest computer:

1. Select Start, Programs, Accessories, Communications, Direct Cable Connection.

2. Activate the Guest option and click Next.

3. Highlight the port and click Next.

4. Click Finish. The guest attempts to connect to the host.

In the future, you establish the connection by launching Direct Cable Connection on both machines. On the host, click Listen, and then on the guest, click Connect. Depending on your setup, you may have to run through the following:

- If the host is protected by a password, you have to enter a password.

- The guest may need to log on to the network, if one exists.

- The guest may ask for the name of the host computer. This is the name specified in the Computer name text box in the Identification tab of the Network dialog box. (Open the Control Panel's Network icon.)

- The guest should automatically display a folder window showing the host's shared resources. You can display this window at any time by clicking the View Host button.

Undocumented
Although there is no direct way for the host com-puter to work with the guest computer, it *is* possible to set this up. First make sure that file and printer sharing is enabled on the guest and that some resources are shared. When everything's ready, select Start, Run on the host and enter *Name**share*, where *Name* is the guest computer's network name, and *Share* is the name of a shared resource.

Using a Briefcase to Synchronize File Sharing

The need to share files between a notebook computer and a desktop computer also creates a problem: How do you ensure that both computers always have the most up-to-date copies of the transferred files? Windows Millennium's solution to this problem is a special folder called a *briefcase*. The files in the

Undocumented
Windows
Millennium
includes an item
for the desktop's
My Briefcase icon
in the Send To
menu. To use this
item for briefcase
on the removable
disk, use
Windows Explorer
to open
the hidden
Windows\SendTo
folder, right-click
the My Briefcase
shortcut, and
then click
Properties. Use
the Target text
box to enter the
path to the
removable disk's
briefcase.

briefcase are always synchronized either with the original files
(that is, the files copied to the briefcase from one computer)
or with the working copies (that is, the files copied from the
briefcase to the other computer). It takes only a simple command to update the briefcase files or the original files, so
everything stays in sync.

Unfortunately, the briefcase feature has always suffered from
an unnecessary complexity. What's the best way to send the
original files to the briefcase? Do you move or copy the briefcase to the floppy disk (or whatever)? On the other computer,
do you work with the files in the Briefcase or send them to the
computer? Fortunately, I've developed a straightforward procedure that cuts through the usual complexity. It's still tedious,
but that's due more to the design flaws inherent in the briefcase concept.

Transferring Files via Floppy Disk

First, when you're transferring files using a floppy disk or some
other removable medium, place a briefcase on the disk using
either of the following methods:

- Move the desktop's My Briefcase icon to the disk.

- Open the disk in Windows Explorer and select File, New,
  Briefcase. Type a name for the new briefcase and press
  Enter.

With that done, follow these steps to use the removable disk to
transfer and synchronize files:

1. On the source machine, send the files you want to work
   with to the briefcase on the removable disk. (If you right-
   drag and drop, make sure you click Make Sync Copy in the
   shortcut menu.)

2. Insert the removable disk in the target computer.

3. Send the files from the briefcase to a folder on the hard
   disk of the target computer.

4. Work on the files on the target computer.

5. Use Windows Explorer to open the briefcase in the remov-

able disk. To see which files were changed, activate the View, Details command. As you can see in Figure 23.5, the Status column reports Needs updating for changed files.

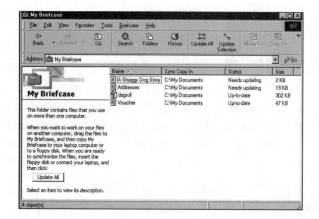

Figure 23.5
In Details view, the Status column tells you which files need to be updated.

6. Select Briefcase, Update All (or click the Update All toolbar button) and, when the list of the updates to be performed appears, click Update. This synchronizes the briefcase with the changed files on the target computer.

7. Insert the removable disk in the source computer.

8. Use Windows Explorer to open the briefcase in the removable disk. Again, use Details view to see which files need updating.

9. Select Briefcase, Update All (or click the Update All toolbar button) and, when the list of the updates to be performed appears, click Update. This synchronizes the original files with the changed files in the briefcase.

Remember
You can update individual files by highlighting them and selecting the Briefcase, Update Selection command, or by clicking the Update Selection toolbar button.

Transferring Files via Direct Cable Connection

If you're using Direct Cable Connection, follow these steps to transfer and synchronize files:

1. Connect the host and guest. *guest ⟶ host* *sync*

2. On the guest computer, copy the files you want to work with from the host computer to a briefcase on the guest computer.

3. Disconnect the host and guest computers (if necessary).

4. Work with the files from the guest computer's briefcase. (Don't move or copy the files to another folder on the guest computer.)

5. When you're ready to synchronize the files, connect the host and guest computers.

6. Open the guest computer's briefcase.

7. Select Briefcase, Update All (or click the Update All toolbar button) and, when the list of the updates to be performed appears, click Update. This synchronizes the host computer's files with the changed files in the guest briefcase.

Essential Information

- Windows Millennium supports the OnNow initiative and ACPI for complete control over a system's power management. Although most older notebooks support only APM, newer machines come with an ACPI BIOS.

- Use the Control Panel's Power Options icon to select and create power schemes, monitor battery life, and set power management options.

- Use the Control Panel's PC Card (PCMCIA) icon to set PC Card options and to stop PC Card devices before removing them.

- For fastest Direct Cable Connection throughput, use a parallel LapLink cable on an Enhanced Parallel Port, or a UCM cable on an Extended Capabilities Port.

- To use a briefcase efficiently, place it on a floppy disk and transfer files back and forth from the briefcase.

Appendixes

PART VIII

A Glossary of Windows Terms

T HIS GLOSSARY OF WINDOWS TERMS is a subset from my How to Speak Geek Web site, a compendium of Windows- and Web-related words and phrases. This site can be found here:

`http://www.howtospeakgeek.com/`

accelerator key   The underlined letter in a menu name or menu command.

ACPI   See *Advanced Configuration and Power Interface.*

active partition   A disk drive's bootable partition. Its boot sector tells the ROM BIOS at startup that this partition contains the operating system's bootstrap code. The active partition is usually the same as the *primary partition.*

ADC   See *analog-to-digital converter.*

Advanced Configuration and Power Interface   A *BIOS* that enables a computer to control the power management capabilities of all the devices on the system.

Advanced Power Management   A specification developed by Microsoft and Intel that lets the operating system, applications, BIOS, and system hardware work cooperatively to manage power and extend battery life.

allocation unit   See *cluster.*

analog-to-digital converter   A chip in a sound card that converts analog sound waves to the digital audio format. See also *digital-to-analog converter.*

APM   See *Advanced Power Management.*

backup job   A Microsoft Backup file that includes a list of files to back up, the type of backup to use (*full, differential,* or *incremental*), and the backup destination.

baud rate   The number of signal changes (which might be variations in voltage or frequency, depending on the *modulation* standard being used) per second that can be exchanged between two *modems.* In most cases, this isn't the same as *bps.*

bi-directional printing   Printing in which not only can Windows Millennium send data to the printer, but the printer can send data to Windows Millennium. So, besides Windows sending print jobs to the printer, the printer could, for example, keep Windows informed of the current printer status (for example, out of paper). See also *Extended Capabilities Port.*

BIOS   Basic Input/Output System. A set of functions that supports the transfer of data to and from the computer's memory, disks, and other components.

bitmap   An array of bits (pixels) that contains data that describes the colors found in an image.

BootKeys   Shortcut keys or key combinations that either invoke the Windows Millennium Startup menu or select a Windows Millennium Startup option (such as *Safe mode*).

bps   Bits per second. The rate at which a *modem* or other communications device transmits data.

bridge   A *network* device that connects two *LANs,* provided that the two LANs are using the same *NOS.* The bridge can either be a standalone device or can be implemented in a server with the addition of a second network card.

CDFS   An *installable file system* for CD-ROM drives. CDFS uses a 32-bit *protected-mode VxD* (VCDFSD.VXD) that replaces MSCDEX.EXE, the 16-bit *real-mode* driver used in previous versions of Windows. See also *VFAT.*

CD-ROM File System   See *CDFS*.

client   In a *client/server network*, a computer that uses the services and resources provided to the network by a *server*.

client/server network   A *network* model that splits the computing workload into two separate but related areas. On one hand, you have users working at intelligent "front-end" systems called *clients*. In turn, these client machines interact with powerful "back-end" systems called *servers*. The basic idea is that the clients have enough processing power to perform tasks on their own, but they rely on the servers to provide them with specialized resources or services, or access to information that would be impractical to implement on a client (such as a large database). See also *peer-to-peer network*.

Clipboard   A memory location used to store data that has been cut or copied from an application.

cluster   The basic unit of storage on a hard disk or floppy disk.

cluster chain   The sequence of *clusters* that defines an entire file.

cluster slack   The amount of unused *cluster* space taken up by a file. For example, if a system uses 4,096-byte clusters and a file is 3,000 bytes, its cluster slack is 1,096 bytes.

codec   A compressor/decompressor device driver. During playback of audio or video data, the codec decompresses the data before sending it to the appropriate multimedia device. During recording, the codec compresses the raw data so that it takes up less disk space. Most codecs offer a variety of compression ratios.

color depth   Determines the number of colors (that is, the color palette) available to your applications and graphics. Color depth is expressed in either bits or total colors. See also *High Color* and *True Color*.

concentrator   See *hub*.

Configuration Manager   A Windows Millennium component (Cnfgmgr.vxd) that enumerates the various *Plug and Play* devices on your system, identifies the *resources* used by each device, resolves resource conflicts, monitors the system for hardware changes, and ensures that the proper *device drivers* are loaded.

connection-oriented protocol See *transport layer protocol.*

connectionless protocol See *network layer protocol.*

context menu See *shortcut menu.*

cooperative multitasking The *multitasking* mode used by Windows 3.*x* and 16-bit applications. It's up to the individual applications to decide when they will relinquish control of the system. See also *preemptive multitasking.*

cross-linked cluster A *cluster* that has somehow been assigned to two different files, or that has two *FAT* entries that refer to the same cluster.

DAC See *digital-to-analog converter.*

data bits In *modem* data transfer, the number of bits used to represent a character.

delay When you press and hold down a key, the time interval between the appearance of the first character and the second character. See also *repeat rate.*

demodulation The conversion into digital data of an analog wave (a series of tones) transmitted over a telephone line. This conversion is performed by a *modem.* See also *modulation.*

device driver Small software programs that serve as intermediaries between hardware devices and the operating system. Device drivers encode software instructions into signals that the device understands, and, conversely, the drivers interpret device signals and report them to the operating system. See also *virtual device drivers.*

Device Manager A tab in the System properties sheet that provides a graphical outline of all the devices on your system. It can show you the current configuration of each device (including the *IRQ, I/O ports,* and *DMA channel* used by each device). It even lets you adjust a device's configuration (assuming that the device doesn't require you to make physical adjustments to, say, a DIP switch or jumper). The Device Manager actually gets its data from, and stores modified data in, the *Registry*.

DHCP   See *Dynamic Host Control Protocol.*

differential backup   Backs up only files in the current *backup job* that have changed since the last *full backup*. See also *incremental backup.*

digital-to-analog converter   A sound card chip that converts digitized audio back into an analog wave so that you can hear it. See also *analog-to-digital converter.*

directory entry   See *file directory.*

disk cache   A section of memory that stores recent or frequently used bits of program code and data. This improves performance by reducing the number of times the system has to retrieve data from the relatively slow hard disk.

Display Power Management Signaling   A specification that lets a *device driver* use the video adapter to send a signal to the monitor that can either blank the screen (standby mode) or turn off the monitor entirely.

DMA   Direct Memory Access. See also *DMA channel.*

DMA channel   A connection that lets a device transfer data to and from memory without going through the processor. The transfer is coordinated by a DMA controller chip.

DNS   See *Domain Name System.*

Domain Name System   On the Internet, a hierarchical distributed database system that converts *host names* into *IP addresses.*

dotted-decimal notation   A format used to represent *IP addresses.* The 32 bits of the address are divided into quads of 8 bits, which are then converted into their decimal equivalent and separated by dots (for example, 123.234.56.7).

dotted-quad notation   See *dotted-decimal notation.*

double-click speed   The time interval that Windows Millennium uses to distinguish between two successive single clicks and a double-click. Anything faster is handled as a double-click; anything slower is handled as two single clicks.

DPMS See *Display Power Management Signaling.*

Dynamic Host Control Protocol A system that manages the dynamic allocation of *IP addresses.*

ECP See *Extended Capabilities Port.*

environment A small memory buffer that holds the DOS *environment variables.*

environment variables Settings used to control certain aspects of DOS and DOS programs. For example, the PATH, the PROMPT, and the values of all SET statements are part of the environment.

Extended Capabilities Port A parallel port that provides support for high-speed printing; new devices that use parallel ports, such as CD-ROMs and modems; and *bi-directional printing.*

extended partition—The hard disk space that isn't allocated to the *primary partition.* For example, if you have a 1.2GB disk and you allocate 300MB to the primary partition, the extended partition will be 900MB. You can then subdivide the extended partition into *logical DOS drives.*

extension In a filename, the part to the right of the period. Windows Millennium uses extensions to determine the file type of a file.

FAT See *File Allocation Table.*

FIFO First in, first out.

FIFO buffer A 16-byte memory buffer included with 16550 and later *UART* chips that enables a serial port handle high-speed data transfers while reducing retransmissions and dropped characters.

File Allocation Table A built-in filing system that is created on every formatted disk. The FAT contains a 16-bit entry for every disk *cluster* that specifies whether the cluster is empty or bad, or else points to the next cluster number in the current file.

file directory A table of contents for the files on a disk that is maintained by the *File Allocation Table.* The entries in the file directory specify each file's name, extension, size, attributes, and more.

file transfer protocol   In *modem* communications, this protocol governs various aspects of the file transfer ritual, including starting and stopping, the size of the data *packets* being sent, how errors are handled, and so on. Windows Millennium supports seven protocols: Xmodem, 1K Xmodem, Ymodem, Ymodem-G, Zmodem, Zmodem with Crash Recovery, and Kermit.

File Transfer Protocol   An Internet protocol that defines file transfers between computers. Part of the *TCP/IP* suite of protocols.

font   A unique set of design characteristics that is common to a group of letters, numbers, and symbols.

FTP   See *File Transfer Protocol.*

full backup   Backs up all the files in the current *backup job.* See also *differential backup* and *incremental backup.*

gateway   A *network* computer or other device that acts as a middleman between two otherwise incompatible systems. The gateway translates the incoming and outgoing *packets* so that each system can work with the data.

GDI   See *Graphical Device Interface.*

Graphical Device Interface   A core Windows Millennium component that manages the operating system's graphical interface. It contains routines that draw graphics primitives (such as lines and circles), manage colors, display fonts, manipulate bitmap images, and interact with graphics drivers. See also *kernel* and *User.*

graphics adapter   The internal component in your system that generates the output you see on your monitor.

hardware flow control   A system whereby the computer and *modem* use individual wires to send signals to each other that indicate whether they're ready to receive data. To stop outgoing data, the modem turns off its CTS (Clear To Send) line. To stop incoming data, the processor turns off its RTS (Request To Send) line. See also *software flow control.*

hardware profile   Hardware configurations in which Windows Millennium loads only specified *device drivers.*

High Color   A *color depth* of 16 bits, or 65,536 colors.

host   A computer on the Internet.

host name   The unique name of an Internet *host* expressed as an English language equivalent of an *IP address.*

HTTP   See *Hypertext Transfer Protocol.*

hub—A central connection point for *network* cables. They range in size from small boxes with four, six, or eight RJ-45 connectors to large cabinets with dozens of ports for various cable types.

hyperlink   In the Windows Millennium Help system, an underlined word or phrase that takes you to another topic or runs a program.

hypertext   In a World Wide Web page, an underlined word or phrase that takes you to a different Web page.

Hypertext Transfer Protocol   An Internet *protocol* that defines the format of *Uniform Resource Locator* addresses and how World Wide Web data is transmitted between a server and a browser. Part of the *TCP/IP* suite of protocols.

idle sensitivity   The amount of time that Windows Millennium waits before declaring a DOS program idle. In the absence of keyboard input, Windows Millennium assumes that a DOS program is in an idle state after this predetermined amount of inactivity, and it then redirects to other running processes the *time slices* that it would otherwise devote to the DOS program.

incremental backup   Backs up only files in the current *backup job* that have changed since the last *full backup* or the last *differential backup.*

installable file system   A file system that can be loaded into the operating system dynamically. Examples in Windows Millennium are *VFAT* and *CDFS.*

Internet Protocol   A network layer protocol that defines the Internet's basic *packet* structure and its addressing scheme, and also handles routing of packets between *hosts*. See also *TCP/IP* and *Transmission Control Protocol*.

internetwork A *network* that combines two or more *LANs* by means of a special device, such as a *bridge* or *router*. Internetworks are often called internets for short, but they shouldn't be confused with *the* Internet, the global collection of networks.

interrupt request An instruction to the CPU that halts processing temporarily so that another operation (such as handling input or output) can take place. Interrupts can be generated by either hardware or software.

intranet The implementation of Internet technologies such as *TCP/IP* and World Wide Web servers for use within a corporate organization rather than for connection to the Internet as a whole.

invalid cluster A *cluster* that falls under one of the following three categories:

- A *FAT* entry that refers to cluster 1. This is illegal, because a disk's cluster numbers start at 2.

- A FAT entry that refers to a cluster number larger than the total number of clusters on the disk.

- A FAT entry of 0 (which normally denotes an unused cluster) that is part of a *cluster chain*.

I/O port A memory address that the processor uses to communicate with a device directly. After a device has used its *IRQ line* to catch the processor's attention, the actual exchange of data or commands takes place through the device's I/O port address.

Io.sys The *real-mode* portion of Windows Millennium. Io.sys processes Msdos.sys, Config.sys, and Autoexec.bat, reads the Registry, switches the processor into *protected mode,* and then calls on Vmm32.vxd to load the Windows Millennium protected-mode drivers.

IP See *Internet Protocol*.

IP address The unique address assigned to every *host* and *router* on the Internet. IP addresses are 32-bit values that are usually expressed in *dotted-decimal notation*. See also *host name*.

IPX/SPX—Internet Packet eXchange/Sequenced Packet eXchange. IPX is a *network layer protocol* that addresses and routes *packets* from one *network* to another on an IPX *internetwork*. SPX, on the other hand, is a *transport layer protocol* that enhances the IPX protocol by providing reliable delivery. IPX/SPX is used by NetWare networks.

IRQ line A hardware line over which peripherals and software can send *interrupt requests*.

Kbps One thousand bits per second (*bps*).

kernel A core Windows Millennium component that loads applications (including any DLLs needed by the program), handles all aspects of file I/O, allocates *virtual memory* and works with the *Memory Pager*, and schedules and runs *threads* started by applications. See also *Graphical Device Interface* and *User*.

LAN See *local area network*.

LIFO Last in, first out.

local area network A *network* in which all the computers occupy a relatively small geographical area, such as a department, office, home, or building. All the connections between computers are made via network cables.

local resource Any peripheral, file, folder, or application that is either attached directly to your computer or resides on your computer's hard disk. See also *remote resource*.

logical DOS drive—A subset of an *extended partition*. For example, if the extended partition is 900MB, you could create three logical DOS drives, each with 300MB, and they would use drive letters D, E, and F. You can assign up to 23 logical DOS drives to an extended partition (letters D through Z).

lost cluster A *cluster* that, according to the *FAT*, is associated with a file but has no link to any entry in the *file directory*. Lost clusters are typically caused by program crashes, power surges, or power outages.

Map Cache   A Windows Millennium feature that enables the system to execute program code directly from the *disk cache*. This saves memory and improves performance because the code doesn't have to be copied to memory.

master boot record   The first 512-byte sector on your system's *active partition* (the partition your system boots from). Most of the MBR consists of a small program that locates and runs the core operating system files (*Io.sys* and *Msdos.sys*).

Mbps   One million bits per second (*bps*).

MBR   See *master boot record.*

MDI   See *Multiple Document Interface.*

metafile   An image that consists of a collection of drawing commands from Windows Millennium's *GDI* component. These commands create the basic primitives (lines, circles, and so on) that make up the image.

MIDI—See *Musical Instrument Digital Interface.*

mini-driver   A small *device driver* that augments the functionality of a *universal driver* by providing the commands and routines necessary to operate a specific device.

miniport driver   A *device driver,* supplied by a SCSI controller manufacturer, that provides support for device-specific I/O requests. See also *mini-driver.*

modem   A device used to transmit data between computers via telephone lines. See also *modulation* and *demodulation.*

modulation   The conversion, performed by a *modem,* of digital data into an analog wave (a series of tones) that can be transmitted over a telephone line. See also *demodulation.*

Moore's Law   Processing power doubles every 18 months (from Gordon Moore, cofounder of Intel).

MS-DOS mode   See *Real mode.*

Msdos.sys   A text file that controls certain Windows Millennium startup parameters.

multimedia   The computer-based presentation of data using multiple modes of communication, including text, graphics, sound, animation, and video.

Multiple Document Interface A Windows Millennium programming interface that lets applications display several documents at once, each in its own window.

multitasking See *cooperative multitasking* and *preemptive multitasking*.

multithreading A multitasking model in which multiple *threads* run simultaneously.

Musical Instrument Digital Interface A communications protocol that standardizes the exchange of data between a computer and a musical synthesizer.

name resolution A process that converts a *host name* into an *IP address*. See *Domain Name System* and *Windows Internet Name Service*.

NetBEUI The NetBIOS Extended User Interface *protocol*. (NetBIOS is an API that enables network applications—such as *redirectors*—to communicate with *networking* protocols.) It's a combined *transport layer protocol* and *network layer protocol* developed by IBM and supported by all Microsoft networks. It's a simple, efficient protocol that works well in small *LANs*.

network A collection of computers connected via special cables or other network media (such as infrared) to share files, folders, disks, peripherals, and applications.

network adapter See *network interface card*.

network interface card An adapter that usually slips into an expansion bus slot inside a *client* or *server* computer. (There are also external *NICs* that plug into parallel ports or PC Card slots.) The NIC's main purpose is to serve as the connection point between the PC and the *network*. The NIC's backplate (the portion of the NIC that you can see after the card is installed) contains one or more ports into which you plug a network cable.

network layer protocol A *protocol* in which no communications channel is established between nodes. Instead, the protocol builds each *packet* with all the information required for the network to deliver each packet and for the destination *node* to assemble everything. See also *transport layer protocol*.

Network News Transport Protocol   An Internet *protocol* that defines how Usenet newsgroups and postings are transmitted. Part of the *TCP/IP* suite of protocols.

network operating system   Operating system software that runs on a *network server* and provides the various network services for the network *clients*.

network redirector   A *virtual device driver* that enables applications to find, open, read, write, and delete files on a remote drive.

NIC   See *network interface card*.

NNTP   See *Network News Transport Protocol*.

node   A computer on a *network*.

NOS   See *network operating system*.

object   A separate entity or component that is distinguished by its properties and actions. In the *OLE* world, an object is not only data—a slice of text, a graphic, a sound, a chunk of a spreadsheet, or whatever—but also one or more functions for creating, accessing, and using that data.

packet   The data transfer unit used in *network* and *modem* communications. Each packet contains not only data, but also a "header" that contains information about which machine sent the data, which machine is supposed to receive the data, and a few extra tidbits that enable the receiving computer to put all the original data together in the correct order and check for errors that might have cropped up during the transmission.

paging file   See *swap file*.

parity bit   In *modem* data transfers that use 7 *data bits,* this is an extra bit that enables the receiving system to check the integrity of each character.

Parkinson's Law of Data   Data expands to fill the space available for storage (from the original Parkinson's Law: Work expands to fill the time available).

peer-to-peer network   A *network* in which no one computer is singled out to provide special services. Instead, all the computers attached to the network have equal status (at least as far as the network is concerned), and all the computers can act as both *servers* and *clients*. See also *client/server network*.

point size   See *type size*.

port driver   A 32-bit *protected-mode device driver* that provides complete functionality for working with devices such as hard disk controllers and floppy disk controllers.

POST   At system startup, the POST detects and tests memory, ports, and basic devices such as the video adapter, keyboard, and disk drives. If everything passes, your system emits a single beep.

Power-On Self Test   See *POST*.

preemptive multitasking   A multitasking model used by 32-bit applications in which Windows Millennium uses a sophisticated algorithm to monitor all running processes, assign each one a priority level, and allocate CPU resources according to the relative priority of each process. See also *cooperative multitasking*.

primary name   In a filename, the part to the left of the period.

primary partition—The first partition (drive C) on a hard disk. See also *active partition* and *extended partition*.

property sheet   A dialog box with controls that let you manipulate various properties of the underlying *object*.

protected mode   An operating mode introduced with the 80286 microprocessor. Unlike *real mode*, which can address only up to 640KB of memory and gives a running program direct access to hardware, protected mode enables software to use memory beyond 640KB. It also sets up a protection scheme so that multiple programs can share the same computer resources without stepping on each other's toes (and, usually, crashing the system).

protocol   A set of standards that defines how information is exchanged between two systems across a *network* connection. See also *transport layer protocol* and *network layer protocol*.

real mode   The operating mode of early Intel microprocessors (the 8088 and 8086). It's a single-tasking mode in which the running program has full access to the computer's memory and peripherals. Windows Millennium does not support real mode. Real mode is also called *MS-DOS mode*. See also *protected mode*.

redirector   A networking driver that provides all the mechanisms needed for an application to communicate with a remote device, including file reads and writes, print job submissions, and resource sharing.

Registry   A central repository that Windows Millennium uses to store anything and everything that applies to your system's configuration. This includes hardware settings, object properties, operating system settings, and application options.

remote resource   Any peripheral, file, folder, or application that exists somewhere on the *network*. See also *local resource*.

repeat rate   When you press and hold down a key, the speed at which the characters appear. See also *delay*.

repeater   A device that boosts a *network* cable's signal so that the length of the network can be extended. Repeaters are needed because copper-based cables suffer from attenuation—a phenomenon in which the degradation of the electrical signal carried over the cable is proportional to the distance the signal has to travel.

router   A device that makes decisions about where to send the *network packets* it receives. Unlike a *bridge*, which merely passes along any data that comes its way, a router examines the address information in each packet and then determines the most efficient route that the packet must take to reach its eventual destination.

routing   The process whereby *packets* travel from *host* to host until they eventually reach their destination.

RTS/CTS flow control   See *hardware flow control*.

Safe mode   A Windows Millennium startup mode that loads a minimal system configuration. Safe mode is useful for troubleshooting problems caused by incorrect or corrupt device drivers.

sans serif   A *typeface* that doesn't contain the cross strokes found in a *serif* typeface.

serif   A *typeface* that contains fine cross strokes (called "feet") at the extremities of each character. See also *sans serif.*

server   In a *client/server network,* a computer that provides and manages services (such as file and print sharing and security) for the users on the network.

shortcut   A pointer to an executable file or a document. Double-clicking the shortcut starts the program or loads the document.

shortcut menu   A menu that appears when you right-click an object. The context menu gives you access to the properties and actions associated with that object. Also called a *context menu.*

signature   A few lines of text at the end of an email message that identify the sender and include his contact information (such as his company name, email address, and fax number). Some people also include snappy quotations or other tidbits. Microsoft Exchange doesn't provide any method of adding a signature automatically. However, if you have WordMail, you can customize one of the included email templates with your signature.

Simple Mail Transport Protocol   An Internet protocol that describes the format of Internet email messages and how messages get delivered. Part of the *TCP/IP* suite of protocols.

software flow control   A system whereby the computer and *modem* send signals to each other that indicate whether they're ready to receive data. To stop the transfer, a device sends an XOFF signal (ASCII 19 or Ctrl-S). To restart the transfer, a device sends an XON signal (ASCII 17 or Ctrl-Q). See also *hardware flow control.*

special drag   Using the right mouse button to drag an object. When you drop the object, Explorer displays a *shortcut menu* with various commands.

start bit   An extra bit added to the beginning of the *data bits* in a *modem* data transfer. This bit marks the beginning of each character. See also *stop bit.*

stop bit   An extra bit (or sometimes two) added to the end of the *data bits* in a *modem* data transfer. This bit marks the end of each character. See also *start bit.*

subnet mask   A 32-bit value, usually expressed in *dotted-decimal notation*, that lets *IP* separate a network ID from a full *IP address* and thus determine whether the source and destination hosts are on the same network.

swap file   A special file used by Windows Millennium to emulate physical memory. If you open enough programs or data files that physical memory becomes exhausted, the paging file is brought into play to augment memory storage. Also called a *paging file.*

system tray   The box on the right side of the taskbar that Windows Millennium uses to display icons that tell you the current state of the system.

TCP   See *Transmission Control Protocol.*

TCP/IP   Transmission Control Protocol/Internet Protocol. TCP/IP is the lingua franca of most UNIX systems and the Internet as a whole. However, TCP/IP is also an excellent choice for other types of *networks* because it's routable, robust, and reliable.

thread   A small chunk of executable code with a very narrow focus. In a spreadsheet, for example, you might have one thread for recalculating, another for printing, and a third for accepting keyboard input. See also *multithreading.*

topology   Describes how the various *nodes* that comprise a *network*—which include not only the computers, but also devices such as *hubs* and *bridges*—are connected.

Transmission Control Protocol—A *transport layer protocol* that sets up a connection between two *hosts* and ensures that data is passed between them reliably. If *packets* are lost or damaged during transmission, TCP takes care of retransmitting the packets. See also *Internet Protocol* and *TCP/IP.*

transport layer protocol   A *protocol* in which a virtual communications channel is established between two systems. The protocol uses this channel to send *packets* between *nodes.* See also *network layer protocol.*

True Color   A *color depth* of 24 bits, or 16,777,216 colors.

type size   A measure of the height of a *font*. Type size is measured from the highest point (the "ascender") of a tall letter, such as "f," to the lowest point (the "descender") of an underhanging letter, such as "g." The standard unit of measurement is the point. There are 72 points in an inch. Also called *point size*.

type style   Extra attributes added to a font's *typeface,* such as **bold** and *italic.* Other type styles (often called type effects) include <u>underlining</u> and ~~strikeout~~ (sometimes called strikethrough).

typeface   A distinctive design that is common to any related set of letters, numbers, and other symbols. This design gives each character a particular shape and thickness that is unique to the typeface and difficult to categorize.

UART   Universal Asynchronous Receiver/Transmitter. A special chip that resides inside every serial port (or sometimes on the computer's motherboard). (For an internal or PC Card modem, the UART chip sits on the card itself.) It's the UART's job (among other things) to take the computer's native parallel data and convert it into a series of bits that can be spit out of the serial port's Transmit Data line. On the other end, individual bits streaming into the destination serial port's Receive Data line are reassembled by the UART into the parallel format that the processor prefers.

Uniform Resource Locator   An Internet addressing scheme that spells out the exact location of a Net resource. Most URLs take the following form:

`protocol://host.domain/directory/file.name`

`protocol`	The TCP/IP protocol to use for retrieving the resource (such as http or ftp).
`host.domain`	The domain name of the host computer where the resource resides.
`directory`	The host directory that contains the resource.
`file.name`	The filename of the resource.

universal driver   A *device driver* that incorporates the code necessary for the devices in a particular hardware class to work with the appropriate Windows Millennium operating system component (such as the printing subsystem). See also *mini-driver*.

URL   See *Uniform Resource Locator*.

User   A core Windows Millennium component that handles all user-related I/O tasks. On the input side, User manages incoming data from the keyboard, mouse, joystick, and any other input devices that are attached to your computer. For output, User sends data to windows, icons, menus, and other components of the Windows Millennium user interface. User also handles the sound driver, the system timer, and the communications ports. See also *Graphical Device Interface* and *kernel*.

user profiles   Separate sets of customization options for each person who uses a computer. Each profile includes most of Windows Millennium's customization options, including the colors, patterns, wallpapers, *shortcut* icons, screen saver, and programs that appear on the Start menu.

VFAT   An *installable file system* that works with the *block I/O subsystem* to access disk services. Because it's a 32-bit *protected-mode VxD* and is multithreaded, VFAT provides superior performance (especially compared to the 16-bit *real-mode* disk access found in Windows 3.1), enhanced reliability, and easier *multitasking*. In particular, VFAT avoids the slow processor mode switches between protected mode and real mode that plagued Windows 3.1. VFAT also supports many more drive and controller types than did Windows 3.*x*. However, it still uses the 16-bit *FAT* for physical storage of files and folders, so it inherits FAT's legendary fragility. See also *CDFS*.

virtual device driver   A 32-bit *protected-mode device driver*.

Virtual File Allocation Table   See *VFAT*.

virtual machine   A separate section of memory that simulates the operation of an entire computer. Virtual machines were born with the release of Intel's 80386 microprocessor. Thanks to *protected mode*, the 80386 circuitry could address up to 4GB of memory. Using this potentially huge address space, the

80386 allowed software to carve out separate chunks of memory and use these areas to emulate the full operation of a computer. This emulation is so complete and so effective that a program running in a virtual machine thinks it's dealing with a real computer. Combined with the resource sharing features of *protected mode,* virtual machines can run their programs simultaneously without bumping into each other.

Virtual Machine Manager   A Windows Millennium driver (Vmm32.vxd) that allocates and manages the resources needed by your system's software—your applications and the various operating system processes. If a program or the operating system needs a resource—whether it's a chunk of memory or access to an I/O port—the Virtual Machine Manager handles the request and allocates the resource appropriately.

virtual memory   Memory created by allocating hard disk space and making it look to applications as though they are dealing with physical RAM.

VxD   See *virtual device driver.*

Windows Internet Name Service   A service that maps NetBIOS names (the names you assign to computers in the Identification tab of the Network properties sheet) to the *IP addresses* assigned via *DHCP.*

WINS   See *Windows Internet Name Service.*

XON/XOFF flow control   See *software flow control.*

Online Resources for Windows Millennium

I F I'VE WHETTED YOUR APPETITE for even more Windows know-how, the Internet is an excellent place to look. This appendix lists a few of my favorite official and unofficial Windows Web sites and Usenet newsgroups.

The World Wide Web

The World Wide Web has tons of pages related to the various flavors of Windows. In this section, I give you addresses and descriptions of my favorite sites.

Microsoft Sites

Let's start with the official Microsoft sites:

Windows Millennium Home Page

URL: `www.microsoft.com/windowsme`

Content: Files, how-to, news, shareware, troubleshooting

Comments: This is the place to begin all your Windows Millennium Web wandering. All the latest Windows news from Microsoft, updates, new Windows programs—it's all here.

Windows Update

URL: windowsupdate.microsoft.com/

Content: Files

Comments: This site can check your system and let you know
              about new components, applications, and device
              drivers that are available. You should check this
              site regularly.

Microsoft Technical Support Search

URL: support.microsoft.com/directory/

Content: How-to, troubleshooting

Comments: If you're scratching your head over some weird
              Windows Millennium behavior, chances are
              someone else has found the same thing and has
              asked Microsoft Tech Support about it, and the
              engineer has posted a solution in the Microsoft
              Knowledge Base. This Web site lets you search
              the Knowledge Base and other support content
              to track down a problem you might be having.
              Note that you have to register with Microsoft to
              use this site.

Windows Software Library

URL: www.microsoft.com/downloads/

Content: Files

Comments: This page contains miscellaneous files from
              Microsoft, including updated components,
              device drivers, and more.

Hardware Compatibility List

URL: www.microsoft.com/hwtest/hcl/

Content: Know-how

Comments: This page presents the complete list of hardware
              that has passed muster with Microsoft and there-
              fore has been deemed compatible with Windows
              Millennium.

Non-Microsoft Sites

Here are a few links to some useful non-Microsoft Windows
pages:

32BIT.com

URL: www.32bit.com

Content: Files, how-to, news, shareware

Comments: This site is dedicated to 32-bit operating systems,
              and so has extensive Windows resources, partic-
              ularly shareware.

Allen's WinApps List

URL: www.winappslist.com

Content: Files, shareware

Comments: An extensive collection of Windows software
              arranged in more than 40 different categories.

Consummate Winsock Apps List

URL: cws.internet.com

Content: Files, shareware

Comments: Not just your average list of Windows shareware
              and files. This site sticks out from the crowd
              thanks to the in-depth reviews given to each pro-
              gram by the site's proprietor: Forrest Stroud.

DOWNLOAD.COM

URL: download.cnet.com

Content: Files, shareware

Comments: An excellent source of Windows files, patches, and programs.

PCWin Resource Center

URL: www.pcwin.com

Content: Files, how-to, news, shareware, troubleshooting

Comments: A nice collection of Windows software and how-to information.

Tech Support Guy

URL: www.helponthe.net

Content: How-to, troubleshooting

Comments: Thousands of troubleshooting articles, many of which are related to Windows problems. Can't find your answer? Ask the Tech Support Guy!

TUCOWS

URL: www.tucows.com

Content: Files, shareware

Comments: One of the premier download sites for Windows shareware. There are dozens of separate software categories.

Windowatch

URL: www.windowatch.com

Content: News

Comments: Subtitled "The Electronic Windows Magazine of the Internet," this site keeps you up to date on the latest developments in the Windows world.

Winmag.com

URL: www.winmag.com

Content: Files, how-to, news, shareware, troubleshooting

Comments: This site is run by Windows Magazine (now online only) and also includes discussion groups, reviews, and much more.

WinFiles.com

URL: www.winfiles.com

Content: Files, how-to, shareware

Comments: This site has loads of useful links, and the shareware collection is second to none. The site's clever layout is designed to resemble the Windows interface.

WinPlanet

URL: www.winplanet.com

Content: How-to, news, troubleshooting

Comments: This is one of the busiest Windows sites on the Net thanks to its large collection of tips and features related to the Windows world.

ZDNet

URL: www.zdnet.com/windows/

Content: How-to, news, shareware, troubleshooting

Comments: This well-done site offers downloads, reviews, and a lot of top-notch advice from the experts at ZDNet.

Usenet Newsgroups

Usenet newsgroups are usually populated with many enthusiastic users, so they're often a great source for getting answers to specific questions. Here's a list of the Windows newsgroups that were available as this book went to press:

Newsgroup	Description
alt.os.windows95.crash.crash.crash	The name sounds like a joke, but this group has plenty of serious posts related to troubleshooting issues.
alt.windows98	A catchall group for Windows questions and answers.
comp.os.ms-windows.advocacy	This is the group to frequent if you enjoy debating the merits of Windows with Linux and Mac fanatics.
comp.os.ms-windows.apps.compatibility	This is the place to look for help related to applications that won't run under Windows.
comp.os.ms-windows.apps.utilities	This group deals with issues related to the Windows accessories.
comp.os.ms-windows.networking.windows	Check out this group if you need help with networking, Internet access, or other connectivity issues.
comp.os.ms-windows.setup	This group covers setup, configuration, and installation issues.
comp.os.ms-windows.misc	This is a catchall group for other Windows issues. A word of warning: This is a very busy group with hundreds of posts each day.
comp.os.ms-windows.moderated	A high-signal, low-noise group that posts about one tenth the number of messages that go through the misc group.
comp.os.ms-windows.video	This group discusses topics related to digital video, scanners, graphics cards, and so on.

Microsoft also runs its own newsgroups. To view them, set up your newsreader to use the server msnews.microsoft.com. The following table lists the newsgroups that deal specifically with Windows topics. (There are many other groups that deal with multimedia, Internet Explorer, and so on.) Note that these are all Windows 98 groups. It's likely that Microsoft will create specific Windows Millennium groups, and that the structure of these groups will mirror those of Windows 98. However, no Millennium-related groups were available as this book went to press.

Newsgroup	Description
microsoft.public.win98.apps	Issues related to running applications in Windows.
microsoft.public.win98.comm.dun	Covers installation, configuration, and use of Dial-Up Networking.
microsoft.public.win98.comm.modem	Deals with issues related to modems, serial ports, HyperTerminal, Phone Dialer, and general telephony.
microsoft.public.win98.disks.general	Primarily a forum for disk drive issues, especially questions related to ScanDisk, DriveSpace, and DoubleSpace.
microsoft.public.win98.display.general	Discussions related to video cards and monitors.
microsoft.public.win98.display.multi_monitor	Covers Windows' support for multiple monitors.
microsoft.public.win98.fat32	Deals with the FAT32 file system.
microsoft.public.win98.gen_discussion	Miscellaneous Windows topics.
microsoft.public.win98.internet	General Windows Internet topics.
microsoft.public.win98.internet.active_desktop	Questions and answers related to the Active Desktop.
microsoft.public.win98.internet.browser	Discussions related to Internet Explorer and other browsers.
microsoft.public.win98.internet.netmeeting	Covers all aspects of NetMeeting conferencing.
microsoft.public.win98.internet.outlookexpress	Deals with email and newsgroup issues in Outlook Express.
microsoft.public.win98.internet.windows_update	Questions and answers related to the Windows Update Web site.
microsoft.public.win98.multimedia	Discussions on audio, video, and other multimedia.
microsoft.public.win98.multimedia.directx5	Covers multimedia topics related to DirectX version 5.

Newsgroup	Description
microsoft.public.win98.networking	Installation, configuration, and troubleshooting of Microsoft and NetWare networks.
microsoft.public.win98.performance	Deals with overcoming poor Windows performance.
microsoft.public.win98.pnp	Windows' Plug and Play support.
microsoft.public.win98.power_mgmt	Questions and answers related to power management.
microsoft.public.win98.printing	Discussions about printing in Windows.
microsoft.public.win98.pws_4	Covers Personal Web Server.
microsoft.public.win98.scanreg	Deals with Windows' Registry Checker system tool.
microsoft.public.win98.setup	Covers issues related to Windows installation.
microsoft.public.win98.setup.win31	Questions and answers related to upgrading to Windows 98 from Windows 3.1.
microsoft.public.win98.shell	Discussions on the Windows shell and user interface.
microsoft.public.win98.sys_file_check	Covers the System File Checker utility.
microsoft.public.win98.taskscheduler	Deals with the Task Scheduler utility.
microsoft.public.win98.webtv	Questions and answers related to WebTV for Windows

Windows Millennium Keyboard Shortcuts

O FFICIALLY, WINDOWS MILLENNIUM was made with the mouse in mind, so most day-to-day tasks are designed to be performed using the standard mouse moves. Unofficially, however, this doesn't mean your keyboard should be ignored when you're not typing. Windows Millennium is loaded with keyboard shortcuts and techniques that can often be used as replacements or enhancements for mouse clicks and drags. (These are also useful if your mouse goes south on you. I once saw an otherwise-competent manager panic badly when, just prior to an important presentation, his mouse died and he didn't know how to use Windows without it!) This appendix consolidates all the Windows Millennium shortcut keys and techniques in one place for handy reference.

Windows Millennium Startup Keys

As described in Chapter 2, "Understanding and Controlling the Windows Millennium Startup," the Windows Millennium Startup menu offers several commands that control how Windows Millennium starts. You can bypass the menu and run some commands directly by using the keys listed in Table C.1. In all cases, press the key or key combination immediately after you hear the beep that signals the end of the Power-On Self Test (POST).

→ **See Also** "Working with the Windows Millennium Startup Menu," **p. 43**.

TABLE C.1: KEYBOARD TECHNIQUES FOR THE WINDOWS MILLENNIUM STARTUP MENU

Press	To
F5	Boot Windows Millennium in safe mode.
F8	Display the Startup menu. (You can also hold down Ctrl during the POST.)
Shift+F8	Boot Windows Millennium using step-by-step confirmation.

Here are a few more startup keyboard techniques to bear in mind:

- Most computers enable you to press a key during the POST to invoke the machine's setup or CMOS settings. The key you press varies depending on the manufacturer, but Delete, Esc, and Ctrl+Esc are common. (You should see a message during the POST that tells you which key to press.)

- Hold down the Shift key during startup to bypass the items in your Startup folder.

- If you use a floppy disk to boot to the DOS prompt, press Ctrl+Alt+Delete to reboot your computer.

Interface Keys

Table C.2 presents a few keyboard shortcuts that you can use with the Windows Millennium interface.

TABLE C.2: KEYBOARD TECHNIQUES FOR THE WINDOWS MILLENNIUM INTERFACE

Press	To
Alt+Double-click	Display the property sheet for the selected object.
Alt+Enter	Display the property sheet for the selected object.
Print Screen	Copy the entire screen image to the Clipboard.
Alt+Print Screen	Copy the active window's image to the Clipboard.
Ctrl+Alt+Delete	Display the Close Program dialog box.
Ctrl+Esc	Open the Start menu.

Press	To
Shift	Prevent an inserted CD from running its AutoPlay application. (Hold down Shift while inserting the CD.)
Shift+F10	Display the shortcut menu for the selected object.
Shift+Right-click	Display the shortcut menu with alternative commands (such as Open With) for the selected object.

Application Keys

You'll spend most of your Windows life working within applications, so knowing a few keyboard shortcuts will save you all kinds of time in the long run. Table C.3 runs through the keys and key combinations available in most Windows applications.

TABLE C.3: KEYBOARD TECHNIQUES FOR APPLICATIONS

Press	To
Working with Application Windows	
Alt	Activate or deactivate the application's menu bar.
Alt+Esc	Cycle through the open application windows.
Alt+F4	Close the active application window.
Alt+Spacebar	Display the system menu for the active application window.
Alt+Tab	Cycle through the active applications. Displays an icon for each application.
F1	Display context-sensitive Help.
F10	Activate the application's menu bar.
Working with Documents	
Alt+-(hyphen)	Display the system menu for the active document window.
Alt+Print Screen	Copy the active window's image to the Clipboard.
Ctrl+F4	Close the active document window.
Ctrl+F6	Cycle through the open documents within an application.
Ctrl+N	Create a new document.
Ctrl+O	Display the Open dialog box.
Ctrl+P	Display the Print dialog box.
Ctrl+S	Save the current file. If the file is new, display the Save As dialog box.

TABLE C.3: CONTINUED

Press	To
	Working with Data
Backspace	Delete the character to the left of the insertion point.
Ctrl+C	Copy the selected data to the Clipboard.
Ctrl+X	Cut the selected data to the Clipboard.
Ctrl+V	Paste the most recently cut or copied data from the Clipboard.
Ctrl+Z	Undo the most recent action.
Delete	Delete the selected data.

Dialog Box Keys

Table C.4 presents a few keyboard shortcuts that come in handy when working with Windows' dialog boxes.

TABLE C.4: KEYBOARD TECHNIQUES FOR DIALOG BOXES

Press	To
Alt+Down arrow	Display the list in a drop-down list box.
Ctrl+Shift+Tab	Move backward through the dialog box tabs.
Ctrl+Tab	Move forward through the dialog box tabs.
Enter	Select the default command button or the active command button.
Spacebar	Toggle a check box on and off; select the active option button or command button.
Esc	Close the dialog box without making any changes.
F4	In the Open and Save As dialog boxes, drop down the Look in list.
F5	Refresh the current folder listing.
Backspace	In the Open and Save As dialog boxes, move up to the parent folder when the folder list has the focus.
Shift+F10	In the Open and Save As dialog boxes, display the shortcut menu for the selected object in the folder list.
Shift+F1	Display "What's This?" help for the control that has the focus.
Shift+Tab	Move backward through the dialog box controls.
Tab	Move forward through the dialog box controls.

Drag-and-Drop Keys

You've seen in several places throughout this book that drag and drop is a useful and efficient method for performing many routine tasks within Windows Millennium. Unfortunately, its rules for copying, moving, and creating shortcuts are convoluted, to say the least. The keyboard techniques shown in Table C.5 can help you avoid drag-and-drop confusion.

TABLE C.5: KEYBOARD TECHNIQUES FOR DRAG AND DROP

Hold Down	To
Ctrl	Copy the dragged object.
Ctrl+Shift	Display a shortcut menu after dropping a left-dragged object.
Esc	Cancel the current drag.
Shift	Move the dragged object.

Windows Explorer Keys

Windows Explorer offers a large number of keyboard shortcuts, as shown in Table C.6.

TABLE C.6: KEYBOARD TECHNIQUES FOR WINDOWS EXPLORER

Press	To
+ (numeric keypad)	Display the next level of subfolders for the current folder.
- (numeric keypad)	Hide the current folder's subfolders.
* (numeric keypad)	Display all levels of subfolders for the current folder.
Alt+Left arrow	Navigate backward to a previously displayed folder.
Alt+Right arrow	Navigate forward to a previously displayed folder.
Backspace	Navigate to the parent folder of the current folder.
Ctrl+arrow key	Scroll up, down, left, or right (depending on the arrow key used) while maintaining the highlight on the currently selected objects.
Ctrl+A	Select all the objects in the current folder.

TABLE C.6: CONTINUED

Press	To
Ctrl+C	Copy the selected objects to the Clipboard.
Ctrl+V	Paste the most recently cut or copied objects from the Clipboard.
Ctrl+X	Cut the selected objects to the Clipboard.
Ctrl+Z	Undo the most recent action.
Delete	Delete the selected objects.
F2	Rename the selected object.
F3	Display the Find dialog box with the current folder displayed in the Look in list.
F4	Open the Address toolbar's drop-down list.
F5	Refresh the contents of the Explorer window.
F6	Cycle the highlight among the All Folders list, the Contents list, and the Address toolbar.
Shift+Delete	Delete the currently selected objects without sending them to the Recycle Bin.
Tab	Cycle the highlight among the All Folders list, the Contents list, and the Address toolbar.

Internet Explorer Keys

Besides typing in the Address bar, most people only use their mouse within Internet Explorer. However, the program comes with quite a few keyboard shortcuts, as you can see from Table C.7.

TABLE C.7: KEYBOARD TECHNIQUES FOR INTERNET EXPLORER

Press	To
Alt+Left arrow	Navigate backward to a previously displayed Web page.
Alt+Right arrow	Navigate forward to a previously displayed Web page.
Ctrl+A	Select the entire Web page.
Ctrl+B	Display the Organize Favorites dialog box.
Ctrl+D	Add the current page to the Favorites list.
Ctrl+F	Display the Find dialog box.
Ctrl+N	Open a new window.

Press	To
Ctrl+O	Display the Open dialog box.
Ctrl+P	Display the Print dialog box.
Ctrl+Shift+Tab	Cycle backward through the Web page frames, the Address toolbar, and the Links toolbar.
Ctrl+Tab	Cycle forward through the Web page frames, the Address toolbar, and the Links toolbar.
Esc	Stop downloading the Web page.
F4	Open the Address toolbar's drop-down list.
F5	Refresh the Web page.
F11	Toggle between Full Screen mode and the regular window.
Spacebar	Scroll down one screenful.
Shift+Spacebar	Scroll up one screenful.
Shift+Tab	Cycle backward through the Links toolbar, the Address toolbar, and the Web page links.
Tab	Cycle forward through the Web page links, the Address toolbar, and the Links toolbar.

Doskey Keys

If you think you'll be spending much time at the DOS prompt, you'll definitely want to learn how to use the Doskey utility, which enables you to recall and edit DOS command lines.

Table C.8 lists Doskey's command-recall keys.

TABLE C.8: KEYBOARD TECHNIQUES FOR COMMAND-RECALL IN DOSKEY

Press	To
Alt+F7	Delete all the commands from the recall list.
Arrow keys	Cycle through the commands in the recall list.
F7	Display the entire recall list.
F8	Recall a command that begins with the letter or letters you've typed on the command line.
F9	Display the Line number: prompt. You then enter the number of the command (as displayed by F7) that you want.
Page Down	Recall the newest command in the list.
Page Up	Recall the oldest command in the list.

Table C.9 runs through Doskey's command-line editing keys.

TABLE C.9: KEYBOARD TECHNIQUES FOR COMMAND-LINE EDITING IN DOSKEY

Press	To
Backspace	Delete the character to the left of the cursor.
Ctrl+End	Delete from the cursor to the end of the line.
Ctrl+Home	Delete from the cursor to the beginning of the line.
Ctrl+Left arrow	Move the cursor one word to the left.
Ctrl+Right arrow	Move the cursor one word to the right.
Delete	Delete the character over the cursor.
End	Move the cursor to the end of the line.
Home	Move the cursor to the beginning of the line.
Insert	Toggle DOSKEY between "insert" mode (your typing is inserted between existing letters on the command line) and "overstrike" mode (your typing replaces existing letters on the command line).
Left arrow	Move the cursor one character to the left.
Right arrow	Move the cursor one character to the right.

Windows Logo (⊞) Keys

The Microsoft Natural Keyboard and most modern keyboards have a Windows logo key (⊞). Table C.10 lists the keyboard shortcuts you can use with this key.

TABLE C.10: KEYBOARD TECHNIQUES FOR THE WINDOWS LOGO (⊞) KEY

Press	To
⊞	Open the Start menu.
⊞+D	Minimize all open windows. Press ⊞+D again to restore the windows.
⊞+E	Open Windows Explorer.
⊞+F	Find a file or folder.
⊞+Ctrl+F	Find a computer.
⊞+M	Minimize all open windows, except those with open modal windows.
⊞+Shift+M	Undo minimize all.
⊞+R	Display the Run dialog box.

Alt-spacebar Display system menu

Press	To
⊞+F1	Display Windows Help.
⊞+Break	Display the System Properties dialog box.
⊞+Spacebar	Scroll down one page (supported only in certain applications, such as Internet Explorer).
⊞+Tab	Cycle through the taskbar buttons.

Note, too, that the Microsoft Natural Keyboard and compatibles also have an Application key. It has a picture of a mouse pointer and a shortcut menu. Pressing this key activates the shortcut menu for the current object.

Symbols

4-bit parallel port, 517
8-bit parallel port, 517
16-bit applications, uninstalling, 281-283
32BIT.com Web site, 547

A

About dialog box, 34
Accelerated graphics adapter, 486
Accelerated Graphics Port. *See* AGP
accelerator keys, Start menu, 403
access control (network clients), 431
access rights
    networks, 448-449
    user-level, 449-451
accessing
    Control Panel, 84-85
    My Network Places folder, 442, 444
    networks, 439
        sharing resources, 448-449
        user-level, 449-451
accounts
    email, 157-160
        digital ID, 195-196
    LANs, 424
ACPI (Advanced Configuration and Power Interface), 508
activating hibernate mode, 510
Active Desktop, 382-383
    Web pages, 385
ActiveX controls, 189
adapters
    drivers, 487-488
    graphics, 486
    secondary, 495
Add Favorite dialog box, 135
Add Network Place Wizard, 446
Add New Hardware Wizard, 471-474
Add New Modem Wizard, 97-104
Add Printer Wizard, 452-453
Add Scheduled Task Wizard, 334
Add Users dialog box, 449
Add/Remove Programs Properties dialog box, 32, 348
Add/Remove Programs wizard, 268, 279

adding
    components, Setup, 32
    folder comments, 373
    places (My Network Places folder), 446
    Scheduled Tasks, 334
    users, networks, 449
    Web sites to security zones, 186-192
Address bar (Internet Explorer), 129, 133-134
    AutoComplete, 134
    features, 133-134
address lines, 286
address space, 286
addresses (Web), 128
    UNC, 445-446
adjusting
    color depth (monitors), 488-492
    monitor resolution, 488, 490-492
Advanced Audio Properties dialog box, 503
Advanced Configuration and Power Interface. *See* ACPI
Advanced Connection Properties dialog box, 107
Advanced File Signature Verification Settings dialog box, 476
Advanced Troubleshooting Settings dialog box, 48, 290
AGP (Accelerated Graphics Port), 487
Alarm Action dialog box, 513
alarms
    batteries, 513
    low battery (notebook), 513
Allen's WinApps list Web site, 547
Application Data folder, 22
application keys (shortcuts), 555
Application Launch Accelerator, 312
applications, 266
    associating extensions, 242-243
    installing, 266-268
        checklist, 266-268
    launching, 273-276
        automatically, 276-278
    multitasking, 278-279
    opening documents, 235-237
    Registry, 270, 272-273
        DLLs, 272-273
        paths, 271
        program settings, 270
        user settings, 271

Index

S